Gower Handbook of Purchasing Management

Third Edition

Edited by
MARC DAY

GOWER

Published by
Gower Publishing Limited
Gower House
Croft Road
Aldershot
Hants GU11 3HR
England

Gower Publishing Company
131 Main Street
Burlington VT 05401–5600 USA

British Library Cataloguing in Publication Data
Gower handbook of purchasing management. - 3rd ed.
  1. Purchasing 2. Purchasing - Management
  I. Day, Marc II. Farmer, David, 1932- III. Weele, A. J. van
  IV. Handbook of purchasing management
  658. 7'2

  ISBN 056608404X

US Library of Congress Cataloging-in-Publication Data
The Library of Congress Control Number: 2002109781

Typeset in 9 point Stone Serif by IML Typographers, Birkenhead, Merseyside and printed in Great Britain by MPG Books Limited, Bodmin

Contents

List of boxes

List of figures

List of tables

List of abbreviations and acronyms

3D	three dimensional
ABC	activity-based costing
AMT	advanced manufacturing technology
ASP	application software provider
AUPO	Association of University Purchasing Officers
B2B	business-to-business
B2C	business-to-consumer
BiE	Business in the Environment
BPR	business process reengineering
CBSP	Centre for Business Strategy and Procurement (Birmingham Business School)
CCL	Climate Change Levy
CFR	cost and freight
CHP	combined heat and power
CIF	cost, insurance, freight
CIP	carriage and insurance paid to
CIPS	Chartered Institute of Purchasing and Supply
CKD	Completely Knocked Down
CMR	Convention de Marchandises par Route
COSHEP	Committee of Scottish Higher Education Principals
COSHH	Control of Substances Hazardous to Health
CPFR	Collaborative Planning, Forecasting and Replenishment
CPT	carriage paid to
CRiSPS	Centre for Research in Strategic Purchasing and Supply (Bath)
CROMTEC	Centre for Research on Organizations, Management and Technical Change (UMIST)
CSSA	Computing Services and Software Association
CVCP	Committee of Vice-Chancellors and Principals
DAF	delivered at frontier
DDP	delivered duty paid
DDU	delivered duty unpaid
DEQ	delivered cx quay
DES	delivered ex ship
DETR	Department of the Environment, Transport and the Regions
DRAMS	dynamic random access memory (chips)
DTI	Department of Trade and Industry
EBEN-UK	European Business Ethics Network (UK)
ECGD	Export Credits Guarantee Department

EDI	electronic data interchange
EMAS	Eco-Management and Auditing Scheme
ERP	Enterprise Resource Planning (system)
ERS	Electronic Registration System
EXW	ex works
FAS	free alongside
FCA	free carrier
FMCG	fast-moving consumer goods
FOB	free on board
FTO	foreign trade organization
GRN	goods received note
HE	higher education
IBIS	Integrated Benchmarking Information Systems
ICS	information communication systems
ICT	information and communications technology
IIP	Investors in People
IMP	Industrial Marketing and Purchasing (Group)
INCOTERMS	International Commercial Terms
IPSERA	International Purchasing and Supply Education and Research Association
IPT	Integrated Project Teams
ISO	International Standards Organization
IT	information technology
ITT	Invitation to Tender
JIT	Just In Time
JPPSG	Joint Procurement Policy and Strategy Group
KM	knowledge management
LDC	less developed country
MoD	Ministry of Defence
MRO	maintenance, repairs and operating
MRP	materials requirements planning
NAO	National Audit Office
NCC	National Computing Centre
NETA	New Electricity Trading Arrangements
NGO	non-governmental organization
NGTA	New Gas Trading Arrangements
OECD	Organization for Economic Cooperation and Development
OFFER	Office of Electricity Regulation
OFGAS	Office of Gas Regulation
OFGEM	Office of Gas and Electricity Markets
OGC	Office of Government Commerce
PO	purchase order
PRS	Public Electricity Supply Regulatory System
QA	quality assurance
R&D	research and development
RBV	resource-based view
REC	regional electricity company

RISP	Regional Information Systems Plan
SCM	supply chain management
SCOP	Standing Conference of Principals
SIC	semi-industrialized country
SLA	service-level agreement
SMP	System Marginal Price
SME	small and medium-sized enterprise
STD	socio-technical design
TIR	Transports Internationaux par Route
TNC	trans-national corporation
WEEE	Waste Electrical and Electronic Equipment (EU Draft Directive)

Notes on contributors

Paul Abbiati is an international e-procurement law consultant and an associate of the PMMS Consulting Group. He researches, writes and speaks on e-law in Europe and Asia. Paul is a presenter at Chartered Institute of Purchasing and Supply (CIPS) legal training courses and seminars in the UK and abroad. His reports and articles are published regularly in UK and international newspapers, magazines and books. He is a member of International Chamber of Commerce (ICC) committees on e-law.

Ken Burnett read for his first degree at Leeds University, followed by a higher degree at the University of Manchester. He joined CIPS in 1991, having previously worked in consultancy organizations, research associations and academia. He is one of three Practice Development Officers in the Professional Practice Team, where he is responsible for answering technical enquiries from both members and non-members. Additionally he is Secretary of a number of Committees which meet on a regular basis to discuss and advise on specific developments in the law and the UK legal system generally. He has also produced several publications, mainly on IT and legal issues, for sale through the CIPS Bookshop, and has contributed papers and book reviews to *Supply Management* and other journals.

Tom Chadwick has 20 years' experience in production and materials management in the defence sector with Ferranti and GEC Marconi. He became Director of Procurement at the University of Edinburgh in 1993, and in 1998 took up his current position in the new post of Director of Procurement Development for the Joint Procurement Policy and Strategy Group (JPPSG) for UK Higher Education. A Fellow of the Chartered Institute of Purchasing and Supply, he is a member of the CIPS appointments board, and a Trustee Director of EduServ, a not-for-profit company working with education for education. He is also part-time lecturer at Heriot-Watt University.

Lorna Chicksand is Lecturer in E-Business at Birmingham Business School. She has published widely on the impact of the Internet on marketing, internal management and procurement and supply chain management. Her research activities include e-business and its impact on marketing.

Christopher Cowton is Professor of Accounting at Huddersfield University Business School. He took up his current appointment in 1996 after ten years at the University of Oxford, where he was University Lecturer in Management Studies and a Fellow of Templeton College. His publications range from philosophy to operations management, but much of his current writing is focused on business and financial ethics. He is Chair of EBEN-UK, the UK Association of the European Business Ethics Network.

Andrew Cox is CIPS-sponsored Professor and Director of the Centre for Business Strategy and Procurement (CBSP) at Birmingham Business School. He is currently involved in two EPSRC-funded research projects developing audit tools and techniques for effective supply chain management. His most recent publications include *The E-Business Report 2001* (Earlsgate Press); *Supply Chains, Markets and Power: Mapping buyer and supplier regimes* (Routledge); *Power Regimes: Mapping the DNA of business and supply chain relationships* (Earlsgate Press); and *Business Success: A way of thinking about strategy, critical assets and operational best practice* (Earlsgate Press).

Marc Day is Head of Research for the Chartered Institute of Purchasing and Supply, a UK-based body for purchasing and supply management personnel. He is a visiting fellow at two universities in the UK, Keele and Birmingham, publishes regularly as an academic scholar and teaches at undergraduate and postgraduate level. His publications range from the theory and philosophy of organization through to the emergent aspects of e-business. He is currently secretary to the International Purchasing and Supply Education and Research Association (IPSERA). He holds a bachelor's degree in business administration and a PhD in manufacturing supply management from Keele University in the UK.

David Ford is Professor of Marketing at the University of Bath, School of Management in the UK. He is an engineer by initial training and before becoming an academic he was Group Planning Manager for the UK operations of American Standard Inc. David Ford specializes in the marketing and purchasing problems of companies in international technology-based markets. He is best known for his work on Business Marketing Strategy, Business Purchasing, the Management of Business Relationships and Technology Strategy. He is a founder member of the international Industrial Marketing and Purchasing (IMP) Group of researchers. The group has carried out a large number of wide-ranging research projects into business, industrial and international marketing. His most recent books, with other members of the IMP group, are *Managing Business Relationships* (Wiley 1998), *Understanding Business Marketing and Purchasing* (3rd edition, International Thomson, 2001) and *Managing and Marketing Technology* (International Thomson, 2001). David Ford has acted as seminar leader or consultant for a large number of international companies, mainly operating in technology-based industries. He also has a strong interest in consumer marketing and has worked with several of the largest UK retailers.

Richard Hall is Professor of Operations and Procurement Strategy at the Durham University Business School. He was appointed to this chair in August 1995; earlier that year Richard won the internationally contested Igor Ansoff Strategy Award. Richard's academic career commenced in 1988 when he joined the Department of Industrial Management at the University of Newcastle upon Tyne; before that he had an extensive career in industry. He initially served as an operations manager for four years with Unilever, then seven years with PA Consulting as a management consultant. Before joining academia he was the managing director of a consumer products manufacturer for 14 years. Richard heads the Centre for the Study of Supply Chain Strategy at Durham, which carries out research on behalf of the Engineering and Physical Sciences Research Council (EPSRC) and the Chartered Institute of Purchasing and Supply.

Christine Harland is Senior Research Fellow and Director of the Centre for Research in

Strategic Purchasing and Supply (CR*i*SPS) in the School of Management, University of Bath. She directs a partnership programme of action research in Supply Strategy with the NHS Purchasing and Supply Agency in addition to conducting private sector based research. Before joining the University of Bath, Christine lectured on the MBA programme at Warwick Business School and had a previous industrial career in supply chain management with GEC Telecommunications and the Dowty Group. As a business consultant Christine has worked with many international organizations in this field, including BT, Ericsson, Hewlett Packard, Volvo, Telia, Nokia, Nestlé, Coats Viyella, Rover, Computer Sciences Corporation and Courtaulds. She is co-author of the world's leading text on Operations Management and is widely published in books, journal articles and research reports. Christine has been an adviser to HM Treasury on Strategic Procurement and was invited to contribute to the recent cabinet office review of civil government procurement.

Simon Harris is a Director of Structured Export Finance at Lloyds TSB Bank plc in London, currently specializing in officially supported export credit financing. He is a career banker with over 30 years' experience, primarily centred on specialized trade finance, recovery techniques and corporate and country risk analysis and management.

Chris Harty is in the Centre for Science Studies, part of the Sociology Department at Lancaster University. His main research interests are the social roles and implications of new technologies. He is currently undertaking research in the construction sector on new design technologies and their effects on the organization of construction-work processes.

Paul Ireland is Research Fellow at the Centre for Business Strategy and Procurement (CBSP) at Birmingham Business School. He has published several papers and books on supply chain management in the information technology and construction industries. His current research interests include e-business applications and their impact on procurement, supply chain management and business strategy.

Neil Jarrett and **Mark Smalley** are consultants from the Warwick Manufacturing Group with considerable experience working with clients and construction organizations to introduce new forms of procurement and improve collaboration of the construction team. Neil is a chartered civil engineer and Mark has considerable experience in implementing Japanese manufacturing practices in UK companies. Their recent experience has been working with clients and construction organizations to introduce processes, tools and techniques for collaborative working. Mark and Neil are currently running a supply chain benchmarking club and a range of construction consultancy projects. Clients include Welsh Water, North British Housing Association, Treasury, Defence Estates, NHS Estates, Portsmouth City Council, National Audit Office, John Laing, Mansell, Tilbury Douglas, Costain, Ballast Wiltshire, White Young Green and Reading Construction Forum, Department of Trade and Industry.

Richard Lamming is the CIPS Professor of Purchasing and Supply Management at the School of Management, University of Bath, in the UK. He was founder of the Centre for Research in Strategic Purchasing and Supply (CR*i*SPS). He is Head of Research for the School of Management. Following an engineering apprenticeship with Jaguar Cars he held positions in purchasing in the UK automotive industry, and spent five years in management consultancy. He has a BSc in Production Engineering and his Doctoral thesis was on strategic management of technological innovation in supply relationships, based upon research in ten countries. He was part of a small team which contributed to the best-selling book, *The Machine That Changed the World* (HarperCollins, 1990). He developed the concept of lean supply in another book in 1993: *Beyond Partnership: Strategies for Innovation and Lean Supply* (Prentice Hall). He is a member of several committees of the UK Chartered Institute of Purchasing and Supply and in 1995 he was awarded the CIPS' highest honour, the Swinbank Medal, for services to the purchasing profession. He has been intimately associated with purchasing and supply management for over 25 years.

Chris Lonsdale is a lecturer in Supply Chain Management at the University of Birmingham. He is the author of *Outsourcing: A Business Guide to Risk Management Tools and Techniques* (Earlsgate Press).

Christopher Low is a management consultant specializing in supply chain issues. He has advised a number of companies on environmental and labour issues and has presented papers on the topic at a number of European conferences. He is presently completing his PhD on labour standards in company supply chains with a particular focus on the role of campaigning NGOs in collaborating with companies in this area of activity. He has been engaged in management education for seven years and lectures at the University of Bradford Management Centre.

Kenneth Lysons spent ten years in purchasing before entering teaching and has held a number of senior appointments in further and higher education. A graduate of three universities, he has written 12 books and over 200 published articles. He currently works as a freelance writer and management consultant.

Douglas Macbeth is Director of Centre for Supply Chain Management. The Centre was co-founded by SCMG Ltd, the University of Glasgow and the Chartered Institute of Purchasing and Supply. It is one of only four centres sponsored by CIPS. Douglas organizes a Supply Chain Club for 150 companies and runs an annual Supply Chain and e-procurement Conference as well as research projects and training events. He is also a Director of SCMG Ltd, which is a specialized consultancy in the strategy and operation of cooperative business relationships for best-value delivery. Professor Macbeth has worked across a range of public and private sector organizations and three UK universities, and has had visiting roles in GSBA Zurich and SUNY at Albany, USA. He is the author of four books and numerous articles and has consulted for and researched in major international companies.

Barbara Morton is based in the Centre for Research on Organizations, Management and Technical Change (CROMTEC) at Manchester School of Management, UMIST. Barbara chairs the Environmental and Green Issues Policy Group of the Chartered Institute of Purchasing and Supply. She is the founder and coordinator of the Environmental Supply Chain Forum, which brings together supply chain and environmental managers from a wide range of organizations to promote good practice in environmental supply chain management. Barbara works with a wide range of organizations, in a number of sectors, including healthcare, electricity and water supply, higher education and retailing. Her work involves assisting organizations to integrate environmental and sustainability criteria into their purchasing and supply chain management practices. Barbara has published widely on environmental supply chain management issues.

Michael Quayle is the Director of the Business School and Bosch Chair in Purchasing and Supply at the University of Glamorgan, UK. Before entering academia he gained significant procurement and project management experience in the European electronics and defence industries. An adviser to the UK HM Treasury, Michael is a registered purchasing and supply management specialist with the United Nations (UNCTAD) and has been published extensively in the fields of management development, purchasing, materials management and logistics. He is also the Chartered Institute of Purchasing and Supply (CIPS) Ambassador to Wales. He has a Doctorate (PhD) in Procurement from the University of Lancaster, UK, a Masters degree (MLitt) in Industrial Relations from the University of Glasgow, UK and a first degree (BSc) in Business Management from the University of Maryland, USA.

Colin Rigby is currently completing his PhD under the PTP scheme between CERAM Research Ltd and Keele University, which is based on examining the theoretical and practical considerations of the agile enterprise. This three-year applied research project is sponsored by the UK DTI and the EPSRC, with further financial support from a number of leading UK ceramics companies. Before beginning his Doctoral research at the Department of Management, Keele University, Colin gained extensive practical experience of production management and engineering-based project work across a number of sectors of the ceramics industry. Before starting his career in engineering, Colin complete his MSc and MPhil at Manchester University and a BSc at UMIST in engineering-based disciplines.

Peter Stannack is an international management consultant specializing in supply management. He is a director of Sourcing Performance, and has contributed to a number of academic and practitioner publications. He is an active contributory member of IPSERA, the international network for purchasing research.

Ken Waters started his early career in shipping where he obtained his Master Mariner's Certificate in 1970. He obtained his BSc (Technology) and then became a lecturer in Maritime Studies, Ship Broking and Export Management before obtaining an MBA in 1986. He teaches courses on distribution and transport systems, export and purchasing and supply. He is a member of the Institute of Logsitics and Transport, Chartered Institute of Marketing and the Nautical Institute.

Richard Wilding is a Senior Lecturer at the Centre for Logistics and Transportation, Cranfield School of Management, UK. Richard works with European and International companies from a variety of industries on logistics and supply chain projects, including the implementation of e-commerce. Richard is both a European and Chartered Engineer; he is a chartered member of the Institute of Logistics and Transport and Institute of Electrical Engineers (Manufacturing Division). He is a steering committee member of the Logistics Research Network, a global network of academics and practitioners involved in state-of-the-art logistics and supply chain research.

Introduction

Marc Day

Since the start of the twentieth century academics and practitioners have tried to understand contracting relations between firms for the sales and supply of materials, goods, services, knowledge and capabilities. We started by terming this purchasing (or procurement); this then moved on to supply management, and then extended to supply chain management. We now (and we are unsure for how long) converse in terms of supply network management and supplier relationship management.

Purchasing has always stood on the boundary of the firm, looking outside and scanning the environment for new opportunities and threats. We are often faced with wide and complex requirements to work within, and in some cases, manage that collection of other companies called suppliers that serve our focal firm. This book will deliver a multifaceted view of the activities that contribute to a holistic understanding of supply management, and how purchasing contributes to general corporate performance.

For many decades we have claimed that activities engaged with business and management have become more and more intensified. It has always been difficult to secure a long-term strategic competitive advantage for generating greater-than-average returns on capital employed. What we now have is a more sophisticated and insightful understanding of the pressures that impinge on us as workers, managers, entrepreneurs, individuals and groups in organizations. In particular, we are constantly hearing of new and more detailed insights from the consulting and academic fields that give us a greater chance to change what we do at work with greater commercial sensitivity. Even when we don't know what will happen, we now have the ability to reason though the subtle evaluation of evidence and use of scenario planning to reach a reasonable conclusion.

If we consider the organization primarily in systems terms, then we have a structure that demands inputs in order to change them into some format, sell them on and generate some value from the performance of these activities. We can see from this very simplistic organizational structure that purchasing (the controller of inputs) holds an important position in organizational terms. This loose grouping of people we often term 'purchasers' are the determinants of both end-product specification and how much revenue is generated from the value added through this transition. With this simplistic approach in mind we can see that the internal and external management and organization of a network is the greatest challenge in performing efficient and effective purchasing.

A great many forces shape the way that purchasing contributes to general corporate performance. In recent years we have been deluged by the potential effects of information technology (IT), somewhat reminiscent of another search for a panacea to control and manage purchasing without the 'people' factor. The general economic conditions that pervade all of the functions of a firm often ride on the waves of economic prosperity and recession, with purchasing playing different roles across these changing times. However, we have some continual and long-running requirements of a competent and professional purchasing function, a particular set of skills brought together in the hands of experienced practitioners and consultants who can play a very active part in corporate prosperity.

What is purchasing?

The scope of purchasing's contribution to corporate management and organization has been gradually growing over the past two to three decades. However, the perception of the contribution (albeit in patches of advanced practice) that the function makes remains variable and incomplete across all manufacturing and service sectors. However, if we consider that purchased goods and services can account for between 50 and 80 per cent of a company's overall expenditure, purchasing does become a key contributor to the profit margin of the corporation. So, can we draw a boundary around purchasing and supply management to aid the practitioner, academic and consultant in identifying where purchasing can make a contribution? We will argue throughout this book that no definition can wholly incorporate the demands placed on a purchasing team's collective set of skills, but we will place a 'stake in the ground'.

For the requirements of defining the scope of this text, purchasing is defined as 'obtaining from external sources all goods, services, capabilities and knowledge which are necessary for running, maintaining, and managing the company's primary and support activities at the most favourable conditions.' (van Weele, 2000, p. 14). In addition, we will argue that the purchasing function should also engage, when appropriate, in activities that identify and exploit activities that directly contribute to business growth by enhancing sales revenue. This mode of purchasing action has often been carried out and labelled as 'business development', but may elevate purchasing from being perceived only as a collection of skills directed predominantly at cost saving.

Changes in the third edition

The third iteration of this successful text is quite different from the previous two, as there has been a mixed set of disruptive and incremental changes in both the landscape for business and the factors that impinge directly on purchasing. In the past two editions it has been the norm to integrate a wide variety of perspectives into a loose framework based on academic, consulting and practitioner contributions about the nebulous concept we call purchasing.

The third edition has been slimmed down and focused to assist the reader by working systematically outwards using a purchasing lens to view the wider business world. The aim of the text is to show the potential contribution that purchasing can make as a driver for organizational efficiency and business development. It is this latter requirement, the need for purchasing to generate revenue, that has become an additional demand on a purchasing directors' time and effort.

Detailed outline of the book

The book is split into three sections. In Part I we lay the foundations for building the organization of purchasing in a corporate environment. We will consider how the processes for purchasing form, what purchasing strategy resembles at different levels of thinking, how to conceptualize the execution of a make–buy decision, and finally how the critical components of finance, management accounting and the interaction with marketing impact on decision making.

Part II will overlay further applications on the foundations of purchasing organization. The assumption will be made that the purchasing activities of the firm will be proactive in outlook, gathering knowledge and measuring their current corporate purchasing performance, but also looking to generate revenues for the business as a result of environmental interaction. These research activities will be compliant with different legal frameworks and exhibit care for the global ecosystem in which modern capitalist modes of operation compete, showing sensitivity to ethical considerations.

The final part of the book will enact some of the learning from the framework built up in the first two tranches of this text. Some key insights will be given about the critical considerations surrounding the purchasing of gas, electricity and information technology (IT). These product-specific chapters will be complemented by insights into the oft-neglected issues surrounding small and medium-sized enterprise (SME) purchasing, procurement practices in the Higher Education sector and finally the practices of purchasing in the UK construction industry.

Chapter configurations

In the first part of the text, entitled 'The Foundations for Organizing Purchasing', Chapter 1 gives an overview of the different types of organization (functional, multi-divisional), and examines the emerging role of networks as intermediate forms of organizing. The unit of analysis for this chapter (the organization) is contrasted with notions of the chain, the value stream and other connected forms of interaction and organizing.

The strategic aspects of supply management have received significant academic and practitioner attention in the past years. Christine Harland, in Chapter 2, outlines these developments in understanding and insight, linking strategic management with the purchasing process and showing how they interact at functional, tactical and strategic levels. The chapter will give readers a basic understanding of strategy in the process of supply management, then guide them through the processes by which strategy is created.

Chapter 3 aims to explain in what ways the function of purchasing is practically organized to operate in an effective and efficient way in the internal organizational environment. Michael Quayle examines the following questions: 'How should the purchasing function be organized?'; 'How should it "fit" with the remainder of the organization?'; 'How should the current organization be reorganized?'; and 'How should it be improved?' The form of organization in purchasing directly links with its function, the subject of the next two chapters.

Douglas Macbeth, in Chapter 4, explains the relationship management task of purchasing, with closer ties between buyers and suppliers being used, when appropriate, as a more productive form of value adding over and above adversarial forms of bargaining and negotiation. This differentiated relationship management strategy is often sparked by the realization that a firm must gain the support of suppliers to reduce costs at a supply chain level as well as internally at the firm level. Although there are no 'ideal' relationship prescriptions for all cases, the selective use of different types of organizational commitment can be exhibited in a number of ways. It is therefore important for the practitioner, academic and consultant that the management of a portfolio of relationships be understood in a more rigorous fashion.

Directly linking with the relationship aspect of purchasing, the critical make–buy decision and outsourcing option is often the end result of a complex decision making and management process that has a many potential pitfalls for the organization as a whole. Chris Lonsdale, in Chapter 5, provides a coherent understanding of the decision points behind outsourcing, the rationale behind a make or buy decision, and how to conclude the process of outsourcing in a successful manner.

The following two chapters focus on the accounting based foundations for purchasing practice. Chapter 6 gives an introductory understanding of the linkages between financial management and the purchasing function, whilst Chapter 7 explores the linkages between management accounting, internal costing and the purchasing function.

Chapter 8 is the first in a series to link non-financial organization functions to purchasing. David Ford explores the linkages between marketing and purchasing, noting the deep ties between the two commonly cited functions of an organization in a systems view of the model corporation. Chapter 9, written by Richard Wilding, adds another externally focused dimension of workplace management and organization, that of logistics, materials planning and inventory control.

We then move to the second part of the book, tactical and operational applications in practice. Chapter 10 discusses the necessity for, and the problems associated with, measuring purchasing performance. Although seen by many as a simple 'cost savings' calculation, the measurement of performance is a complex and difficult process that requires an appreciation of context, the limits of a measurement system and their wider applicability in the organization. The questions answered in this chapter include: 'Why should purchasing be measured?'; 'What should be measured?'; and 'What methods exist in order to perform such evaluations?'

Chapter 11 links closely with the preceding chapter about performance measurement and even more closely with the subsequent chapter about the use of IS and IT in purchasing practice. Chris Harty and Marc Day extend the process view of the firm discussed by Richard Lamming in Chapter 1. In a critical review-based piece they set out how purchasing process organization should be viewed, and what potential caveats to business process management may emerge as a result of breaking down the functional silos that are clearly evident in a great many organizations.

Chapter 12, written by a group of researchers from the Centre for Business Strategy and Procurement (CBSP) at Birmingham University in the UK, assesses the use of IS/IT software for the purchase of goods and services over the Internet. As its backbone, this chapter examines the development of purchasing information systems, and the relationship between them and those used in other parts of the organization. Rather than just concentrating on the devolvement of responsibility for purchasing to 'users', the chapter gives a basic knowledge of the information systems that are key to many purchasing functions.

In Chapter 13 Richard Hall explains purchasing's role in the 'knowledge management' (KM) phenomenon that has pervaded strategic thinking in recent years. This chapter gives a basic understanding of the issues surrounding knowledge management, in particular leveraging knowledge as a key contributor to sustained competitive advantage. Case examples of the techniques used to harness and codify tacit knowledge assist in explaining the complex processes of KM, especially for practitioners who have not yet acquainted themselves with KM and resource-based strategy theory.

The next three chapters position the process of identifying new purchasing sources and practices according to ethical, legal and environmental dimensions. Chapter 14, by Barbara Morton, allows the purchasing practitioner to implement strategies that minimize the potential environmental impact of their activities. The contents reflect how to implement an environmentally aware purchasing strategy, and how to show the value of this to the wider organization. This chapter equips the practitioner with the basic tools to understand the need for developing an environmentally conscious strategy in action.

Directly linked with the previous contribution, Chapter 15 shows how ethical standards adopted by the purchasing function can have a considerable impact on the wider corporate ethical perspective. Chris Cowton and Chris Low show, from a different number of perspectives, that sound ethical standards are a prerequisite for effective purchasing.

Chapter 16 shows how effective information gathering about supply markets and the practice of purchasing has always been an important aspect of purchasing and supply management. Given the choice of alternative global sourcing options, environmental and ethical considerations, turbulence in world markets, different legal terms and conditions, the impact of the Internet and variable macroeconomic conditions, the purchaser must be equipped with the right skill set to source effectively and efficiently. This chapter gives practitioners and consultants insights using the following questions: 'What is purchasing research?'; 'How can the purchaser build an effective portfolio of market intelligence based on sound and rigorous research skills?'; 'What is the role of desk research and how is it performed?'

Chapter 17 gives a basic overview of the different legal frameworks that regulate the purchasing function, illustrating how to work within several different legal frameworks that comprise the global business scene. The main result of this chapter will be to equip the practitioner with the basic tools needed to understand and use international contracts. Chapter 18, the final contribution in Part II of the book, uses this global legal and contractual framework to explain the significance of countertrade and show its significance for purchasing.

The third part of the book, insights into purchasing practice, starts with Chapter 19, which gives some key insights into the purchasing activities surrounding procurement in small firms. The emphasis should be on explanation, primarily providing the practitioner with some actionable points that can be implemented in the workplace. In particular, this chapter makes the theory of purchasing and supply applicable to buyers who often have to contend with strongly differential power structures, smaller spend amounts and challenges to create ways to leverage spend. The chapter also examines the organizational role that purchasing takes within small firms, and how the SME purchasing practitioner can enhance their role in the wider organizational context.

Chapters 20 and 21, both written by Ken Burnett, give some key insights into the purchasing activities surrounding the buying of IS/IT software, gas and electricity. This triad of expenditure accounts, a key cumulative expense for the firm, and one in which professional purchasing can make a sound impact.

Chapter 22 investigates the specific challenges faced by the purchasing community of the Higher Education (HE) sector in the UK. Written by a key player in the sector, it gives the reader an understanding in context of the decisions made to streamline and make an effective purchasing contribution to this large proportion of public spending.

Chapter 23 provides a practitioner viewpoint of purchasing and supply management in transportation, often a mixed area of responsibility between purchasers, supply chain managers and logisticians. The chapter outlines INCOTERMS 2000 and gives a qualitative and statistical account of the transportation field.

The final contribution, Chapter 24, focuses on a section of the UK economy in which purchasing has been identified as a potentially large contributor to commercial success. Purchasing in the construction sector explains how the 'project'-based organization of construction can be matched to appropriate purchasing and supply management practices. This chapter concentrates on procedures and practices that are strongly associated with the difficult conditions of project-based purchasing, and suggests alternative forms of good-practice purchasing in construction. Supporting information is included from the large number of 'best-practice' projects and guidance notes published by the UK government and other industry bodies.

In the final pages of this book we give an extensive list of further reading and details of global professional purchasing institutes. This should prove an invaluable start for identifying more resources to assist you in your research and practice-based activities. There are many sources of help for academics, practitioners, and consultants over and beyond one book, all ready and available to be accessed by those that show an interest.

Reference

Van Weele, A.J., (2000), *Purchasing and Supply Chain Management*, London: Thomson Learning Business Press.

The Foundations for Organizing Purchasing

1 Purchasing and organizational design

Richard Lamming

New pressures for an old problem

As purchasing becomes a strategic part of the business organization and a significant contributor to its commercial, competitive success, so its position, shape and form within the organizational structure become more critical. The nature of the business will inevitably affect the choice of these dimensions although trends such as outsourcing, information and communications technology (ICT) and globalization may have an overarching impact.

Many of the modern strategic challenges facing organizations on the supply side do not fit within traditional purchasing perspectives. It is probable that new types of individual role will emerge within the function – possibly dividing it into two parts: day-to-day operations and leading edge deal making. The people who have been trained for traditional purchasing may find it hard to deal with these radical challenges and new perspectives. Whether they survive – and whether purchasing as a function remains in the organizational structure – depends to a great extent on how it is structured to meet the organization's needs.

The long-running debate in the organizational design of purchasing has been whether it should be *centralized* or *decentralized*. Much has been written on this, but even more has been formulated by consultants. This may be because the moves between central and distributed functional organization are not limited to purchasing: they form a bread-and-butter activity for consultants keen to develop organizational change. In this chapter, we shall review this debate and also consider some more recent aspects that must be taken into account in embarking on the design of purchasing's shape, form and position within the organizational structure.

The types and extent of competition faced by business organizations in almost all sectors have changed fundamentally over the past two decades. Central to this change has been the advance in information systems and telecommunications. As long ago as 1990, Venkatramen pointed out that information systems now represented a possibility for completely redesigning the organization and the ways in which it earned its income.[1] His point was not that this was an interesting option but that organizations which did not do this would not survive. The chief executive of American Airlines at the time was famously quoted as saying that if he had to sell his aeroplanes or his information system, he would sell the planes. Venkatramen showed how information systems required organizations first to evolve and then go through a revolution. In the 1990s, the rise of electronic commerce (variously including e-purchasing, e-procurement, e-business, e-connectivity, etc.) has been seen as a revolutionary stage in information systems, and there is general agreement with Venkatraman's prediction: everyone has to join this wave or simply get left behind. The implications for purchasing are extreme – we shall examine these in this chapter.

The broader implication of Venkatramen – that organizations would have to look anew at how they earned their keep – subtly combines with the technological impacts of the micro-processor (starting in the 1970s) and global labour markets to provide organizations with the need to reallocate activities, only performing those they are best at (some would say, 'world class'). This has meant that many organizations have stopped doing some of the things they used to do and now have those activities carried out for them by others: subcontractors. This is not new, of course, for purchasing, the 'make or buy?' (or 'do or buy?') decision has long been a staple of the function. However, the stakes are so high in outsourcing that a new language has been invented for it – the concept of 'core competencies'. It is wrong to think that these are things that an organization must do for itself, however. As Roberto Testore, Chief Executive of Fiat Auto, said in 1997, his company's core competencies were 'styling and engines.' Despite this, Fiat has always outsourced both of these to some extent (for example, having its styling done by famous automotive studios such as Pininfarina, Giugiaro and Bertone). The point is that Fiat needed to know about these competencies – to be an intelligent, well-briefed customer.

In practice, however, 'make or buy?' decisions rarely involve purchasing people in anything other than an information-providing role. This is because they are essentially political decisions, rather than commercial. Matters such as the closure of factories, mass transfer of employees, legal complexities (e.g. TUPE), relinquishing technical competence and so on are the subject of board decisions. After such a decision is made, purchasing is usually left with the task of dealing with disappointed suppliers and – even more complex – setting up outsourcing relationships with companies that now conduct vital parts of the organization's business. This is why no producer of personal computers now makes its own circuit assemblies, and pharmaceutical companies do not make their own pills – the internal workings of the PC and the blister packs of pills are all made by 'contract manufacturers'. The contract manufacturing sectors have quickly become dominated by a small number of large players. Dealing with these powerful partners is not a new duty for purchasing but it is one whose importance has recently increased significantly. We shall look at how purchasing can be organized to face this challenge.

The purpose of organizational design

Most business organizations are still designed the way that nineteenth-century mass production concepts demanded – close to a Weberian model of traditional bureaucracy. A hierarchy is constructed beneath the board of directors, with vertical functional 'chimneys' or 'silos' – ladders up which career paths are seen to lead – taking responsibility for the activities and specialisms into which the organization divides itself (finance, marketing and sales, operations, human resources, and so on). Purchasing is rarely one of these silos – more often it fits within one of the first three. The silos were strengthened over the twentieth century by the 'professionalization' of specialism, complete with self-governing associations (mimicking the craft-based guilds of two centuries before), centrally controlled examinations and qualifications (sometimes self-referential), and status differentials, largely based on time serving and practical experience – reinforcing the new *status quo*.

During the 1970s, much discussion began on the need for a more practical approach to the horizontal flows of communication (i.e. a member of staff might be permitted speak to their opposite number in another department [silo] without 'going through' their manager). This was driven by the need to remove operational anomalies that the previous system had accommodated. Such accommodation was no longer possible because markets at this time began to demand responsiveness and price performance that had not been seen previously. The concept of bringing a product to market in a specific time (more quickly than a competitor) meant that organizations could not wait for procedures to run their course – short circuits were needed: hence horizontal communication and the beginning of the end for functional silos. The operational level impact of this was the concept of 'cross-functional teams' in which people from different functional silos were put together to work as a unit, for a specific purpose. Breaking down the silo walls in this way was not easy, and cross-functional teams still appear to present major problems for some organizations today. For employees in purchasing, many of the people with whom they work on a daily basis are from other organizations (suppliers and contractors) and their cross-functional teams should logically break not only the silo walls but also the organization's own boundaries. A good example of this is given by the Integrated Project Teams (IPT) developed within the UK Ministry of Defence (for example, at the major centre at Abbey Wood, just north of Bristol), where secondees from several defence contractors and MOD personnel are co-located on a long-term basis (actually working together as an integrated team and sharing one large office) in order to focus their activities on a specific objective (e.g. developing a new submarine). The IPT initiative has not been without its teething problems but is widely seen as a success; it is now being copied by organizations within the defence industry for working on their own new products by collaborating with their suppliers in this way.

The purpose of organizational design, then, is to arrange the intelligent resources of the organization (people and ICT) in such a way that it can engage with the market effectively. It follows that, as the needs of the market change (e.g. computers have to become communicators in addition to calculators, or long-term peace breaks out in a previously troubled region, reducing the need for fighter aircraft), so the design of the organization must be reviewed. As globalization of customer markets forces organizations to face the need to be able to compete anywhere in the world – selling product and procuring goods and services – so their operations must reflect a strong core and flexible operating divisions. Purchasing is directly and profoundly affected by such design changes and cannot expect to live cosily within a traditional silo. The forces have been under way for some time and few people in purchasing have not already felt the wind of change.

Principal choices for organizing purchasing

In this section, we shall consider the basic choices that are available to the purchasing strategist when deploying people and resources to provide the organization with effective service. The actual choice made will depend upon the market pressures – there can never be one best way. It is also not possible to make simple connections between external pressures and organizational design; for example, globalization might mean entirely different things to an insurance company and a producer of motor cars. A buyer sourcing indirect materials, or 'MRO' (the American term – maintenance, repairs and operating[2] expenses – is now being popularized outside its home country by the wave of e-commerce providers) may have different concerns about e-procurement from those of a colleague buying components for production. However, in discussing the differing structure types, we shall consider situations in which each might appear *prima facie* appropriate.

CENTRALIZATION

The original silo format of organizations was based on all the functions being co-located on one site – often quite literally 'beneath' the board of directors (who would occupy the top floor of the office block). This simple idea naturally brought the purchasing department together as one entity. When divisions were formed in the organization, so satellite plants would be managed from the centre, where the expertise, records and political power lay. Once the divisions began to gain different political power and expertise (local knowledge, language, etc.), tensions built up between them and the centre. From these early developments in the twentieth century, centralized purchasing inherited advantages and disadvantages (see Figure 1.1). Naturally, when the divisions originated outside the organization (i.e. acquisitions) the political difficulties in centralizing purchasing might be very complicated.

Economies of scale

Perhaps the most obvious advantage of centralization is the ability of the organization to amalgamate its requirements – across the divisions – and purchase in large quantities, negotiating for lower prices: traditional economies of scale. If commodities are to be bought, this makes even more sense – the size of requirements is a powerful bargaining tool in such purchasing and even more important if the trader is to balance a portfolio of futures and stocks in various places in the world – perhaps dealing on several exchanges at once. In some industries this is not even seen as purchasing – for example, in the UK, chocolate bar producer Mars refers to the people who buy cocoa, sugar, and butter for them as 'Economists'. (We shall look at this in more detail later.)

The amalgamation of requirements is only a paper exercise, of course. The delivery requirements may be much more diverse (for example, head office in London might make a corporate deal on photocopier paper but require it to be delivered to several operating

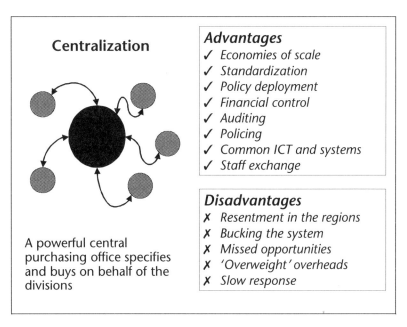

Figure 1.1   *Centralization of purchasing*

divisions on sites across Europe). This can detract from the economies of scale, as the supplier will need to charge for the delivery complexity – thus removing the single, optimized price (note that the supplier will have to charge for this, whether the customer realizes it or not).

Standardization

With the amalgamation of requirements comes the ability to standardize. This should provide operating cost reductions as well as the possibility of a lower overall price. For example, in 1999, SmithKline Beecham developed a global purchasing database that enabled its purchasing staff and divisional managers to know the price that should be paid for many items across a wide range of requirements, wherever in the world they were purchased. At the same time, head office did a deal with Compaq for laptop computers. Through this deal, an SB person in, say, Sydney, Australia could buy a computer at the lowest price possible (price saving). When she brought her laptop to a meeting in London and needed to replace a part that had been broken on the flight, the standardization meant that her machine was the same as that used by her UK colleagues, and the part could be procured and fitted easily. The Internet hardware manufacturer Cisco has a similar policy, linked to its strategy of growth through acquisition: when it takes over another company, all existing computers are removed and replaced with a standard model (also a Compaq) so that all PCs throughout the organization are the same.

Policy deployment

Standardizing should support the vital concept of policy deployment. This means constructing organizational mechanisms that ensure the policies developed by the directors are actually followed in practice. (Note that policy is a much more profound and long-term feature than strategy, which may change at a moment's notice. Policy is a public statement – to the community, shareholders, employees, customers and suppliers – of what the organization stands for.) Failure to deploy policy is a key weakness in many organizations (for example, it is often the case that the chief executive tells the shareholders that the firm now operates a policy of collaborating with suppliers, while at the purchasing interface the buyer is still instructed to negotiate for every penny possible, regardless of the impact on the supplier, who is seen as a disposable resource). The weakness comes from a lack of credibility in the marketplace (first the supply market, then the stock market).

Centralized purchasing should mean that the decisions taken centrally can be manifested in divisions by controlling what is bought. The logic is that procedures to control purchasing in the organization as a whole can be more easily managed if they are run by one office (rather than several, perhaps located in countries thousands of miles apart, by people who speak different languages and have different customs).

Financial control

Centralized purchasing should lead to better control of financial issues, for similar reasons to those applying to policy deployment. This should include the costs of purchase, the financial implications for investment (capital) and cashflow (revenue) and the integration with other parts of the organization that are responsible for such matters. Once again it is the geographical proximity and the homogeneity of the business culture that are employed to engender the benefits.

Auditing

The inspection of procedures is a complex and difficult process, made simpler by the co-location of all the areas that must be examined – and is rarely popular with those whose actions are under scrutiny! Centralizing the purchasing activity should ease the complexity (and thus reduce its process costs) and make for more effective, responsive auditing.

Policing

The bane of the purchaser's life is so-called 'maverick' buying – where an individual decides to procure something outside the agreed specifications, or takes action which compromises the commercial freedom of the buyer to gain value for money from the organization. Even when individuals are spending their own budgets, the lapse in control represented by non-standard choices is perceived as a weakness in the system. We shall visit this again later – it is not that simple, of course – but for now, it appears that a basic advantage of centralization should be the ability of the purchasing system to stop maverick buying, or any other departure from the agreed procedure (whether or not the act itself represents criminal, moral or ethical corruption, or just someone exercising their imagination).

Common information and communications technology and systems

For three decades, business has struggled to get to grips with the information systems presented to it by an avid and avaricious supply industry (hardware and software manufacturers and consultants). The complexity of the systems coupled with the complexity of the processes and structures they are attempting to manage has meant that stories of failure and duplication are legion. The addition of the need to incorporate communications in the package (and thus move from IT to ICT) has complicated matters even further. From Materials Requirements Planning in the 1970s to Enterprise Resources Planning in the 1990s (and e-procurement at the turn of the century), IT/ICT systems appear to have provided solutions in theory and problems in practice. They are seen, nevertheless, as a *sine qua non*, and purchasing is required to fall in line with its share of them. This may be seen as a generalization but it is depressingly obvious in practice.

This is not the place to explore all this complexity (and the despair in implementation). Suffice it to say that a centralized system should logically be simpler to develop, implement and run than one that has to take in the complexity of decentralized decision making. This should be reinforced by the possibilities represented by the Internet. That said, the need to communicate between the centre and the operating units can never be assumed to be a simple matter in a divisionalized organization.

Staff exchange

The staff in a centralized purchasing organization develop skills and expertise, coupled with an overview of the corporate position, which may be rare and valuable attributes within the divisionalized organization. This 'view from the hill' may be shared with divisions by seconding staff from the centre. It is an assumed benefit of centralization, therefore, that someone has a view of the total organization. Whether or not this is so will depend on the degree to which there is transparency and communication within the organization, as we shall see.

Disadvantages

The disadvantages of centralization stem largely from attitudinal problems and the difficulty of controlling processes remotely. The feelings of people in divisions towards headquarters may include resentment of perceived hierarchy or privilege, and it is likely that any anomaly or mishap will be blamed upon those in the central office who 'don't know what is going on at the coalface'. Thus, a system that runs well may still be criticized simply because it is imposed, while one that leads to errors will be grasped with enthusiasm as an opportunity to show dissent.

Beyond criticism, of course, lies sabotage. Staff in divisions (in purchasing offices or operating units who are, in effect, the 'customers' for purchasing's services) often feel they have a right to autonomy, since it is they who answer for the performance of their operation. This commonly leads to 'bucking the system' (the maverick buying referred to above). Local staff express their preference by ignoring the standard systems and preferred sources, and conceal this in order to avoid penalties. Once this starts (and it is traditionally a very common practice), the integrity of the centralized system can never be assured.

The people in the divisions who criticize the central system may not be wrong to do so. Local knowledge at the divisional level may be very valuable, and a system that seeks to suppress this may lead to missed opportunities. For example, when the Japanese television manufacturers came to South Wales in the 1970s, they set about developing local supply bases. This was not just for political or even logistical reasons – the need to localize design of televisions begins with the people who will watch them. When their *Accord* saloon was redesigned in 1996, Honda ended up with three different models for the three principal regions, allowing for varying tastes. 'Global' need not mean standardized (Akio Morita of Sony invented the word 'glocalization' to describe this combination of global economies of scale combined with local preferences). This may apply to ways of working (including systems and procedures) as well as to products and services.

A negative feature of centralized control that grew during the first three quarters of the twentieth century was what might be called 'corporate obesity' – excessive overhead costs and even opulence in some cases. In the UK, companies would boast elaborate headquarters buildings in fashionable areas, justifying them as symbols of success which would appear to potential shareholders. Centralized purchasing can also suffer in this way – another reason for those in divisions to criticize it. Oversized central offices also typically work with a slow response to divisional matters – despite the extra people, the system did not provide good service to its remote customers. (The corporate palaces came down in the last two decades of the twentieth century, as funds were redirected to improve operations, and takeover deals often revealed decadence and profligacy at the heart of the old empires.)

DECENTRALIZATION

Many of the advantages of decentralization (see Figure 1.2) come from removing the disadvantages of centralization, discussed above. As the constraints of the centrally run system are removed, those in the divisions gradually take more control of their day-to-day affairs and can develop previously unexploited opportunities.

Autonomy

For staff in divisions to control their own purchasing, critical resources must be made available by corporate planners. Such resources will include information systems which are inevitably designed in one location (centrally). For the divisions to enjoy autonomy, therefore, means consulting staff there about standardized ICT provisions. This seemingly obvious requirement apparently eluded purchasing and IT strategists for many years (and still does in some fields).

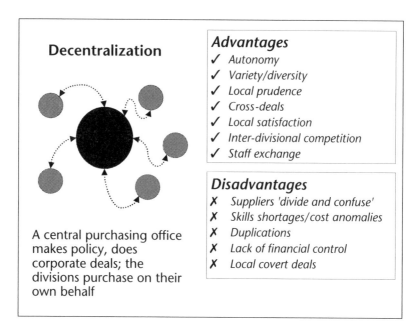

Figure 1.2 *Decentralization of purchasing*

Autonomy, once agreed, should enable divisional purchasing staff to exploit the diversity and variety of local supplies, and to exercise prudence (which may reflect, for example, local culture that would be offended by insensitive edicts from a remote central office). As the responsibility for divisional purchasing to obtain best value for money for their funds becomes real, so the carping about anomalous systems must logically disappear ('If it doesn't work for you then change it yourself – to your own requirements').

Cross-deals

The divisions themselves become the focus for activity and planning although in decentralized systems, however, a central office usually remains, often in a 'staff' role (as opposed to a 'line function') or internal consultancy. In very large global organizations, the central (or 'corporate') office often has no executive control over purchasing in the divisions and may be chiefly concerned with consolidating policies (removing anomalies between divisions), education and training, and process development (i.e. genuine consultancy). This may need to be funded as an overhead, or on the basis of the central team charging its customers (divisional purchasing directors) for its services. The latter is often fraught with difficulty in practice because hard-pressed operating divisions are likely to remove, say, 'education' from their budgets in favour of more immediately beneficial investments, even though they would probably all agree that education is vital, in the long term.

Partly as a result of the 'bridging' mechanism of a central office (as described above) but also as a part of everyday operating, it is likely that senior staff in the divisions will communicate amongst themselves as a natural network. This can lead to opportunities in one region being exploited by purchasing in another – a 'cross-deal'. This can include making other divisions aware of especially good suppliers, exchanging members of staff on secondment, and so on. Often, however, such sharing of benefits is curtailed by a buyer in one region fearing that, by sharing a good supplier, they might lose the position of preferred customer, with a consequent drop-off in service. This is a good example of the failure of organizational logic in the face of human nature. Intra-corporate (sometimes internecine!) secrecy and competition remain alive and well in decentralized purchasing systems.

Being able to respond to local requirements without the need for central approval of plans should lead to purchasing offices in divisions improving the satisfaction felt by their 'customers' in their operating units.

Disadvantages

The disadvantages of decentralization, however, can lead to situations as corrupted as the one we saw above under the opposite arrangement. The lack of communication or collaboration between divisions, unchecked by a central common system, can provide a perfect opportunity for suppliers to exploit their customers by charging different prices across the corporate organization. This was the situation in the National Health Service as recently as the early 1990s, where one health authority would typically be paying significantly higher prices for an item (e.g. hypodermic syringes) than its neighbour, just a few miles away. The problem was addressed by the formation of central purchasing authority for the NHS, but the predictable wrangles over local autonomy continued (for example, a surgeon often likes to use one particular brand of latex gloves, and is not prepared to have this preference compromised by a clerk in a central purchasing office, simply to save a few pounds when lives might be put at risk).

Decentralization inevitably involves duplication of resources – each divisional office has to have its own range of skills and competences. In addition to the obvious corporate cost of this (which might, however, not exceed the cost of the excessive overheads in the centralized system, as discussed above), a situation of scarcity may arise (e.g. just how many e-commerce experts can a corporation hope to employ?).

A combination of these factors may give rise to difficulty in controlling the financial reporting in a decentralized organization – if only for purposes of corporate reporting. The tendency for divisions to conduct local, covert deals may lead, in fact, to a loss of intelligence at the corporate level that could be considered destabilizing for the organization – not a situation that is tolerable for long. For example, the Walt Disney corporation reached a point in the 1980s where the chief financial officer did not know how much was being spent on the very diverse and exotic range of products and services that a company such as this must procure. Decentralization had gone haywire. His only chance of regaining control was to stop all payments being made and see who complained! Then, one small central office was set up where all cheques would be raised for payment. Gradually, a picture emerged of the spend that was being made across the corporation.

ATOMIZATION

So far we have considered corporations in which there is a central 'headquarters' office (which presumably doesn't do anything productive – i.e. it is an overhead cost) and operating divisions, where all the action takes place. It is not just in such a large, divisionalized organization that the debate on central control takes place – in any situation where purchasing provides a service to budget-holding 'internal customers' there will be a tension between the constraints of a formal system in the former and the wishes and preferences of the latter.

One way of overcoming this is to *atomize* responsibility for expenditure – to 'explode' it from the centre to the budget holders. This has radical implications for both purchasing and the organization as a whole (see Figure 1.3). The budget holders may assume that they can make their own purchases but find that it is not as simple as it seems to get good value. Rather than fall back on traditional central purchasing, they may require different types of support, including advice on policy, tactical activity, legal and contractual matters, and so on.

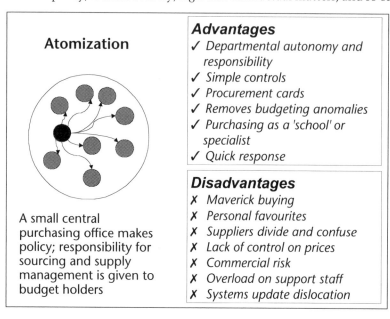

Atomization	**Advantages**
	✓ Departmental autonomy and responsibility
	✓ Simple controls
	✓ Procurement cards
	✓ Removes budgeting anomalies
	✓ Purchasing as a 'school' or specialist
	✓ Quick response
A small central purchasing office makes policy; responsibility for sourcing and supply management is given to budget holders	**Disadvantages**
	✗ Maverick buying
	✗ Personal favourites
	✗ Suppliers divide and confuse
	✗ Lack of control on prices
	✗ Commercial risk
	✗ Overload on support staff
	✗ Systems update dislocation

Figure 1.3   *Atomization of purchasing*

As with decentralization, atomization brings autonomy to the budget holder. It may be possible to temper this with fairly simple controls; for example, the advent of credit cards for budget holders – the so-called procurement cards of the 1990s – represented an attempt to do just this. The early offerings from e-procurement systems suppliers take this concept to a more advanced level: budget holders can buy materials and services through a computer interface that can actually show them the product.

Budgets are a complex (and, some would say, conceptually flawed) concept in themselves. It is not in the interests of someone to whom an annual operating budget is given to reduce the amount allocated to them. So, if purchasing offers to reduce the cost of the items which the budget holder needs to acquire, it might easily be seen as a threat to the level of budget that could be claimed next year. Giving budget holders responsibility for purchasing may not result in corporate savings, therefore, and is open to all the problems of maverick buying, local preferences and supplier exploitation that we saw earlier. Atomization of purchasing may thus require a review of budgeting procedures.

The budget holders may see atomization as increasing their workload and bid to employ their own specialist (i.e. a purchaser in every department or project). This has all the resourcing problems (scarcity and duplication) that we saw above. The activity involved in purchasing by the budget holders must thus be reduced to a minimum. To do this, the purchasing department has an important role as a 'school' or internal consultancy – to help the budget holders buy for themselves with all the commercial skill and wisdom of a traditional purchasing person. This must be held together with a robust policy, which makes it clear to everyone how the organization conducts its relationships with other parties, and how dealings must proceed.

Atomization is still a relatively rare approach to structuring purchasing within an organization, even in those that are project-based; as technology (e-procurement) eases the physical burden associated with conducting one's own buying, so the concept appears to have major attractions, in reducing organizational dislocations that traditionally occur between the person who wants something (whether it is a piece of equipment or components to be used in production) and the remote purchaser who acquires it for them.

FEDERAL STRUCTURE

The expression 'federal' has suffered from a bad press in recent times, perhaps due to its use as a derogatory manner in political and economic reform in Europe. It is actually a more general concept and has major implications and opportunities for business organizations (see Figure 1.4).

Charles Handy, in his book *The Age of Unreason*, explains the basic rules of federalism.[3] Briefly put, Handy explains them as:

- Common rules and procedures: basic ground rules are agreed and used throughout the organization. Within these, local ways of working may vary, but not in conflict with the corporate policies and strategies.
- Dual citizenship: people in the organization are genuinely content to wear two hats – showing concern for the good of the corporation as a whole, and for their own local division.
- Subsidiarity: literally 'giving away power' by the centre to the divisions. This concept means that activities are carried out, and decisions taken, at the lowest level possible. The centre then becomes a coordinating device, but answerable to the divisions.

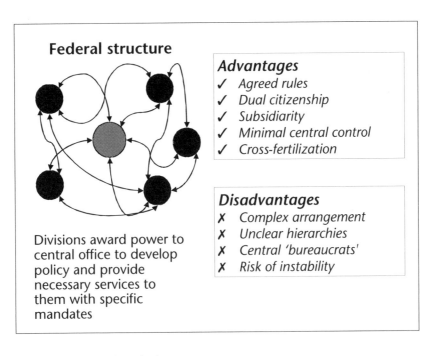

Figure 1.4   *Federal structures in puchasing*

For purchasing, the implications are profound. The role of the central office is to serve the divisions, not control them. Since its personnel are seconded from the divisions, there should be less chance of the centre becoming remote – the headquarters syndrome may be avoided. For their part, the divisions are in constant and intimate contact with one another – sharing sourcing information and maintaining a dual perspective – and they are as concerned for the success of the whole organization as they are for their own local prosperity. This is not easy in a business organization because it is quite possible for one division to be set against another in the need to decide, for example, which plant to invest in and which to close (especially if the two are in different countries). Thus, Ford's decision in 2000 to cease car production at its highly visible main plant in Dagenham was eased because the motor giant's purchasing is closely controlled globally from Dearborn in Michigan, and locally from Cologne, in Germany. The same company had, of course, long before realized the benefits to it of central control on purchasing, enabling it to economize on 'platforms' (the standardized base for a car, on which several different bodies might be produced, appearing to be independent designs). For example, this enabled Ford to produce new Jaguar saloons (the 'S' type, which is effectively a remodelled Linclon Town Car, and the X400, which is based on the Ford Mondeo).

In fact, Ford's purchasing, like that in many global giants, has to be a hybrid of the forms discussed above – combining the strengths of central planning with the necessities and opportunities of local sourcing. When the company began making its famous Model T, all the parts were produced in Michigan and then shipped to assembly plants around the USA. This technique was used throughout the twentieth century to enable developing countries to produce complex products from a kit of parts which could not possibly be sourced locally. The practice is called CKD, (standing for Completely Knocked Down) and is still in use today. As developing countries grow, however, their politicians want jobs for their people not just in assembly (in 'screwdriver plants') but in the more valuable activities (i.e. greater value is added in creating components from raw material than in simply screwing them together). The implication for purchasing is to be able to source locally (sometimes under the pressure for 'import substitution' or, in the more complicated world of defence procurement, as part of an 'offset' or 'counter-trade' deal).

HYBRID SYSTEMS

The most common form of hybrid is seen in organizations that decide to buy some commodities centrally and others locally. The rationale is typically based upon the principle of economies of scale – major deals that can be struck for items such as energy (often an organization's largest spend after labour), company cars, legal services, information systems, travel services, etc. True commodities (the word is used loosely for many items that are not actually commodities in the economic sense) such as cocoa and sugar for confectioners or steel for car producers, are almost always bought centrally unless the global nature of the organization provides sufficient bargaining strength for traders in several countries to buy independently. Even then, such traders within the organization will need to keep constantly in touch, to share market intelligence and trading dynamics such as the chance of arbitrage (buying in one market where the price is low and selling in another where it is high – a practice that helps to reduce anomalies on world markets).

Meanwhile, the organization requires (or allows) its divisions to purchase other requirements locally. Take the example of a catering company firm with a chain of restaurants (which may be owned or franchised); items where large-scale deals can bring low prices, reliable delivery and quality, resulting in standardized offerings to customers, will be bought centrally. Items such as fresh vegetables or bread, meanwhile, will be bought in local markets at the discretion of the local manager (or chef), to take advantage of daily deals and specialities.

Pseudo-commodities (such as technological items whose supply and demand fluctuate with innovation and fashion) pose a problem for manufacturers: the latest technology must be available globally but there is no formal market (i.e. a network with all the information, analysis, communication and stable dealing of a true commodity market) to support sourcing. An example of this would be 'dynamic random access memory' chips (DRAMs) in the computer industry. Producers of such vitally important components regularly employ the oldest form of economic power (make an item scarce and thus drive up the price) to support their industry. Consequently, computer manufacturers have to vie with one another to get hold of the precious components (which are said to be worth more than their weight in gold). To inform themselves, such producers set up mechanisms within their global structures to ensure that they know what is going on. One global giant, IBM, calls these 'commodity councils'. The members of such councils become the experts for IBM on the commodity in focus (e.g. 'memory' or 'packaging'), communicating constantly through electronic mail and video conferencing, etc.) and meeting occasionally. The councils are features of the purchasing structure within the global organization although they may include specialist non-purchasing people (such as engineers or logisticians).

Another traditional approach to the problem of intelligence on sourcing and technology is to appoint one division as 'lead buyer' for the commodity; the organization's 'brain' for sourcing, say, high-performance metals, might lie in its Singapore purchasing office: all others communicate with colleagues in Singapore for direction on this commodity. The problem with this approach, of course, is that the commodity becomes global (e.g. a new source for high-performance metals is set up in Brazil) and the single specialist division may find it difficult to maintain sufficient intelligence. The solution to this would seem to be IBM's commodity council approach.

TRENDS

Inevitably, structuring purchasing within organizations is a matter of 'horses for courses'. There are, however, some trends that might shed some light on where the topic is heading.

The twin forces of globalization and technology development (which are, of course, heavily intertwined) encourage both traditional approaches such as economies of scale, and radical concepts such as networked intelligence and atomization. A large organization with stable infrastructure (e.g. a local government system in one country) may face constant change but is unlikely to shut down divisions quite as readily as, say, a producer of televisions or a retailer. A federal system may work well in such a situation, since the divisions themselves compete in only some respects (e.g. for inward investment) but collaborate in most others (e.g. to drive down prices and improve quality levels for basic services).

The advent of electronic exchanges may be expected to encourage centralization, or perhaps federal structures, since the Internet makes geography almost irrelevant – at least at the sourcing stage. It is too early to assess the impact of such 'rational' approaches to purchasing on the strategic approaches of collaboration and partnering, in which, it would seem, personal connections and face-to-face meetings are all-important.

The possibilities of e-procurement may be extrapolated to a scenario in which much day-to-day purchasing is done by computers with minimal human input (as, for example, wages are managed currently) while the really value-adding deals in the supply market are done by powerful and dynamic individuals who see the world as their marketplace and work in very short timescales, possibly from a remote location. This scenario would encourage a centralized basis for the majority of purchases, coupled with a high degree of flexibility in the entire system for divisions to take advantage of special opportunities which must be managed as projects of change. The lesson for the structure of purchasing is clear in all these possibilities: it must change to adapt to the requirements of the organization. Such requirements cannot be assumed static, even over the briefest planning period.

Notes

1. For a good development of Venkatramen's work and many other linked concepts, see Scott Morton, M. (ed.) (1991), *The Corporation of the 1990s: Information Technology and Organizational Transformation*, Cambridge MA: MIT Press.
2. MRO is also sometimes used to stand for 'maintenance, repair and overhaul'.
3. Handy, C. (1989), *The Age of Unreason*, Business Books Ltd, London: Hutchinson.

2 *Purchasing strategy process*

Christine Harland

Introduction

Before examining purchasing strategy and the process for formulating it, first it should be considered in the wider context of business strategy.

Business strategy is a relatively new subject, and knowledge about it is evolving and developing in a fragmented way. Business strategy academics argue alternative views and approaches with each other and practitioners remain somewhat perplexed about how to actually *do* it. This is in no way a criticism or suggestion of failure of the subject and those who are involved in its development, but rather a recognition that the concepts, frameworks, theories and research community and their activities are still relatively young, dynamic and exciting. The subject of business strategy is not, therefore, evident in a relatively stable body of knowledge, fine-tuned and perfected over time. Rather, as a subject it takes small steps and large leaps in many different directions, testing and re-examining its assumptions based on perceptions of what appears to be the 'reality' of the business world. It can be argued that currently business strategists, both academics and practitioners, are in a phase of trying to make sense of dynamic, complex business decisions and practice in various business contexts. The contexts themselves are becoming more 'fuzzy'.

The focus for business strategy theory originated in private sector, firm-based decision making. However, the boundary for 'doing' strategy is no longer clear. Partnerships, alliances, outsourcing, strategic collaboration, joint ventures are all terms that have been applied to strategy being 'done' beyond the firm boundary. The Private Finance Initiative, Public Private Partnerships, privatization, liberalization and contractorization embody strategies that span the public and private sectors. Indeed there is evidence of public services around the world becoming more strategic, stretching, changing and spanning the boundaries that differentiated public from private sector responsibility and, therefore, strategy to effect that responsibility.

So, does the subject of business strategy provide clear rules and guidance for purchasing strategy? The short answer to this question is 'no'. How relevant is the study of business strategy to the understanding and improving of the purchasing strategy process? Understanding of the subject of business strategy can help provide a backcloth to set the scene for examining the purchasing strategy process.

Purchasing strategy in itself is in a state of dynamic development and there is no one stable body of knowledge to guide practitioners on how to 'do' it. Purchasing strategy has been mutating through the development of supply chain strategy and more recently the broader concept of supply strategy. This leaves purchasing practitioners with a multi-faceted dilemma incorporating the changing business world, the changing nature of business strategy and the changing nature of purchasing strategy. It is unlikely that academics will solve the dilemma for purchasing strategy practitioners with a recipe book derived from theory development. Rather, academics researching purchasing, supply relationships, supply chains, supply networks and supply strategy are attempting to catch up with what is happening in business practice. It is more pressing that we find out from practice and managers' views of practice how they 'do' strategy and try to make some sense of that.

This stage of knowledge development could sound like a one-way flow, with academics taking from practitioners and practitioners receiving nothing in return. Making sense of strategy in different purchasing and supply contexts enables academia to form frameworks, taxonomies and methodologies that provide guidance to managers on what appears to be *appropriate* action and decisions at different times, in different situations and for different purposes. But to date there has not been sufficient empirical research to help form theory to inform practitioners how to do supply strategy with a level of confidence that, if they follow the process, it will work for them in their situations. Therefore, generic purchasing and supply strategy processes, recipes for success, toolkits and methodologies are still largely the stuff of consultancy, much of which is underpinned by an assumption that 'one size fits all' and, if it doesn't, your situation can be squashed into one size, one way or another.

The rest of this chapter, therefore, is not for those who are looking for answers, but rather for those who are struggling to identify the particular questions they should ask of organizations and individuals who are involved in the complex, inter-organization networks that are engaged in strategic supply. Asking these questions, thinking about the answers, experimenting and learning through informed action is as much, today, as can be expected. The need for questioning, thinking, experimenting and learning increases the requirement for action research.[1]

The chapter is structured to provide the backcloth of understanding of business strategy, discuss the development from purchasing to supply chain management to supply strategies and to provide a conceptual framework for understanding the variables and questions relevant to forming strategy.

Business strategy

In *What is Strategy and Does it Matter?* Whittington (1993) classifies business strategies into four main types – classical, evolutionary, systemic and processual. *Classical strategies* dominate most textbooks and business strategy and planning processes. These are rational methods of planning that aim to maximize profits using deliberate calculation and analysis; such is the stuff of Porter (1980, 1985) and Ansoff (1965, 1991) and originally the 'visible hand' in the work of Alfred Chandler (1962, 1977). Classicists believe that internal and external environments can be mastered and use strategy formulation processes based on understanding these environments, then rationally calculate what action to take to gain and sustain competitive advantage.

Evolutionary strategies, such as those proposed by Williamson (1991), accept that the environment is too unpredictable to plan or control; therefore rational plans are irrelevant. Instead Darwinian evolution occurs where those with efficient business processes survive and the less efficient become extinct. Evolutionists believe it is beyond the power of managers to determine this outcome in the long term; the 'market' (whatever that is) determines this for them.

Systemic strategies are based on the principle that rational plans are formed and do have effect, and therefore share this belief in common with classicists. However, unlike classicists, who believe strategies are formed by corporations for the good of corporations, proponents of systemic strategies believe they are instead formed by individuals for individual benefit. Individuals operate in social systems using their own social beliefs and principles – Granovetter's (1985) ideas of 'social embeddedness'. This view has more recently been developed to form the concept of 'corporate social capital' that is the 'set of resources, tangible or virtual, that accrue to organizations through social structure, facilitating the attainment of organizational goals' (Gabbay and Leenders, 1999).

Processual strategies, like evolutionary ones, are formed on the basis that planning, in the sense of a grand plan, is a waste of time. Grand plans are forgotten as things change, and business becomes complicated and confused as many day-to-day decisions are taken. Rather, as Mintzberg (1987, 1994) proposed, strategies emerge as a pattern in the stream of decisions taken as individuals learn, adapt and impose their own personal influence.

The above four groups are only summaries of the various approaches to business strategy evident today; some have argued that up to 16 different schools of business strategy exist. This doesn't bode well for practising managers looking for clear guidance. In practice, most organizations don't engage in worrying about these differences, and instead buy or develop some process that takes them through a sequence of relatively logical, hierarchical steps, at the end of which out drops a strategy. This is usually a document that is communicated and used to form plans and measure performance against, and one that is recreated annually in another document. These are classical strategies and they guide the business functions of operations, purchasing, marketing, finance and accounting, human resource management and information systems.

Purchasing strategy

The traditional view of purchasing and purchasing strategy perceives the function and the strategy as subordinate to business strategy. In fact business strategists, such as Porter, did not even credit purchasing as a value-adding activity but rather as a support to the value chain of inbound logistics, operations, outbound logistics, marketing and sales and service (Porter, 1985). The mission and corporate objectives contained within the business strategy provided direction and a framework within which the purchasing strategy would be designed to support the achievement of the objectives. This is similar to the traditional views of strategy evident in other functional business subjects. Each functional area had its own area of activities, its own bounded set of resources, its own budgets, targets and performance measures, the aggregate of which made some coherent, corporate, strategic whole. During the 1960s and 1970s, articles emerged from most of the business function areas highlighting the important role and contribution their area made to corporate planning. From the purchasing area, the work of David Farmer was fundamental to the subject becoming more strategic (see, for example, Farmer, 1972, 1974 and 1976).

In purchasing, like other functional areas of business, the function had its own set of variables and decisions to take that supported the achievement of its goals which, in turn, would support the achievement of the corporate goals. Various authors on purchasing strategy have provided their own lists of these (such as Scheuing, 1989; Browning et al., 1983; Spekman, 1985), and they include the following:

- make or buy decisions
- single vs multi-sourcing

- lease or buy
- variety reduction/variety management/standardization decisions
- responsibility/ownership/location of inbound materials
- timing of purchase
- local/domestic/international sourcing
- type of relationship/contract
- sourcing from distributor vs manufacturer
- responding to changes in supply markets.

Whilst it was being recognized that purchasing should be contributing more to corporate strategy and planning, purchasing strategies were still functional and supportive. At the time there was little evidence of opportunity in theory to turn the hierarchy of business strategy upside down to drive the business through supply market advantage, for example. Also, purchasing strategies were constrained by the functional boundary; integration across functional boundaries was not encouraged by hierarchical, classical planning.

During the 1980s three significant themes emerged in work on purchasing strategy that fundamentally impacted on the development of the area in theory and on the purchasing strategy process in practice. These three themes were:

1   recognition of a staged approach
2   development of a contingent/portfolio approach
3   broadening of the subject into supply chain management.

RECOGNITION OF A STAGED APPROACH

Again, in common with other functional areas of business, articles emerged during the 1980s that highlighted an evolutionary or development path for purchasing strategies. Similar to Wheelwright and Hayes's (1985) four-stage model for manufacturing strategy, Reck and Long (1988) described the following four stages of purchasing strategy:

1   *Passive* is where the function is reactive and in crisis, applying quick fixes and focused on day-to-day routine operations.
2   *Independent* is where the function is adopting latest techniques and 'best practice', but its strategic direction is not in harmony with the corporate strategy.
3   *Supportive* is the stage where purchasing strengthens the corporate competitive position.
4   *Integrative* is where purchasing strategy is fully integrated with other functions and with corporate strategy in a much more cross-functional way.

Recognition of stages of purchasing strategy was an important step as it raised awareness that purchasing functions had to progress and develop; if an organization's purchasing function was in stage 1, then aspiring to reach stage 4 during the next year would seem highly ambitious. Certain fundamentals had to be in place first to move the function out of crisis.

DEVELOPMENT OF A CONTINGENT/PORTFOLIO APPROACH

The second key development in purchasing strategy was the appreciation that one size didn't fit all and that a 'horses for courses' approach was more appropriate. This involved firms viewing their total spend as a portfolio, different parts of which would be treated differently. Early adoption of a portfolio approach was evident in firms using ABC or Pareto analysis, where the smaller number of higher-value (A) items were managed differently to B and C items in terms of their procurement, inventory management and stores management. However, lower-value items could have been critical, so variations of ABC analysis were used to create multi-criteria groupings. For example, a CA item could be C by volume value criterion but A by criticality. It was also common practice for firms to divide the portfolio into product/service families, each with a team to purchase those items and who were able to form their own strategies relevant to their particular supply markets. However, both ABC analysis and product/service family-driven strategies did not address or highlight critical supply issues such as 'risk' and 'trust'.

Peter Kraljic (1983) created a 2 × 2 matrix to divide the spend portfolio into four types according to supply market complexity/risk and importance of purchasing. The top right-hand box contained 'strategic' items that were important to the firm and where there was high risk/complexity in the supply market. Kraljic proposed that these items required 'supply management'. He advocated different approaches for each of the other three boxes – purchasing management for the low-risk, low-importance box containing routine purchases, materials management for the low-risk but highly important 'leverage' items, and sourcing management for the high-risk, low-importance 'bottleneck' items. Kraljic led a wave of variations of the portfolio theme. Figure 2.1 shows Elliott-Shircore and Steele's version that differentiated particularly between strategic and tactical approaches dependent on risk/vulnerability and potential value/profit.

In Figure 2.2, Ring and Van de Ven's variation specified the appropriate type of relationship according to the balance of trust and risk.

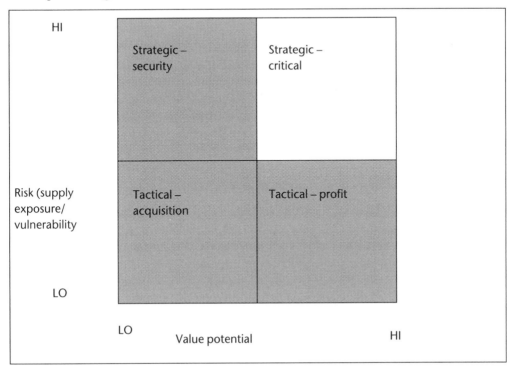

Source: Adapted from Elliott-Shircore and Steele (1985).

Figure 2.1   *Elliott-Shircore and Steele's portfolio approach*

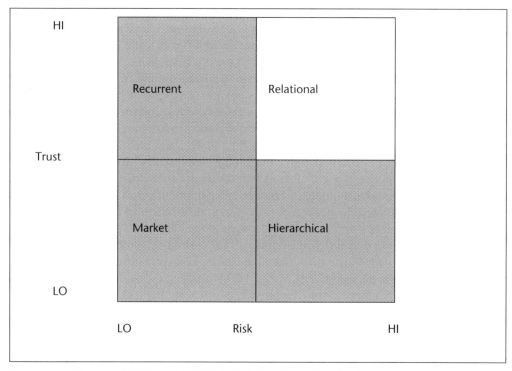

Figure 2.2   *Ring and Van de Ven's portfolio approach*

These 2 × 2 matrices using different axes highlighted the complexity of deciding how best to cut the cake. Instead of a 2 × 2 matrix, combinations of multiple variables in a multi-dimensional table would lead to a larger number of strategy options. For example, combining three factors such as value, trust and risk with high and low scale would lead to eight strategic options. There is no one universal 'best' 2 × 2 matrix, therefore. Also, four different strategy options might not be appropriate in every situation. Individual organizations need to decide which variables are critical to them in differentiating within their purchasing strategy.

BROADENING OF THE SUBJECT INTO SUPPLY CHAIN MANAGEMENT

The term 'supply chain management' has been used since the early 1980s to refer to many different systems, organization structures and practices; there is no consistency or clarity of meaning (Harland, 1995). There are four distinct levels of organization that supply chain management has been used to relate to – the internal supply chain, the buyer/supplier relationship, the external supply chain and the supply network (Harland 1996).

The term supply chain management first appeared in a publication by Oliver and Webber (1982). They used it to represent the integration of the internal business functions of purchasing, manufacturing, sales and distribution, i.e. the internal chain. This relates closely to the concept of materials management pioneered in the 1960s (see, e.g., Ammer, 1968 and Lee and Dobler, 1965) and also has similarities to Porter's (1985) value chain. The focus for attention at this level of supply chain management was logistical, concentrating on materials and information flows from inbound to outbound ends of the business. Strategies for the internal supply chain that necessarily impacted on the purchasing function were largely aimed to reduce delivery lead time and reduce costs through inventory reduction. The process of strategy formulation for purchasing became less functionally bounded.

Some authors and practitioners used the term supply chain management to refer to the management of supply relationships. Ellram (1991) positioned supply chain management as an intermediate type of relationship within a spectrum ranging from hierarchy to market. Others used the term interchangeably with 'partnership' and 'partnership sourcing' (e.g. Macbeth and Ferguson, 1994). Using this definition, purchasing strategy and supply chain management strategy have substantial overlap.

A third level of supply chain management can be viewed as the 'external supply chain'. This is similar to Hayes and Wheelwright's (1984) commercial chain for manufacturing connecting raw material producers, material fabricators, component parts producers, the manufacturer/assembler, wholesalers/distributors, retailers and consumers. The focus at this level has been logistics oriented with strategies to coordinate and balance flows of materials and information to remove dynamic 'noise' such as the Forrester (1961) or bullwhip effect (Burbidge, 1961; Towill, 1991). In practice and in theory some have viewed this as expanding the strategic role for purchasing.

A fourth level of supply chain management is the strategic management of inter-business networks. This view incorporates more than just traditional functional purchasing, logistics or buyer/supplier relationships. It positions supply chain management as managing '. . . the network of organisations that are involved, through upstream and downstream linkages, in the different processes and activities that produce value in the form of products and services in the hands of the ultimate consumer' (Christopher, 1992). Some have stretched the definition of 'purchasing' to include this, stating 'New styles of purchasing involve careful analysis and planning, requiring an understanding of supplier relationships, product development processes, quality driven management and industrial networks' (Gadde and Håkansson, 1993). The concept of 'lean supply' (Lamming, 1993), increasing 'buy' rather than 'make' decisions (Nishiguchi, 1994) and greater focus on relationship management in complex inter-organization networks has stretched the area of consideration for purchasing beyond immediate relationships with suppliers and beyond merely the buying and acquisition role. This has shifted purchasing strategy, therefore, beyond supply chain management towards 'supply strategy'.

Supply strategy

The concept of Supply Strategy integrates various existing bodies of knowledge and concepts, to form an holistic, strategic perspective of management of operations, stretching across inter-organisational boundaries. Central to the concept of Supply are the purchasing, use and transformation of resources to provide goods or service packages to satisfy end customers today and in the future, and the organisational structuring decisions that accommodate global markets. (Harland et al., 1999)

Supply strategies are implemented decisions of supply interventions across organizational boundaries. There are three main dimensions of supply strategy decision making.

1   the *extent* to which you choose to intervene
2   the *type* of intervention you choose to make
3   the *level* at which you intervene.

Clearly there are other important variables such as *when* to intervene but these form part of the content of the decision.

THE EXTENT OF SUPPLY INTERVENTION

Figure 2.3 shows a spectrum for the extent of intervention you can choose to make, ranging from doing nothing, through to dominating.

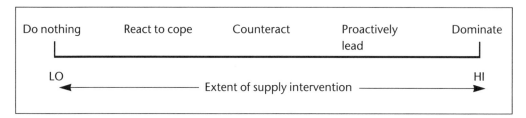

Figure 2.3   *Extent of supply intervention*

Faced with a situation of a supply market that has become dominated by one powerful supplier, different choices of extent of intervention have different implications.

Do nothing is one extreme choice, i.e. you accept the market imbalance and any subsequent price increases through exploitation of dominance as unavoidable without passing them on to your customers.

React to cope might involve negotiating a price increase with your customers to maintain your current position. This may enable you to cope in the short term but does not guarantee that your customers won't take action in the medium to long term to resource or innovate supply alternatives.

Counteract might involve investigating and developing alternative suppliers.

Proactively lead means you wouldn't have been in this situation in the first place. You would have been assessing and evaluating the market structure and setting several alternative strategies in motion, such as setting up a competitive source and funding innovation to provide a stream of alternatives for the future.

Dominate also means you wouldn't be in the situation but may have caused it yourself by acquiring the dominant supplier and driving price increases through for your competitors, while protecting the costs of your own supply line.

THE TYPE OF SUPPLY INTERVENTION

Supply interventions can be of different types; Harland et al. (2000) classified the types as *operational, managerial, strategic* and *policy.*

Operational supply intervention is the basic transactional process of buying and acquiring goods and services. *Managerial* supply interventions involve planning and controlling; for example, forming a plan with your suppliers for a set of contracts over a particular time and monitoring that this plan has been effected. *Strategic* supply intervention involves direction setting in the form of a set of strategic decisions. *Policy* supply intervention is about enforcing your long-term beliefs about supply, such as environmental or ethical beliefs.

THE LEVEL OF SUPPLY INTERVENTION

The *level* of supply intervention refers to the systems level at which the intervention takes place.

Individual or teams within an organization may be empowered to intervene, either through management procedures or through budgetary empowerment. This type of intervention is usually quick and easy to effect, and ensures the users are happy with the decision. However, this extent of decentralization of intervention can lead to lack of consistency, irregularities arising through unchecked spending and increased transaction costs through many parts of the organization all dealing with potentially the same supplier.

Individual organizations might intervene, possibly through a purchasing department in which particular decisions must be taken, i.e. individuals or teams would have to request the intervention from the functional specialists within the organization. This can lead to organizational consistency and learning, though it can cause frustration within the organization. It may also be at odds with other organizations you deal with in the supply network.

Supply networks (or two-party relationships within those networks) can intervene in supply decisions. For example, a large manufacturer might represent a set of smaller component suppliers in their dealings with a large powerful raw material supplier and effectively pass round them to exert influence on prices and delivery lead times they are being quoted in the supply network.

Regional supply intervention can occur when groups of organizations club together locally to share certain services and pool their purchasing power. Regions in Italy such as Emilia-Romagna, Modena, Reggio, Bologna and Parma contain examples of regional clusters of organizations that collectively take supply decisions for their region.

Government department or divisional supply intervention is a multi-organizational decision taken by some form of organizational superstructure, such as the Department of Health intervening for all hospitals, or a divisional purchasing organization intervening for all firms within the division. This differs from the collective decision making of the region, which requires more cooperation and consensus; this type of intervention can be quite dictatorial and mandated to other organizations.

National supply intervention often occurs in politically sensitive supply decisions and may involve national trade treaties and agreements. For example, many of the reciprocal trade deals involving China were made in this way. China purchased various types of capital equipment and paid years later with the products it had produced using the equipment.

International supply intervention is across territories. For example, the South American countries collaborated in their contracts for supply of vaccines and contraception to gain more leverage and consistency of supply.

Choices are made relating to the three main dimensions of supply strategy decision making. The combination of choices made for each dimension provides a 3D decision-making cube as shown in Figure 2.4. The mix of these choices on a day-by-day basis represents your real strategy.

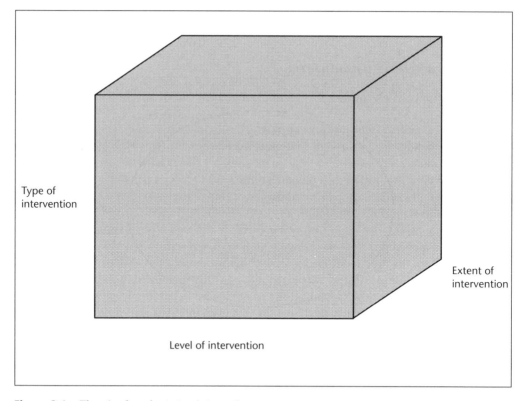

Figure 2.4   *The mix of supply strategy intervention*

A FRAMEWORK FOR SUPPLY STRATEGY

The mix of decisions can be different for different parts of your spend. The context for the decisions impacts on the choices. In some circumstances large, macro issues such as political influence may drive the strategy. Supply market or customer market factors might dominate thinking and decision making. Figure 2.5 provides a framework for supply strategy intervention.

Summary

To summarize, therefore, purchasing strategy has evolved to supply strategy. The supply strategy process contains the following key elements:

1   The decision variables
   - make or buy decisions
   - single vs multi-sourcing
   - lease or buy
   - variety reduction/variety management/standardization decisions
   - responsibility/ownership/location of inbound materials
   - timing of purchase
   - local/domestic/international sourcing

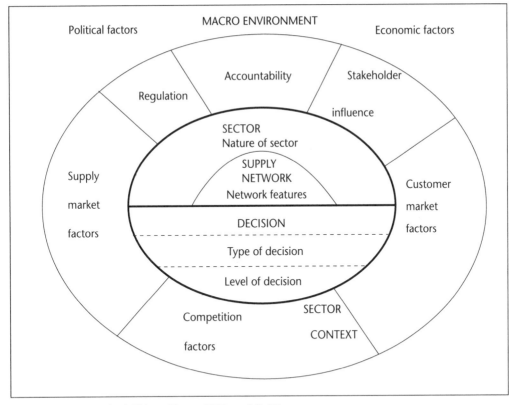

Source: Derived from Harland, Gibbs and Sutton (2000, pp. 342–52).

Figure 2.5   *Framework for supply strategy intervention*

- type of relationship/contract
- sourcing from distributor vs manufacturer
- responding to changes in supply markets

2   Division of the spend portfolio – cutting the cake in the most appropriate manner
3   The extent of intervention – ranging from doing nothing to dominating
4   The type of intervention – operational, managerial, strategic or policy
5   The level of intervention – individual, team, organization, supply network, region, government department, company division, national, international.

The particular decision is influenced by the context for the decision and by the stage of development you are currently at.

Note

1.   Most of the conceptual development that helped to form the ideas in this chapter are based on action research conducted collaboratively between the Centre for Research in Strategic Purchasing and Supply (CRiSPS), School of Management, University of Bath, and its partners in public and private sector, manufacturing and service settings.

References

Ammer, D.S. (1968), *Materials Management,* Homewood, IL: Irwin.

Ansoff, H.I. (1965) *Corporate Strategy,* Harmondsworth: Penguin.

Ansoff, H.I. (1991) 'Critique of Henry Mintzberg's "The Design School"', *Strategic Management Journal,* Vol. 12, pp. 449–61.

Browning, J.M., Zabriskie, N.B. and Huellmantel, A.B. (1983) 'Strategic Purchasing Planning', *Journal of Purchasing and Materials Management,* Spring, pp. 19–24.

Burbidge, J.L. (1961), 'The New Approach to Production', *Production Engineer,* Vol. 40, No. 12, December, pp. 769–84.

Chandler, A.D. (1962), *Strategy and Structure: Chapters in the History of the American Industrial Enterprise,* Cambridge, MA, MIT Press.

Chandler, A.D. (1977), *The Visible Hand: The Managerial Revolution in American Business,* Cambridge, MA: Harvard University Press.

Christopher, M. (1992), *Logistics and Supply Chain Management,* London: Pitman.

Elliott-Shircore, T.I. and Steele, P.T. (1985), 'Procurement Positioning Overview', *Purchasing and Supply Management,* December, pp. 23–6.

Ellram, L.M. (1991), 'A Managerial Guideline for the Development and Implementation of Purchasing Partnerships', *International Journal of Purchasing and Materials Management,* Vol. 27, No. 2, pp. 2–8.

Farmer, D.H. (1972), 'The Impact of Supply Markets on Corporate Planning', *Long Range Planning,* March, pp. 10–16.

Farmer, D.H. (1974), 'Corporate Planning and Procurement in Multi-National Firms', *Journal of Purchasing and Materials Management,* Vol. 10, No. 2, pp. 55–67.

Farmer, D.H. (1976) 'The Role of Procurement in Corporate Planning', *Purchasing and Supply,* November, pp. 44–6.

Forrester, J.W. (1961), *Industrial Dynamics,* Boston: MIT Press.

Gabbay, S.M. and Leenders, R.T.A.J, (1999), 'Corporate Social Capital: The Structure of Advantage and Disadvantage', in R.T.A.J. Leenders and S.M. Gabbay (eds), *Corporate Social Capital and Liability,* London: Kluwer Academic Publishers.

Gadde, L.E. and Håkansson, H. (1993), *Professional Purchasing,* London: Routledge.

Granovetter, M. (1985), 'Economic Action and Social Structure: The Problem of Embeddedness', *American Journal of Sociology,* Vol. 91, No. 3, pp. 481–510.

Harland, C.M. (1995), 'The Dynamics of Customer Dissatisfaction in Supply Chains', *Production Planning and Control,* Vol. 6, No. 3, May/June, pp. 209–17.

Harland, C.M. (1996), 'Supply Chain Management: Relationships, Chains and Networks', *British Journal of Management,* Vol. 7, Special Issue, March, pp. S63–S81.

Harland, C.M., Gibbs, J. and Sutton R.Y. (2000), 'Supply Strategy for the Public Sector: Framing the Issues', *Proceedings of the 9th International IPSERA Conference and the 3rd Annual North American Research Symposium of Purchasing and Supply Chain Management,* 24–27 May, Toronto, Canada, pp. 342–52.

Harland, C.M., Lamming, R.C. and Cousins, P.D. (1999), 'Developing the Concept of Supply Strategy', *International Journal of Operations and Production Management,* Vol. 19, pp. 650–73.

Hayes, R.H. and Wheelwright, S.C. (1984), *Restoring our Competitive Edge: Competing Through Manufacturing,* New York: John Wiley.

Kraljic, P. (1983), 'Purchasing Must Become Supply Management', *Harvard Business Review,* September/October, pp. 109–17.

Lamming, R.C. (1993), *Beyond Partnership: Strategies for Innovation and Lean Supply,* Hemel Hampstead: Prentice-Hall.

Lee, L. and Dobler, D. (1965), *Purchasing and Materials Management,* New York: McGraw-Hill.

Macbeth, D.K. and Ferguson, N. (1994) *Partnership Sourcing: An Integrated Supply Chain Approach,* London: Pitman Publishing.

Mintzberg, H. (1987), 'Crafting Strategy', *Harvard Business Review,* July– August, pp. 65–75.

Mintzberg, H. (1994), *The Rise and Fall of Strategic Planning,* New York: Prentice-Hall.

Nishiguchi, T. (1994), *Strategic Industrial Sourcing,* Oxford and New York: Oxford University Press.

Oliver, R.K. and Webber, M.D. (1982), 'Supply Chain Management: Logistics Catches Up With Strategy', in M. Christopher (1992), *Logistics: The Strategic Issues,* pp. 63–75, London: Chapman and Hall.

Porter, M.E. (1980), *Competitive Strategy: Techniques for Analysing Industries and Firms,* New York: Free Press and Macmillan.

Porter, M.E. (1985), *Competitive Advantage: Creating and Sustaining Superior Performance*, New York: Free Press.

Reck, R.F. and Long, B.G. (1988), 'Purchasing: A Competitive Weapon', *Journal of Purchasing and Materials Management*, Fall, pp. 2–8.

Ring, P.S. and Van de Ven, A.H. (1992), 'Structuring Co-operative Relationships Between Organisations', *Strategic Management Journal*, Vol. 13, pp. 483–98.

Scheuing, E.E. (1989) *Purchasing Management*, Englewood Cliffs, NJ: Prentice-Hall.

Spekman, R.E. (1985), 'Competitive Procurement Strategies: Building Strength and Reducing Vulnerability', *Long Range Planning*, Vol. 18, No. 1, pp. 94–99.

Towill, D.R. (1991), 'Supply Chain Dynamics', *Computer Integrated Manufacturing*, Vol. 4, No. 4, pp.197–208.

Wheelwright, S.C. and Hayes, R. (1985) 'Competing Through Manufacturing', *Harvard Business Review*, January–February, pp. 99–109.

Whittington, R. (1993), *What is Strategy and Does it Matter?*, London: International Thompson Businss Press.

Williamson, O.E. (1991), 'Comparative Economic Organization – The Analysis of Discrete Structural Alternatives', *Administrative Science Quarterly*, Vol. 36, No. 2, pp. 269–96.

3 *Organizing the purchasing function*

Michael Quayle

Introduction

This chapter provides information about the various purchasing organizational policies that can be adopted to support an organization's corporate plan. It is important that a long-term view of activities should be prepared and that this should provide a framework within which day-to-day problems can be tackled. It is especially important for large companies to develop conscious long-term strategies in order that their monopolistic powers should be used wisely. Concentrated buying power may be able to dictate to smaller suppliers in the short term, but it is essential to estimate the long-term effects. The pursuit of low prices may bankrupt suppliers and such tactics may, therefore, alter the market structure and reduce competition. Purchasing, therefore, must decide whether its long-term objective on continuity of supply is more important than achievement of price objectives in the short term. The dominant buyer should seek to maintain 'effective' or workable competition which produces fair prices in relation to cost, prompt service and a reasonable rate of innovation. The buyer must also remember the five rights of purchasing shown in Figure 3.1.

Smith and Conway (1993) identified seven key success factors which characterize effective purchasing. These were, and arguably remain, valid: a clear purchasing strategy, effective

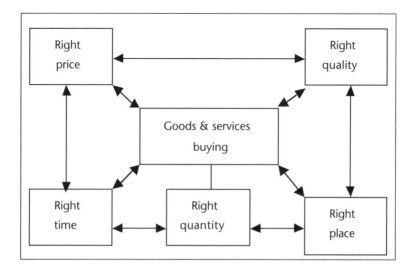

Figure 3.1   *The five rights of purchasing*

management information and control systems, development of expertise, a role in corporate management, an entrepreneurial and proactive approach, coordination, and focused efforts. Arguably these seven success factors are the key to effective purchasing; however, an eighth is fundamental – effective communication of the key success factors to all levels of the organization (public or private sector).

Structure of purchasing organization

Classical management writers have emphasized the importance of the activity of organizing as a key function of management. Whilst their views have been modified in many respects, this function is still important and, therefore, the purchasing manager should pay close attention to the development of the organizational structure for the purchasing function. Organization is concerned with the division of work and the delegation of authority and responsibility in such a way that the objectives of the organization can be achieved. It also involves defining the duties of personnel and the relationships between them.

The task of developing an organization structure has become a complex one and there is no longer a simple prescriptive model that can be applied in all situations. The business environment is now populated by a wide variety of different types of organization. What is suitable for one would not necessarily be copied by another. In discussing organizational problems for purchasing management it is essential to take into account some of the important differences. Of course, the development of an organization for the purchasing function is but part of a general problem of developing a structure for the organization as a whole. Thus purchasing considerations will reflect the needs of this broader framework as well as internal factors (Quayle, 1998a).

In a simple organization example it is necessary to concentrate upon the organization of a centralized purchasing function within a relatively simple, single-product, single-site firm, assess the advantages of specialization and then map out the possible range of activities that could be included.

Benefits of a centralized purchasing function

In very small organizations the scope for specialization is limited and purchasing activities may not be sufficient to occupy a person full time. Once an organization employs around 50 people or above, however, it should be possible to introduce purchasing as a specialist job. As the volume of work expands, so the number of purchasing personnel will grow and the opportunities for specialization within the function increase. Parallel with this growth, therefore, the problem of organization assumes greater importance.

The introduction of a specialist department to handle purchasing activities means that its members see purchasing as their major responsibility and can develop expertise in conducting their work. Previously, purchasing jobs would have been done by other people for whom it would have been a major activity and for which they had no particular skills. Thus full-time specialists can develop their abilities and use progressive purchasing techniques to obtain better value for money. The department can coordinate the previously fragmented purchasing pattern and can introduce a common system of procedures. Knowledge of supply markets can be built up, an efficient record system introduced and negotiating skills can be applied. What may have started as a simple clerical function can become a sophisticated independent department.

The basic argument for the development of the centralized function rests on the point that efficiency in controlling the flow of inputs to the organization is increased by the application of specialist expertise. The opportunities to make such improvements in efficiency can be found in different types of organization in all sectors of the economy. The purchasing function can make a major contribution towards the achievement of corporate objectives in both the public and private sectors.

Activities in the purchasing function

A wide variety of arrangements can be found concerning the activities which should be included under the control of the purchasing manager. The most effective pattern is one in which the purchasing manager is given authority for all those activities which lead to the supply of goods and services to user departments. Such a range might include the following.

CATEGORIES OF GOODS PURCHASED

In manufacturing companies, the purchase of industrial materials is regarded as the major area of expenditure to be controlled, but many purchasing managers, even in the twenty-first century, have no control over the purchase of plant and equipment at all. In spite of this difference in delegation of authority, the arguments in favour of the application of specialist purchasing skills are relevant to all purchases. It follows that the purchasing department should be given responsibility for purchasing all bought-out goods that are required. This does not mean that other departments should be excluded from the decision-making process, but that the purchasing department should contribute its commercial expertise to this process to complement the technical skills of the other departments. A purchasing research team should also be attached to the buying area to provide information to the buyers which may include cost analysis.

PURCHASING IN DISTRIBUTIVE ORGANIZATIONS

Whilst the principles of purchasing management apply equally to the wholesale and retail sections of industry as to manufacture, procedures differ. Since there is normally no production process involved (the raw material stockholder may offer a cutting or shearing service), sales and purchasing personnel are involved in product selection and programming as a total merchandising operation. Many large organizations are headed as far as supplies are concerned by a merchandise executive or director responsible for purchasing, organized to coordinate the expertise and information available to both. In a dynamic, consumer demand situation – retail multi-stores or supermarket – purchasing requirement forecasting and expenditure based on product sales, subject to changing preferences, promotions and seasonal peaks and troughs, requires continuous updating to data and flexible purchasing arrangements. Product knowledge, ability to interpret sales data, short- and long-term, allied to continuous supply market research, are essential to successful buying for direct resale to the consumer.

STORES AND STOCK CONTROL, INCLUDING GOODS RECEIVING

It can be argued that there are advantages to be gained by grouping stores and stock control activities under the control of the purchasing manager. The achievement of the objective of lowest cost of supply implies that both purchasing and stock control considerations are relevant in deciding how many and when to purchase goods required to reprovision the stores. Goods receiving activities complete the purchasing cycle and transfer the purchases to user departments or, more frequently, to the stores. These, too should be integrated into the purchasing organization.

Typical structure of a purchasing department

Figure 3.2 shows a typical structure for a supplies organization in a medium to large-sized organization.

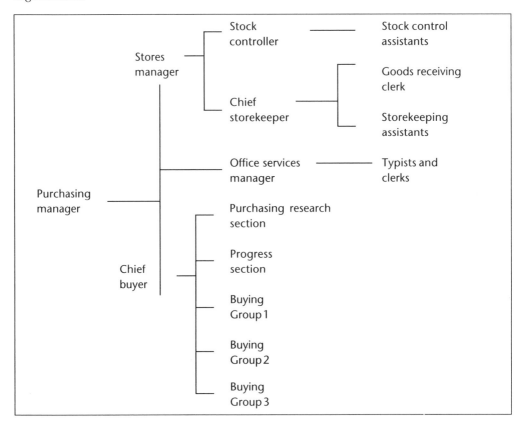

Source: Quayle and Jones (1999).

Figure 3.2   *Supplies organization structure*

Division of work amongst buying groups

It is worth remembering that there are many links in the negotiation chain. These include bidding, bargaining and agreement; which in turn include introductions, negotiation research and planning. The information flow may be complex, partnerships may be under consideration (or existing) and there is a need for continuous improvement allied to value for money. This is illustrated in Figure 3.3, where each link is reviewed and assessed in order to develop the full strength of the whole chain.

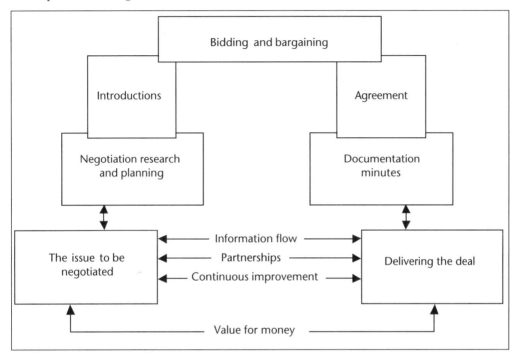

Figure 3.3   *Negotiating links*

In single-product, single-site organizations the major principle adopted is to divide purchasing work according to commodities. Each section and each buyer would be given responsibilities for particular groups of products. Thus Buying Group 1 might be authorized to purchase all the industrial materials, Group 2 might be responsible for industrial equipment and Group 3 might be given industrial supplies and services. Individual buyers would then be given narrower ranges within each section. However, a second principle might also be followed in so far as more senior buyers would be responsible for high-value orders. Specialization on a commodity or product basis allows buyers to build up expertise in a limited number of markets and they have the opportunity to get to know the nature of these products and the characteristics of the suppliers.

In more complex multi-product, multi-site organizations, however, two further principles which can be adopted in the division of work may arise. Buyers may be appointed to handle purchases for a particular product line or manufacturing division. In addition, workloads can be divided according to geographical locations.

The position of purchasing management in the organization

Carter and Narasimhan (1996) suggest that the status accorded the purchasing function in an organization is frequently determined by the image the function projects to personnel outside purchasing. Support through the firm will determine the status of purchasing and the role purchasing plays in the firm. Unfortunately, most non-purchasing personnel have a very simplistic view of the purchasing function, and they understandably demonstrate little regard for internal purchasing performance measures, which they view as mainly tactical (Cavinato, 1987). Carter and Narasimhan also suggest the linkage between purchasing strategy and organizational performance began to be established when organizations started to realize the impact the purchasing function can have on their competitive position, and they gradually shifted the role of purchasing from tactical to strategic (see also Saunders, 1994).

Where there is an integrated supplies organization or, indeed, where there is a significant purchasing team, a case can be made out for the purchasing manager or director of purchasing to have a senior and meaningful position within the management structure. This allows the manager and the department to give full weight to commercial aspects of purchasing decisions. It can be argued, therefore, that the purchasing manager should be a member of the senior management team, with a direct reporting responsibility to the managing director. The purchasing manager may also be a member of the board of directors. Thus the management organization might be as shown in Figure 3.4.

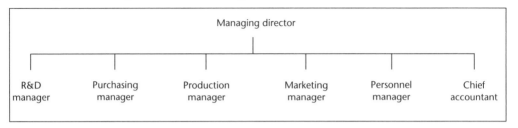

Figure 3.4   *Management organization*

The position of the purchasing manager within the organization hierarchy is an important determinant of the impact that the department can have. A high position and high status enables an effective, progressive approach to purchasing work to be implemented. In the last analysis, however, it is successful performance that earns the respect of others in the organization.

Structure of the purchasing function in complex organizations

There has been an emergence of large multi-product, multi-site organizations which often employ marketing strategies that can alter product ranges as they seek growth. They have, therefore, moved away from the relatively simple situation of operating one production site to manufacture one product line. Thus, some have diversified into other product areas on one or more sites and others have duplicated production facilities by opening establishments in different geographical locations. Policy decisions which have brought about these transformations have also influenced the development and adoption of different organizational structures to cope with the added complexity.

In the simple organization the basic breakdown of tasks was achieved by splitting work up according to the main functional activities. In the multi-divisional organization function tasks are grouped around different product lines. Each product organization might be a separate limited company, with a holding company as headquarters. In others, each division and the head office may all be part of the same legal entity. At both divisional and head office level, further divisions of work can be made on a functional basis. What emerges is shown in Figure 3.5.

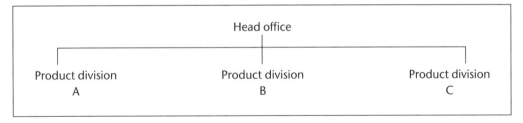

Figure 3.5   *Division of work by product*

Each division may have a management structure as above and the same functions may be present at head office level to act in a coordinating capacity. However, the extent of head office activities of the divisions tends to vary. Some multi-level organizations are relatively centralized and head office personnel play a detailed part in the activities of the divisions. Other decentralized arrangements, however, give more autonomous powers to the divisions. These are established as separate profit centres, with minimal interference from headquarters, and the relationship between the division and the headquarters is mainly a financial one. The division is responsible for achieving satisfactory profit figures and must apply for approval of corporate plans and investment finance. It can be argued that the more unrelated in terms of technology, materials requirements and markets the divisions are, the more decentralized should be the method of control. There is little scope for central coordination as each division operates in an entirely different sphere.

Alternative structures for the purchasing function in complex companies

There are four possible solutions to the problem of organizing the purchasing function in complex organizations. Each will be examined in turn to establish the advantages and disadvantages inherent in each solution. The four solutions are as follows:

1   Complete centralization – one central purchasing department controls the purchasing of all supplies for various scattered units or factories.
2   Complete decentralization – each separate unit or factory has its own purchasing department and is responsible for obtaining its own requirements.
3   Multi-level structure – each unit has its own purchasing department, but a central purchasing department has some powers to coordinate the activities of the local departments.
4   The virtual organization.

ADVANTAGES OF CENTRALIZATION

The advantages to be gained from the establishment of one central purchasing department are as follows:

- Economies of bulk buying of items commonly used at each unit. The central department can negotiate cheaper prices on the basis of total consumption throughout the company.
- Avoidance of 'competitive' buying by individual departments of materials in short supply.
- Opportunities for development of greater knowledge about products because buyers can specialize in a narrower range of commodities which can be handled more expertly, i.e. buyers place orders for the whole company for a small range of products, whereas local buyers have to handle a more general range of local requirements.
- Savings in operating costs. Fewer, but larger orders are placed and hence a reduction in administrative costs can be made.
- Development of common procedures, forms, standards and specifications.
- Simpler relationship with suppliers as a result of single, direct contact.
- Investigations of new products and materials can benefit all units in the company.
- Centralization of stock control can reduce overall stock levels through greater flexibility and establishment of strategic reserves, i.e. flow of stocks between factories to meet short-ages.
- Development of improved support services made possible, e.g. purchasing research and statistical information services.
- Enhanced importance of the supplies department and higher position of the supplies manager in management hierarchy.
- More scope for purchasing strategy and contribution to corporate plans.
- More scope for manpower planning in the function and development of training programmes.

ADVANTAGES OF DECENTRALIZATION

The advantages of decentralization can be seen as a remedy for the weaknesses of centralization. The main advantages are as follows:

- Closer coordination with local organization and buyers can build up close contacts with other departments.
- Buyer is in direct touch with the problems where they arise and can handle emergencies more easily than a distant office.
- Local buyers are better informed about local markets which may offer possibilities to a local customer which could not be offered on a national basis.
- Clear responsibility of buyers to local management.
- Local plants may need a different range of products and, thus, a local buyer may have a more specialized knowledge of these.

A MULTI-LEVEL STRUCTURE FOR PURCHASING MANAGEMENT

The multi-level approach attempts to obtain the advantages of both the previous models. The division of duties between the two levels which is designed to achieve this are as follows:

Central office:

- determination of purchasing strategies and development of purchasing policies
- standardization of procedures, specifications, codes and forms

- negotiation of contracts for commonly used items against which local departments can place delivery orders for supplies as required
- purchase of major plant and equipment
- importation of supplies from overseas
- responsibility for legal matters
- inter-plant stock transfers and stocking policy
- responsibility for training
- research and information service.

Local offices:

- responsibility for placing orders for 'non-contract' items
- placing delivery orders for contract items.

In this group purchasing system, the manager at the local level would be responsible to his local line management. The manager at the central office would usually act in a staff capacity. That is, the latter would not have executive authority, as such, over the local manager, but would act in an advisory capacity.

A number of difficulties can arise in this multi-level approach. First, there is a danger that local initiative will be stifled by having group contracts imposed by a remote head office. The relationship between the two levels may be difficult to control. The local department may resent interference and there may be a conflict of interest between local interests and head office views. The staff/line division of responsibilities does not successfully resolve the problem of the local purchasing manager who has dual responsibilities to his local management team and to the group purchasing manager, when the latter has a more senior position, but no executive authority.

THE VIRTUAL ORGANIZATION

Van Weele and Rozemeijer (1996) suggest that a possible model for future purchasing organizations to make simultaneous improvements in both increasing functional expertise and horizontal synergy, and in improving focus and flexibility at the business unit level, could be the hard core/soft organization. In this organization a small centralized hard core of corporate purchasing professionals is surrounded by a rather fluid soft core of business specialists. The hard core is responsible for the purchasing process, the strategy, professional development, and the recruitment, training and development of the people involved in the purchasing process. Van Weele and Rozemeijer also use the term 'the virtual purchasing organisation' to describe their vision of what is now required. There appears to be absolutely no reason why a group of small and medium-sized enterprises could not develop a 'core' purchasing activity to operate independently or as a consortium.

Sourcing Form

Whatever the form of organization, the choice of sourcing is a complex issue. In some cases the sourcing policy dictates the organization. Arguably there are contingencies such as the individual, markets, products and organizations and there are criteria such as economic, power, risk and social factors; the contingencies and criteria prevailing at the decision point will result in single or multiple sourcing. This is illustrated in Figure 3.6.

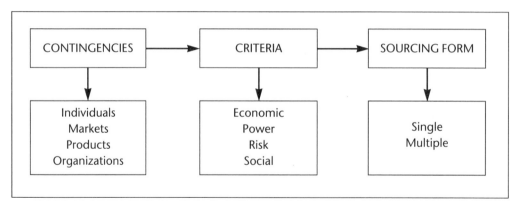

Source: Quayle (1998b).

Figure 3.6   *Factors resulting in sourcing form*

In larger organizations policies of single or multiple sourcing are often set; often where purchasing is 'centralized', the sourcing form is left to the 'decentralized' units.

The selection of an appropriate structure for particular circumstances

There is no single method of organizing the purchasing function which is appropriate for all complex organizations. In developing a suitable structure, it is important to analyse the circumstances of the particular organization for which it is intended. Perhaps the key question that needs to be asked is how common are the purchasing problems that have to be faced at each site. The greater the similarity of purchases, the greater is the potential for centralizing control. Conversely, the greater the variety, the greater the opportunity to decentralize activities. Four different situations are worth examining:

1   single-product/multi-site operations
2   multi-product/multi-site operations in which products are related
3   multi-product/multi-site operations in which products are unrelated
4   very large multi-product/multi-site operations in which there is scope for multi-level structures in each division.

SINGLE-PRODUCT/MULTI-SITE OPERATIONS

Where each factory is concerned with manufacturing the same products, the purchasing requirements are the same. Demand arises for the same products which are purchased from the same markets. There is scope for a fully centralized purchasing function, therefore, to gain the maximum benefit of the purchasing power of the company and to provide common solutions to common problems. In the tertiary sector, a central purchasing department would be able to control the purchasing for individual branches of a retail or distribution network and organize central storage points from which supplies of many items could be delivered. Buying consortia for several local authorities base their arguments on such a premise.

MULTI-PRODUCT/MULTI-SITE OPERATIONS IN WHICH PRODUCTS ARE RELATED

In organizations which have several product divisions, but whose products are related, in the sense that similar technology and similar materials are used, a multi-level purchasing system could be employed. Sufficient common items and associated purchasing problems exist for a central department to make a valuable contribution, whilst local supply departments maintain close contact with local factories.

MULTI-PRODUCT/MULTI-SITE OPERATIONS IN WHICH PRODUCTS ARE UNRELATED

Conglomerate or diversified organizations may consist of manufacturing divisions which are entirely different in terms of technology and materials used. In such a situation, few common problems arise and there is little to be gained, therefore, from having a central department. Each divisional purchasing manager, however, should be given a high position of responsibility within the divisional management structure and should play a significant part in the planning process for the division.

VERY LARGE MULTI-PRODUCT/MULTI-SITE OPERATIONS

In very large organizations, individual divisions may themselves have a multi-level organizational structure. In such a situation, there may be local purchasing departments under the control of a divisional purchasing manager. At the top there may be a corporate purchasing department to coordinate the activities of the divisions, depending on how similar their needs are.

Multinational supplies structures

The multinational character of big organizations creates additional complications. Wide variations in terms of political, economic, social and industrial conditions may exist in the countries in which operations are located. It may be necessary, therefore, to allow a local purchasing department greater latitude in determining its own supply policy and controlling its own supplies. Nevertheless, if there are opportunities to be gained from closer coordination, such objectives should not be ignored and the local department should be encouraged to follow group policy. The central office could be used to organize the supply of goods being imported into other countries for local factories.

Public sector

Within the UK there has been a drive to squeeze costs and inefficiencies out of government purchasing (Schachter, 1994; Edmonds and McCready, 1994; Mintzberg, 1997; Pullen, 1994; Fee and Erridge, 1999). Similarly the UK government has pursued greater purchasing effectiveness (Hein, 1990 and Quayle, 1998a). Since the later 1980s, the UK government sector has taken a close interest in its ability to maximize resources. Amongst other initiatives, this has led to a plethora of appointments of purchasing staff, with very few at director level.

Clearly the rationale for such appointments is based on either improving or introducing professionalism within institutions of disparate cultures. The impact of purchasing in UK government is driven by the contribution of the function to overall corporate performance and its interface relationships; much has been written about purchasing strategy, but the actual impact of purchasing organization on corporate performance has been neither empirically substantiated nor rigorously examined.

Both in central government and local authority purchasing, the emphasis is on *public accountability*. This is not to underestimate the vital necessity for efficiency in purchasing, as in the private sector, and the move towards centralization is evident in both central and local organizations.

Cox (1996) identifies the need for proactive rather than reactive strategic purchasing management. His approach links competencies, relationships and asset specificity in order to procure a supply and value chain which reduces the costs of transactions and improves profitability. Chadwick (1995) argues, however, that performance assessment can only be truly effective when the circumstances and environment surrounding an organization are taken into account, and when measurement is closely linked to the means of improving performance. He suggests that an evaluation of purchasing effectiveness should include an estimate of how much the purchasing operation actually costs. How much value does it deliver to the overall organization? Is the function targeted on goals that align with the strategic plan of the overall organization? What progress is being made towards meeting these goals? Is purchasing accountable for the basic load of the organization? Is the infrastructure being developed to meet the needs of the organization, by optimizing administration and inventory management? How effective is the staff development plan at increasing the professional competence and standing of the suppliers' management function? These are all valid questions and are all applicable to both the private and public sector.

Conclusion

There are no simple prescriptions to help designers prepare a plan for the organization of the purchasing function in a complex organization. It is necessary to examine the conditions in which each is operating. An additional determinant will be the view of senior managers at the corporate level who are the key decision makers regarding the structure of the organization as a whole. A further feature which may require diplomatic treatment is the relationship between the parent company and newly taken-over subsidiaries. Personnel in the latter are often reluctant to alter systems and procedures and to adopt new policies. Even within old established organizations, plans to restructure an organization can also cause much conflict unless the task is carried out carefully.

This chapter has been concerned with the problem of organization with respect to the purchasing function. There are no simple solutions which have general applicability to all organizations. It is, nevertheless, extremely important to design an *effective structure* if purchasing activities are to make a significant contribution to the success of the company. Structural arrangements have a significant effect on the performance of individuals in the function, because it is these arrangements that circumscribe the duties to be carried out by them.

References

Carter, J.R. and Narasimhan, R. (1996), 'Is Purchasing Really Strategic?', *International Journal of Purchasing and Materials Management*, Winter, pp. 20–28.

Cavinato, J.L. (1987), 'Purchasing Performance: What Makes the Magic?', *Journal of Purchasing and Materials Management*, Vol. 23, No. 4, pp. 20–25.

Chadwick, T. (1995), *Strategic Supply Management*, Oxford: Butterworth Heinemann.

Cox, A. (1996), 'Relational Competence and Strategic Procurement Management', *European Journal of Purchasing and Supply Management*, Vol. 2, No. 1, pp. 57–70.

Edmonds, D. and McCready, D. (1994), 'Costing and Pricing of Police Services', *International Journal of Public Sector Management*, Vol. 7, No. 5, pp. 4–14.

Fee, R. and Erridge, A. (1999), 'Contract Compliance in Canada and Northern Ireland: A Comparative Analysis', *Proceedings of 8th IPSERA Conference*, Belfast and Dublin.

Hein, W. (1990), 'Government Organisations and Their Customers in the Netherlands: Strategy, Tactics and Operations', *European Journal of Marketing*, Vol. 24, No. 7, pp. 31–42.

Mintzberg, H. (1997), 'Managing On The Edges', *International Journal of Public Sector Management*, Vol. 10, No. 3, pp. 131–53.

Pullen, W. (1994), 'Eyes On The Prize Strategy in Government Agencies', *International Journal of Public Sector Management*, Vol. 7, No. 1, pp. 5–14.

Quayle, M. (1998a), 'The Impact of Strategic Procurement in the UK Government Sector', *International Journal of Public Sector Management*, Vol. 11, No. 5, pp. 397–413.

Quayle, M. (1998b), 'Industrial Procurement: Factors Affecting Sourcing Decisions', *European Journal of Purchasing and Supply Management*, Vol. 4, No. 4, pp. 199–205.

Quayle, M. and Jones B. (1999), *Logistics: An Integrated Approach*, Wirral, UK: Tudor Business Publishing.

Saunders, M. (1994), *Strategic Purchasing & Supply Chain Management*, London: Pitman.

Schachter, H. (1994), 'Revolution from Within', *Canadian Business*, November, pp. 31–47.

Smith, R. and Conway, G. (1993), 'Organisation of Procurement in Government Departments and their Agencies,' London: HM Treasury Consultancy and Inspection Services Division.

Van Weele, A. and Rozemeijer, F. (1996), 'Revolution in Purchasing', *European Journal of Purchasing and Supply Management*, Vol. 2, No. 4, pp. 153–60.

4 Managing a portfolio of supplier relationships

Douglas K. Macbeth

Introduction

In the eyes of some traditional business people, purchasing staff are seen as routine order placers with little effect on business strategy. While this has often been the case, the new reality is that, for certain aspects of the business, the opportunity to have a major impact is very large indeed. It will remain the case, however, that some traditional practice will still be necessary. What now needs to be recognized is that there is a variety of suppliers and therefore there needs to be a variety of supplier relationships.

Pareto law

In any population of interest a property first observed by an economist in Italy at the start of the twentieth century is that there is not an equal distribution of value across all members of that population. Pareto was looking at wealth in human populations, but the same 'law' seems to apply in many different situations. This is also expressed as the 80:20 rule, which says that roughly 80 per cent of the total value in a population will be represented in only 20 per cent of the number of that population. This is borne out for our purposes in the realization that, given an uneven spread of value contributed across the supplier population, we should consider how best to allocate our managerial resources to each supplier to be more in line with their relative importance to us as purchasers. Looked at from the other point of view (to which we will return later), a supplier looking at its customer base will find the same rough relationships to exist in that there will be relatively few customers who represent the most important proportion of their total business while there might be a great many whose contribution might be better removed than supported at an excessive relative cost.

The further logic of this differentiated strategy is that, from the customer point of view, we need to have a clear picture of what is purchased from whom. This sounds an obvious thing to do, but the reality, in many organizations, is that these data are often not available in the form necessary for a sensible analysis.

Spend analysis

In order to analyse the spend pattern we can create a 2×2 matrix with a vertical scale which indicates an increasing level of risk to the customer's operation should the supplier fail to

deliver. The horizontal axis increases with the total value of the spend with that supplier. Generating these data can be a challenge in some organizations. Often they will not be readily available since until the power of such analysis is recognized the need to ask for the data is not apparent.

Figure 4.1 shows the results of performing this analysis in a large organization with significant amounts spent in all areas of activity. Interestingly, no one had ever tried to do the analysis before this time.

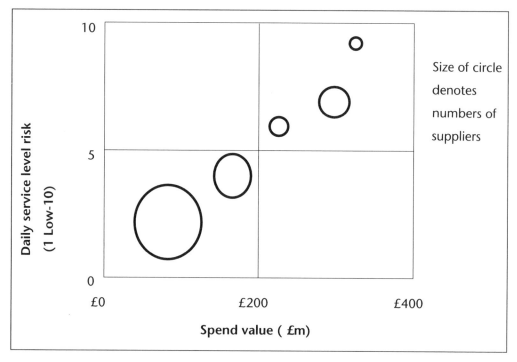

Figure 4.1   *Risk–value analysis, top 100 suppliers*
© SCMG Ltd

Of course the process of gathering and grouping the data is an exercise in strategic analysis in itself (Wind and Mahajan, 1981). The process therefore has a number of benefits. First it raises the issues of data availability, access and accuracy or believability. Second it causes debate and decision about relative risks and what these terms mean in the context of the business situation. By its very nature the attempt to construct the matrix causes managers to consider a differentiated strategy for the four quadrants and helps prepare the ground for the detailed implementation to follow.

Figure 4.2 shows the generic framework as used by SCMG Ltd (www.scmg.co.uk) as the basis of their approach. Olsen and Ellram (1997, p. 111) have similarly argued that this is a sensible first step in a portfolio analysis. Both approaches draw on the original work by Kraljic (1983).

This basic approach has been found by Bensaou (1999) to be one of the routes to successful supply chain management.

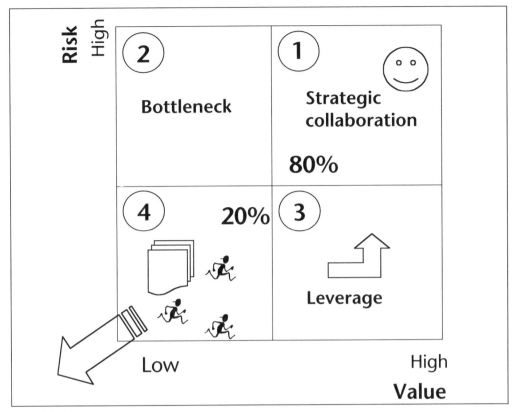

Source: Adapted from Kraljic (1983).

Figure 4.2   *Portfolio of relationships: customer's perspective*

View from the customer

QUADRANT 4: THE TRIVIAL MANY

In this quadrant are 80 per cent of the numbers of items purchased but they are individually of low value. As a result, their overall contribution to the total spend is 20 per cent. This is the quadrant that covers commodity type purchases where the only differentiating factor in the products or services bought is the price of the item or service. It is in this quadrant that the rules of the market apply, and the normal expectation is that there are many suppliers and many customers and the market is so competitive that prices find their lowest level through these market pressures since comparisons are easy and the costs of switching from one supplier to another are negligible.

Conversely, this is the quadrant where traditionally most of the purchasing efforts are directed such that the allocation of effort is usually in the reverse proportion to the value one. That is, in this quadrant there is usually 80 per cent of the organizational effort involved in finding and re-sourcing suppliers, solving delivery problems and quality issues, often in highly stressful fire-fighting mode. This is therefore the quadrant where measures to remove the costs of all of these numerous transactions are concentrated. These include the use of purchasing cards and some of the e-commerce solutions, including e-markets which offer the potential to perform the tasks more efficiently. Please recognize, however, that these solutions do not remove the need for the items or services purchased; they will still be needed in the business but the cost to purchase them can be reduced dramatically.

QUADRANT 3: LEVERAGE

In this quadrant are located those items of value in themselves but available without difficulty from a variety of suppliers. By definition there is a ready market for these items and they are not high risk to the customer's business since a particular source of supply is easily replaced. Here the logic of the pure market can apply and it is possible to exert pressure on suppliers to reduce their cost to supply, under threat to replace them with other equally qualified competitors who are prepared to meet the cost targets.

QUADRANT 2: BOTTLENECK

The items in this quadrant represent problems for the buyer since the items, although not significant in individual value terms, represent significant risk to the business if supply is interrupted. The items are often unique in some way. Sometimes this will be because the supplier has a monopoly and there are no other sources available. This is not a healthy place to be for a buyer, and steps should be taken to either design the unique requirement out of the product or find some suitable alternative to the item which is more freely available. Sometimes the uniqueness is the fault of the buyer's technical specialists who have so designed the item that a supplier has to do something special to supply it. Specials usually cause problems to production schedulers, so often there are frantic periods of action to expedite the delivery process.

Thus there are two options: find an alternative supplier for the unique item or replace the need for the supply by redesign.

QUADRANT 1: STRATEGIC COLLABORATION

In this quadrant are 'the important few' – 20 per cent of items which contribute 80 per cent of the value of all of the items. This is where the key relationship partners for the future of the buyer's business can be found. These are the providers of the items and/or services whose presence is crucial to any success of the buyer organization. The buyer is dependent on both the availability of these items and on receiving both a fair price in their purchase and the benefits of continuous improvement efforts to reduce the costs of providing the items and managing their supply. It is in this quadrant that the strategic leverage of good-practice business relationships is evident and where the opportunity to conduct business in more co-operative ways has a real prospect of delivering mutual benefit.

There will be relatively few of such suppliers to consider. In Japanese automotive examples there might be up to 200 of such first-tier suppliers on whom the assembler is totally dependent, but for Western-style companies moving from traditional adversarial, price-driven relationships, the likelihood is that the effort to initiate and manage more than 20 per cent of all relationships in this way will be unrealistic. In fact, most organizations move slowly, a few at a time, to test their methods and demonstrate the benefits of closer working. Empirically the data suggest that it is difficult to do this well, and many efforts fail (Boddy et al., 1998). There are, however, ways in which the prospects for success can be dramatically improved (Macbeth et al., 1998).

Priorities and roles of purchasing staff

The nature of the risk–value calculation in each of these quadrants implies different priorities and roles for the purchasing staff engaged in such activities.

QUADRANT 4: THE TRIVIAL MANY

In this quadrant the smart thing to do is not to do this work at all. This is the area of simple order placing, monitoring and expediting the progress of the order and trouble-shooting as things go wrong. They go wrong because no one regards this business as other than a nuisance: the buyers because it is low risk, low value, and the suppliers because they are being squeezed on price and cannot afford to increase their costs by investing in the items or their delivery processes since their margins are already very small. In addition, since they know that the buyer has many supply options available, the supplier might easily lose the business to an undercutting competitor and therefore investment is again hard to justify.

A number of options offer themselves to buyers in this quadrant.

First, they can reduce the costs of the very many individual transactions involved by using purchasing cards (company credit cards for specified purchase ranges and values) to simplify the buying process and especially the accounting process after purchase. This is also the quadrant in which the simplest form of electronic marketplace has an application. Since the conditions of the pure market apply, it is possible to create an even bigger electronic market; the items are commodities in type, undifferentiated on other than price; there are ready suppliers in some number worldwide; and the risk of supplier delivery failure or quality non-conformance on delivered items is not a big consideration.

A second option is to outsource the problems in this quadrant to someone else who will manage the complexities. Thus, rather than have individual contracts with many suppliers, of, for example, stationery items, one integrator provides one point of contact with the buyer and then manages all the other suppliers on the buyer's behalf. Of course, given that the buyer is still spending the same overall amount of money, i.e. the demand for all of the variety has not disappeared, the new integrator supplier is no longer a trivial party, easily replaced. Instead the integrator supplier moves towards quadrant 1 since a failure now is much more likely to have a major impact on the business activity.

Buyers in this quadrant therefore have a set of changing challenges depending on how the procurement strategy is developed. They can continue as traditional, transactional buyers aggressively looking for reducing costs and alternative supply sources but looking to reduce their process costs at the same time. If purchasing cards are decided upon, there is a major strategic decision to be made on which organization provides the card service, but this is a quadrant 1 concern. If e-markets are the chosen option, again this becomes a strategic quadrant 1 decision. Similarly, once the integrator supplier is selected, the management moves to a quadrant 1 mode and the traditional role of the buyer is removed from the scene. Thus the operational or transactional buyer role in this quadrant is most at risk from evolutions in business practice.

Note, however, that this is the quadrant that typically employs most of the purchasing resource, so there are serious management of change issues emerging from such considerations.

QUADRANT 3: LEVERAGE

Traditional skills of finding alternative sources, re-tendering contracts, pressurizing and negotiating for reduced supply costs are the priorities in this quadrant. This is the area where buyers are probably most experienced. Given the high values of the individual items, savings in supply costs on this range of items are possibly large and the effort relatively low risk because of the alternatives in the marketplace.

E-markets or consortium buying can also be considered since the opportunity to aggregate a set of similar demands from diverse customers might offer the possibilities of negotiating bulk discounts from the suppliers who win the bigger orders. Here again, skills development might be needed to cope with the e-market procedures effectively and to learn how best to interface with and operate in a consortium.

QUADRANT 2: BOTTLENECK

This is a difficult area for buyers to operate in. The items represented here are very difficult to influence or control. In the situation of a supplier monopoly there is little to do but wait for the supplier to deign to provide you with your requirements or the allocation allotted to you by the supplier in a constrained marketplace where demand exceeds supply capability. The best that a supplier can do is get close to the buyer to recognize the changes in the supplier's business around which the buyer can plan.

If the item purchased is unique to that customer, then two possibilities appear. One is internally focused and the other externally, but covertly. Internally the challenge is to re-engineer the uniqueness away. The risk is not balanced by the value of the item and this is bad design. That is not to say that the engineers or designers will agree readily; after all, they devoted their expertise to the original design in the first place and clearly the item still provides the utility intended; it is simply not good business even if it remains the best engineering!

If this proves an insurmountable challenge because of personalities, power structures or simply the time and systems costs to effect a change, then the buyers must still source the item as is but perhaps the risk can be reduced by having an alternative source of supply. The danger is that the existing supplier is probably not that interested in this item since it is unique to this customer and therefore cannot be produced for others. As a result they may not be that concerned if the order disappears, but if they realize that an alternative source is under investigation they might believe that this is to replace them and might stop supplying the business before the alternative source is fully operational. The search for a second source therefore needs to proceed with some care, and hidden from the direct view of the current supplier. The skills needed for such covert operations are likely to include a creative view of capabilities in the supply base to identify suppliers who do not supply this item (they cannot because of its uniqueness) but who could use their existing expertise in the new direction. This also must be done in a way that does not arouse suspicions in the current supplier. Indirect means to access the marketplace are required since an invitation to tender notice will be quickly spotted. Here the nature of the Internet can allow the investigation of alternative supplier's web sites and other indirect evaluations before any serious approach is made. It might also be sensible to consider the building of stocks of the item ready for potential interruptions in supply at the change-over or second source. It is important to produce at least a dual-source solution or else the buyer is no further forward, having replaced a single supplier with a different single supplier at no reduced risk but possible increased costs through the resourcing exercise.

QUADRANT 1: STRATEGIC COLLABORATION

In this quadrant the suppliers will be truly of strategic importance to the customer. These will be the suppliers on whom the customer's future business will depend. These are the people whose expertise the customer will call on to support their forward plans and who are likely to be involved in product or service design for those parts of the product or service which the customer has decided are not a core competence. These suppliers will also act as the eyes and ears of the customer in their own marketplaces, watching for new opportunities and technological developments that the customer might be able to use and which can allow both parties to share in increased market benefit and/or reduced real cost. This relationship can also include serious discussions about risk and reward sharing on mutually important future projects. As such the challenges are many and varied. Getting it right can reap major benefits but needs a lot of up-front investment in finding the correct partner organization, agreeing the matching process and making it all work to full potential. The lessons learned in each relationship can be built into other relationships and the capability to become good at the collaborative form of business is a skill which will be of value to other customers and or suppliers, making it easier to be the customer or supplier of choice.

In this sector the changes to the roles and responsibilities of the purchasing staff are at their most extreme.

The business associates involved from the supplier side are in this quadrant because their continued support is crucial to the continued success of the buyer's business. In some cases these suppliers are obvious choices and no selection is necessary, but in other cases some supply base rationalization might be needed in order to concentrate efforts and interactions.

SCMG Ltd have a five-step methodology to examine the issues involved in this sector and it serves as a useful guide to the issues to be managed (see Figure 4.3).

To move to a new business relationship between legally separate and independent businesses will require a serious examination of many aspects of the company's business practices. This cannot happen without understanding and commitment from the top of both organizations. The top team in each organization needs to work with lower-level teams to set the boundaries for agreements and to support the effort involved to change ways of working and joint procedures. Selecting the appropriate supplier partner to work with is a crucial step, since by definition the relationship is expected to continue for an extended period of time. Of course the selection process has unique aspects for each product and service, but often the task is to assess whether the partner has the right mind set and will to work in the more collaborative way proposed. As already indicated, sometimes this step has no meaning since the choice is unreal or already made for other historical reasons. Of course both sides in this arrangement need to want to do the same things and both will have to change their practices to some extent. So the next stage is for the supplier to replicate what went on in the customer organization at step one and also to formalize the agreements on the nature of interactions and joint procedures. Once this is committed to, the next stage is to start a continuous improvement loop in which benchmarks of current performance can be developed, analysed and used as input to reviews of improvement projects.

In all of this the role of the purchasing personnel will be important if they choose to be part of it. If they do not so choose, then others, more in tune with the new requirements, will

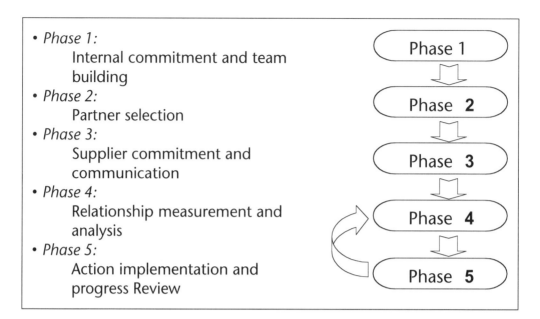

- *Phase 1:*
    Internal commitment and team building
- *Phase 2:*
    Partner selection
- *Phase 3:*
    Supplier commitment and communication
- *Phase 4:*
    Relationship measurement and analysis
- *Phase 5:*
    Action implementation and progress Review

Figure 4.3   *Supply chain improvement process (SCIP)*
© SCMG Ltd

replace their positions. The purchasing personnel have the existing supplier contacts, experience with the company and its individuals, and will be best placed to advise on issues of whom to talk to and when.

The role, however, changes quite dramatically since this is much more of a shared venture arrangement, and so any last vestiges of adversarial behaviour are very dangerous since they can destroy the building of mutual trust which is the source of real cost reductions. The opportunity exists, however, to become the relationship manager for the chosen supplier and to become much more of a total business manager working in new product development, shared reengineering and redesign projects, in supply chain performance improvement and in areas associated with interactive and electronic business planning. This is the opportunity to be truly strategic in focus and to make a major contribution while learning a range of skills which will be career enhancing.

The suppliers' quadrants and their implications

There are two sides to these considerations: if the customer is playing games with its strategic choices in terms of positioning its interactions with suppliers, then by the expectations of good business, so are they.

A concept similar to the customer's spend analysis, and using some of the same thinking from a supplier perspective, produces another portfolio diagram as shown in Figure 4.4.

Attractiveness will need specification in the particular context of that supplier, but it can include reputation, payment record, openness regarding future business plans, growth and innovation intentions, market ambition, readiness to listen and incorporate ideas and any other aspects of a good customer. Whatever these are, the range of current customers can

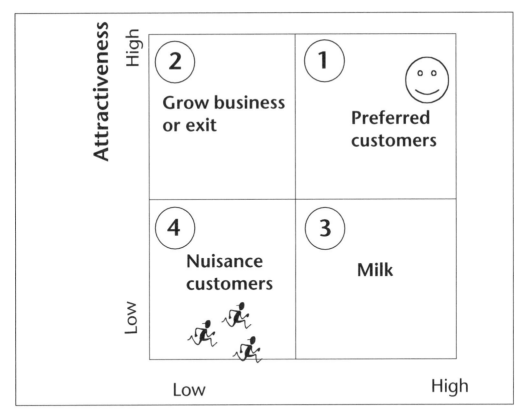

Figure 4.4   *Customer attractiveness and value*
© SCMG Ltd

be ranked against these criteria related to the value of the total supplier business that such a customer represents.

We therefore produce another 2 × 2 matrix. Here quadrant 4 represents customers whose value contribution is not covered by the difficulty and cost of satisfying them. Customers cannot always be right if satisfying them causes a supplier to become bankrupt! In this situation, unless something drastic changes, a supplier's financial position improves if the customer's business is removed. It takes a strong supplier to tell a customer that their business is a nuisance and the supplier can no longer afford to do business with them, but that is the exit strategy if all else fails.

Quadrant 3 represents good business that is not going anywhere in particular (otherwise the attractiveness would be higher). Nevertheless the value obtained from the customer is high and the supplier essentially tries to get as much as possible from this cash cow before a change occurs. The strategy then is to put sufficient resource into continued, reliable supply but to minimize the transaction costs of dealing with the customer.

Quadrant 2 represents customers who are attractive in some sense but have not yet translated this into sufficient value to ensure that it will continue to make sense to service their needs. Such a customer might be in a market that is new and attractive or is launching new products or services or represents kudos in being their supplier. In some sense this is business which is a loss leader, allowing the supplier to be associated with the customer's business. However, it is not sustainable over an extended period, since in that time they will have moved from quadrant 2 to quadrant 4 and subsequently exit from the supplier's portfolio. In these circumstances the supplier must put some effort into increasing the amount spent by that customer so that they move from quadrant 2 to quadrant 1.

Quadrant 1 represents the happy outcome for the supplier. Here we have an attractive customer spending enough to justify continuing investment and support. These are the customers that suppliers need and must have. Often these will be relatively few in number out of a much wider range of customers, and so Pareto reappears as the important few customers. These are the ones that the supplier's future will depend on.

Preferred supplier and the preferred customer

Customers are too often strange organizations. They seem to behave as if they are the only customers a supplier has and yet in almost the same breath will decree that it is their policy not to take more than, say, 30 per cent of the supplier's business. By that simple statement they send a series of messages to the supplier. The first is that they are prepared to cancel the order and walk away from the supplier with no concern that the action will force bankruptcy and bad press in the supplier's local environment or further afield. That same limit forces the supplier to find other customers, so customer one is in fact creating its own competition for the supplier's support and service. Third, the very fact that the business might not continue means that it is difficult for the supplier to justify any specific asset investment to support customer one's business. Finally, the need to find alternative customers causes the supplier to spend on marketing and sales to fill their capacity and in so doing the supplier's costs of doing business increase, further reducing their capacity to invest while the added number of customers causes increased complexity in scheduling and delivering the service. It is therefore in the supplier's interest, as it is in the customer's, to reduce the number of transactions in which they are involved to a level where the benefits of fewer but more productive relationships can provide mutual benefits.

Given the tendency of customers to assume that there is no one else more important in the supplier's world, it is no surprise to hear customers talking of choosing their preferred supplier but, as Figure 4.4 has shown, suppliers will have preferred customers. The difference is that since suppliers always say yes (the customer is always right, after all!), the customer will not necessarily know if they are not the preferred customer. Nevertheless, when a number of customers all need a scarce resource in a hurry, then the supplier must choose who gets first response and best support. The insularity of the typical customer means that they will have no way of knowing that they were anywhere but first in the queue, even though the reality may be completely different.

The ideal match is when a customer chooses a supplier as its preferred one and the supplier analysis indicated the customer as the preferred one – in effect both analyses producing the correct name in quadrant 1. When such happens, the smiles on the faces will be real. In order for this to happen there needs to be a recognition that in this matching there are benefits to be sought and shared by both parties to create a true win-win solution.

POWER

It is worth saying something at this stage about the role of power in these transactions.

To some extent customers will always have some power over a supplier, since they can choose not to spend. Power is a dangerous and sometimes spurious benefit, however. Whoever exercises their perceived power is in some senses often diminished by its use. In quadrant 1 that will very evidently be the case since any collaboration benefits soon disappear as preferred status turns to the target for retribution. In any integrated, close relationship the danger of using power is that the relationship is damaged irretrievably. It is perhaps for this reason that the businesses represented in the collaboration quadrant will often recognize a degree of equality in their relative power over the other. If the power is vastly different in either the customer or the supplier, then the benefits of mutual destiny arguments are unlikely to hold. It is for this reason that any monopolist is unlikely to need to get close to a supplier or a customer since their monopoly avoids any requirement to collaborate. Their future is more dependent on the monopoly than anything else.

Gelderman and van Weele (2000) develop the power/importance aspects of relationships further to represent the relative dominance of buyer and supplier in each of the quadrants.

In business there will always be choices in the longer term even if there appear to be few in the short term. Certainly in quadrant 1 both parties have to want to work in a collaborative way or the prospects are alarming. In other quadrants traditional practices will still be relevant.

In quadrants 2, 3 and 4 the relationships are distant at best and fleeting in many cases. An efficient e-market in quadrant 4 allows little relationship between buyer and seller on a single transaction where price is all. On the other hand, the relationship either party has with the provider of the market service might well be a quadrant 1 relationship if the volume of business transacted through that service provider is significant enough.

It is worth recognizing that in any relationship the power to destroy, and the ability to do so instantly, resides in every actor involved. Operating in the preferred mode is not a comfortable, easy or risk-free option. The benefits are there but they have to be worked for and the effort will need to be continuous. This, then, is the challenge for all in each organization (not just the purchasing personnel, who might still be the major contact or relationship managers) for many more people will now be crossing the boundaries between the organizations and the messages they carry must be consistent and thoughtful.

Managing the portfolio

The implication of this approach for portfolio relationships is that purchasing functions must recognize the need to differentiate their supplier bases and then manage each of the sub-sectors in different ways. Since the management objectives are different, the skills required to operate the relationship are also different. It is often hard for individuals to be able to switch easily between different operating modes, so this also implies that the purchasing department should look carefully at the inherent skills and attitudes of its staff members and consider the training needs in order to fill any identified gaps.

It is, however, not a single function's responsibility to operate in portfolio mode. Certainly in quadrant 1 the importance of managing the relationship with the critical few customers or suppliers means that everyone in both organizations needs to understand the rules of engagement and the mutual responsibilities inherent in this form of working. Senior managers from both sides will need to commit publicly and often to ensure that their operational colleagues have a full mandate to continue along the chosen path. However, given that the world changes and circumstances might indicate that the path cannot continue indefinitely, there is also the responsibility to monitor and evaluate the contributions made in this sector and to initiate remedial actions (including replacement of the partner) if all is not as well as it should be.

In the other quadrants the roles of the purchasing staff previously discussed need to be overseen and managed. Above all, the need for more data about changing patterns of spend, risk and dependence should be recognized and procedures put in place to gather, analyse and review achievements against the planned strategic direction.

References

Bensaou, E. (1999), 'Portfolios of Buyer–Supplier Relationships', *Sloan Management Review*, Vol. 4, No. 4, pp. 35–44.

Boddy, D., Cahill, C., Charles, M., Fraser-Kraus, M., and Macbeth, D.K. (1998), 'Success and Failure in Implementing Supply Chain Partnering: an empirical study', *European Journal of Purchasing and Supply Management*, Vol. 4, Nos 2–3, pp. 143–51.

Gelderman, K. and van Weele, A. (2000), 'New Perspectives on Kraljic's Purchasing Portfolio Approach,' *Proceedings of the 9th International IPSERA Conference*, Richard Ivey School of Business, London, Ontario, Canada.

Kraljic, P. (1983), 'Purchasing Must Become Supply Management', *Harvard Business Review*, Vol. 61, September/October, pp. 109–17.

Macbeth, D.K., Boddy, D., Wagner, B. and Charles, M. (1998) 'Implementing Partnering Relationships: A Change Process Model', in R. Berndt (ed.), *Managing Change*, Berlin: Springer-Verlag, pp. 59–74.

Olsen, R.F. and Ellram, L.M. (1997), 'A Portfolio Approach to Supplier Relationships', *Industrial Marketing Management*, Vol. 26, pp. 101–13, www.scmg.co.uk.

Wind, Y. and Mahajan, V. (1981), 'Designing Product and Business Portfolios', *Harvard Business Review*, Vol. 59, January/February, pp. 156–65.

5 *Outsourcing*

Chris Lonsdale

Introduction

During the 1990s managers from both the public and private sectors found themselves under ever-greater pressure to improve the performance of their organizations. In the public sector, managers were expected to deliver better services to the public at lower cost whilst, in the private sector, many firms found their margins being eroded by ever-increasing competition. These pressures left managers looking for techniques that would promote better organizational performance. One such technique that was used was outsourcing. Outsourcing is defined in this chapter as the transfer of an existing organizational activity to a third party.

Despite the high hopes of managers, however, the extent to which outsourcing has actually contributed to improved organizational performance has been uneven. Many managers have been left disappointed. (PA Consulting Group, 1996; KPMG, 1997; Cox and Lonsdale, 1997). Yet the variability of outcome has not been random and success not the result of dumb luck. Rather, the most favourable results have been achieved when managers have undertaken outsourcing with an awareness of the practice's many risks. In this chapter what the author considers to be the most important of these risks are investigated. Following this, the remainder of the chapter is dedicated to a brief discussion of the issues that arise after the decision has been made to outsource. The chapter begins, however, with a review of why managers consider the option of outsourcing in the first place.

The organizational objectives of outsourcing

There are many reasons why organizations may wish to employ the practice of outsourcing. Those that will be discussed in this chapter are: the reduction of headcount, the reduction of cost, the desire for greater flexibility, the desire to focus on 'core' activities, the desire to gain access to a supplier's expertise or innovation and the desire to reduce time to market. None of these reasons are inherently right or wrong, although they may be considered to be more or less respectable. The key, as will be discussed later in the chapter, is that whatever the motivation for outsourcing managers should not make the decision before they have undertaken a comprehensive risk assessment.

HEADCOUNT REDUCTION

Perhaps the most maligned reason for undertaking outsourcing is a desire to reduce the organization's headcount. Reducing headcount became a major objective of senior management in the 1990s, not least because fund managers and others involved in trading shares looked favourably upon those private sector firms that made significant reductions. Outsourcing, as well as the infamous practice of 'downsizing', has helped managers achieve this objective, although many practitioners report that the aim of reducing headcount is usually dressed up in more respectable rhetoric.

COST REDUCTION

The most common motivation for outsourcing is cost reduction. The view taken by many managers is that, as a rule, specialist third-party providers are more cost efficient than internal providers. A desire to reduce costs will usually underpin the decision to outsource what are considered to be the organization's support services, for example catering, reprographics, security and cleaning. Part of the greater efficiency, it is argued, comes from the supplier's specialist skills, economies of scale and leading edge equipment. What can also reduce cost, however, are lower labour rates. Getting access to low-cost labour is, of course, one of the main motivations for sourcing globally and will often involve activities that are much more significant than the aforementioned support services. Many clothing firms, for example, have outsourced production to places such as Indonesia, where pay rates are a fraction of those paid in Europe or the USA.

GREATER FLEXIBILITY

A third motivation for outsourcing is a desire to obtain greater flexibility in the provision of certain goods or services. When an organization outsources, it turns a fixed cost into a variable cost. In other words, rather than maintaining an internal operation 365 days of the year, organizations can simply call upon a supplier or suppliers when necessary. This has been a compelling argument in the case of component machining in manufacturing firms.

Historically, many manufacturing firms have produced in-house almost all of the components for their end products. To do so has almost been an act of faith, especially in medium-sized firms. However, the machining operations to produce such components will often only be used for three or four runs a year, the rest of the time they just stand expensively idle. As margins have tightened many such firms have had finally to embrace outsourcing and shut down certain of their machine shops.

GREATER FOCUS ON 'CORE' ACTIVITIES

This reason for outsourcing was heard a great deal during the 1990s. Over the past ten years public and private sector organizations have been encouraged to focus on their 'core competencies', outsourcing other activities to third parties that have such activities as their core business. It is argued that, especially in the private sector, organizations need to concentrate their scarce resources on certain core activities, otherwise they will discover over time that they no longer hold a superior competence in anything.

Hewlett-Packard (as was) provides a good example of a firm that paid heed to this message. In the 1980s, managers in the firm's mobile phone testing equipment division came to the conclusion that they could not continue as a highly vertically integrated business entity. After an in-depth internal review they decided that their core activities lay in research and development, final assembly, certain key components and equipment testing. Nearly all other activities were outsourced. This outsourcing strategy freed up management time and also allowed investment resources to be concentrated on certain key activities within the firm.

ACCESS TO SUPPLIER EXPERTISE AND INNOVATION

The other side of a core competence strategy is the opportunity it provides to access the core competencies of other firms. This has been an argument that has informed the trend towards information technology (IT) outsourcing. Organizational spending on IT has, of course, increased dramatically over the past 20 years. However, many senior executives have come to see the IT function as a black hole and have grown increasingly frustrated by the fact that the large sums of money invested have not been turned into an effective and up-to-date IT function. It was felt that internal IT departments were always one step behind the IT market and during the 1990s many executives finally came to the conclusion that outsourcing was the only way in which the firm was ever going to access leading edge processes. Rather than try to develop leading edge expertise themselves, it was argued that firms should instead access the expertise and innovation of the major IT consultancies and smaller specialist firms.

As a result, we have seen the development of an enormous market for IT service provision, involving the older-established IT players such as IBM, but also the newer entrants into the market such as Accenture, which have stretched their brands out of different market sectors. IT outsourcing is now commonplace and has been undertaken by organizations as disparate as local councils in the UK and large multinationals such as BP.

IMPROVE TIME TO MARKET

The final objective to be discussed is the hope that outsourcing will reduce the time it takes a firm to get its product or service to market. A high level of vertical integration can significantly affect a firm's lead times because any changes that have to be made to an updated product have to be made by the firm itself. These changes could require new equipment, new research, the enhancement of skills or the acquisition of new employees.

The time it takes for the firm to make these changes can make the existing level of vertical integration a major barrier to competitiveness. The firm may find that it is simply unable to get its latest product to market before the rest of the competition has made it obsolete. Reducing the time it took to get its product to market was another driver of the aforementioned division of Hewlett-Packard. Following its outsourcing programme, the firm no longer had to update its circuit boards etc., but simply sourced them from what was a highly competent and competitive marketplace. In this situation outsourcing was credited with cutting the firm's lead times from six months to two weeks, a dramatic difference and one crucial to its competitive position.

Managing the risks of outsourcing

In the previous section it was seen that there are many reasons why an organization might decide to outsource an existing business activity. Indeed, it may be that on certain occasions managers hope to achieve a number of objectives simultaneously. These are just aspirations, however, they do not provide any criteria by which to make the decision. The way in which the need for criteria will be addressed in this section is through investigating the risks of the practice. The slant of this section, therefore, will be towards providing criteria for *not* outsourcing rather than providing criteria *for* outsourcing. The end result is the same. In general terms, the risks divide into two main types: those that concern competitive advantage and those that concern supply management. The former will be dealt with first.

Outsourcing and competitive advantage

The first consideration of a risk management model for outsourcing concerns the protection of a firm's competitive advantage. Many firms have undertaken outsourcing in the hope of achieving cost reduction. On some occasions decisions have been made solely on this basis, without managers considering the importance of an activity to the firm's competitive position. Such a narrow focus is dangerous, especially if a firm's outsourcing becomes extensive. In this section three issues relating to competitive advantage are explored: the loss of core activities, the loss of intellectual property and damage to brand reputation.

THE RISK OF LOSING CORE ACTIVITIES

Over the past ten years both public and private sector managers have been encouraged to outsource around their core activities. This is reasonable advice. However, it does raise an important issue of how managers might interpret what is core to their organization. The idea of organizations having core and non-core activities has long been around, but became particularly fashionable in the early 1990s following the work of C.K. Prahalad and Gary Hamel. Prahalad and Hamel introduced the concept of 'core competence' and argued that the development of such competencies was essential for the creation and maintenance of competitive advantage. (Prahalad and Hamel, 1990). Two further academics, James Brian Quinn and Frederick Hilmer, then took the core competence concept and used it in the development of an outsourcing model. In a 1994 article, they stated:

> Two new strategic approaches, when properly combined, allow managers to leverage their companies' skills and resources well beyond levels available with other strategies:
>
> - Concentrate the firm's own resources on a set of 'core competencies' where it can achieve definable pre-eminence and provide unique value for customers.
> - Strategically outsource other activities – including many traditionally considered integral to any company – for which the firm has neither a critical strategic need nor special capabilities. (Quinn and Hilmer, 1994)

All this may seem perfectly straightforward, but if we look at the business strategy literature we are alerted to three issues that threaten to complicate matters. First, Prahalad and Hamel were taking part in what is actually quite a heated debate about how firms create and sustain competitive advantage over rivals. For example, their ideas are criticized by probably the best known of recent management theorists, Michael Porter. Furthermore, Porter is particularly critical of the type of advice that has been given by Quinn and Hilmer. He argues that one of the main sources of competitive advantage is the way firms are able to configure and link the different activities in what he calls the 'value chain', or what others refer to as the internal supply chain. Extensive outsourcing can upset the configuration of and linkages between these activities and reduce the firm's ability to establish and sustain cost leadership or uniqueness (Porter, 1980, 1991, 1996).

Second, even if we set aside the previous point and go along with the ideas of Prahalad and Hamel, identifying what is core is not an easy exercise. This is not least because the authors make clear that core competencies are never defined in terms of a firm's product or in terms of a firm's business functions. Intel's core competence, for example, is not and has never been their microprocessor chip. Nor has it ever been their research and development or marketing *function*. Rather, contemporary strategic theory states that the causes of competitive advantage are often very intangible and hard to identify or create (Hall, 1993; Teece and Pisano, 1995; Nonaka and Takeuchi, 1992). Competencies that allow competitive advantage are often the product of a combination of know-how, organizational routines and organizational infrastructure (Grant, 1998). It is not surprising, therefore, that many managers are not totally clear about exactly how above-average performance is created or might be sustained.

The implications of this complexity for an outsourcing strategy are clear. If it is ambiguous as to which activities within the firm contribute directly or, just as importantly, indirectly to competitive advantage there will always be a risk that certain key activities are outsourced by mistake. Valuable competencies can be outsourced or delicate organizational routines disrupted.

Finally, managers also need to think about the outsourcing decision in longitudinal terms. A decision over what is core and non-core needs to be taken with an eye on the future. Managers must ask themselves not just about what are the core activities in their market today, but also about what are likely to be the core activities in the future. To understand this point we only need to think about how the key competencies in the personal computer market have changed over the past 30 years. The game is, of course, going to change even more profoundly in the future.

Towards the virtual company?

Managers undertake outsourcing with a range of objectives in their mind. Yet whatever the reason for outsourcing, consideration must be made of the risk of losing core activities. Obviously this is never going to happen to firms just outsourcing facilities and the like. In the 1990s, however, a new vision for corporate management was propagated. This was the idea of the 'virtual corporation', where firms become almost a contract management operation (for example Andersen Consulting, 1997). However, taking this idea to its logical conclusion would, given what we know about the complex nature of competitive advantage, almost certainly lead to core activities being outsourced.

LOSS OF INTELLECTUAL PROPERTY

A similar issue concerns an organization's intellectual property. As many sectors are now said to be 'knowledge driven', it is crucial that organizations tenaciously protect their intellectual property. Many academics in the USA have argued that the outsourcing that numerous American corporations undertook in the 1960s led to the decline in their competitiveness in the 1970s and 1980s (Bettis, Bradley and Hamel, 1992; Reich and Mankin, 1986). Firms in industries as diverse as televisions and bicycles outsourced many production tasks to firms in Japan. The American firms immediately experienced dramatic reductions in their costs of production, improving their short-term profitability. As a result, the firms outsourced more of their production, including processes that required the Japanese firms to have knowledge of key technology.

The low prices that the Japanese contract manufacturers were charging their American customers were, of course, merely part of a much bigger game. They were willing to service these unprofitable contracts because their main aim was to learn from the American firms. Eventually, of course, the Japanese firms learnt enough to become competitors and began to take market share from their former 'masters'. In this case, therefore, it was not that the American firms outsourced their core activities, although in some cases they undoubtedly did. Rather, they outsourced to the extent that they exposed their key intellectual property and allowed it to be replicated. Many believe that the same mistakes are being made again 40 years on, with Western firms again thinking about the short-term cost advantage of teaming up with firms from lower-wage economies.

LOSS OF CORPORATE REPUTATION

A different aspect of outsourcing risk worth mentioning briefly is the damage it can cause to a firm's reputation. Earlier in the chapter we saw how outsourcing is often utilized by managers in order to cut costs. One way in which this can be achieved is by outsourcing to a country with lower labour costs. Whilst this may achieve that immediate objective, there can also be problems with such a move. For many firms the basis of their competitive advantage is brand and they therefore invest heavily in promoting that brand identity, providing it with a positive image. Outsourcing used recklessly can damage a firm's brand identity, as recent examples have shown.

One such example is Nike, a firm that was very aggressive in outsourcing and used as an outsourcing role model by many writers, including Quinn and Hilmer. Nike's core competencies were said to reside in the areas of research and development, sales, distribution and, crucially, marketing. As a result, Nike outsourced all of its production, except for that of specialist components.

Nike obtained tremendous benefits from their programme of outsourcing, reducing headcount and cutting their cost base. However, in the mid-1990s the company came under attack as it became alleged that the suppliers to whom it had outsourced were operating 'sweatshop' labour practices. Indeed, it was reported that in 1992 Nike paid more (about $20 million) to basketball hero Michael Jordan for endorsing its trainers than it paid to its entire 30,000-strong Indonesian workforce that made them. Reports such as these have made Nike a target of those who are protesting about the wider issue of global free trade. Specifically, Nike shops in the USA have been subject to demonstrations and other action (Viner, 2000).

This is clearly not a happy state of affairs for a brand-led firm like Nike. Its chief executive admitted in 1998 that the company's image had deteriorated from being 'the spirit of sport' to being a company whose trainers had 'become synonymous with slave wages, forced overtime and arbitrary abuse'. Gap has also received similar criticism and Katherine Viner commented recently, 'When [competitive positioning is] no longer just about products, when the corporations have promised so much more – a way of life! – they have very much more to lose' (Viner, 2000)

Outsourcing and supply management risk

There is no question that outsourcing, if managed badly, can have a deleterious effect on the firm's competitive position. Recent research on outsourcing, however, does not suggest that it is the most common problem caused by the practice. The greatest difficulties concern supply management. That supply management problems are more common than problems relating to the loss of competitive advantage is not surprising given the profile of most firms' outsourcing. The vast majority of firms have confined their outsourcing to functions such as facilities management and basic financial services such as payroll, which are far away from anything that could be considered 'core'.

There are many outsourcing risks relating to supply management. Recent research has shown that communication problems between buyers and suppliers are a major cause of underperformance (3i, 1994). There is also the risk of supplier failure causing interruptions to supply. For example, if a firm single-sources for a particular item of spend it has outsourced, it could be vulnerable to unexpected crises, such as an IT failure or the proverbial fire at the factory. A third risk reported in the literature is one of cultural fit between the buyer and supplier. Organizations possess distinctive operational practices and sets of values and attitudes that can often combine badly with those of other organizations.

However, because of the limited space available only two supply management risks will be discussed in detail in this section. These are the risk of dependency on suppliers and the risk of having a low level of transparency over supply. To the author these are the two most significant supply management related risks of outsourcing.

DEPENDENCY ON SUPPLIERS

The first rule of purchasing and supply is that managers should try to ensure that they keep their options open and do not become too reliant on one or a small number of suppliers. Consequently, it goes without saying that managers should think extremely carefully before outsourcing into a supply market with very few players, or with very few players that can deal with the manager's particular requirements. It is possible, however, to become dependent on a supplier even when there is a relatively competitive supply market. This is when the activity concerned involves either one or both parties incurring significant sunk and switching costs.

Sunk costs are the investments that an organization has to make during the term of a contract in order to make the relationship work effectively. These investments could include the training of employees, the adaptation of equipment or the transfer of data between two different information systems. The key point is that sometimes these investments are what are termed 'dedicated investments'. Dedicated investments are those investments made during the term of a contract that are specific to the relationship with the particular supplier. They cannot be transferred to a relationship with a different supplier should the organization wish to change suppliers. When such investments are non-transferable they are referred as highly specific assets (Williamson, 1985).

The concept can be illustrated by considering a contract with a supplier providing an enterprise resource planning system (ERP). When an organization contracts with an ERP supplier it has to make a number of investments in order to make the system work effectively. First, it will need to train its staff to use the system. Given that an ERP system is trying to link more effectively different parts of the organization, there is likely to be a wide range of employees requiring the training. Second, what often happens in the case of ERP systems is that the buying firm is required to adapt its own systems to suit the specifications of the software. There ensues, therefore, something of a business process re-engineering phase. Third, there will also often be a data transfer exercise. What is also often the case with ERP systems is that these investments are non-transferable. If managers decide to change ERP systems they have to write off much of the above investment.

This all seems fairly routine, but here comes the rub. In many buyer–supplier relationships for ERP systems the majority of the dedicated investment is undertaken by the *buyer*. A similar degree of dedicated investment to that described above is not made by the supplier. This puts the supplier in an advantageous position because it knows that the buyer's exit from the relationship is constrained – the buyer has become dependent. The buyer can still change suppliers, but the buyer and the supplier both know that there are significant costs attached to such a decision. Suppliers will often use that advantageous position to renegotiate the contract or negotiate a much better contract next time (Lonsdale and Cox, 1998; Lonsdale, 1999, 2001).

Sunk costs are usually accompanied by switching costs, that is the costs associated with the process of installing a new supplier. These costs include search costs, selection costs and contracting costs. In the case of ERP systems, it can often take well over a year to undertake the process of switching suppliers.

However, not all activities require dedicated investments. When an organization contracts with a supplier to provide a catering service, for example, it is unlikely to build up significant sunk and switching costs, however long the relationship. The market for catering services can be accessed at relatively low cost should the buyer not be satisfied with its existing supplier, and this ease of access allows it to retain control over the relationship. A key criterion for the outsourcing decision, therefore, is the extent to which the activity concerned is characterized by medium or high asset specificity. If it has a reasonable level of asset specificity, then managers need to think carefully about whether they will be able to structure the relationship in a manner that will enable them to retain control. If the buyer becomes dependent through the making of significant dedicated investments then it will often lose control and find its ability to achieve its objectives, especially that of cost reduction, significantly constrained.

LACK OF TRANSPARENCY OVER SUPPLY

The ability of an organization to achieve cost reduction from outsourcing can also be constrained if the activity passed to a third party is one that leads to information asymmetry between the two parties. Information asymmetry arises when one party to a transaction has more or better information than the other. This concept is probably one of the most important in the whole of the business management literature as it explains why many firms are able to make above-average profits without possessing any distinctive skills or products at all.

The easiest way to understand the significance of the concept for outsourcing is simply to think about what happens when we take our car to be serviced at the local garage. When we return to the garage to retrieve our car and pay the bill, we are faced with an invoice containing a number of elements. We can acquire quite easily the information necessary to check that the spare parts are being charged at the market rate. We can also check without too much difficulty that the labour rates are competitive. However, in respect of the most crucial aspect of the transaction we are at an enormous information disadvantage *vis-à-vis* the garage-owner. Our problem as a buyer is that we have no way of knowing whether or not the tasks that were done were actually necessary in the first place, or whether they were as problematic and time-consuming as claimed.

What is true in this situation is true in business in general. Indeed, the economics literature has a term for a market that is characterized by a high degree of information asymmetry. It is referred to as a 'lemons market' (Akerlof, 1970). What the economics literature has also done is segment goods or services in respect of the ease with which the buyer can ascertain value for money (Nelson and Winter, 1982). Those goods where the buyer can assess value for money before making the purchase are referred to as 'search goods'. Those goods where the buyer has to purchase the good or service before being able to ascertain value for money are called 'experience goods'. Those goods where value for money cannot be ascertained even after the buyer has made the purchase are called 'credence goods'. A search good could be a type of paper used for marketing materials, an experience good could be a software system, whilst a credence good could be management consultancy advice.

To return to the outsourcing context, it should be obvious from the above that if managers outsource business activities that are characterized by a high degree of information asymmetry they run the risk that suppliers might take advantage of their position, eroding and possibly reversing the hoped-for benefits.

A model for the outsourcing decision

Having considered both the risk of outsourcing for the firm's competitive position and the risks that arise from supply management issues, we can develop a simple model that brings the two elements together. This can be seen in Figure 5.1. The message of the model is 'safety first'. There is only one segment on the model where there is a high likelihood of achieving a successful outcome.

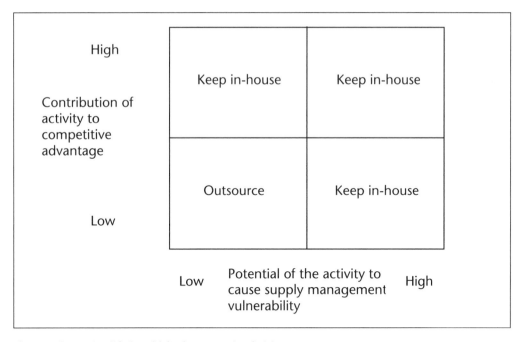

Figure 5.1   *A simplified model for the outsourcing decision*

Managing the outsourcing process

The final concern of this chapter is with providing a process for outsourcing. A summary of this can be seen in Figure 5.2. At the most basic level, a process for outsourcing consists of two parts. The first part relates to the consideration of whether or not to outsource an activity

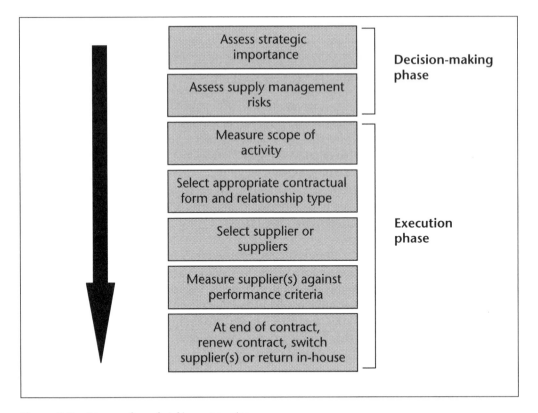

Figure 5.2   *A process for undertaking outsourcing*

– the decision-making phase. Some of the criteria that should be used to make the decision have been discussed in this chapter. The second part of the process, applicable to those occasions where managers have decided to go ahead with outsourcing, relates to the execution phase. The execution phase is really nothing more than a standard procurement process.

The execution phase starts with the scoping of the activity, with whatever costing tool is deemed most applicable. Managers then need to decide what form of contract and what type of relationship is most appropriate for the given activity. This will need to include consideration of whether the firm should single- or multi-source. Following this comes the actual selection of suppliers, involving the usual process of quotation analysis and negotiation. Once the contract or contracts have been signed there is the job of managing the supplier or suppliers, measuring their performance against appropriate metrics. Finally, when the contract comes towards its expiration, managers must decide whether they are going to renew the contract or contracts, switch suppliers or, if the experience has been particularly unsuccessful, take the activity back in-house, assuming the capability still exists.

Space precludes a detailed discussion of all the aspects of the execution phase. In the space that does remain, however, we can discuss one issue that has been hotly debated in outsourcing circles over the past ten years. This is the issue of contract and relationship management in outsourcing scenarios. A view was expressed above that the execution phase of outsourcing was nothing more than a standard procurement process. This view was actually contested in the 1990s, both by academics and by suppliers themselves. Getting this part of the outsourcing process right, however, is crucial, as research reported below can confirm.

CONTRACT AND RELATIONSHIP MANAGEMENT

A popular view over the past decade, which most in procurement will be familiar with, went like this. When outsourcing, managers should consider suppliers as 'partners'. These partners make it their business to improve the performance of their clients. They can only do this, however, if they are given time to develop and if the relationship with the customer is close, open, collaborative and based on trust. As the term of the contract with a partner needs to be long, it is difficult for it to be drawn up precisely. What should happen, therefore, is that the two parties proceed on the basis of a 'general clause' or incomplete contract. Yet as the relationship is a partnership, the customer need have no concerns about its lack of contractual protection. This sort of policy has often been recommended for logistics or IT outsourcing.

However, an overwhelming body of research has indicated that managers should be very wary of such a recommendation, not least when it comes from the supplier itself. Furthermore, research has shown that the greater the sunk and switching costs, the greater the need for contractual protection. It just so happens that many logistics or IT outsourcing contracts are characterized by extremely high sunk and switching costs. Research shows that when incomplete or general clause contracts are used for relationships where the buyer has made most of the dedicated investments, the supplier often simply uses the looseness of the contract and the dependency of the supplier to act opportunistically and raise prices or reduce service levels.

Indeed, research undertaken by Lacity and Willcocks showed that 0 per cent of IT outsourcing deals involving significant sunk and switching costs were successful in delivering anticipated cost savings if they were supported by an incomplete or general clause contract. They commented:

> Typically we found that, when operationalising the concept [of strategic partnerships], managers and academics under-estimated the importance of the contract, [and] over-estimated the ease with which companies can balance risks and rewards [and build] mutual as opposed to asymmetric dependencies. Senior executives ... were persuaded by vendors to sign flimsy contracts in the spirit and trust of a 'strategic partnership'. This contracting model is a poor way to manage outsourcing – primarily because outsourcing vendors and customers are fundamentally opposed. Vendor account managers are usually rewarded for maximising profits. These can be achieved by charging customers additional fees for services beyond the original contract, or not made clear in that contract. (Lacity and Willcocks, 1996)

Contrary to the fashion of the 1990s, Lacity and Willcocks found that the best results were achieved from IT outsourcing when organizations were (a) selective in the aspects of their IT that they outsourced, when (b) they signed short-term contracts and when (c) they ignored the advice about incomplete contracts. It is just a pity that the UK government, amongst others, wasn't listening.

Conclusion

There is nothing new about outsourcing; organizations have always made decisions about their boundaries. The practice can provide organizations with tremendous benefits – benefits that go far beyond basic headcount and cost reduction. Benefits will only be achieved, however, if managers undertake the practice using a robust management process. This process first concerns decision making and then turns its attention to execution. There are many more aspects to outsourcing than those included in this short chapter. The basic elements discussed, however, should steer managers away from the mistakes that have made the practice such a dirty word in so many organizations over the past ten years.

References

3i (1994), *Outsourcing*, London; 3i.

Akerlof, G. (1970), 'The Market for "Lemons": Quality, Uncertainty and the Market Mechanism', *Quarterly Journal of Economics*, August.

Andersen Consulting (1997), *Outsourcing: Gaining Competitive Advantage*, Proceedings of the SMI Outsourcing for Utilities Conference, London.

Bettis, R., Bradley, S. and Hamel, G. (1992), 'Outsourcing and Industrial Decline', *Academy of Management Executive*, Vol. 6, No. 1, pp. 7–22.

Cox, A. and Lonsdale, C. (1997) *Strategic Outsourcing Methodologies in UK Companies*, University of Birmingham Working Paper.

Grant, R. (1998), *Contemporary Strategy Analysis*, Oxford: Blackwell.

Hall, R. (1993), 'The Strategic Analysis of Intangible Resources', *Strategic Management Journal*, Vol. 13, No. 2, pp. 135–44.

KPMG (1997) *The Maturing of Outsourcing*, London: KPMG.

Lacity, M. and Willcocks, L. (1996), *Best Practices in Information Technology Sourcing*, Oxford, Oxford: Executive Research Briefings.

Lonsdale, C. (1999), 'Effectively Managing Vertical Supply Relationships: A Risk Management Model for Outsourcing', *Supply Chain Management: An International Journal*, Vol. 4, No. 4, pp. 176–83.

Lonsdale, C. (2001), 'Locked-in to Supplier Dominance: On the Dangers of Asset Specificity for the Outsourcing Decision', *Journal of Supply Chain Management*, Vol. 37, No. 2 (Spring 2001), pp. 22–7.

Lonsdale, C. and Cox, A. (1998), *Outsourcing: A Business Guide to Risk Management Tools and Techniques*, Boston: Earlsgate Press.

Nelson, R.R. and Winter, S.G. (1982), *An Evolutionary Theory of Economic Change*, Cambridge: The Bellknap Press.

Nonaka, I. and Takeuchi, H. (1992), *The Knowledge Creating Company*, Oxford: Oxford University Press.

PA Consulting Group (1996), *Strategic Sourcing: International Survey*, London: PA Consulting Group.

Porter, M. (1980), *Competitive Strategy*, New York: Free Press.

Porter, M. (1991), 'Towards a Dynamic Theory of the Firm', *Strategic Management Journal*, Vol. 12, pp. 72–85.

Porter, M. (1996), 'What is Strategy?', *Harvard Business Review*, November–December, pp. 61–78.

Prahalad, C.K. and Hamel, G. (1990), 'The Core Competence of the Corporation', *Harvard Business Review*, May–June, pp. 79–91.

Quinn, J.B. and Hilmer, F. (1994), 'Strategic Outsourcing', *Sloan Management Review*, Summer, pp. 43–55.

Reich, R. and Mankin, E. (1986), 'Joint Ventures with Japan give away our Future', *Harvard Business Review*, March–April, pp. 78–86.

Teece, D. and Pisano, G. (1995), 'The Dynamic Capabilities of Firms: An Introduction', *Industrial and Corporate Change*, Vol. 3, No. 3, pp. 537–56.

Teece, D., Pisano, G. and Shuen, A. (1997), 'Dynamic Capabilities and Strategic Management', *Strategic Management Journal*, Vol. 18, No. 7, pp. 509–33.

Viner, K. (2000), 'Hand to Brand Combat', *The Guardian Weekend*, 23 September, pp. 12–21.

Williamson, O.E. (1985), *The Economic Institutions of Capitalism*, New York: Free Press.

6 Financial aspects of purchasing*

Colin Rigby

Introduction

Credit taken from suppliers of goods and services constitutes the single largest source of short-term funds to many companies. Therefore, it should scarcely be surprising that corporate treasurers and finance directors will display a keen interest in those policies pursued by their purchasing colleagues, in so far as they affect the crucial task of corporate funding. And yet purchasing executives could be forgiven for concluding that the glamour and technical sophistication of stock market share issues, and the like, cause credit management to be artificially relegated in the minds of their financial colleagues – until, that is, a parlous cash position provokes crash stock reduction programmes and the clarion call.

'Stretch the creditors for all you can get!'

In this chapter the origin of the several sources of relationship between purchasing and financial management will be examined. The purpose will be to identify the nature of the many competing interests that can arise and the means by which they may be resolved efficiently in the pursuit of mutually accepted corporate objectives. Although it is true that constructive, and sometimes destructive, tension will often characterize the resolution of these dilemmas, there is much territory where coincidence of purpose and responsibility can be found. The latter is illustrated by the joint pursuit of raw material and other costs designed to maximize profitability. Nevertheless, conflicting pressures do arise when, for example, attractive input costs can only be 'bought' at the expense of early settlement or abnormally rapid delivery dates.

This chapter reflects the principal areas in which the responsibilities of purchasing and financial management interact. It begins with an exploration of the roles of price and credit terms in the negotiating armoury of the buyer in so far as these affect the profitability and liquidity positions of the business. This will lead to an evaluation of the cost of trade credit as a source of capital, paying particular attention to the implications of abnormally short or long credit terms. The management of credit as a key component of financial policy is then examined. The problems of growth and inflation receive special attention. Finally, some attention is devoted to the financial evaluation of suppliers.

---

*This chapter originally appeared in the second edition of this book and has been updated by Colin Rigby.

Motives in purchasing and finance

If asked to provide three policy guidelines to his purchasing colleague, a finance manager or accountant might typically respond:

'Get the lowest you can . . .
　　　. . . on longest credit terms possible . . .
　　　　　. . . but make sure the supplier not us, holds the stocks.'

Of course there is an assumption here that trade and its management is either cost-less or at least cheaper than some alternative source of finance, e.g. a bank overdraft. As will be seen later, this often merits greater attention than is generally assumed necessary.

This will raise questions along the following lines:

- Why should a treasurer respond in the manner suggested?
- What are his motives?
- Are they rational? And if so, for how long and under what conditions?

These are some of the key questions which purchasing managers need to bear in mind when pursuing policies which are both rational to them and sensible from a general management point of view.

Simple economic intuition might be sufficient to explain the main motives behind the advice given to our purchasing executive. Unfortunately this will not provide a set of tangible, operational guidelines sufficient to recognize not only the complex interrelationships which may exist, but also the very real limits for manoeuvre which the likes of common-sense prudence and custom and practice will dictate. Analysis of the so-called 'operating cycle' does, however, provide a useful means for disentangling the impact of several key variables that affect profitability and the funds needed to generate it.

The operating cycle is a generalized picture of the time interval which elapses between the initial investment in materials and services required to produce a product and the eventual receipt of cash for the sale of that product. For the typical multi-product process company the length of the cycle is in the nature of some hypothetical 'average' of all the individual patterns of buying, stockholding and production, together with the supplier and customer credit lines associated with each product or product group in the company's portfolio. The start and finish of the operating cycle cannot, of course, be identified as discrete points in time. However, for most businesses, it is possible to calculate the approximate length of the cycle. In the case of a manufacturing business, reference must be made to the average duration of the activities shown in Table 6.1.

The data required should be readily accessible from the firm's accounting or finance department, although it must be stressed that a number of simplifying assumptions will often prove necessary, even if these do cause some concern for the more pedantic breed of accountant! It is also worth mentioning, in advance of the more detailed examination of the financial health of supplier companies that will be undertaken later, that a crude version of the operating cycle can be gleaned from published annual reports and accounts. The cycle length can be calculated in terms of days, if the necessary information is of sufficient quality. However, typically it is adequate to work in units of one week.

Table 6.1 *Duration of operating cycle elements*

Activity sequence	Duration calculation
Credit taken from suppliers	Average level of trade credit
	Period supply of raw material
Holding raw materials inventories	Average investment in raw material
	Period consumption of raw materials
Production/conversion process	Average investment in work in progress
	Period of production output
Holding finished goods inventories	Average investment in finished goods
	Period cost of sales
Credit given to customers	Average level of trade debtors
	Period value of sales turnover

The length of the operating cycle can now be determined and, for best effect, portrayed graphically (see Figure 6.1). It can be seen that the overall length of the operating cycle is 20 weeks, made up from each of the five key components.

Whilst the absolute length of the operating cycle can provide startling news for the uninitiated and, usually, inefficient business, it has little intrinsic value except to highlight the relative significance of each of the corporate functions involved. Its real potential derives from two sources:

1   Informative comparisons can be made between different products produced by the same organization and between similar products produced by different organizations. Analysis of this type can serve to highlight product priorities in the first case and comparative efficiency in the second.

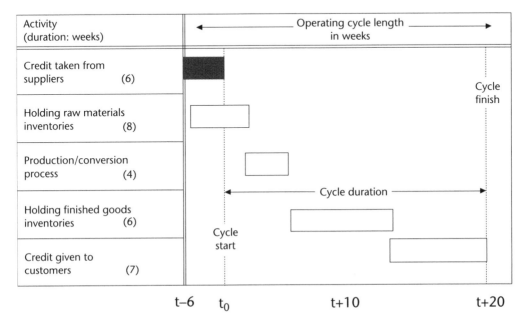

Figure 6.1   *The operating cycle length*

2   There is the opportunity to contemplate variations both in the length of the operating cycle as a whole and to each of its constituent parts.

However, in order to appreciate the full range of influences that the purchasing function may exert on corporate efficiency, the financial consequences of the extant cycle need to be recognized. In Figure 6.2 the cash flow consequences of each of the operating activities are shown in the form of a cumulative profile.

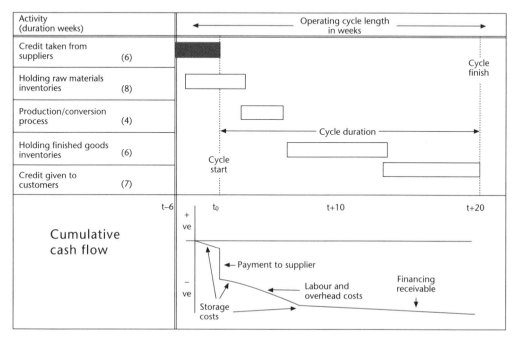

Figure 6.2   *The operating cycle: cash flow profile*

It can be seen that the operating cycle constitutes an ever-increasing hole in the corporate purse, until such time as the product's customer actually delivers his cash.

There are two key messages here. First, both the length and depth of the operating cycle will have a vital impact upon the cash flow and liquidity positions of the business, not only at the level of the individual product or product group but also for the business in total. Second, the level of holding costs will directly influence the firm's profitability, this will include financing charges incurred as a function of the length and depth of the cycle.

If the length of the cycle can be curtailed, then both cash flow and profits will improve; if the depth of the cycle can be reduced, then profits and cash flow will also improve; and if both can be achieved simultaneously, then the effects will be multiplicative.

Where, precisely, can purchasing management influence the shape and duration of the operating cycle? Plainly, there are several sources:

1   Extend the period of credit taken from the suppliers of raw materials and thereby reduce the period during which the cash deficit is at its most sizeable.
2   Organize delivery of supplies so as to reduce inventory levels and thereby the 'tie-up' of own capital, at the expense of the supplier.

3 Negotiate input prices not only of raw materials but also of other goods and services consumed in production, distribution and the like so as to minimize product costs and thereby maximize profitability.

Although the analysis so far does not capture the contribution which purchasing management may make through decisions covering, for example, capital expenditure and 'make or buy', it should already be clear that there is ample scope for enhancing corporate prosperity.

Naturally, the objective of efficient purchasing must be to achieve a sensible mix of priorities when negotiating supplier contracts. The purchasing levers that have been mentioned cannot, usually, be operated entirely independently of each other, nor will their travel be unencumbered by the objectives and instincts of the suppliers themselves. Moreover, the skill of the purchasing manager lies in the ability to accommodate important financial motives while recognizing the more subtle qualitative attributes of the supplier/buyer relationship.

Supplier credit and corporate funding

The importance of trade creditors or accounts payable as a source of corporate finance has already been stressed, at least in general terms. A specific example will better illustrate the point. The following table summarizes the manner in which a British company funded its multinational operations at its financial year end:

Short term	£m	£m
Trade creditors	669	
Other creditors	880	
Short-term borrowings	538	2,087

Long term	£m	£m
Grants and deferred liabilities	792	
Loans	1,400	
Capital and reserves	3,342	5,534
		7,621

If we assume that this position is typical of the company's funding policy over time, then it can be seen that trade creditors accounted for some 9 per cent of total funds. This is equivalent to 12 per cent of the long-term capital invested in the business. Plainly this item will feature strongly in the mind of that company's finance director as he seeks to organize an efficient portfolio of liabilities. In principle, the volume of credit taken from suppliers will reflect the commercial conditions prevailing in those sectors in which the company operates, the current liquidity position of the business and several other factors that include the cost of this particular source of finance. For like any other source of capital, supplier credit attracts a cost even though it may be less conspicuous than that of dividends on share capital or interest on bank and other borrowings.

Leaving aside the above example, corporate treasurers will be concerned to:

• optimize the use of cash discounts for early settlement
• manage cost-effectively the administration of supplier accounts

- evaluate late stage payment opportunities
- optimize the mix of short-term sources finance which may include payables, bank overdrafts, acceptance credits and trade bills.

The cost of trade credit

The cost of supplier credit normally has two components. These are administrative cost of managing supplier accounts – e.g. computers, account clerks – and the opportunity cost entailed in forgoing options to take cash discounts. Both of these costs will normally fall within the responsibility of the finance and accounting department, even though cash discounts may be a potent ingredient in supplier/buyer negotiations. It is important in these circumstances for the buyer to appreciate the true benefit of discount opportunities as well as the cost of disturbing established methods and systems supplier payment. In other words, though we are concerned with what primarily amounts to a financing decision, the purchasing function should recognize the financial dimension of its work and be prepared to simultaneously exert and accede to pressures on the finance function.

In general, credit terms will offer two alternative means of settlement, i.e. payment within a specified period following the transaction date, or settlement within a prescribed shorter period in exchange for deduction of a specified discount. The difference between the two options constitutes an opportunity to borrow for the duration of the difference between the two settlement dates at the cost of the cash discount to be foregone. The annualized cost of this source of funds is illustrated in the following example.

COMPUTING THE COST OF CASH DISCOUNTS

Assume that normal settlement terms call for payment of the entire debt within 30 days of the invoice date. A cash discount of 2.5 per cent is available if settlement is made within seven days of the invoice date.

$$
\begin{aligned}
\text{Annualized discount cost} &= \frac{2.5}{(100{-}2.5)} \times \frac{365}{(30{-}7)} \times 100 \\[2mm]
&= \frac{2.5}{97.5} \times \frac{365}{23} \times 100 \\[2mm]
&= 40.7\%
\end{aligned}
$$

It is plain that the cost of credit terms such as these is not trivial! Where annualized costs are of this order of magnitude, then serious consideration must be given to the use of alternative cheaper sources of finance such as bank overdrafts. In fact, where overdraft finance is judged to be the realistic alternative, then comparative interest costs must be expressed in compound rather than simple terms. If, in the example, interest were to be compounded at 23-day intervals, then the effective annualized cost would rise to approximately 48 per cent. Whichever method of calculation is used, there is a clear incentive for the buying function to recognize credit costs when negotiating suppliers' prices and to convey the significance of these to the treasurer's department. Two problems arise here. First, costs expressed in percentage terms are not readily identifiable in their 'bottom-line' effect. Second, the circumstances envisaged in the example are incomplete in the sense that an extra administrative charge may need to be incurred in order to give special treatment to an account which would normally be settled by standard accounting and computing systems. The following example illustrates how credit costs may be expressed more informatively:

Invoice value	£10,000
Supplier's normal credit terms	30 days following invoice date
Early payment (2.5 per cent discount)	7 days following invoice date
Marginal administration cost	£20
Bank overdraft cost	15 per cent p.a.
Value of normal credit period	$\dfrac{30}{365} \times 15\% \times £10,000$
	$= £123$

Value of early payment credit period =

$$\left(\frac{7}{365} \times 15\% + 2.5\% \right) \times £10,000 - £20$$

$$= £259$$

Net cost saved by taking cash discount = £136

Practical difficulties can be encountered in estimating the true incremental cost of special administrative arrangements to handle early payment opportunities. However, once these are known, the profitability consequences of early or normal settlement can readily be seen in the example: £136 of additional profit arises by adopting early payment. But one word of warning! The temptation often arises to ascribe excessive potency to arithmetic calculations and conclusions such as illustrated. It is vital to stand back in order to judge whether or not other, perhaps non-quantifiable, factors should be taken into account. For instance, adoption of early settlement terms may serve to reduce flexibility in negotiations or the risk may arise that the supplier will become excessively dependent upon the buyer's liquidity position, to the detriment of his own financial standing.

Other points to watch out for include:

- difficulties in recovering overpayment where insufficient time exists to check the quantity and quality of supplies before early payment is due
- reduced leverage on suppliers when contractual disputes or litigation arise
- the risk of being locked into early payment when financial exigency may make it essential to delay payment as long as possible.

DEVELOPING CREDITOR PAYMENT POLICIES

In addition to recognizing cash discounts in terms of their annualized percentage cost or absolute value, it is also essential to appreciate their effects in relation to the volume of credit settlement transactions. Broadly, the higher the proportion of 'credit input costs' to the total costs of the organization, the greater will be the significance of discounts policy for profit-ability and cash flow planning. Figure 6.3 illustrates this point, where a company's projected revenue, cost and profit plans are divided as shown.

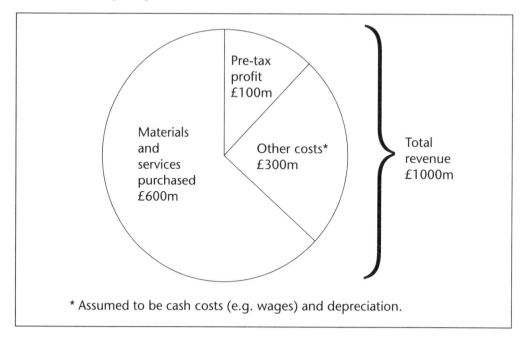

Figure 6.3   *Breakdown of company costs and revenues*

Assume that this company planned on obtaining an average 2.5 per cent cash discount on all materials and services to be purchased during the forthcoming year. Pre-discount purchases would be:

$$£600m \times \frac{100}{97.5} = £615m$$

That is, a cost saving of £15m (£615m–£600m) would have been anticipated in the process of earning pre-tax profits of £100m.

If, for whatever reason, cash discounts were assumed to be unobtainable, then, other things being equal, pre-tax profits of only £85m would be expected. Taking cash discounts at an average level of 2.5 per cent will generate pre-tax profits some 17 per cent (£15m/£85m × 100) greater than otherwise possible. The scale of this profit impact is of course the direct consequence of creditor costs constituting two-thirds of total costs. A simple calculation will show that when the relationship between creditor and cash costs respectively is inverted, then the leverage effect of discount policy on profits is correspondingly reduced. It can be seen then that the profitability consequences of a specified early settlement policy are a direct function of both the rate of cash discounts and the volume of transactions to which they apply.

Cash discounts apart, frequently settlement policy will involve opportunities to take extended credit, even perhaps where these involve late payment penalties. In general, these opportunities should be evaluated on lines similar to those for early settlement. For the large organization which has ready access to a greater variety of cheaper sources of finance than its smaller counterpart, the cost of extended credit is likely to be uncompetitive. Nevertheless, these opportunities should not be discounted altogether where, for example, the supplier refuses to negotiate on price or is employing credit as a marketing device and will not reflect the credit benefit in an alternative, cash price. Complex financial subsidy packages can also be encountered and, again, it is important to stress that other commercial considerations may be sufficient to sway the balance of the decision.

In any event, the development of coherent policy must be based upon a realistic judgement of the costs and benefits of routine payment and processes that should apply in the majority of cases, together with the special costs or benefits of early and late settlement opportunities. Moreover, it is vital that whatever policy is ultimately agreed on, it should not be allowed to become sterile or, worse still, a straitjacket which inhibits entrepreneurial skill and refuses to accommodate fundamental changes in the financial and commercial circumstances of the organization and its environment. It is to two particular types of change – actual and apparent growth – that attention is now turned.

Managing growth

Paradoxically, the task of financial management becomes the more exacting when growth, rather than contraction, is the order of the day. The economic recession in the UK manufacturing sector of recent years has served to cause many companies to accumulate large quantities of cash, as surplus assets have been sold or run down to levels consistent with reduced activity. In sharp contrast, the most prevalent cause of corporate collapse, other than that caused by sustained loss making, is mismanagement of growth and the financial strain that it frequently imposes. In short, this discussion is concerned with the problems of cash management and the impact which purchasing management may have on them.

Before proceeding it is necessary to distinguish between two types of growth which may occur independently or simultaneously. 'Real growth', as the term suggests, implies progressive expansion of the physical attributes of the firm; this could be the number of personnel employed, the physical volume of output generated, the number of customers or the size of market share. None of them needs be measured by means of money – other measures will suffice to capture genuine rates of change. Once the yardstick of money is used, its inherent instability can serve to distort or disguise the underlying real position. Inflation will make growth apparent rather than real and deflation the opposite. Whilst this problem besets the interpretation of financial statements (as shown later), the present concern is for the real demands for cash which derive from unreal changes to the substance of the business. Nowhere is this phenomenon better illustrated than in the increasing need for cash to finance the inflating prices of supplies whose physical levels do not change. The financial consequences of real growth are examined first.

REAL GROWTH

Real growth may be achieved either organically or by acquisition. The route chosen will depend on a number of factors including the degree of hunger for growth as well as diversification objectives. Whilst these two routes may be pursued simultaneously, the choice of appropriate strategy will need to reflect, for example, preferences in terms of horizontal and vertical integration. The former may arise from a desire to obtain a suitable measure of market dominance, whereas the latter is frequently motivated by the need to secure a guaranteed supply of critical downstream resources, such as pulp supply in papermaking.

The problems of financing rapid growth, particularly of the organic variety, lie in the freedom or lack of it with which the particular firm may exercise choice between different alternative sources of finance. Notwithstanding the existence of a highly developed capital market, UK companies typically fund 60–70 per cent of their capital requirements by means of profit retention. This dependence is often exaggerated for the small firm, which does not have access to stock market share issues or long-term institutional lending. Therefore, heavy reliance will often be placed on bank borrowings, retained profits and, of course, trade credit. The next example illustrates some of the issues involved.

Visualize a company, perhaps one of your own suppliers, which seeks to expand operations (see Figure 6.4). It aims to achieve this result by offering new extended credit terms to its existing and potential customer base. What cash flow consequences would be encountered by this change of policy?

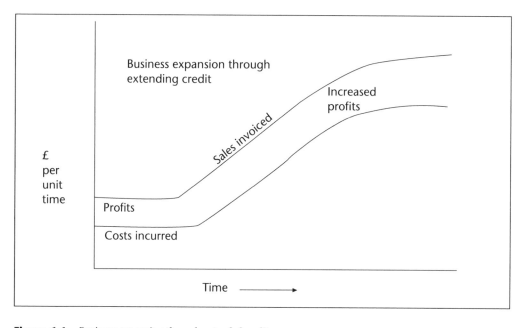

Figure 6.4   *Business expansion through extended credit*

Whereas in the small, steady-state condition to the left of the diagram, the rate of cash remittances per week or month would have been virtually identical to the rate at which sales were being achieved, the effects of the new promotion would be first to generate additional sales turnover, but then to experience a delay in the rate at which cash receipts would accelerate until the new credit terms began to 'bite'. Eventually, it is reasonable to expect a new steady-state condition reflecting the increased size of the business where the rates of sales turnover and cash receipts once again coincided at the new, higher level shown in Figure 6.5. The key question for the treasurer of this company concerns his ability to tolerate the delay in cash receipts, given that he must fund the purchase and production of the additional output in advance of its sale; moreover, he must also be prepared to finance a larger permanent

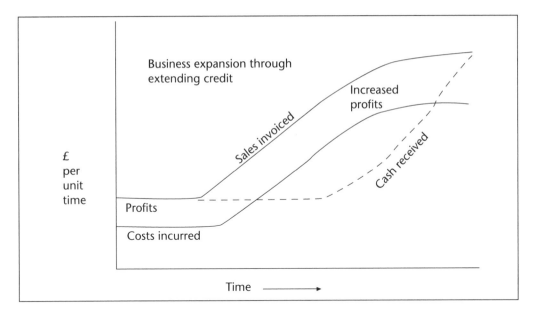

Figure 6.5 *Delay in cash receipts*

investment in customer debts. What are the options open to him and will they be sufficient to meet the full requirement?

An important contribution to solving this funding problem could be the purchasing function of the company. As Figure 6.6 shows, it might be able to mitigate the scale of the expected cash flow deficit by obtaining extended credit terms on the additional inputs required by the intended expansion.

It can be seen that the size and duration of the cash flow deficiency (hatched) are both substantially smaller than would have been the case had the 'cash paid' line continued to coincide with the 'costs incurred' line, perhaps to the critical extent that the expansion exercise could not be sustained.

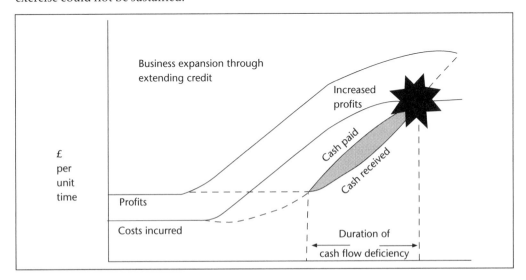

Figure 6.6 *Effect of extended credit*

In this sense, it is worth stressing the financial and other strains which a customer company, intent on growing itself, may impose upon suppliers who are exhorted to participate in such growth. Such interdependency of fortune has, of course, prompted the very intimate relationships which can be encountered between high street retailers of clothing and furniture and their manufacturing suppliers, particularly where the latter's output is heavily or even exclusively devoted to one major customer.

Two important conclusions emerge for purchasing managers:

1 As a party to the real growth of their own businesses they can influence materially both the scale and the nature of the funding tasks required of their financial colleagues. Growth is not easy to manage, and it should be apparent that procurement plans can assume crucial significance in exacerbating and/or solving its attainment.
2 Informed susceptibility by purchasing managers to the problems they may pose when stimulating rapid growth in supplier companies can pre-empt unpleasant surprises and even demises.

COPING WITH INFLATION

Inflation holds two threats to corporate prosperity and survival. The first danger manifests itself in declining real margins. This problem can be particularly acute for the business that depends upon fine margins and high volume, i.e. characterized by high break-even points, in highly competitive markets. If retained profits hold the dominant place that they do in corporate financing, then the importance of maintaining profit margins is self-evident. However, the ability to maintain margins is governed typically by several variables, many of which are within the purchasing sphere of responsibility. These variables are dealt with elsewhere in this and other chapters, but one in particular is worth emphasizing here. As much as anything else, speed of response to changing price levels is the key to maintaining profitability and this requires quick, efficient management accounting systems. These systems will need to anticipate and convey the consequences of price increases which purchasing management can neither directly nor indirectly avoid to those other functions which will become affected. Surprising though it may seem, many management accountants responsible for such systems are frequently amenable to constructive ideas from their non-financial colleagues! Purchasing managers are in a unique position to influence the design of information systems which will alert the organization to the threat of inflationary input costs and it is vital that they take this initiative.

The second major risk attending inflation derives from the fact that it consumes real cash for no productive purpose. Not only is this effect felt in escalating cost of replacing obsolete or worn-out fixed assets, e.g. plant machinery (magnified frequently by deteriorating exchange rates on imported equipment), but it can have an insidious impact on the various components of working capital which themselves affect the solvency position of the firm.

The latter phenomenon can be readily observed in the following illustration. Imagine two companies, A and B, which are identical in all respects except for the different requirements for working capital which each experiences to achieve the same sales turnover and pre-tax profits. The results for both companies in year 1 are shown in Table 6.2. It can be seen that the consequence of B requiring twice the level of working capital of A, whether the reasons be valid or not, is that B incurs higher bank interest charges. Thereby it achieves lower

Table 6.2 *Comparison of requirements for working capital*

		Company A £	Company B £
Trading account			
Sales		1,200,000	1,200,000
Depreciation		30,000	30,000
Surplus on trading (7½%)		90,000	90,000
Bank interest (see below)		(16,000)	(32,000)
Profit before tax		74,000	58,000
Tax at 50%		37,000	29,000
Profit after tax		37,000	29,000
Working capital			
Debtors	(A = 2 months of sales)	200,000	
	(B = 3 months of sales)		300,000
Stocks	(A = 1½ months of sales)	150,000	
	(B = 2½ months of sales)		250,000
Creditors	(A = equivalent to stocks)	(150,000)	
	(B = same as A)		(150,000)
Working capital		200,000	400,000
Bank interest at 12% on facilities, being equivalent to two-thirds of working capital		16,000	32,000
Cash flow			
Profit after tax		37,000	29,000
Depreciation		30,000	30,000
Capital expenditure		(30,000)	(30,000)
Positive cash flow		37,000	29,000
Difference between A and B cash flows		£8,000	

post-tax profits than A. This difference of fortunes is also realized at the level of net cash inflows for each company.

Table 6.3 sets out the results for both companies on the assumption that each experiences 15 per cent inflation in the following year's trading. The results for the two companies can be summarized as follows:

- Both achieve identical levels of sales turnover and trading profit, although margins have suffered during the inflationary period.
- Whereas the working capital requirement of A has risen by £30,000 to £230,000, B has experienced an increase of £60,000 even though the credit and stock cover periods of each have not altered between the two years.
- The bank interest charges arising from the overdrafts required to fund two-thirds of the working capital in both companies have risen as a product of the higher interest rates required to discount debasement of the currency.

- Higher bank interest charges, especially for B, have dented the pre- and post-tax profits of both companies.
- The cash flow positions of the two companies are entirely different. Whereas A has achieved a modest cash surplus even after consuming £30,000 in inflated stocks and debtors, B experiences a major cash deficiency all and more of which can be attributed to its adverse working capital position.

The essential point to grasp is that the different profit and cash flow conditions of the two companies arise as the exclusive product of inflation – not real growth.

The role of purchasing in maintaining margins has already been discussed, but there are other forms of assistance which can mitigate the effects of inflation. In so far as trade credit is

Table 6.3 *Comparison of results*

		Company A *£*	*Company B* *£*
Trading account			
Sales		1,380,000	1,380,000
Depreciation		30,000	30,000
Surplus on trading (7½%)		90,000	90,000
Bank interest (see below)		(21,500)	(43,000)
Profit before tax		68,500	47,000
Tax at 50%		34,250	23,000
Profit after tax		34,250	23,500
Working capital			
Debtors	(A = 2 months of sales)	230,000	
	(B = 3 months of sales)		345,000
Stocks	(A = 1½ months of sales)	172,500	
	(B = 2½ months of sales)		287,500
Creditors	(A = equivalent to stocks)	(172,500)	
	(B = same as A)		(172,500)
Working capital		230,000	460,000
Bank interest at 15% on facilities, being equivalent			
to two-thirds of working capital		21,500	43,000
Cash flow			
Profit after tax		34,250	23,500
Depreciation		30,000	30,000
Capital expenditure		(30,000)	(30,000)
Positive cash flow		4,250	36,000
Difference between A and B cash flows		£40,750	

Note: Bank interest at 15 per cent (up from 12 per cent in year 1) has been applied to the average working capital for year 2.

a cost-competitive source of finance, then it should be used to counterbalance inflationary pressures on stocks and debtors particularly. Of course, the degree to which this is feasible will depend upon the circumstances of the individual company, its suppliers and the several interacting considerations which have already been discussed. Excessive investment in stocks is a further source of vulnerability in inflationary conditions. If the debilitating effects of savage stock reduction programmes on supplier relations are to be avoided, then purchasing management must look for opportunities to curtail stock build-up. These may include resisting the temptation of bulk purchases, rescheduling supplier deliveries on to a more continuous pattern, thereby reducing buffer stocks, and, sometimes, reducing the speculative purchase of goods expected to rise in price.

The last point may seem perverse, yet it precisely epitomizes the need to shift emphasis away from profitability and towards cash flow in severely inflationary times – better profits tomorrow than insolvency today!

This section has dealt with the financial problems involved in securing growth (be it real or illusory). When these two forms of growth occur simultaneously it is to be expected that the task of funding, and purchasing management's contribution to it, will be magnified. But the task of integrating the aspirations and motives of purchasing, financial and other functions lies not only with the buyer's own organization; it also faces suppliers. The success or failure that they achieve can have direct and often substantial influence upon the buying company's destiny. It is incumbent, then, to assess the strengths and weaknesses of supplier companies and it is the financial aspects of that task that will now be discussed.

Assessing suppliers

The following quotations come from an interview that the author held recently with the purchasing manager of a major photographic company:

> I like to review the financial viability of a concern I am dealing with ... It would be bad news to get three months into a project, to find that a company failed. There may not be any direct cash lost but the failure may indirectly affect our concern by slowing or cancelling a project.
>
> I look to make sure that my purchases do not exceed a certain proportion of a company's sales ... Not so bad with an extraneous purchase, but on a regular basis it could become morally difficult to drop a company, i.e. that company may fall when your business is taken away.
>
> I review suppliers' accounts regularly to make sure they are consistent, e.g. I would be concerned if R and D was suddenly arrested, or ...
>
> When discussing/negotiating with suppliers I look for signs of financial pressure, i.e. specific pressure to pay bills earlier.
>
> ... during negotiation I try to obtain breakdowns of costs from suppliers. It may be possible to get a percentage split of their product ... This will help in following years to substantiate changes/increases. I always keep notes of discussions with suppliers.

These observations serve to highlight many of the strategic and tactical responsibilities of purchasing management when developing relationships with suppliers.

At the strategic level, a key preoccupation will be to decide on the merits of single or multiple sourcing and the risks of buyer/supplier dependency that may arise.

This problem is illustrated in Figure 6.7, where the concern is with the strategic stance of company B_1 in each of two different scenarios.

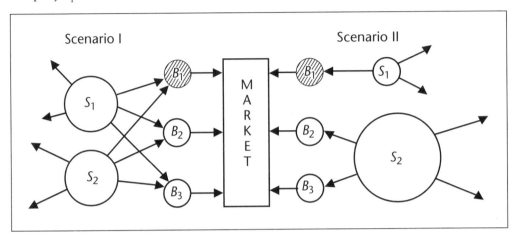

Note: Disc sizes to give approximate effect to corporate size/strength.

Figure 6.7   *Alternative consumer/supplier relationships*

In scenario I the market is supplied equally by three competitors, B_1, B_2 and B_3. Each of these companies buys inputs from two similar suppliers, S_1 and S_2. By contrast, scenario II assumes the same competitors as in scenario I but that B_1 is supplied exclusively by S_1, and B_2 and B_3 are supplied jointly by S_2.

In scenario I, B_1 has no obvious strategic strengths or weaknesses when compared with its competitors. Suppliers S_1 and S_2 are both of sufficient size and stability that the demise of either is unlikely. If either should fail when B_1 loses little or no strategic strength *vis-à-vis* its competitors. In scenario II, however, B_1 is supplied exclusively by S_1, which is comparatively smaller and weaker than its competitor S_2.

Plainly there are different policy implications for B_1 in each of the two scenarios. In the first case, the company will need to develop competitive strategies so as not to suffer to the advantage of competitors B_2 and B_3. In the absence of any serious concern about the financial viability of its two large suppliers, B_1 may find it sufficient to ensure that it is not taking substantially more or less than one-third of the output of each of its two suppliers.

In scenario II, B_1 may need to shift the emphasis of its intelligence gathering. Whilst the incentives for a solus relationship with S_1 may be substantial, B_1 will need to guard itself against two key sources of risk. First, it will need to monitor the extent to which S_1's survival and prosperity may become dependent on B_1, by virtue of its own growth or the retreat of S_1's other customers. Second, it will need to appraise, regularly, the financial stability of S_1 so that, in advance of the possible failure of that firm, either supply links can be established with S_2, or S_1 can be acquired to ensure continuity. Of course, this implies a need for B_1 to monitor the position of S_2 even though no commercial relationship exists at present.

An abstraction perhaps, but the illustration serves to highlight the need for purchasing management to gather important commercial and financial intelligence about existing and potential key suppliers, as a matter of routine. This will serve to develop not only intelligent strategy over the choice of suppliers, it will also provide powerful levers when negotiating supply contracts. But what specific types of financial intelligence are actually useful?

Financial intelligence

Experience shows that information is a seductive creature! The more we can get, the more assured we feel – even if much of it is of the 'nice to know' rather than the 'need to know' variety. Analysing a set of published accounts is no exception. It is a very time-consuming process even for the skilled analyst who knows his needs precisely. However, the exercise can be made relatively straightforward by asking four simple questions at the outset:

1   What do we need to know?
2   Where can we find the answers and how reliable are they?
3   How much reliance can we place on supplier survival?
4   How are they performing *vis-à-vis* their key competitors?

Each of these questions will typically spawn subsidiary lines of enquiry, which reflect the particular circumstances of the buyer/supplier relationship. Consequently, generalizations about the types of question and answer which may be relevant are of limited value. Nevertheless it is useful to speculate on one or two of the more important ones, bearing in mind that access to suitable information will typically extend beyond the scope of published annual reports and accounts. Indeed, one of the key objectives of financial appraisal should be to use its results either to stimulate questions whose answers can and should be found elsewhere, or to confirm qualitative intelligence gleaned from the marketplace, trade and financial press, business contacts and other sources.

DEFINING NECESSARY INFORMATION

At the outset it is necessary to be clear about just which existing or potential suppliers should merit close scrutiny. Often the 80:20 rule will apply: that is, 20 per cent by number of suppliers will account for 80 per cent of purchasing activity. Whilst modest intelligence may be sufficient for the bulk of suppliers, the weight of investigative effort should be devoted only to those of substance, or those which are new but which could become important.

Central to the understanding of annual reports and similar data is the body of knowledge that all users will need to have, whatever their standpoint. The following types of question will usually be relevant:

• What do I already know about the company?
• What sort and mix of products does the company make?
• What principal industry(s) is the company in?
• Does the company operate at home and overseas?
• Do the company's products have a worthwhile reputation for being advanced and reliable?
• What do other people think about the company?
• Is the company in the news?
• Who are the leaders of the company and are they in the news?

- How do I expect the current economic situation to affect the company?
- What are the market trends for the company's products?

By beginning with a checklist such as this it quickly becomes apparent that a company's report and accounts serve to complement or supplement the knowledge already gleaned from financial or other sources.

With this 'broad brush' picture in mind, the next task should be to formulate specific questions about the existing or potential supplier. The precise nature of these questions will vary according to the perspective of the enquirer, but for the purchasing executive the following will probably be uppermost in importance:

- Is this supplier progressing, stagnating or withering?
- Do we/will we feature significantly in the interests and future of this supplier?
- Can this supplier survive, given the financial and other risks to which it is exposed?

Of course there may be other questions that can acquire special significance in non-routine situations. These can include: 'Is this supplier worthy of acquisition?' or 'Are there signs that this supplier might be taken over by a competitor in its own field or in ours?' or 'Would this supplier collapse if we were to cease trading with it?' Questions such as these are very broad in their scope and the financial acumen required to answer them will typically lie with specialists elsewhere in the organization. Nevertheless the purchasing executive can be expected to discover for himself, largely if not exclusively, the answers to the three basic questions.

FINDING THE ANSWERS

An early exercise in any task of intelligence gathering is to familiarize oneself with the form of the information available. This applies not only to annual accounts but also to other sources of financial information to which we shall refer shortly.

Whilst it is true that annual reports are subject to legal and other requirements, it is also true that companies have a fair measure of discretion over the way in which information is compiled and displayed. Regrettably it is commonplace for particular information located in one section of one company's report to be found in an entirely different section of another company's report. Be prepared to keep your eyes wide open!

The content of an annual report can be broken down into a number of separate sections. All reports will contain the following:

- the annual accounts and notes relating to them
- the auditor's report
- the directors' report.

Most company reports will also contain the following:

- the chairman's statement
- a review of the company's activities
- a short summary of the company's results
- a statement summarizing the company's principal results for the past five or ten years.

Once familiarity has been obtained with the layout of an annual report, a crucial first step is to examine the auditor's report. This will not indicate whether the company is in good financial shape, but it will show whether the accounts have been prepared correctly or not. Beware particularly of reports that contain such phraseology as 'The financial statements have been drawn up on a going concern basis that assumes that additional borrowing facilities will be obtained. We have been unable to satisfy ourselves . . .' If, nevertheless, you have a real interest in such a company, it is worthwhile seeking professional advice either within or outside your own organization.

Assuming that the supplier company has a 'clean bill of health' from the auditors, the next important stage is to review the Statement of Accounting Policies. Here it is important to look for any major changes in accounting policies which may affect your interpretation of the results of the company, year on year. A quick check should also be made to discover whether the account policies that are used differ from those normally adopted by similar companies. Once again, professional advice may be worthwhile.

Protected by the two 'early warning' tests which have been suggested, the recent progress of the target supplier can be investigated. The best source for a quick overall view of the company's performance is the five- or ten-year statistical summary. The purpose here is to look for trends over a number of years without attempting to undertake any complex calculations.

These summaries typically include financial and non-financial information which can be used to trace such variables as sales turnover, number of employees, capital expenditure, number of sales or production units and earnings per share. Graphical presentation of these figures will often serve to dramatize and make transparent the progress, or lack of it, which the company has achieved. Frequently this stage of the analysis provides the best opportunity to gauge the scale and impact of your own dealings with the company in question. Growth trends of your business and those of the supplier can be correlated to discover significant patterns or discontinuities. But a word of warning! There are two key limitations of annual accounts to be aware of:

1   Although it is true that the accounting profession has been wrestling with the problem of inflation for many years, heavy reliance is still placed on so-called 'historic cost' figures. Although this is but one of a series of technical principles or conventions underpinning accounting statements, the fact is that historic cost data can easily distort the true progress implied by time-series comparisons. The more enlightened of publicly listed companies will provide inflation-adjusted figures to aid your interpretation. For other companies it can suffice to recalculate published figures by reference to a suitable price index, e.g. RPI.
2   Annual accounts need make no mention of the plans which companies have in mind. In special situations such as share issues or take-over bids, forecast information may be publicized in prospectuses or offer documents. More fruitful sources can include stockbroker's reports, press cuttings and trade publications.

Although the emphasis so far has been on published financial information, several other sources of data are available and can be used to build up a picture of the target company – including its history, its present status and at least some indication of its future. These may be listed under two headings:

1   possibly within your own organization or the commercial section of a public/central library, e.g. *The Financial Times*
2   commercial organizations, e.g. Extel.

ASSESSING CORPORATE SURVIVAL

Predicting corporate failure is itself a hazardous business. Many attempts have been made to construct predictive models which, by means of combining a series of more or less conventional financial ratios, aim to anticipate incipient failure. Some of these approaches are more successful than others. However, their common disability is that they impute a degree of inexorability about decline which self-aware and intelligent management teams should find intolerable. Nevertheless, the following are key financial ratios for which declining trends should be a source of concern, if not panic!

1   Current ratio   = current assets:current liabilities
2   Liquid ratio (or acid test)   = liquid assets:current liabilities
3   Gearing ratio   = $\dfrac{\text{Interest-bearing capital}}{\text{ordinary shareholders' equity.}}$

4   Interest cover   = $\dfrac{\text{operating profit before interest}}{\text{interest on borrowing}}$

Current ratio

This ratio can be constructed by reference to the current assets and current liabilities listed in the company's balance sheet. It is a crude measure of liquidity but useful as a first indicator of a company's ability to pay its creditors. It is difficult to specify what the current ratio for a particular company ought to be. As a 'rule of thumb' there should be at least £1 of current assets for every £1 of current liabilities; for complete safety, some analysts prefer to see certain types of company exhibiting a substantial excess of current assets, that is with a current ratio approaching 2:1.

Liquid ratio or acid test

A more incisive measure of liquidity, this ratio excludes those items in current assets that may not be immediately available as cash to meet short-term liabilities. Normally this means excluding stocks from the calculation, although in food retailing, for example, this may be thought an artificial restriction. A rule of thumb relationship of 1:1 is often suggested for this ratio but, again, circumspection is required in the application of such yardsticks – like most averages they seldom apply to any one individual! Both the current ratio and the acid test are absolute measures of solvency and, as with all 'snapshot' ratios, their real value lies in comparison over time or across similar businesses. The supplier that displays steadily deteriorating solvency ratios may be heading for disaster, but it is almost certain that it will wish to exert pressure on its customers to settle their accounts rapidly. If, as a buyer, you are sure that failure is not imminent, then, of course, such weakness can be capitalized on in price negotiations.

Gearing ratio

Sometimes known as leverage, this ratio expresses the relationship between interest-bearing capital (debt + preference shares) and equity capital (including reserves). A company with a large proportion of debt to equity is said to be highly geared and vice versa. High gearing may be interpreted as a source of vulnerability in the sense that the company concerned may be subjected to distracting pressure from its lenders. Moreover, in the event of receivership the providers of secured borrowings will naturally hold preferential rights over the assets of the company. These are usually sufficient to ensure that any residue for unsecured creditors will be small to zero. Again caution must be exercised in the interpretation of gearing ratios, for they vary greatly between business sectors according to the mortgageable nature of the fixed assets involved, e.g. land and buildings for property companies.

Interest cover

This measure illustrates the extent to which profits are pre-empted by the need to make interest payments. If interest cover begins to decline, perhaps to the point where profits are scarcely sufficient to meet them, pressure can be anticipated from the providers of loan capital. In fact, inspection of trust deeds attaching to borrowings, which can be undertaken in the UK, for example at Companies House or via a company search service, will often reveal very precise stipulations for interest cover which can be tested against the annual accounts.

Whilst none of these ratios is capable individually of anticipating collapse, they can be used in combination to good effect. But beware of slavish adherence to arithmetic; it is its origins that matter. In this respect it is worthwhile mentioning the availability of credit ratings from such organizations as Dunn & Bradstreet in the UK, and Moodys in the USA. These ratings are obtained as an amalgam of several ratios of the type discussed and can give useful indications of the creditworthiness of supplier and other companies. Whilst UK ratings have yet to acquire the status of their US counterparts, the latter provide ample evidence of the degree to which financial manoeuvrability may be restricted or enhanced by the level of the rating. Changes to these ratings are often publicized and can give useful indications of the financial community's shifting mood.

7 *Purchasing and costing**

Marc Day

As regimes of management and organization adapts to more intense pressures to generate revenues under regimes of tighter cost controls, it can be argued that demands for new insights to identify and nurture sustainable competitive advantage become equally inensive. Many writers, for example Bessant (1991) and Womack (1990), have provided accounts which lend substance to such a viewpoint.

The communist world may have collapsed, but the capitalist world is experiencing its own changes, largely perhaps as a result of the apparent success of Japanese business practices. The continued two-pronged approach to procurement (cost saving and business development) is keey to making a strong contribution to the overall corporate strategy.

These more general developments have, among other issues, directed attention to the relevance and significance of purchasing and supply practice and performance. They have also emphasized the importance of managing and creating value in the supply network, and have prompted innovations in supply relationship strategy.

Whilst emphasis has been on the need to improve quality, shorten delivery times and foster innovation in controlling purchases and making a contribution to corporate performance, the importance of cost and price cannot be neglected. The return of economic recession in the early part of the 1990s tended to remind those who advocated that quality and delivery were what mattered that price is still a pertinent issue.

Analysts from North America and Europe, who have studied Japanese business practices either in Japan or in Japanese transplant firms in the West, have drawn attention to the need for an enhanced strategic role for the purchasing function. They have also emphasized its importance in managing suppliers and creating value in the supply chain, and have, too, promoted many strategic courses of action – readers will be aware of such possibilities as long-term 'Partnership Sourcing', rationalization of the supply base and structuring of the supply chain.

At the same time, elimination and reduction of non-value-added activities and their costs also contribute to improved performance. Japanese subcontracting practices are seen to be a major element in gaining a competitive advantage both in producing current products and in developing innovative products for the future, Japanese buyers being keen to obtain price reductions as well as other improvements. However, in order to allow their partner suppliers to remain commercially viable, the Japanese are concerned to see that their suppliers exploit cost reduction opportunities as well. Thus, management of suppliers includes the need to manage and influence the activities and associated costs in supplier firms. If this role is accepted by buyers, then it is important that they understand the behaviour of costs in relation to the products they have responsibility for purchasing.

*This chapter originally appeared in the second edition of this book and has been updated by Marc Day.

In this atmosphere of change, observers have commented that cost profiles of firms are altering as a result of the upheaval in manufacturing and sourcing practices. The introduction of AMT (Harrison, 1990), the application of techniques embodied in the JIT concept, changing product technologies and their associated processes, and an increase in the outsourcing of supplies have tended to increase materials and overheads costs and to reduce direct labour costs. An example is in the telecommunications industry in which the move from mechanical to electronic telephone exchanges changed the methods of operation and the profile of manufacturing costs. The bought-out content increased from less than 40 per cent to more than 60 per cent. In the electronics industry, direct labour costs in some firms are less than 10 per cent and are treated as fixed costs and are included in overheads. There is, therefore, an increased concern to both understand and control overheads costs more effectively inside the buyer's firm and also in suppliers' operations.

The changes discussed in the previous paragraph represent a challenge to both the theory and practice of cost and management accounting. A fierce debate rages in accounting circles about the value of traditional cost accounting principles and their application by firms (Johnson and Kaplan 1987). New approaches, such as Activity Based Costing and Throughput Accounting, have been proposed as alternatives to traditional standard costing and budgetary control practices. Whatever the final outcome of this debate, it is clear that a deeper understanding of cost behaviour has emerged from the conflict and firms have introduced changes in their costing systems. Those involved in implementing the more sophisticated purchasing strategies need to be aware of these developments.

The costs incurred in making and supplying both goods and services are not just simple matters of fact which can be determined easily. Their determination involves the application of accepted rules and conventions. The selection of a costing approach introduces elements of choice and subjective judgement in the perceptions formed by both suppliers and buyers of cost behaviour. Cost analysis is a technique which has been in the buyer's toolbag for many years, but the approach has been based on traditional costing perspectives and primarily on those costs incurred by the seller. The adoption of a wider supply chain perspective, emphasizing 'total costs of supply', as well as recognition of the new approaches to cost accounting, open up scope for discussion as to how buyers should consider costs and performance in purchasing work. As an example, a 'ship to line' strategy can reduce the costs of goods inward inspection and of materials inventory. However, costing should not be thought of purely as a technical issue: there are behavioural implications for both buyers and sellers. These implications arise from both what is monitored and the methods of measurement selected. Measurements have a motivational influence and help to direct activities and the decisions which people make. The choice of approach is therefore important. If the wrong signals are generated, undesirable and dysfunctional performance might result.

The foregoing has served to identify the current background with regard to an understanding of costs in a changing business world and its relevance to purchasing and supply management. Its relevance applies to buyers as they develop appropriate supply arrangements and manage relationships with suppliers. Longer-term strategies for achieving cost reductions in product sourcing arrangements can also be investigated. However, there are also implications for managers inside and outside the purchasing and supply function as they consider the development of strategies, policies and procedures to both direct and account for purchasing activities. A more detailed analysis of these changing ideas with regard to costing and purchasing work now follows.

Supply chain costs

Changing perceptions of the role of purchasing have broadened the perspective of the factors and activities which need to be taken into account. Traditional views of managing organizations had tended to emphasize departments with clearly defined and separate objectives and duties. Such boundaries also constrained decision making and performance measurement. However, concern for improved corporate performance and the search for a competitive advantage has encouraged the adoption of more holistic perceptions which emphasize the interdependencies of activities and the recognition of processes or chains of activity which cut across the conventional functional boundaries. Horizontal flows of information are given more attention, whereas vertical flows were emphasized in a more hierarchically organized firm. A supply chain perspective concentrates on 'total costs of supply', whereas a more limited perception of purchasing tends to emphasize 'purchase price' and purchase expenditure. There is some value in this latter perspective, as it does draw attention to the importance of bought-out content in the corporate financial picture and the potential contribution purchasing can make to profitability. Nevertheless, there are dangers in giving too much weight to purchase price alone. A supply chain or supply pipeline view makes more transparent the additional activities and costs in managing material flows.

Buyers, when operating under a regime which sees purchase price as the main factor to be monitored (as, for instance, by price variance analysis in standard costing systems), can be given encouragement to make decisions which lead to increased costs in other areas. The net result may be sub-optimal from the broader corporate point of view. For example, the purchase of larger quantities to take advantage of discounts may contribute to higher levels of stock and increased investment costs. Buying too far ahead of demand may result in another form of 'waste' – namely obsolescence. Quality and delivery performance might also be sacrificed on the altar of low prices and the company will incur extra costs in overcoming these problems. A supply chain or pipeline perspective encourages an awareness of all these activities and costs associated with the control of material and product flows and the possibility of modelling the total supply costs of alternative supply plans is opened up. A multi-functional approach and the use of buying teams to amass the appropriate knowledge and expertise may be effective in implementing this approach. Internal cooperation of this kind alters the way in which buyers operate and they need to demonstrate capability and credibility in such teams. As far as the purchase of capital equipment is concerned, perspectives can be expanded to encompass 'lifecycle costs', which include aspects such as maintenance and repair and running costs.

At a time when shorter lifecycles of products and processes are adding to the competitive nature of markets, corporate and business strategies place increased emphasis on innovation. From a purchasing and supply management point of view, this accentuates the need to introduce changes into purchasing arrangements, covering both the products and services being bought and the activities employed in producing and controlling them. Thus, the goal of cost reduction applies not only to existing products and operations, but also to new product and material developments and their sourcing agreements. Techniques such as value engineering, simultaneous engineering and early supplier involvement all place a requirement for relevant cost information and provide opportunities for cost reductions. Indeed, it can be shown that approximately 75 per cent of the costs of the product are determined at the design stage, as material and component specifications and the required process plans are decided. Buyers and suppliers should be involved in this 'upstream' activity to ensure that all avenues are investigated in looking for cost reduction opportunities within the framework of long-term partnerships.

A more complete picture of the possible applications of cost data for decision making in purchasing and supply management is illustrated by the following list.

1   Analysis of supplier costs for price negotiations, often based on an 'open book' approach and including search for cost reduction opportunities as part of 'cost down/price down' strategies. The need to control suppliers' overhead activities and costs is of growing importance as cost profiles change.
2   Analysis of bought-out costs in new product development and in product modifications.
3   Product costing in both strategic and tactical 'make or buy' studies for goods or services.
4   Costing and pricing of products in 'intra-firm trading'.
5   Comparison of 'home' versus 'foreign' sourcing alternatives, allowing for different procedures and operations involved.
6   Evaluating the 'total costs of supply' of alternative supply arrangements when developing plans.
7   Preparation of material and departmental budgets and variance analysis.
8   Analysis of the different activities and the associated distribution of administrative costs in purchasing and supply management – the 'overheads' associated with the function. Activities include categories such as order placing, expediting, supplier assessment and supplier development.
9   Measurement of purchasing and buyer performance.

The challenge to traditional cost and management accounting

As global competition has increased and has added pressure for firms to pursue excellence in terms of quality, delivery and cost, the view has emerged that an obstacle to progress was the continued use of outdated costing systems. Indeed, as long ago as 1984, Kaplan (1984) wrote:

> There remains, however, a major – and largely unnoticed – obstacle to the lasting success of this revolution in the organization and technology of manufacturing operations. Most companies still use the same cost accounting and management control systems that were developed decades ago for a competitive environment drastically different from that of today.

Briefly, this traditional approach which was being criticized uses a cost model in which product costs were seen to be made up of the familiar elements of:

• direct labour costs
• direct material costs
• manufacturing overheads
• administrative and selling costs.

The allocation of manufacturing overheads was seen to be generally based upon a percentage of direct labour costs and a single rate used to allocate all overheads.

It is not possible to do full justice to the ensuing debate which has taken place in the last ten years or so, but some of the main points have been summarized by Kaplan (1988). These are:

1   Companies tend to operate a single system, but try to satisfy different purposes simultaneously:
    (a) inventory valuation for financial and tax statements;
    (b) feedback of performance for operational control of the resources of labour, material and overheads used;
    (c) measurement of individual product costs and profits.
    Purpose (a) is usually taken to be the primary purpose, but methods of collecting and classifying costs for this purpose can be less than helpful when considering (b) and (c).

2   Accounting principles were developed in the early part of the twentieth century when conditions were different and direct labour costs were the most significant element. Continuing to use direct labour as a basis for recovery, when the proportions of direct labour and manufacturing overheads have changed, may not account accurately for the varying consumption of overheads by different products. Product costs might, therefore, be distorted. There is an underlying assumption, which may not be valid, that overheads relate to volume, such as labour hours, in these overhead allocation mechanisms. Data suggest that high-volume standardized products might be unfairly penalized and low-volume special products might be underloaded with regard to the allocation of overheads based on the traditional approach. Thus, high-volume products might be subsidizing low-volume products. If this is the case, then firms may form the wrong impressions of the potential of their product ranges and may make the wrong marketing, manufacturing and sourcing decisions as a result. Firms may not realize where their competitive advantages lie in relation to outside competitors and suppliers.

    A further weakness of dealing with overheads in the traditional way is that it does not draw attention to the main causes of overhead cost – the activities which generate them. These activities are not linked accurately to the centres and products which consume the resources required by them. A lack of a proper understanding of overhead behaviour has severely limited efforts to tightly control and reduce it. Attacks on what has been called the 'hidden factory' (Miller and Vollman, 1985) have not taken place effectively. Alternatively, firms may have looked for only 'overhead quick fixes' (Blaxhill and Hout, 1991); they fail to examine the processes and activities which cause the costs.

3   Traditional costing and budgetary systems tend to target existing products and the control of current activities. However, business strategies in today's environment demand change and continuous improvement of performance. Control systems constructed around conventional departmental or functional boundaries are not helpful in showing savings and wasteful costs that might show up in other operational areas. Apparently optimal performance of one part may be sub-optimal when considered from the point of view of the wider system. Many of the current recommended techniques embodied in such 'umbrella' concepts as JIT and TQM require this more holistic view if the benefits are to be recognized. Organizational changes being introduced into many companies mean that they are becoming less hierarchical and departmental in their outlook. The increased use of cross-functional team approaches, however, highlights the need for supporting

accounting data. How many firms can provide this? How many firms, for example, can easily estimate the total cost of quality?

4   Measures of performance based on traditional perspectives may provide the wrong signals. Concern for high machine utilization rates may encourage overproduction ahead of demand to absorb overheads and keep direct labour employed, but at the expense of high inventory. Should inventory be regarded as an asset or a penalty or sunk cost? A rigid distinction and demarcation between direct and indirect employees can also lead to the inflexible use of labour resources. Quantity of output, at the expense of quality, may also be encouraged if the true costs of poor quality are not traced back to their origins.

It is easier to agree with many of these criticisms of the traditional approach than to agree with proposed solutions to the problems. Having said this, however, there is a disagreement as to whether the root cause of these problems lies in the accounting principles themselves or in the way in which they have been implemented. The view taken over this question will, of course, help to determine solutions which are preferred. The proposed solutions, thus, fall into two groups:

• Those who criticize the practice of traditional principles suggest that the way forward lies in a more sophisticated application of the existing theory. They argue that scope exists for a more varied approach in the uses of overhead recovery rates. Different rates for different work centres or the use of different bases, such as materials or machine hours, are the two main steps which are put forward.
• Others who believe the problems are fundamental in relation to the traditional principles favour the search for more radical solutions and are keen to look for new accounting approaches. Advocates of 'Activity-Based Costing' (ABC) and 'Throughput Accounting' fall into this school of thought. The well-known doyen of management writers, Peter Drucker (1990), suggests that the 'bean counters' need to count the beans differently. He also underlines the need to adopt a systemic or integrated perspective of manufacturing as a stage in the flow of materials from suppliers to customers.

The potential of 'Activity-Based Costing'

The ABC approach adopts the view of the firm as a 'collection of activities that are performed to design, produce, market, deliver, and support its products or services' (Ward and Patel, 1990).

It is these activities which require resources and it is their costs which need to be established. (The omission in the definition of any reference to purchasing in the list of activities can be ignored in the interests of establishing the fundamental principles of the approach.)

Some costs are directly concerned with product or service production; others are overhead activities needed to support direct activities. As many of these activity costs as possible need to be traced (not arbitrarily allocated) to products or services which 'consume' these activities. In addition to activities, products still consume materials which remain as direct costs and vary in the short term in relation to the volume of products produced.

What causes the support costs, though, are the transactions, or 'cost drivers'. Examples are the processing of requisitions or placing of purchase orders in the purchasing department or the receiving of deliveries in goods receiving departments. Cost centres or cost pools can be established for each 'cost driver' and a charging rate for the transactions can be determined and then traced to products on the basis of the demands products make for these activities.

By a more specific tracing of support costs to products using ABC principles, more accurate product costs can be established. It has also been recognized that overhead costs can arise at different levels. Set-up, materials handling and scheduling activities occur at a batch, rather than a unit, level. Design and process planning activities and design modification work arise at a product, or product line, level and contribute to product lifecycle costs. Thus, a more sophisticated picture of overhead activities and costs can be painted.

One benefit of the ABC approach is that it illuminates activities and can lead to investigations of underlying causes of the activities. Studies can be conducted to inquire whether they are necessary or whether they are being carried out in the most efficient manner. The approach can lead to Activity-Based Cost Management (ABCM) studies of processes and, therefore, emphasis being placed on the search for improvements. The use of common parts or the reduction in the number of parts and components in product designs can reduce the number of transactions in supply operations. Sourcing policies, such as stockless purchasing systems, for consumables or MRO items, can reduce and simplify purchasing administration costs, as well as remove the need to hold inventories.

The ABCM approach, as MacErlean (1993) has suggested, is not so much a new accounting technique but more a new way of running the business. It changes 'mind sets', or ways of thinking about business. New organizational structures and the redesign of processes and procedures can emerge as a result.

Many companies, such as IBM, Unipart and Cummins, at least in parts of their organizations, have found ABC an approach worthy of pilot studies, for later evaluation based upon experience. It can also be used in particular exercises rather than necessarily as an ongoing approach supplementing or replacing existing schemes.

Use of information technology can enhance the practicality of operating more than one accounting system at the same time to satisfy different needs or purposes. Experiments being conducted by firms are also designed to investigate the costs involved in setting up and operating ABC systems, as well as to establish what are the most significant 'cost drivers'. ABC profiles (in the Pareto sense) have been found to exist and, thus, firms need to exercise judgement in identifying key 'drivers' in their operations. There is no point in attempting to monitor a large number of relatively insignificant factors.

What have been claimed as the advantages which firms might expect to find from the adoption of ABC? Innes and Falconer (1991) have provided a helpful summary, which includes the following:

1   It provides more accurate product costings for decision-making purposes and profitability analysis.
2   New performance measures can be developed based on chosen cost drivers.
3   It emphasizes activities across departments (and across organizational boundaries in supply chains).
4   Overhead visibility is enhanced.
5   Overheads are more clearly understood.
6   Overhead costs can be controlled and reduced by reorganizing or eliminating activities.

Implications for purchasing and supply management

Whether the ABC approach is formally adopted or not as an operational system, as a replacement or as an addition to existing costing systems, the debate has enriched significantly an understanding of cost behaviour and, especially, of overhead cost behaviour. This should be of benefit to not only cost and management accountants, but also to those who are in effect the 'customers' of such accountants' services, including those in purchasing and supply management.

Some might argue that purchasing personnel in controlling prices of bought-out goods can rely on 'market testing', via tendering or request for quotation procedures, to find out what prices are being created by competitive market forces. For many years, others have argued that only a detailed analysis of a supplier's actual or estimated costs can provide a basis on which to form judgements of what the price ought to be. However, this latter method probably contributed to more meaningful discussions of direct labour and direct material costs in negotiations than of overhead rates. Disputes about percentage rates reflected less than a full understanding of actual overhead activities by both buyers and sellers. It is suggested that buyers need to have a better understanding and more accurate information of these activities, not only in the supplier's firm, but along the supply chain as a whole. Cooperative or collaborative approaches between buyers and sellers, as adopted by Japanese firms, which make use of value engineering techniques and target costing (see Lamming, 1993, pp. 200–201), require clearer insights into these activities and their costs as a basis for implementing a 'KAIZEN' philosophy. If partnerships are to succeed, then price reductions need to be gained as the result of driving down costs, rather than forcing down profit margins to levels which threaten the viability of the supplier. Professional purchasing, as the new century begins, needs to be based on managing value added and non-value added activities in the supply chain more effectively and efficiently.

References

Bessant, J. (1991), *Managing Advanced Manufacturing Technology: The Challenge of the Fifth Wave*, Oxford: Blackwell,.
Blaxhill, M.F. and Hout, T.M. (1991), 'The Fallacy of the Overhead Quick Fix', *Harvard Business Review*, July/August, pp. 93–101.
Drucker, P.E. (1990), 'The Emerging Theory of Manufacturing', *Harvard Business Review*, May/June, pp. 94–102.
Harrison, M. (1990), *Advanced Manufacturing Technology*, London: Pitman.
Innes, J. and Falconer, M. (1991), 'Managing with Activity Based Costing', *Professional Engineering*, July/August.
Johnson, H.J. and Kaplan, R.S. (1987), *Relevance Lost: The Rise and Fall of Management Accounting*, Cambridge, MA: Harvard Business School Press.
Kaplan, R.S. (1984), 'Yesterday's Accounting Undermines Production', *Harvard Business Review*, July/August, pp. 95–101.
Kaplan, R.S. (1988), 'One System Isn't Enough', *Harvard Business Review*, January/February, pp. 61–6.
Lamming, R. (1993), *Beyond Partnership: Strategies for Innovation and Lean Supply*, Hemel Hempstead: Prentice Hall.
MacErlean, N. (1993), 'A New Dawn for Western Management', *Accountancy*, June.
Miller, J.G. and Vollman, T.E. (1985), 'The Hidden Factory', *Harvard Business Review*, September/October, pp. 142–50.
Ward, T. and Patel, K. (1990), 'ABC – A Framework for Improving Shareholder Value', *Management Accounting*, July/August, pp. 34–6.

Womack, J.P., Jones, D.T., and Roos, D. (1990), *The Machine which Changed the World*, New York: Rawson Associates.

8 *The interrelationship between purchasing and marketing*

David Ford

Introduction

The idea behind this chapter is that purchasing and marketing are closely interrelated. The development of sound purchasing strategy and practice depends on the purchasing manager having a close understanding of the concepts and techniques of marketing and of the ways it is practised in his or her own company and the companies with which he or she deals. Additionally, purchasers must be able to work effectively with both of these marketing functions in order to carry out the increasing demands which they face. Throughout this chapter we will use recent ideas on the nature of business marketing and examine purchasing in terms of the emerging trends in the profession, using the most recent ideas on the nature of the purchasing task, rather than looking at the historical way it has been carried out. The chapter is based on the work of the IMP (Industrial Marketing and Purchasing) Group. For a full discussion of the group's research see Axelsson and Easton (1992).

Purchasing and marketing have a number of interrelationships and we can list some of these as follows:

1   Purchasing and marketing are similar activities in many ways and they require similar skills to carry them out. Both exist on the boundaries of their companies and so have the problems of relating the logic of the marketplace to the particular conditions inside their own companies and the possible inadequate understanding of their colleagues in relation to market realities. Both earn their livings by knowing about the dynamics of markets and the attitudes of competing marketers and competing buyers. Both have a similar and limited set of variables which they can manipulate to achieve an acceptable outcome in their interactions with others. Both must be skilled negotiators so as to satisfy not only themselves, but also all the different groups in their companies. Hence each function can gather ideas from the other in order to improve their own effectiveness. One way in which this learning can take place is by a company accepting the similarities between the skills required for the two jobs and switching staff more frequently between them.

2   Purchasing and marketing personnel carry out their work by interacting with each other. They have to learn to understand the methods and motivations of the other party and the problems which they face in order to deal effectively with each other. This goes far beyond the obvious issue of trying to think through the negotiating position of a counterpart. Instead it means that the buyer needs to analyse the marketing strategy of a counterpart and whether this involves, for example, share building, profit taking, action against a specific competitor, etc. He or she must examine the position that the marketer

is trying to build when compared to competitors, and the variables on which he or she is seeking to differentiate. Finally, the buyer must understand the portfolio of customers that the marketer has and form an idea of where the marketer sees its relationship with his company within that portfolio.

3   The task of a purchasing function is strongly affected by the characteristics of the marketing strategy of its own company and by the short- and long-term actions of marketing people. Purchasing has to be at the very least aware of these strategies and actions and, preferably, it must be consulted about them and even involved in some. For example, the growing trends towards more rapid changes in products and marketing methods mean that purchasing must be much more closely in touch with the thinking, plans and pressures which influence marketing. Purchasing must supply an analysis of the likely developments and thinking of potential suppliers and how these might affect the company's own marketing offering. Similarly, if purchasing is going to be able to develop its own coherent strategic approach and its long-term supplier relationships, it will need to understand the needs of the marketing function in its own company and work effectively with marketing to translate these needs into requirements expected from its suppliers. In return, purchasing strategy has an increasingly strong influence on the success of marketing's strategy. There are many aspects to this. For example, good purchasing strategy will involve the development of close strategic relationships with a number of suppliers. The development of these relationships will depend on the way in which these suppliers understand, and have a stake in, the developing and interrelated purchasing and marketing strategies of their customer.

4   Many companies operate in markets where competition has become much more intense and often comes from non-traditional sources. These same markets are often in a state of 'technological turbulence', where change is both rapid and unpredictable. Companies are faced with frequent decisions on whether they should continue with products based on current technologies or make a technological shift. Such a shift carries obvious cost implications. It also carries great risk, both technologically and in terms of the possibility of market loss during development. All such change is occurring at a time when companies are ever more dependent on the technology of their suppliers and other partners. Unfortunately, many marketers are 'technologically illiterate'. They are often unable to understand the issues, problems and opportunities which the skills of suppliers offer towards enhancing new products. Providing this understanding should be paramount in the purchasing function.

   At the more detailed level, these conditions mean that product lifecycles are shortening. So marketers must provide a better analysis of customer requirements so that products are immediately right for the market. Short lifecycles also produce two potentially conflicting pressures on marketers. On the one hand they must maximize their short-term returns on product development investment, while those products are still marketable. On the other hand they must carefully plan and control the features in their products so that they can ensure the success of successive generations of products. Hence the saying, 'Don't give them too much today or they won't come back tomorrow!'. The increasing complexity and costs of developing new products and services mean that marketers are seeking to liaise more closely with potential customers and to involve them in the product development process and its costs and risks. This means that purchasing has an important role in assisting *its* suppliers in *their* product development for the future success of both companies. Inside their own companies buyers must be involved earlier and more fully with marketing in the new-product development process. Despite considerable efforts, many companies have failed substantially to reduce this development cycle time. Successive generations of products often overlap and this emphasizes the importance of purchasing/marketing interaction to organize and control the use of new technology in each successive generation.

5   The activities of purchasing are an integral part of the marketing strategy of a company's suppliers. Business marketers are very properly obsessed with understanding and manipulating the purchasing processes of their customers. In the same way, purchasing must be obsessed with understanding and manipulating the marketing processes of its suppliers. Business marketing is perhaps best defined as the process of selecting, establishing and managing a portfolio of customer relationships, for mutual advantage. If we change the word customer to supplier then this becomes a very suitable definition of business purchasing. The similarity in definitions of the two activities reinforces the similarity of the two activities. It also emphasizes that neither of the parties involved can ever completely manage a business relationship on their own, although many act as if they can or do. The two parties to a business relationship will never have the same view of what it is for or what they expect from it. Both parties seek to manage the actions of each other and the relationship between them. So it is vital for the purchaser to understand how a relationship fits into the supplier's strategy and into its portfolio of relationships, as well as to understand the purpose of the relationship for his own company.

6   Perhaps most importantly, the purchasing and marketing functions in buying and selling companies exist in a symbiotic relationship. Each acts as boundary personnel for their respective companies. A company's purchasing and marketing relationships are its primary assets, without which its other physical and technological assets have little value. Each company can only achieve long-term success through the success of the other companies with which it has relationships. This means that the successful interaction between the two functions is the primary task of both purchasing and marketing, although of course they may not always have the same view of what constitutes success!

Ideas of purchasing strategy

The idea of purchasing strategy is now viewed in much wider terms than the task of acquiring the right goods at the right time and the right price. There are a number of aspects of an emerging view of the nature of purchasing strategy that are relevant to our tasks of understanding the interrelationships between purchasing and marketing. The first of these relates to the idea of technology strategy, the second to the ideas of business networks, and the third to the nature of relationship strategy in them.

TECHNOLOGY STRATEGY

No supplier has all the technologies that are necessary to satisfy the requirements of its customers. All are dependent on the technologies of others and this dependence is increasing, for at least two reasons: first, the technological content of all suppliers' offerings tends to become *wider* because each generation is likely to involve more and different technologies; and second, the technological content also tends to become *deeper* because each generation of technology is likely to cost more to develop than previous ones.

For these reasons, decisions on which technologies to develop in-house are critical, not only because of the costs involved but also because they may well be once-and-for-ever decisions. Once a company decides to stop development in a technology it may never be able to start and catch up again. On the other hand a decision to start or continue a particular technological development may well commit the company to a particular strategic direction for years to come. Decisions must be made on which technologies to make or keep in-house – the company's *internal technologies*. They must also be made on the technologies for which the company will rely on its suppliers of products and services, the so-called *external technologies*. In these cases the products or services that the company buys are the vehicles by which the *benefits* of the supplier's technologies are delivered to the customer. These technology decisions are clearly more profound than make-or-buy decisions about individual products that are often made on narrow, short-term cost criteria. Such short-term decisions to buy a product rather than make it may mean that the company is giving up a presence in an area of technology and effectively barring itself from re-entering it in the future. Similarly, a short-term decision to save money by making a product, often without a full appreciation of the costs of staying in a technology, can rule out a productive relationship with a technology leader. Not only can this mean that the company's product costs may be higher, but also that it does not have the best technological input into the company in that area. Technology decisions fundamentally affect the nature of a company's relationships with its supplier portfolio that has to be managed by purchasing.

An understanding of the company's technological strategy also enables a buyer to determine exactly which of a potential supplier's technologies or skills he or she wishes to benefit from. For example, the buyer may choose between vendors based on the excellence or innovativeness of their product design (their product technology) and be at that time prepared to accept lower levels of consistent product quality (perhaps because of inadequacies in the supplier's process technology). Alternatively, the buyer may be seeking vendors which will make to its own design ('make to print'). In this case he or she is likely to be looking for a supplier with the most consistent or lowest-cost production (its process technology).

More generally, buying companies face major strategic decisions about whether they will require suppliers to provide innovation in product or process development and be prepared to pay for that. If buyers do expect this from suppliers, then they gain the advantage of input of the development skills of suppliers. We shall see later that these buyers may develop a close relationship with suppliers and benefit from the supplier's greater commitment to the buyer. However, the approach also means that the buying company is conciously or unconsciously taking a decision to de-emphasize its investment in some technologies and rely for them on its supplier. This has strong long-term implications as it may be extremely difficult and expensive to re-enter this technology area at a later date if it should wish to do so.

Alternatively, the buyer could adopt a strategy which involves choosing between suppliers which will make products to their own or to an industry standard, at the lowest price. The approach based on buying for price provides obvious short-term cost advantages for the buyer, but its suppliers are unlikely to invest heavily in technological development or in meeting the requirements of the buyer.

Whatever the decisions taken in relationship to particular suppliers, those decisions need to be made in the context of the overall technology strategy of the company. Technology strategy cannot be the responsibility of a single functional area within the company. But it is one of the ways in which the interrelationships between marketing and purchasing can be managed. Marketing is responsible for managing relationships with the company's customers, on whose requirements all strategy must ultimately be based. Technology strategy relates these requirements to the company's own product and process development, and to the technologies for which it depends on its suppliers, and hence to the management of relationships with those suppliers that are the responsibilities of purchasing.

NETWORKS

The world in which business buyers operate has few of the characteristics conventionally associated with a market. It is not a world of individually insignificant, single transactions between a large number of anonymous buyers and sellers, each based on similar, easily described offerings and similar requirements. Instead, business sellers have individual and complex offerings of product, service, logistics, adaptation and advice, developed within relationships with particular customers, each of which has its own specific requirements. Each relationship is likely to be significant, although some are much more important than others. These relationships are separate from each other. What happens in any relationship between a customer and a supplier will affect, and be affected by, the other relationships that both parties have and in turn what happens in relationships in which they have no direct involvement. Thus business marketing companies operate in a complex *network* of companies and the relationships between them (Håkansson and Snehota, 1995; Axelsson and Easton, 1992). The idea of a network has at least two implications for business purchasing and marketing and their interrelationships:

1   Business networks are not neatly structured lines of companies designed and managed by a customer into 'supply chains'. Instead they consist of a very wide range of companies, each of which has numerous relationships with many suppliers and customers simultaneously. Each of the companies in a network will have its own technological and other resources and it is a combination of the resources from a number of companies that together can satisfy the requirements of any final customer. This complexity means that no single company can design or control a network. Even those companies that appear powerful enough to control many of their suppliers are in fact only a small part of the total network that affects their business. Complete network control may not only be impossible to achieve, but too much control by a single buying or supplying company may not be in the best interests of either that company or the network as a whole (Håkansson and Ford, 2000). This is because a major feature of business networks is the value of innovation emanating from many points in the network. The monitoring, encouragement and exploitation of that innovation are increasingly important aspects of the tasks of business buyers and marketers.

2   A business network cannot be separated into neat categories of 'manufacturers' who sell to 'distributors' who, in turn sell to 'retailers', etc. Instead, any one customer is likely to have relationships with a wide variety of companies that operate in different ways, but all of which are potential 'suppliers'. Each supplier will offer different benefits to the customer and each relationship will affect the others to a greater or lesser extent. For example, a customer for business software may have a well-developed relationship with a computer *distributor* that it uses for the supply of its personal computers and networking. This supplier may be able to offer its own 'tailored', but more expensive, solution when compared with the more standardized offering from the software *manufacturer*. Similarly, the customer may have worked closely with a *hardware manufacturer* in the past and this

company may offer the customer a solution to its problems previously developed by the hardware company in another relationship. The software purchase may have been suggested by some of the customer's own customers who have been concerned about its lack of flexibility in meeting their individual equipment requirements or delivery schedule. The need to 'rescue' these relationships may be an important factor in the customer's software purchase. The software customer will also have relationships with suppliers of other types of equipment. Its ability to make purchases in these relationships will be affected by the software purchase. Also, its use of any new equipment may be affected by how compatible it is with the functionality of the new software.

This example indicates the complexity of business networks. It also shows that neither business buyers nor marketers can restrict their attention to their *immediate* relationships. Instead, they must work *together* to understand what is happening in the wider network in which they both must operate to see how its dynamics will affect their own operations and those of their customers and suppliers. In other words, the buyer and the marketer must try to understand the technological resources and the network position, or pattern of relationships of those around them.

RELATIONSHIP STRATEGY

An understanding of the interrelationships between purchasing and marketing requires a clear view of what happens between them in a business relationship as well as the strategic choices open to them in managing each relationship individually and as a portfolio. An examination of business relationships shows the similarity of the tasks facing both purchasing and marketing and the nature of their interdependence. This similarity occurs if the relationship spans just a single major transaction, which may take years before a deal is made or delivery is complete, such as in the case of the purchase of an electricity generating station. It also occurs in those relationships that involve many purchases, whether for components continuously delivered to a production line or successive generations of capital equipment, some of which are bought from one supplier, others from its competitors or if the relationship consists of only a series of brief encounters by telephone, each for a small order.

Obviously any one relationship may be very productive for both parties and the volume of business between them may grow rapidly. Other relationships are unsatisfactory for one or both of the companies involved and simply become inert or a source of constant argument and recrimination. A third group may stabilize at a low level of interaction so that the customer buys only a small proportion of its requirements from the supplier and the supplier makes little effort to develop business. These variations are partially because of the different requirements that the companies have from each of their relationships and the different uncertainties and resources that each company brings to them. But relationships also vary in their development on the basis of the respective skills of the purchasing and marketing counterparts who are involved in them.

The way in which a company's relationships with both suppliers and customers develops should be of major concern to it and the skills of the company's marketing and purchasing staff in managing this development will be a key factor in its business success. We can examine the process of relationship change and development and highlight the management tasks involved by considering a number of factors that both buyers and marketers need to monitor in their relationships. The discussion of these that follows is drawn from Ford (1982) and Ford et al. (1998).

Learning

The way in which a relationship develops and the interaction between the individuals involved will relate closely to what both buyer and seller *learn* about each other and what each needs from the relationship and what they can offer to it. They will also have to learn about more subtle and complex issues, such as what their counterparts mean by the things they say and the attitudes they show. Learning is the process by which companies reduce their uncertainties. But it is also the process of learning how to *live with* some uncertainties that cannot be reduced. Listening and learning are not usually listed as prime characteristics for success in business markets. But relationship success will depend on the extent to which buyers and sellers feel that they *need* to learn, on their *willingness* to learn and on their *ability* to learn (Håkansson and Ford, 2000).

Investment

The development of business relationships involves the investment of tangible and intangible resources by both parties. This includes using human resources to develop contacts with the counterpart and investing in order-processing procedures to simplify and reduce the cost of interaction. It may also include developing new products or services in the relationship or dedicating existing or new plant and equipment to it. Companies also invest their expertise in a relationship, either directly or by transferring it to their counterpart, whether deliberately or not. Investment also occurs through many small changes that a company makes to cope with problems, such as altering a production sequence to cope with a rush order from a particular customer. Many of these relationship investments are made almost unconsciously and it would be very difficult for a company to effectively account for the sum total of the investments that it had made in even its most significant relationships.

Adaptations

Adaptations are unique investments by a customer or supplier company to suit the requirements of a particular customer or supplier. Both buyer and seller may modify their product, production processes or administrative procedures to suit the other. Over time these adaptations are a major factor through which the companies come to rely on each other. Many of the adaptations that each company makes to its normal operations will be *formally* laid out in the contract between the buyer and seller. Others will be *informal adaptations* and will be agreed to cope with a problem that arises or at the request of the counterpart. For example, the supplier could agree to reduce deliveries from the contractually agreed level for a short time to cope with a sales down-turn at the customer, or the buyer could change the design of its own product to cope with a production difficulty at its supplier. Adaptations are likely to be expensive and companies need to manage their informal adaptations carefully. They are likely to try to reduce their costs by making common investments for a number of relationships. These investments make relationships important assets and companies must always assess their relationship investments against the benefits they can realistically expect to receive from them.

Commitment

Sometimes a company will not be committed to the long-term future of a relationship and will try to take short-term advantage. For example, a buyer may encourage a supplier to invest in their relationship even though its requirements are likely to change in the near future. At other times, one or both of the parties will try to show that it is committed to the long-term future of the relationship and seek to achieve mutual advantage. Each may be prepared to incur considerable costs so that both companies gain in the longer term. The level of trust in a relationship can also vary widely. Sometimes the parties will be entirely open in their dealings; sometimes they will behave with guile. On some occasions they will show genuine altruism, but at other times they will simply cheat. The behaviour of the two companies won't always be predictable, or indeed make any sense when set against their stated individual aims, individual best interest or the good of their relationship. Every single relationship will have a specific history in terms of how the parties have treated each other and the degree of trust and commitment that has been built up. Clearly, this will affect how the parties will act towards each other, how they will handle cooperation opportunities and the degree to which they will wish to favour each other in the future.

Distance

The distance between companies in business relationships has a number of aspects (Johanson and Wiedersheim-Paul, 1975). *Social distance* is a measure of the extent to which the individuals in the two organizations are familiar with each other's ways of thinking and working and are at ease with them. *Cultural distance* is the degree to which the norms and values of the two companies differ because of their place of origin. When the two companies don't know each other well, this distance will often show up in national stereotypes, such as the boring Swedes, the arrogant Germans, the unreliable English or the untrustworthy Italians. *Technological distance* is the result of the differences between the product and production technologies of the two companies and hence the degree of 'fit' between them. It also arises because of the differences between the understanding that each company has of the technologies involved in the purchase. For example, interaction between a Western retailer seeking to buy products to its own specification from a low labour-cost supplier in East Asia is likely to be very different to that between a manufacturer of industrial robotics and an experienced buyer from the automotive industry. *Time distance* refers to the time between when a deal is being negotiated and the time when either party has to deliver the goods or make payment. The greater this distance then the more likely that there will be an air of unreality in the interactions between the companies.

AUDITING BUSINESS RELATIONSHIPS

The business relationships of a company are its primary assets and both purchasing and marketing need to maximize the rate of return on the assets for which they are responsible. In the case of marketing, it is possible to develop a simple *financial* model of rate of return by looking at the sales volume achieved within each significant relationship and relate these to the direct costs of purchased items, production, service delivery, sales effort and logistics. Less significant relationships will have to be treated in aggregate. It is also possible for marketing to assign less direct costs to particular relationships, such as those of developing or adapting an offering or investing in production facilities or providing dedicated logistics. Similarly, purchasing can develop a simple financial model of the costs of a relationship (as opposed to the direct costs of the offerings purchased within it) by adding the costs of investment and adaptations in its offerings and operations that are made to accommodate a supplier. But these financial models will not give a complete picture of the costs of developing a relationship, nor will they account for the actual or potential benefits of that relationship. A more qualitative assessment is required and this can be provided by the 'relationship audit'. An outline of the questions in such an audit is provided in Figure 8.1.

1	What is the history of the relationship?
2	What is the purpose of the relationship for both parties?
3	What is the potential of the relationship for both parties?
4	What are the resources required from both parties to fulfil that potential, and are those resources available?
5	What are the threats to the relationship?
6	Where does the relationship fit within the company's overall operation and resource allocation?
7	What is the portfolio and network position of the relationship?
8	Do current efforts relate to overall strategy?
9	How committed are both companies to the relationship?
10	Are the ways of dealing with each other appropriate?

Figure 8.1   *The relationship audit*

The history of a business relationship is an important element in an audit. This question leads to analysis of which company started the relationship and why, what has happened in the relationship and what has gone right and wrong and why crises may have occurred.

'What is the purpose of a relationship?' may seem an obvious question. But no two companies will have the same idea of that purpose. The buyer may see the relationship as a convenient source of basic items and view its potential as very restricted (Question 3). In contrast, the supplier may see the relationship as a source of learning about the operations of this type of customer so that he can use that learning in other relationships. The buyer may see another relationship as a source of technologically intense offerings with the potential to transform his company's own offerings in the future. The buyer may be committed to that relationship (Question 9). In contrast, the relationship may be unimportant to the supplier, for whom it is just one of many similar relationships. Even if the buyer could convince the marketer of the potential development of new technology between them, that development will not take place unless both buyer and seller have a clear idea of the necessary resources required to develop the relationship and the ability to supply them (Question 4). An audit of any one relationship must take place within the context of both the buying and marketing companies' total portfolio of relationships (Turnbull and Zolkiewski, 1997). It is important for both companies to develop a portfolio where each relationship has a complementary role to the others (Question 7). For example, one supplier relationship may be heavily oriented towards technology development, others will be seen as a way of learning new commercial practices or will provide access to a part of the network to which the company has had no previous contact, while others will be seen to be in decline and with no future. The relationship audit provides a way of checking whether a relationship is being operated within the company's overall strategy (Question 8). This is a much more important question than whether it is simply the current source of the right offering at the right price and at the right time. Finally, Question 10 asks if the company deals with the supplier in the right way. In some ways this is the least important of all the questions, but it often receives the most attention. This question is concerned with such issues as whether a senior or a junior buyer should be involved and with what terms and deals should be requested. Although these are part of the process of buying, they are essentially short-term and tactical and must be placed within the context of the overall management of each relationship and the portfolio that they constitute.

Conclusion

This chapter has tried to examine the interrelationships between purchasing and marketing. These interrelationships are based on the close proximity in which buying must work with the marketers inside its own company and in its suppliers. They are also based on the essential similarity between the tasks of purchasing and marketing. Both are concerned with the management of single relationships and portfolios of relationships and both are involved with questions about the technologies of their own company and those of counterparts.

However, it is important to finish by saying that the views of the purchasing function on which this chapter is based are somewhat distant from the day-to-day reality facing many buyers. Many buyers still have to operate in a reactive mode by responding to the requests of colleague functions and to the sales efforts of suppliers. Many do not have the resources to take the approach that we have outlined here. But the need for purchasing to be involved in long-term technology decisions in their own company and to manage a portfolio of supplier relationships to provide access to the technologies of their suppliers is paramount. A final indication of this importance can be provided by the idea that technology is not exploited by individual companies, nor is it developed inside them, whether they are suppliers or customers. Technology is increasingly exploited, developed and is located in the relationships between companies. Both purchasing and marketing have an interrelated role in these processes and companies will neglect this at their peril.

References

Axelsson, B. and Easton, G. (1992), *Industrial Networks: A New View of Reality*, London: Routledge.

Ford, D. (1982), 'The Development of Buyer–Seller Relationships in Industrial Markets', in H. Håkansson (ed.), *International Marketing and Purchasing of Industrial Goods – An Interaction Approach*. New York: Wiley.

Ford, D., Gadde, L.E., Håkansson, H., Lundgren, A., Snehota, I., Turnbull, P. and Wilson, D. (1998), *Managing Business Relationships*, Chichester: John Wiley.

Håkansson, H. and Snehota, I. (1995), *Developing Relationships in Business Networks*, London, Routledge.

Håkansson, H. and Ford, D. (2000), 'How Should Companies Interact?' *Journal of Business Research*, pp. 1–7.

Johanson, J. and Wiedersheim-Paul, F. (1975), 'The Internationalisation Process of the Firm, Four Swedish Case Studies', *Journal of Management Studies*, October, pp. 305–22.

Turnbull, P. and Zolkiewski, J. (1997), 'Profitability in Customer Portfolio Planning', in D. Ford (ed.), *Understanding Business Markets*, 2nd edn, London: The Dryden Press.

9 *Purchasing, logistics and supply chain management*

Richard Wilding

Today's marketplace is increasingly dynamic and volatile. Customer responsiveness is generally the key differentiator in markets today. Globalization is resulting in many organizations experiencing market pressures that are forcing a fundamental rethink of the way business is conducted. Trade-offs between, for example labour costs, transportation costs, inventory costs and response time to customer are becoming increasingly complex. It is no longer seen as possible to focus only on one's individual organization to gain competitive advantage. It has been recognized that the success of the individual organization is dependent on the performance and reliability of its suppliers and also its customers.

Christopher (1998) emphasizes this by stating:

> Competition in the future will not be between individual organisations but between competing supply chains.

It is not the intention of this chapter to discuss every facet of logistics and supply chain management but to demonstrate the importance of these areas in relation to the activities undertaken within the purchasing function. It is critical that the supply chain is aligned on the customer-perceived benefits of products and services and it can be argued that activities that do not contribute to benefiting a customer should not be undertaken at all.

In this chapter the concept of the supply chain will be presented and the strategic drivers and requirements for the successful application of this approach will be presented and briefly discussed.

Definitions of logistics and supply chain management

A supply chain has been defined by Stevens (1989) as follows:

> A supply chain is a system whose constituent parts include material suppliers, production facilities, distribution services and customers linked together via a feed forward flow of materials and the feedback flow of information.

This definition emphasizes the linkage between organizations and the movement of material and information between them.

The term supply chain is a simplification of reality. A complex network of organizations is generally present; organizations are frequently part of many different supply chains or channels. Harland et al. (1993), investigating automotive supply chains, demonstrate that component suppliers are part of many chains, with differing characteristics due to the customers being served. Automotive components are not just supplied to the automotive manufacturers, but also to the parts and service providers. Parts and service providers then supply a number of distinct markets through a variety of supply chains; these include fleet garages, the DIY market, motor factors etc. Complex interactions occur within this supply network. For example, I recently came across a problem in supplying air-conditioning units to an automotive manufacturer caused by the automotive manufacturer's dealers ordering large quantities of units for fitting to vehicles after they had been purchased. This resulted in a shortage of units for the manufacturer to fit to vehicles on the production line and subsequently the lead-time to delivery of air-conditioned vehicles increased dramatically, resulting in a loss of sales.

Supply chains exhibit many complex interactions between organizations and ultimately the end customer and the market that customer represents.

The management of the supply chain is accomplished through logistics. The British Standards definition of logistics is as follows:

> Logistics is the planning, execution and control of the movement of people, goods and related support in order to achieve an objective within a system. (British Standards Institute, 1997)

Harland et al. (1993) define supply chain management as:

> The management of the flow of goods and services to end customers to satisfy their requirements.

The British Standards definition raises two questions; what is the system and what is the objective? Wild (1989) defines an operating system as:

> A configuration of resources combined for the function of manufacture, transport, supply or service.

The above definition of a system would also make an excellent definition for a supply chain.

Harland et al.'s definition provides the objective of 'satisfying the customers' requirements'. This is often achieved through ensuring the right products are in the right place, at the right time and at the right price. To achieve this objective we require effective logistics management.

The Institute of Logistics & Transport, UK summarizes this relationship as follows:

> The management of logistics makes possible the optimised flow and positioning of goods, materials, information and all other resources of an enterprise.
>
> The supply chain is the flow of materials through procurement, manufacture, distribution, sales and disposal, together with the associated transport and storage.
>
> The application of logistics is essential to the efficient management of the supply chain. (Institute of Logistics, 1997)

The fundamental elements of logistics and supply chain management

Supply chain management differs from traditional material control in a number of key areas. Jones and Riley (1985) suggest that fundamental to effective supply chain management is the need for organizations to integrate by:

- recognizing end customer service level requirements
- defining where to position inventories along the supply chain, and how much to stock at each point
- developing the appropriate policies and procedures for managing the supply chain as a single entity.

Christine Jones (1989) emphasizes the importance of focusing on the end customer. She argues that if all members of the supply chain do not focus on the end customer, improvements made in one link of the supply chain will not necessarily improve the overall competitive position of the organizations in that chain. By achieving 'supply chain synergy' additional benefits are gained from managing a supply chain as a whole rather than its individual elements.

Oliver and Webber (1982) identify four fundamental differences between the supply chain approach and traditional approaches to management. These can be summarized as follows:

1   The supply chain is viewed as a single entity.
2   An emphasis on strategic decision making is required.
3   Inventories are viewed with a different perspective; they are used as a last, not first, resort.
4   A focus on systems integration is required, not systems 'interfacing'.

A key element of both Oliver and Webber's and Riley and Jones's analysis is the need for effective inventory management within the supply chain. This is driven from the recognition that within most manufacturing organisations 70–80 per cent of total annual costs are spent on materials (Christopher, 1998 p. 244); the effective management of this resource is therefore a focal point of many organizations.

In summary, effective logistics and supply chain management are characterized by an emphasis on the end customer, the integration of systems, and policies and inventory within the supply chain, thus achieving a 'synergy' where all organizations gain competitive advantage and subsequently prosper.

Classification of literature

The diversity of literature on aspects of supply chain management is a result of large numbers of activities that impact on the efficiency of the supply chain. I have classified the subject area under two main headings. These are:

1   The drivers for supply chain management. These are the issues that enable organizations to recognize the need for the application of supply chain management techniques. The

drivers are generally the need to gain competitive advantage and/or the need for cost reduction.

2   The requirements and methods for supply chain management. These are the policies and systems that must be in place to undertake effective management and thus the integration of the supply chain. These policies and systems relate to five broad areas: material logistics; information systems; time compression; quality of products; and service and finance and costing systems.

In the following sections an overview of these areas will be presented.

Drivers for supply chain management

COMPETITIVE ADVANTAGE

When gaining an understanding of drivers for supply chain management it is first necessary to look at the nature of competitive advantage. Ohmae (1983) defines a useful framework within which to view competitive advantage. This is depicted in Figure 9.1.

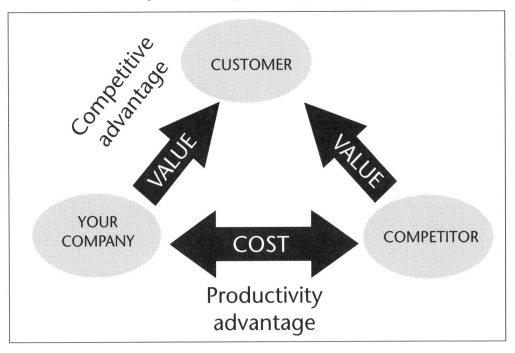

Source: Adapted from Ohmae (1983).

Figure 9.1   *The strategic three 'C's*

The objective of a business is to make a profit by delivering more value to a customer at a similar cost to the competition, or the same value as the competition at a lower cost.

Value is based on customer perception and is a mixture of tangible and intangible benefits, specific product features and also image, reputation and responsiveness (see Figure 9.2). As the old marketing saying states, 'Customers don't buy products; they buy benefits'.

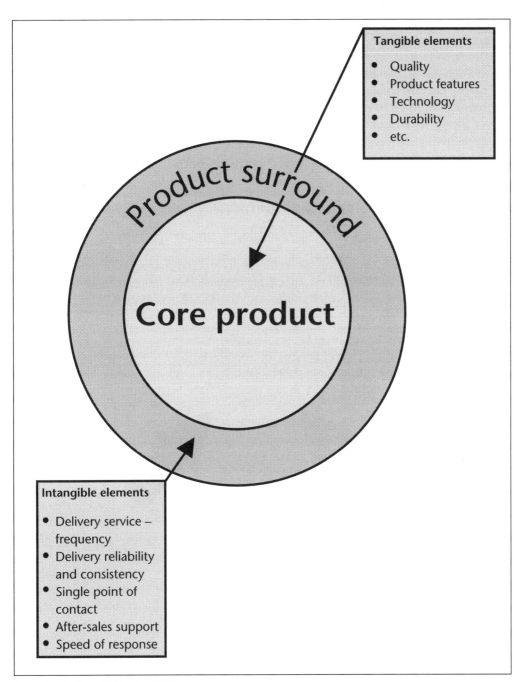

Tangible elements

- Quality
- Product features
- Technology
- Durability
- etc.

Product surround

Core product

Intangible elements

- Delivery service – frequency
- Delivery reliability and consistency
- Single point of contact
- After-sales support
- Speed of response

Source: Adapted from Christopher (1998).

Figure 9.2   *The customer product perception*

If a business is very effective it might be possible to achieve differentiation (more value) and cost-leadership (lower cost) at the same time. Expert in competitive strategy, Professor Michael Porter, argues that there are irreconcilable differences in approach between these two objectives, and achieving both over a long time-scale is unlikely (Porter, 1985, pp. 17–18).

However, experience shows that supply chain management can support both the drive to add more value and the drive to produce at lower cost.

The success or failure of any firm depends on its ability to define an effective strategy, to achieve the elusive goal of sustainable competitive advantage. Unfortunately strategic advantages rarely last. The competition learns, understands the approach, applies it and it becomes the industry norm. As a result approaches have evolved over time and companies have moved through a range of strategies.

It has been proven that companies that seek and exploit innovation in business strategy grow faster and are more profitable than their competitors (Stalk and Hout, 1990 p. 4). This is probably more a reflection on the ability of senior management to review and adapt their current strategy rather than the fact that all new strategy is good strategy. A word that is increasingly used to describe such organizations is 'agile' (Wilding, 1999). Agile competition demands that the supply chain processes that support the creation, production and distribution of goods and services are centred on the customer-perceived value of products. Successful agile companies therefore know a great deal about individual customers and interact routinely and intensively (Goldman et al., 1995, pp. 3–7).

CUSTOMER SERVICE

Defining what is meant by customer service depends on the expectations of each individual customer. However, all attempts to define customer service tend to focus on relationships at the buyer/seller interface (Christopher, 1998 p. 39).

Effective customer service requires three key elements to be in place. These are customer-focused systems, measurements and people (Wilding, 1995). These elements are all inter-related, and each element requires the other elements to be in place to achieve the customer service levels expected. For example, a computer system developed to aid customer service requires trained personnel to operate it. The effectiveness of the systems operation requires measurement, as does the effectiveness of people.

I witnessed a recent example of these relationships with a leading telephone banking organization. After many months of exceptional service I, the customer, noticed that it was becoming difficult to contact the organization. After I had complained about the situation, the organization explained that due to a recent advertising campaign the number of customers had increased dramatically, which had resulted in an increase in the response time (a key measure for the organization). The organization responded by increasing the number of telephone lines and improving communication systems; however, this resulted in increased stress on the telephone banking assistants resulting in errors occurring (another key measure for the organization). This led to the recruitment and training of new telephone banking assistants. The service I now experience has returned to the high level witnessed before the advertising campaign. This example demonstrates the importance to customer service of systems (the telephone system), people (telephone banking assistants) and measurements: response time (a systems measure) and error rate (a people measure).

LaLonde and Zinszer (1976) suggest that the requirements to achieve customer service can be categorized as:

- pre-transaction elements
- transaction elements
- post-transaction elements.

Pre-transaction elements relate to policies and programmes within the organization, such as written statements of service policy and adequate organizational structure. The transaction elements are those focusing on order processing and delivery of the product. Post-transaction elements are generally in support of the product after purchase, for instance service call-out time, warranty length, and customer complaints handling.

For effective customer service, organizations need to ensure that for each of these key categories the systems, measurements and people are in place to respond to each customer group or market.

The driver of improving customer service and hence competitive advantage results in the re-engineering of the supply chain. Christopher (1998, p. 47) states that the role of logistics is the provision of systems and the supporting coordination process to ensure the customer service goals of an organization are met. Supply chain management can enable all organizations to focus on the customer through integrating activities and policies. This can result in a reduction of non-value adding activity within the supply chain, leading to cost reduction.

COST REDUCTION

From the definitions of supply chain management given earlier in this chapter, it is concluded that inventory management across the supply chain is a key emphasis. This is due to the fact that this is a major area where cost reduction can be achieved for all players in the supply chain. It is estimated that typically a 25 per cent reduction in inventory is possible in the best-run supply chains if proper tools and understanding can be applied (Davis, 1993). It is recognized that the supplier's finished goods stock becomes the customer's raw material stock, and by working together organizations can remove this duplication and place the inventory at the best location to benefit the end customers and subsequently the organizations in the supply chain.

Further cost benefits are achieved by effective supply chain management. Some of these costs are easily quantified by current accounting techniques; some, however, are less easy to quantify. Savings can be made within the ordering process by electronic data interchange and in design and lifetime costs by involving suppliers in the design phase for new products. Concurrent engineering with a focus on the supply chain can also benefit ownership and service costs for products. This may be the result of careful engineering to reduce the complexity of the products and subsequently the supply chain (Wilding and Yazdani, 1997). These areas will be discussed in more detail in later sections.

Cost reduction through supply chain management is often a major driver for organizations. However, both competitive advantage and cost reduction can be achieved concurrently by applying a holistic approach to the management of the supply chain.

Requirements and methods for supply chain management

The implementation of effective supply chain management requires an organization to focus on a number of key areas, which can be categorized as follows:

• *Material logistics*. This focuses on the movement and management of material and the physical processes undertaken on that material. It is planned and controlled by a number of functions within an organization, from purchasing and manufacturing through to distribution. Supply chain management requires that the movement and processing of material should be as seamless as possible.

- *Information requirements.* Information is passed between organizations and within organizations within the supply chain. This may take the form of orders, invoices and schedules; the accuracy and timeliness of this information is critical to the effective management of the supply chain. The electronic transmission of information is having a major impact on the effectiveness of supply chains and can enable a more detailed picture of customer requirements and habits to be gathered.
- *Time compression.* This is becoming a widely used approach enabling the integration of the supply chain and subsequently gaining competitive advantage. Time compression focuses on maximizing the proportion of added value time that is spent on key resources such as materials and information.
- *Quality of products and service.* This is essential to the effective management of the supply chain. Earlier in this chapter the importance of customer service was discussed; customer service requires both quality in the tangible product and intangible product.
- *Costing systems.* These also require reviewing when undertaking effective supply chain management. Total lifecycle costing, focusing not just on the initial purchase costs but also the service and ultimately disposal costs of a product, may be applied, such as activity-based costing.

In the following sections each of these areas will be discussed in relation to the management of the supply chain.

MATERIAL LOGISTICS

Capacity, inventory and scheduling

The effective management of a supply chain system may be considered as dependent on three interacting factors: scheduling; capacity management; and inventory management (Wild, 1989). Figure 9.3 depicts the relationship between these closely related areas; decisions made to address problems in one area may have a major (and sometimes detrimental) impact on another area.

The type of problems experienced in each of these principal areas is influenced by the structure of the organization and its supply chain. The trade-offs between each of these areas is often industry dependent. Managers in different types of organization will use different strategies and techniques to manage the inventory, capacity and scheduling problems. The schedule reflects the needs of the customers, while inventory and capacity are managed to match the output of the system to the customer's needs. However, due to the close relationship of the three areas, decisions in one area may result in additional uncertainty being generated within the system.

Inventory management

Waters (1992) defines inventory management as follows:

> Inventory management consists of all the activities and procedures to ensure the right amount of each item is held in stock.

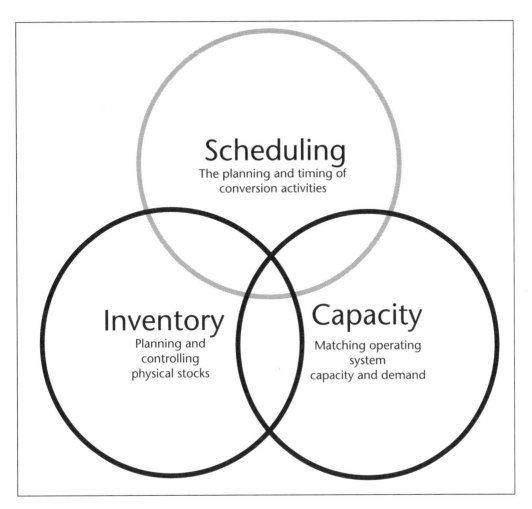

Scheduling
The planning and timing of
conversion activities

Inventory
Planning and
controlling
physical stocks

Capacity
Matching operating
system
capacity and demand

Source: Adapted from Wild (1989).

Figure 9.3   *The principal problem areas of materials logistics*

The main purpose of holding inventory is to act as a buffer between supply and demand. However, inventory may also be used strategically to give value to a product by its geographical position. Waters discusses ten reasons for holding inventory. These are:

1   to act as a buffer (decoupling) between different operations
2   to allow for mismatches between supply and demand
3   to allow for demands which are larger than expected, or at unexpected times
4   to allow for delayed deliveries or deliveries that are short of items
5   to avoid delays in passing products to customers
6   to take advantage of price discounts on large orders
7   to buy items that may be going out of production or are difficult to find
8   to buy items when price is low and is expected to rise
9   to make full loads and thus reduce transport costs
10   to maintain stable levels of operations.

The above list highlights that inventory can be used strategically, but is often used as a way of managing uncertainty. This uncertainty may be the result of problems with capacity management or poor scheduling.

The location and management of inventories has a major impact on both resource productivity and customer service. The existence of finished goods inventory may result in organizations being able to achieve high customer service levels, in terms of availability, but their existence may be costly. A focus on holding raw materials stock may also benefit customer service, but productivity may be adversely affected because more resources may stand idle while waiting for customer orders. Planning the quantity and location of inventory may be costly but is also necessary. Inventory can tie up a considerable amount of an organization's capital, so a trade-off between the high costs, and using inventory to increase flexibility, customer service levels and insulating against uncertainty in demand, needs to be constantly reviewed.

Scheduling

The schedule is responsible for delivery performance. Vollmann et al. (1992) define a schedule as:

> A plan with reference to the sequence of and time allocated for each item or operation necessary to complete each item.

To develop an effective schedule the entire sequence of operations, time estimates for each operation, and the resource capacities for each operation are required. Scheduling is a process; the schedule is prepared, actual performance is observed and rescheduling takes place as uncertainty becomes resolved, i.e. forecast demand becomes actual customer orders. Due to the necessary forecasting of future requirements, schedules are rarely 100 per cent effective and 'right'. This therefore requires some buffering in the form of inventory or flexibility in capacity.

The nature of the scheduling problem is influenced by the presence and location of inventories, which in turn are related to the customers of the system. Scheduling relates to the 'timing' of the physical flow or transfer of goods; the complexity of this is clearly dependent on the number of stages that are within the system. Where stock is held in a warehouse the customer demand will be met by the scheduled output from stock; these stocks will be replenished by scheduled inputs either from other warehouses or direct from suppliers. In the absence of finished goods inventory the customer demand will be met by the scheduled output from the manufacturing function; this requires scheduled input of raw materials and scheduled deliveries from suppliers.

Capacity management

Capacity creates flexibility that can be used to buffer against uncertainty. Chase and Aquilano (1995) define capacity as:

> The amount of resource inputs available relative to output requirements at a particular time.

This definition does not differentiate between good and bad use of capacity. Chase and Aquilano also provide the US government definition of capacity, which is as follows:

That output attained within the normal operating *schedule* of shifts per day and days per week including the use of high cost inefficient systems.

This definition recognizes that the amount of capacity present is linked to the schedule for a given period. A schedule involving many machine set-ups reduces the overall productive time of a machine and hence its capacity.

When designing any system, the determination of capacity is a key planning and design problem, the adjustment of capacity is a major control problem impacting on both the scheduling and inventory management. Effective capacity management can improve resource productivity and customer service. Poor capacity management can result in low resource utilization and poor customer service.

All functions within an organization and all players in a supply chain are concerned with inventory, scheduling and capacity decisions.

Purchasing

Purchasing is critical to the effective management of material logistics. Positioned at the interface between the customer and the supplier, responsibility often falls on this function for managing the relationship between the customers and suppliers in the supply chain. Leenders et al. (1994) describe purchasing's role as the gateway to suppliers so the other business functions can communicate with their counterparts within the supplier organizations. Leenders et al. also comment that purchasing can often block access to suppliers and this is detrimental to effective management of the supply chain.

The purchasing strategy must address the question of how many sources should be used for each component or service and what type of relationship should be formed with each supplier. The purchasing department will not give all suppliers the same level of attention. The purchasing matrix is a useful tool to assess the supply base according to supplier risk factors that may generate uncertainty for the customer (Syson, 1992). Table 9.1 shows the categories and the risks involved.

The matrix is dynamic and the leverage items of today may become the bottleneck or non-critical items of tomorrow. Depending on the sector within which the purchased item falls, different purchasing and inventory policies are required. The selection of the suppliers and inventory strategy employed is dictated by the position of an item on the matrix.

Two key areas that the purchasing function is actively involved in are supplier selection and the development of customer/supplier relationships.

Supplier selection

Dickson (1966) identifies from the literature over 50 distinct factors presented as meaningful to consider during the vendor selection decision. This demonstrates that supplier selection is multi-objective in nature. The nature of supplier selection has resulted in the development of decision support tools (Weber and Ellram, 1993).

Traditionally supplier selection focuses on the quantifiable aspects of the purchasing decision such as cost, delivery reliability and quality. Ellram (1990) identifies additional factors that should be considered when selecting supply partners for effective supply chain management. Ellram categorizes these factors under the headings of financial issues, organizational culture and strategy, technology and miscellaneous factors.

Table 9.1   *The purchasing matrix*

		Bottleneck items:	Strategic items:
Level of risk	*High*	<ul><li>Need to handle efficiently</li><li>Focus on systems/automation EDI/Internet)</li><li>Use forecasts based on past demand</li><li>Shortage of supply/high risk of non-availability</li><li>Minimum order quantities</li><li>Political factors may influence demand, e.g. patents</li><li>Security of inventory</li></ul>	<ul><li>High-value items</li><li>Balance of power between buyer and seller</li><li>Parties are dependent on each other</li><li>High-level relationship</li><li>Development of long-term relationships</li><li>Strategic inventory</li></ul>
		Non-critical items:	**Leverage items:**
	Low	<ul><li>Need to handle efficiently High volumes</li><li>Wide choice of suppliers</li><li>Focus on systems/automation (EDI/Internet)</li><li>Use forecasts based on past demand</li><li>Inventory optimization</li></ul>	<ul><li>Significant buying power in favourable market conditions</li><li>Wide choice of suppliers</li><li>Spot and long-term deals</li></ul>
		Low	*High*
		Degree of influence customer has on relationship	

Source: Adapted from Syson (1992).

- Financial issues focus on the supplier's historical economic performance and stability.
- The organizational culture and strategy includes a number of intangible factors including a feeling of trust, the outlook and attitude of the management, strategic fit, and the compatibility across levels and functions between the supplier and buyer organizations. These factors are seen as important to the long-term future of the supply relationship.

- Technology factors are important to organizations selecting suppliers for supply partnerships where future technological capability is of importance. To assess these issues the supplier's design capability, speed of new product development and also current and future manufacturing capabilities require assessment and benchmarking.
- The miscellaneous factors include safety record of the supplier, business references and the supplier's customer base.

Managing the customer/supplier relationship

The Bose Corporation, manufacturer of quality audio equipment, has taken partnership sourcing a step further. To manage supplier relationships to the level required Bose recognized that more people were needed within their organization, but due to budget restraints no further people could be employed in this role. This acted as a driver to develop the JIT2 concept.

The just-in-time concept was seen to eliminate inventory and bring the customer and supplier closer together on an operational basis (Greenblatt, 1994). The JIT2 approach eliminates the buyer and the salesman from the customer/supplier relationship, thus fostering increased communication between the parties. A supplier employee who resides full time in the customer's purchasing office replaces the buyer and supplier. This 'supplier in-plant' is empowered to use the customers' purchase orders and place orders on their own company. The 'supplier in-plant' also does the material planning for the materials supplied by his company. The 'in-plant' is also part of the production planning process so that production is planned concurrently with the supplier organization. This streamlines the supply process by removing the 'planner to buyer to salesman to supplier's plant' process by making this the responsibility of one individual. This has dramatically reduced the uncertainty experienced by the supplier organizations. The benefits of this streamlining have also resulted in major business improvements for Bose. These include (Greenblatt, 1994):

- 50 per cent improvement relating to on time deliveries, damage and shortages
- 6 per cent reduction in material costs
- 26 per cent improvement in equipment utilization
- major reductions in inventory holdings.

Amongst the authors presenting detailed discussion of the importance of supplier development and purchasing to supply chain performance are Hines (1994), Lamming (1993) and Syson (1992).

Manufacturing planning and control

Figure 9.4 depicts a generic manufacturing planning system. The total demand for end items is collected from customer orders and also forecasts from the marketing function. A high-level master production schedule is developed by viewing the current finished goods inventory files, forecasts, orders and any policy decisions which may be applied (for example, at certain times of year a policy of building up stock may be applied). To prevent unreasonable demands on manufacturing resources, 'rough-cut capacity planning' is carried out. This focuses, for example, on possible material shortages and the purchase of additional tooling. After the 'rough-cut capacity planning' the master production schedule should be broadly feasible.

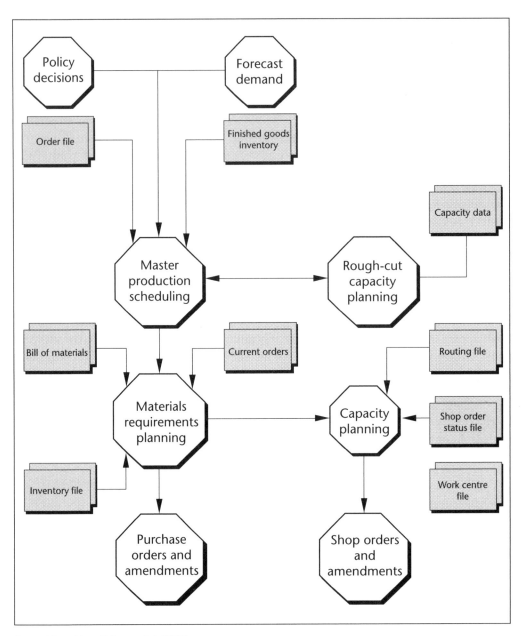

Source: Adapted from Vollmann et al. (1992).

Figure 9.4   *Generic manufacturing planning system*

The aim of the master production schedule is to timetable the arrival of finished product into the warehouse in order to meet customer demand. Due to manufacturing constraints production may be in batches and customer demand usually fluctuates, resulting in a difference between the desired production batch size and the demand quantity.

Once a feasible master production schedule is obtained, detailed capacity requirements planning, materials requirements planning and scheduling take place. This procedure defines what needs to be made, what needs to be purchased and the timing of these events.

Unfortunately, due to uncertainty within the system the schedules developed may not be fulfilled exactly and hour-by-hour changes may take place.

It is not uncommon for the manufacturing planning systems to be run on a monthly basis due to the computer time required to do all the various calculations.

It should be emphasized that materials requirements planning (MRP), as its name suggests, is a planning tool, not a control tool. A survey of best practice revealed that of the 'leaders' in logistics only 20 per cent professed to use MRP, while of the 'laggers' 50 per cent used MRP systems (A.T. Kearney Consultants, 1991). Braithwaite (1996) comments that most of the 'laggers' have also achieved Class A certification for the quality with which the MRP systems have been installed. Good practice in the use of MRP involves using the system for planning and then using simple materials control techniques such as 'Kanban control' to manage the flow of materials through the operation. This policy was confirmed by the A.T. Kearney investigation.

For detailed discussions on materials requirements planning, Kanban and hybrids of these approaches, both Vollmann et al. (1992) and Wild (1989) are texts worth referring to.

SUPPLY CHAIN INFORMATION

Bowersox and Closs (1996) classify supply chain information under two main headings: planning and coordination flows and operational requirement flows. The overall relationship between these two information flows is illustrated in Figure 9.5.

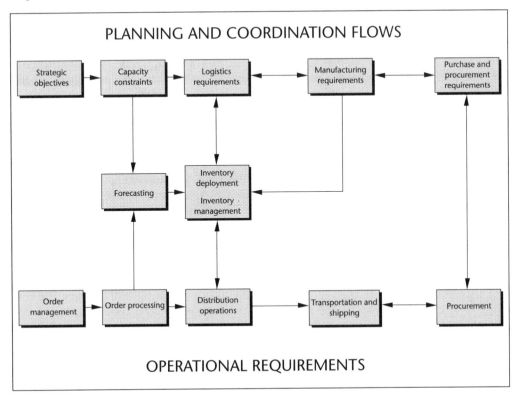

Source: Adapted from Bowersox (1996).

Figure 9.5 *Supply chain information requirements*

Planning and coordination flows

Information is vital to ensure the effective coordination of the supply chain. The coordination activity results in plans which specify the strategic objectives, capacity constraints, logistical requirements, inventory deployment, manufacturing requirements, purchasing and procurement requirements, and finally forecasting. The key driver for these plans should be the supply chain's strategic objectives, focusing on customer service but related to the financial and marketing objectives.

The capacity constraints identify limitations or bottlenecks within the supply chain organizations. The result of understanding these constraints is a schedule that can be used to achieve the strategic objectives. Logistics requirements apply to the work that the distribution facilities equipment and labour must undertake in order to implement the capacity plan. This requires information inputs from forecasting, customer orders, inventory status and marketing. Inventory deployments detail the composition and location of where inventory is held in the supply chain. The planning and coordination activity defines the type of inventory, where it is positioned and when it should be in a given location. The operational requirements of inventory require it to be managed on a day-to-day basis. Manufacturing requirements are derived from the inventory deployment and logistics requirements areas. Materials requirements planning (MRP) defines what needs to be purchased, what needs to be manufactured and when. Manufacturing requirements define the day-to-day production schedule to satisfy the strategic objectives of the business. Purchasing and procurement schedule and plan the components to support the manufacturing requirements. Purchasing coordinates decisions regarding supplier selection and the type of relationship required with the supplier. Finally forecasting utilizes historical data and current activity levels in order to predict future activity levels.

The overall purpose of the planning and coordination of information flow is to integrate the plans and activities within the individual organizations and wherever possible across the complete supply chain.

Operational requirement flows

The second category defined by Bowersox and Closs (1996) is the informational requirements for operations. Operational information enables order management, order processing, distribution operations, inventory management, transportation and procurement.

Order management refers to the transmission of resource requirement information between the supply chain members. Key to this activity is the accuracy and timeliness of the information. The transfer of information between supply chain members can be achieved by a variety of methods, including phone, fax or electronic data interchange. Order processing assigns inventory to customer orders. Distribution operations are responsible for coordinating the information to provide the product assortments required by the customer; the key emphasis is to store and handle inventory as little as possible while still meeting the customer service requirements defined through the strategic objectives. The role of inventory management information is to ensure the various supply chain operations have adequate inventory to perform as planned. Transportation and shipping information directs the movement of inventory. Change in ownership and the movement across national boundaries also requires supporting documentation. The procurement information is necessary to complete purchase order preparation, modification and release.

Operational information's overall purpose is to provide the detailed data required for integrating the supply chain's operation on a short-term basis.

Electronic data interchange (EDI) and the Internet

Palmer (1989) defines EDI as:

> The electronic transfer from one computer to another of computer processable data, using an agreed standard to structure the data.

The emphasis of this definition is the computer-to-computer communication. The data exchange should be without manual intervention, thus resulting in seamless data transfer and processing between suppliers and all echelons in the supply chain.

Emmelhainz (1990) describes the following direct benefits of using EDI. These include:

- increased internal and external productivity
- improved supply chain relationships
- improved ability to compete internationally
- reduced operation costs.

The reduced operating costs can be attributed to a variety of issues, including a reduction in clerical and labour costs, reduced inventory due to improved planning and, due to the reduction in lead-times, a reduction in pipeline inventory.

To achieve the transmission of data, agreed standards for data transmission are needed. This has resulted in a number of industry- and country-specific standards being developed. However, there is concern between users that what should be a reasonably simple exercise in order transmission is becoming increasingly complex, resulting in inefficient EDI use and consequently inefficient internal IT system usage within supply chain organizations. McGuffog (in Fenton et al., 1997) defines the key obstacles to cost-effective EDI as the unnecessary complexity of the messages and the processes they relate to; this results in inconsistent interpretations of the data elements and messages by some EDI hub organizations. This problem is currently being addressed by the UK Confederation of EDI standards, which is proposing a replacement standard 'SIMPL-EDI'.

The e-revolution is enabling organizations to attain supply chain integration with trading partners which was unthinkable just a few years ago. Collaborative Planning, Forecasting and Replenishment (CPFR) is one approach that has been receiving increasing attention (Wilding, 2000). The first industrial pilots of this approach were completed in 1999.

The basis of CPFR is that trading partners share forecast and results data over the Internet. Pure CPFR has one forecast for all trading partners; unfortunately this is still rare within trading relationships, but the ultimate goal is 'one number' that all supply chain members work to. However, the visibility generated by the CPFR concept means that today trading partners can have visibility of all the forecasts being used in the supply chain. This results in forecasts that all the trading partners understand so they can start to plan together.

CPFR technology analyses the forecast and results data and alerts planners at each organization to exceptional situations that could affect delivery and sales performance. The trading partners then work together to resolve these exceptions – adjusting plans, expediting orders and correcting data entry errors, thus achieving better business outcomes for all the members of the supply chain. With increasingly large amounts of data being generated within the supply chain, exception reporting is becoming a way to manage in such situations.

Three major developments have resulted in CPFR being an accessible and viable proposition for organizations to consider. First, new strategies for how companies can work together in the supply chain have enabled trust to develop and the recognition of win–win scenarios as a reality within the supply chain. Second, the technological improvements in both software and hardware have resulted in systems able to cope with the significant amounts of information that are being communicated, and finally the recognition that the Internet is a viable business-to-business (B2B) medium.

CPFR requires an agreement between trading partners to develop a jointly owned, market-specific plan based on category management principles. The plan will include information on what is to be sold, how it may be promoted, in what marketplace and at what time. This plan is accessible to all trading partners by the use of communications standards. Each trading partner can adjust the plan within established limits. Changes outside these limits need approval from other trading partners, and may require further negotiation. This plan becomes the key input into the forecast. The forecast is frozen at a mutually agreed time and can be automatically converted into a shipping plan for the trading partners, thus avoiding the traditional order processing. CPFR systems also capture critical information on promotional activity and supply constraints enabling better planning and overall reduced inventory.

The benefits that have been experienced through the CPFR pilots are as follows. Wal-mart has undertaken CPFR trials with a number of suppliers. Wal-mart and Sara Lee tested CPFR and experienced sales increases of 45 per cent and a decline in weeks-on-hand inventory of 23 per cent. Proctor and Gamble has initiated CPFR trials with Sainsbury, Tesco and Wal-mart. The benefits experienced by Proctor and Gamble include a reduction in replenishment cycle time of 20 per cent. The increased visibility of the supply chain resulted in a reduction of instore availability from 99 per cent to 88 per cent being detected with sufficient lead-time to respond. This saved three to four days of out-of-stocks for the retailer. Forecast accuracy improvements of 20 per cent have also been experienced.

Randy Mott of Wal-mart has stated, 'I believe that CPFR is the single largest opportunity to move inventory management forward in the next 5 years. We plan to implement collaborative relationships with well over 100 suppliers in the next 12 months. We believe that CPFR is the driver for moving the next era of buyer–seller relationships.'

TIME COMPRESSION

Time is becoming more important in the value perception of customers. It is also an important cost driver. Removing time from company processes therefore reduces cost. Time-based strategies can increase competitive advantage on both the value and cost sides of the equation (Wilding, 1999).

A definition proposed by the Institute of Logistics & Transport, UK (Canadine, 1994, p. 21) states that:

Logistics is the time-related positioning of resources.

It follows that effective logistics management is the process required to effect the positioning of resources (i.e. manpower, machines, facilities, materials, products, money, energy and information) in the right position in the supply chain at the right time. Logistics focuses on the total system design, integration of one process with another, system efficiency, deployment of resources and, above all, the effective management of time.

Research over the past ten years has indicated that it is not uncommon for the average time spent actually 'adding value' within a manufacturing environment to be as little as 5 per cent of the total process time. In effect this means that in such a situation we waste 95 per cent of the time (Bhattacharyya, 1995; Peters, 1991; Stalk, 1987). For the total supply chain things are generally even worse. As little as one-tenth of 1 per cent has been found to be 'adding value' time. In effect this means 'time-related positioning' is not achieved in such a supply chain for over 99 per cent of the time!

Experience indicates that focusing on the effective management of the key resources of the business can derive major benefits (Wilding and Sweeney, 1994). The key to success involves understanding what constitutes good practice in management of these resources with respect to time, and how this can be applied, given the unique characteristics of a particular business. Henry Ford said when comparing the management of the material resource with time:

Time waste differs from material waste in that there can be no salvage.

Time-based systems with an emphasis on speeding up process times result in a reduction in cumulative lead-times. This results in lower inventory and thus a further reduction in response time. A time compression 'virtuous circle' is produced (Wilding and Newton, 1996), as depicted in Figure 9.6.

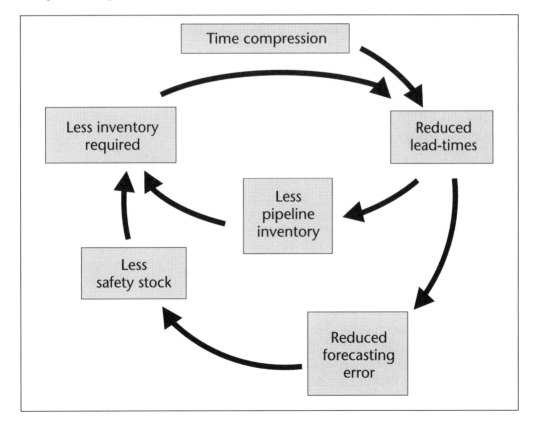

Source: Wilding and Newton (1996, pp. 32–3).

Figure 9.6   *The time-compression 'virtuous circle'*

Within a manufacturing environment it is easy to focus on the actual shop floor production process. However, this is only a small part of the processes required to qualify as a manufacturing company. Customer service, marketing, purchasing etc. all have direct and indirect inputs to the production process. The production process, as stated above, may add value for only 5 per cent of the time. For example, the time to schedule orders into production (up to four weeks in some major automotive companies) and the time to replenish stocks both have a major impact on the effectiveness of a supply chain. These areas have also become prime focus areas for time compression.

Focusing on the flow of information in the supply chain often brings opportunities to improve response time dramatically and hence reduce inventory, working capital and therefore cost.

Wilding and Newton (1996) demonstrate the effectiveness of this approach with a simple example. In one large multinational company, the European sales companies did not understand the needs and operation of the factories and vice versa. Simple analysis of the internal ordering and replenishment process opened communication channels and the company as a whole has benefited.

In the same organization re-order point planning was used in each of the sales outlets. Large orders placed infrequently on the central factory often overloaded the capacity of the factory, warehouse, packing and shipping departments and caused long and unreliable lead-times. Sales outlets lost confidence in the ability of the factory to supply to quoted lead-times and relationships rapidly deteriorated. In fact the factory had sufficient capacity to meet end customer demand. It was the internal inventory planning systems that were causing the problems.

After only three days' data gathering and analysis of its European supply chain, and using a time-based process map developed on a standard spreadsheet package, the team was able to reduce a key lead-time from eight weeks to under three weeks.

QUALITY OF PRODUCTS AND SERVICE

To achieve customer satisfaction, quality needs to be maintained in both the tangible and intangible parts of the product. Quality should be defined as conformance to the total customer requirement. Over-engineering products for a particular market can be as costly to the organization as under-engineered 'poor quality' items. Over-engineered products may incur increased costs in design and material costs, which may result in the product being too costly for the market needs. Hines (1994) describes how Hewlett Packard defines quality. Hewlett Packard classifies quality under two main categories: quality of products and quality of sales. Each of these categories is further divided into three sub-groups. These will be briefly discussed.

Service quality
Quality of sales is broken into two key areas relating to the service component of the product.

- 'Before sales quality' is the quality of collecting information on market needs, the quality of advertising, sales literature, product sales and training. The quality of the sales activity is dependent on quality of customer seminars, ease of use of sales literature, proposal for solution to customer, distribution, installation and delivery.
- 'After-sales quality' is dependent on the quality of maintenance, repairs, parts and claim management and the delivery of replacement parts.

In many markets today the service quality may be more important to the customer than the tangible product.

Product quality

Product quality is subdivided into three main areas: product planning, design and manufacturing.

Product planning quality depends on the analysis of market needs and the matching of product characteristics to those needs. Design quality focuses on the marketability of the product, the product performance, reliability, serviceability, the adaptability of the product to changing market needs and the lasting value of the product. Manufacturing quality is the quality of the components, production process, inspection and packaging. Product quality is intended to satisfy the tangible needs of the customer.

For effective supply chain management all the above categories of quality need to be addressed by the organizations in the supply chain. The fashionable concept of exceeding customer expectations may be costly and gain little competitive advantage for the organization. Similarly, products that do not meet the customers' requirements are just as costly to the organization. This further emphasizes the need to work closely with customers.

COSTING SYSTEMS

Costing systems used within the supply chain can have an indirect effect on the performance of the supply chain. Traditional cost accounting approaches tend to focus on historical data and merely record the cost of the product. The rather arbitrary way in which overhead costs are accounted for has been a concern to many. This has resulted in the development of approaches such as activity-based costing that can be used dynamically to predict cost and also target areas of non-value-adding activity. Yoshikawa et al. (1993) have produced an excellent discussion on the various approaches used to costing within industry.

Accounting cycles should be aligned across the supply chain. For example, organizations using a four-week month can have conflicts with those using a 4-4-5 week accounting cycle because account systems may pass on a forecast for a five-week period to another with a four-week period. This may result in the misinterpretation of the weekly production requirements within one of the organizations, resulting in excesses or shortages within the supply chain.

Summary

This chapter has defined logistics and supply chain management and presented the drivers and requirements for this approach. It can be seen that the purchasing function has significant influence on the effective operation of the supply chain and logistics processes. If purchasing does not operate in isolation from the other functions within an organization and focuses on integrating suppliers and customers within the supply chain, significant competitive advantage can be gained.

References

A.T. Kearney Consultants (1991), *Leaders and Laggers in Logistics '91,* UK: The Institute of Materials Management.

Bhattacharyya, S.K. (1995), 'Time Compression – Strategic Threat or Competitive Opportunity?' *Proceedings of 'Profit from Time Compression Conference'*, Warwick: University of Warwick Print Services.

Bowersox, D.J. and Closs, D.J. (1996), *Logistical Management*, New York: McGraw-Hill.

Braithwaite, A. (1996), 'MRP – Partially Discredited Solution in Decline', *Logistics Focus: The Journal of the Institute of Logistics (U.K.)*, Vol. 4, Issue 4, pp. 5–7.

British Standards Institute (1997), 'EN 12777: Logistics – Structure, Basic Terms and Definitions in Logistics', Draft for public comment, London: BSI.

Canadine, I. (1994), *The Institute of Logistics Yearbook 1994*, Corby, UK: The Institute of Logistics.

Chase, R.B., and Aquilano, N.J. (1995), *Production and Operations Management: Manufacturing and Services*, 7th edn, Boston, MA: Irwin.

Christopher, M. (1998), *Logistics and Supply Chain Management: Strategies for Reducing Costs and Improving Services*, 2nd edn, London: Financial Times/Pitman Publishing.

Davis, T. (1993), 'Effective Supply Chain Management', *Sloan Management Review*, Summer, pp. 35–46.

Dickson, G.W. (1966), 'An Analysis of Vendor Selection Systems and Decisions', *Journal of Purchasing*, Vol. 2, Issue 1, pp. 5–17.

Ellram, L.M. (1990), 'The Supplier Selection Decision in Strategic Partnerships', *Journal of Purchasing and Materials Management*, Fall, pp. 8–14.

Emmelhainz, M. (1990), *EDI: The total management guide*, New York: Van Nostrand Reinhold.

Fenton, N., McGuffog, T. and Wadsley, N. (1997), *SIMPL-IT – The Simplest Value Chain Message*, London: ANA.

Goldman, S.L., Nagel, R.N. and Preiss, K. (1995), *Agile Competitors and Virtual Organizations*, New York: Van Nostrand Reinhold.

Greenblatt, S. (1994), 'The JIT II supply chain' in Gordon Brace (ed.), *Logistic Information Management 1994*, London: Sterling Publishing.

Harland, C., Williams, D. and Fitzgerald, L. (1993), 'Supply Chain Methodology', *Human Systems Management*, Vol. 12, pp. 17–23.

Hines, P. (1994), *Creating World Class Suppliers: Unlocking mutual competitive advantage*, London: Pitman/Financial Times.

Institute of Logistics (1997), *The Institute of Logistics 1997 Membership Directory*, eds A. Davey and G. Fisher, Corby, UK: Institute of Logistics.

Jones, C. (1989), 'Supply Chain Management – The Key Issues,' *BPICS Control*, October/November, pp. 23–27.

Jones, T.C. and Riley, D.W. (1985), 'Using Inventory for Competitive Advantage through Supply Chain Management', *International Journal of Physical Distribution and Material Management*, Vol. 15, Issue 5, pp. 16–26.

LaLonde, B.J. and Zinszer, P.H. (1976), *Customer Service: Meaning and Measurement*, Chicago: National Council of Physical Distribution Management.

Lamming, R. (1993), *Beyond Partnership: Strategies for Innovation and Lean Supply*, London: Prentice Hall.

Leenders, M.R., Nollet, J. and Ellram, L.M. (1994), 'Adapting Purchasing to Supply Chain Management', *International Journal of Physical Distribution & Logistics Management [IPD]*, Vol. 24, Issue 1, pp. 40–42.

Ohmae, K. (1983). *The Mind of the Strategist*, Harmondsworth: Penguin.

Oliver, R.K. and Webber, M.D. (1982), 'Supply-Chain Management; Logistics Catches up with Strategy', *Outlook*, Booz, Allen & Hamilton Inc.

Palmer, D. (1989), 'EDI: A Status Report', *Logistics World*, March, pp. 25–9.

Peters, T. (1991), *Speed is Life: Get Fast or Go Broke*, 68-minute video, ed. The Tom Peters Organization .

Porter, M. (1985), *Competitive Advantage*, New York: Free Press.

Stalk, G. (1987), 'Rules of Response', in *Perspectives Series*, Boston, MA: The Boston Consulting Group Inc.

Stalk, G. and Hout, T.M. (1990), *Competing Against Time*, New York: Free Press.

Stevens, G.C. (1989), 'Integrating the Supply Chain', *International Journal of Physical Distribution & Logistics Management [IPD]*, Vol. 9, Issue 8.

Syson, R. (1992), *Improving Purchase Performance*, London: Pitman.

Vollmann, T.E., Berry, W.L. and Whybark, D.C. (1992), *Manufacturing Planning and Control Systems*. 3rd edn, Boston: Irwin.

Waters, C.D.J. (1992), *Inventory Control and Management*, Chichester: John Wiley.

Weber, C.A. and Ellram, L.M. (1993), 'Supplier Selection Using Multi-objective Programming: A Decision Support System Approach', *International Journal of Physical Distribution & Logistics Management [IPD]*, Vol. 23, Issue 2, pp. 3–14.

Wild, R. (1989), *Production and Operations Management: Principles and Techniques*, 4th edn, London: Cassell.

Wilding, R.D. (1995), 'Chairmans Introduction', *Proceedings of the 1995 Supply Chain Management Conference*, London: Turret Press.

Wilding, R.D. and Newton, J.M. (1996), 'Enabling Time-based Strategy Through Logistics: Using Time to Competitive Advantage', *Logistics Information Management [LIM]*, Vol. 9, Issue 1, pp. 26–31.

Wilding, R.D. and Sweeney, E.T. (1994), 'Effective Manufacturing Logistics', *Logistics Focus: The Journal of the Institute of Logistics (U.K.)*, Vol. 2, Issue 6, pp. 2–5.

Wilding R.D. and Yazdani, B. (1997), 'Concurrent engineering in the supply chain', *Logistics Focus: The Journal of the Institute of Logistics (U.K.)*, Vol. 5, Issue 2, pp. 16–22.

Wilding, R. (1999), 'The Role of Time Compression and Emotional Intelligence in the Agile Supply Chain', *Supply Chain Practice*, Vol. 1, Issue 4 (December), pp. 14–24.

Wilding, R. (2000), 'Collaborative Planning in the Supply Chain', *Manufacturing and Supply Chain Excellence – Management Today Reports*, London: Haymarket Business Publications, May, pp. 6–9.

Yoshikawa, T., Innes, J., Michell, F. and Tanaka, M. (1993), *Contemporary Cost Management*, London: Chapman Hall.

Tactical and Operational Applications in Purchasing Management

10 *Managing and measuring for purchasing performance*

Peter Stannack

Introduction

In the 1990s, organizations have seen many changes in the business environment. The key ingredient that binds all of them together is a recognition of the need for a focus on markets, customers and consumers. A number of key drivers that the enterprise will face in the future include:

- getting *closer to the customer* – understanding and building customer relationships to reduce marketing costs
- making it easier for customers *to maintain this relationship* by eliminating 'switching costs' so that customers can obtain what they need from one source – either one company or one company and its partners offering a complete continuum of products and services
- restructuring the enterprise so that it focuses on the customer to *integrate strategy and operations*
- changing the *attitude and culture* of people within the enterprise to reflect the need to be responsive, agile and customer-centred
- *integrating the supply chain* and the value chain to flex in response to fast-changing customer needs
- introducing and integrating additional *channels of distribution*
- *segmenting and targeting markets* to maximize the effectiveness of each channel
- *reducing the total cost* throughout the business network, not just within one node
- *reaching the market faster* with new products and services
- deciding, acting, reacting, and practically doing everything in *real time*.

To support these shifts companies increasingly have to look beyond the boundaries of the organization for competitive advantage. According to many experts and practitioners, the most significant management breakthrough in the late 1990s, as the strategic issue for the twenty-first century, has been a realization that the basis of competition is now between supply chains rather than individual businesses. Experts variously call this 'network' competition achieved through webs of supply chain relationships, value streams and value webs – all enabled by integrated business models. Sector examples include pharmaceuticals, telecommunications, retailing, financial services, e-commerce businesses, and so on.

If purchasing professionals are going to take an active role in these processes, they will increasingly need to demonstrate that they can add value to the enterprise. This means that they will increasingly rely on more sophisticated measures that support this demonstration. Designing and using measurement systems is, however, something between a science and an art (see Box 10.1). If the measurement system is poorly designed and implemented, it will often have a major negative impact on the business and the purchasing department. If well designed and implemented, this can be an equally positive impact.

Box 10.1 Definition and key terms in measurement

Measurement is filled with sloppy language. People often don't differentiate between terms when they are talking about measurement, and this can lead to problems in measurement itself. This chapter will talk about:

Metrics – the units of measurement
Measurement – the act of measuring
Efficiency – the ratio between resources used and outputs created
Effectiveness – the way in which an entity meets targets
Validity – the degree to which measures actually describe the entity or process being measured
Benchmarking – the process of measurement and comparison against another entity, outcome, or process

It is also useful to recall that measurement should always be related to objectives. There is little point in measuring something unless you can actually use the information you obtain. Without a set of objectives that you want to achieve, measurement is meaningless. Because all organizations have different objectives, they need different combinations of metrics and measurement tools. This is not to say that it is not possible to create a menu of metrics that can be chosen for different situations. Nor are all combinations of metrics and measurement tools equally useful. Competitive advantage comes from having a better measurement system than other businesses or functions.

There are often difficulties in designing and implementing sophisticated measurement systems for purchasing. Equally often, there are very simple reasons behind some of the difficulties. Perhaps the first of these problems is *measurement system design*.

We often take measurement for granted. People think that because a metric exists, it is set in stone, and not to be questioned. Metrics are designed to help us communicate: without standardized metrics, we cannot communicate properly. Often, customers and suppliers speak different 'languages', where words such as 'quality' mean completely different things.

One of the best examples of the growth of a standard measurement system is that pertaining to baking and cooking. Up until the twentieth century, there were no 'standard' measurements of oven heat. This made it difficult to pass recipes from one location to another because a 'hot' or 'very hot' oven was different for different people. In order to calibrate ovens, people were forced to put in a piece of bread dough, and wait for it to turn 'brown' or 'very brown'. They could then work backwards to establish the proper cooking time for the recipe in their own oven. In the twentieth century, standard oven temperatures began to be established, and we are now able, with some certainty, to cook using different recipes.

Unfortunately, there has been little work done to develop a common measurement system for purchasing. Measurement generally is in its infancy, and in purchasing it has not really left the new-born-baby stage. There is little theoretical basis for measurement systems, and many measurement systems are inadequate for the purposes that they attempt to achieve. These shortcomings are not unique to purchasing. They can be identified in disciplines as wide ranging as accounting or human resource management. In purchasing and supply management, many supplier assessment or vendor rating programmes fail to meet the most basic of criteria for measurement.

A second problem lies in *measurement strategy*. The objectives of measurement, and the measurement processes that are designed to meet these objectives, are often tactical rather than strategic. This means that measures are only designed to do part of the task they need to fulfil, with often disastrous consequences. It can be useful to think of a measurement system as a machine or a production line, with certain outputs. These outputs need to have certain characteristics if they are to be saleable.

Unless your system can create these outcomes, it is unlikely to fulfil the measurement requirements of your business or organization (see Box 10.2).

Box 10.2 Checking your measurement system

Successful measurement systems should be:

- *Accurate*, i.e. accurately describe what is going on
- *Complete*, i.e. comprehensively describe what's going on
- *Augmentative*, i.e. tell us more than we already know
- *Timely*, i.e. reach us in time to use
- *Credible*, i.e. everybody believes it
- *Relevant*, i.e. meet our current and future needs
- *Usable*, i.e. we can do something with it
- *Scalable*, i.e. it should measure both 'large' and 'small' effects
- *Predictive*, i.e. we can use it to avoid problems
- *Cost-effective*, i.e. not too expensive to manage

The third issue involves *measurement system implementation*. Purchasing departments will often put measurement systems in place and not have any way of using the information that they collect. Implementation also fails because of measurement system conflict and integration. When we consider the question of measuring purchasing performance, we need also to consider the other types of measurement system within the organization. The most salient of these is the accounting system in place. Accounting systems are designed to measure inflows and outflows of funds. Consequently purchasing staff often need to measure their own performance in terms of the reduction of outflows–price reduction.

It is therefore imperative, when thinking about measuring purchasing performance, to be aware of the potential sources of conflict with existing systems when designing and implementing a measurement system. There is little point in overlaying new measurement systems on top of old measurement systems, obscuring the meaning of the information being measured.

This chapter looks at the fundamental requirements involved in implementing a new or refining an existing performance measurement system.

Who is this chapter for?

We often hear that measurement is a key activity in purchasing, and indeed we might expect that buyers would want to measure exactly what it is they are receiving for the money they pay. Although it is fairly easy to measure the quantity and quality of goods we receive, it is often seen as too difficult to measure the effect received from a purchased good or service. As a consequence, purchasing professionals will often look internally at the savings that they can make. This is often less than useful because:

1 price reductions will often have an impact on other measures such as quality, delivery, innovation
2 price measures are often not seen as credible by other stakeholders within the organization.

This chapter is aimed at purchasing professionals and staff seeking to measure purchasing performance effectively, and understand the benefits that they receive and the risks involved in the measurement process.

Planning for measurement

This section deals with the basics of measurement, and how these affect planning and introducing a measurement system in purchasing.

Measurement is a complex process, and not to be taken lightly. The measures that businesses choose can often dictate their success or failure. Measure the right things, and a business can flourish. Measure the wrong things, and hidden costs and risks can cause the business to fail catastrophically. Increasingly, there is a recognition that traditional measurement systems no longer give businesses the information they require. Increasingly businesses are turning to new key performance indicators to set strategy and define performance.

Despite the complexity of measurement, few educational establishments teach measurement other than in the form of research methods, which is just a rigorous form of measurement. Traditionally, purchasing measurement was held to involve getting the right thing to the right place at the right time in the right quantity, and at the right price. Today, we can suggest that purchasing needs to be a little more sophisticated in measuring.

WHY DO WE MEASURE?

Understanding the purposes of your measurement system is critical. There are a number of reasons for implementing a measurement system, which generally fall into five groups.

The first group is about acquiring the information we need to make decisions. Perhaps the most basic decision involves comparing one item with another. Without some sort of measurement, we cannot compare items. If we cannot compare, we cannot make the best decision. If we cannot make the best decision, we leave ourselves, and our organization, open to risk. Perhaps the easiest and most common measure is price. We can compare two items very easily using price. Comparison is less easy when we consider effects, and more complex measures such as 'quality'.

It is also useful to remember that there are only two ways of comparing something. We can either compare *normatively* – against a 'norm' or sample of other things (making sure that our sample is adequate) or we can compare using *criteria* or standards (making sure that our standards are adequate). If we fail to make our sample or standards explicit, our measurement system will often perform badly.

The second set of purposes is linked with the first and is about control or management. Here we may measure to ascertain the benefit that an item might bring to us. In this sense we are trying to measure the effect of an item, and here measurement becomes much more complex. Here we have to look at a wide range of measures such as reliability, consistency and fitness for purpose.

The third group is about risk. Here we may need to assess supplier capacity in order to develop a risk management strategy, or we may need to assess the impact of new technology on an existing marketplace, and the implications that may have for sourcing and negotiating policies.

The fourth group of reasons is about politics. In this case, individuals or groups may set up a measurement system to gain advantage ('We have charts and graphs to back us up . . .') over other groups.

The fifth set of reasons is about learning and developing a business and business network. Without good measurement we cannot 'learn' effectively from our failures and successes. This makes performance improvement difficult, if not impossible. Without a path to performance improvement, management and purchasing practitioners are forced to experiment. Such business experiments become more and more extreme, but less and less effective.

In designing a measurement system, ensure that your objectives for measurement are clear and explicit. Without clear objectives, the rest of the measurement system design process is likely to fail. When we look at implementing a measurement system, later in the chapter, we will consider some useful objectives for the different types of purchasing measurement system.

HOW DO WE MEASURE?

In carrying out the measurement, it is critical to bear in mind your objectives. As we have seen, there are a number of potential motivations for measurement. These range from the managerial through to the political. When measuring, you constantly need to calibrate your measures. Calibration can be carried out in a number of ways, using the criteria identified in the introduction, i.e. 'Do these measures accurately identify what is going on in our purchasing organization and our supply network?'.

Once you have carried out your measurement, the next critical task is to decide exactly what measures mean. What is your measure telling you? For example, a rise in the number of defective parts per million may be because of poor quality assurance methods, but may also be the result of the installation of new tooling. Likewise, a rise in the number of supplier visits by a purchasing department may be a measure of proactivity in purchasing, or it may be a sign of staff looking to get out of the office for a range of reasons.

When deciding the 'how' of measurement, one way of improving the validity of the measures used is to employ *ratios*. Ratios allow you to compare one measure with another and, if properly selected, will improve the usability of the measure.

Ratios here may consist of:

1   Number of purchasing staff vs spend
2   Number of purchasing staff vs number of active suppliers
3   Number of purchasing staff vs number of contracts
4   Purchasing spend vs sales revenue
5   Purchasing operating expenses vs sales revenue
6   Number of suppliers vs total spend
7   Type of supplier communication vs frequency of supplier communication
8   Number of suppliers vs proportion of spend
9   Percentage of spend handled by purchasing

The critical issue here is to decide what your ratios are telling you. It can often be useful to share the metrics that you have chosen with the people responsible for the processes being measured, so that you can generate consensus about what the measures mean. The Centre for Advanced Purchasing Studies (www.capsresearch.org) at Arizona State University provides a range of purchasing 'benchmarks' for different industries.

WHO MEASURES?

The critical question in designing a measurement system is ownership. In Box 10.2 we identified relevance and credibility as being key factors. If measures are perceived as irrelevant or lacking in credibility, they will largely be ignored. A good example of measures that lack credibility are supplier assessment models that use 'culture' as a measure of supplier dependability. 'Culture' is a word with so many meanings that it is almost meaningless as a measure. Few suppliers would take such a measure seriously – unless they saw some advantage in doing so.

We can promote ownership in measurement by identifying common objectives and common processes for the design of the measurement system. Measurement may be carried out by purchasing staff, warehousing staff, purchasing managers production managers or suppliers.

Key questions when deciding who measures are: how much it will cost to set up a measurement system, and who will benefit? Try to remember that the best measure will come from the person closest to the process, and that this is often the cheapest place to measure. Remember that cost-effectiveness is a factor in measurement.

WHAT DO WE MEASURE?

Another issue in considering the basics of measurement is: what do we measure, when we measure? It is useful to remember that we measure a property or a characteristic of something. We cannot measure a thing itself. A measurement is only an indicator of some characteristic of the thing we are attempting to measure. Some indicators of a property or characteristic might be size, weight, price, or conformance to specification.

Although it may seem too obvious to need restating, within the buying business or organization some of these characteristics may be more important than others. In engineering businesses the size of the thing or its tensile strength might be of more importance than its price or delivery date.

Reconciling these measures is difficult, as is understanding the trade-offs between price and (say) quality. It is of little benefit to the buyer to reduce price, if quality suffers.

WHERE DO WE MEASURE?

In the introduction, we considered the fact that different, conflicting measurement systems can actively damage the organization. One reasons for this is that purchasing can become too specialist and may forget that other parts of the business exist. Purchasing professionals need to remember that purchasing is part of the wider organization, and need to 'think corporately' to integrate with other business disciplines, including marketing, production and HRM.

In order to do this, purchasing can demonstrate clearly the contribution that it can make to the overall strategic direction of the business by reconciling internal client needs, contract strategy and supplier capacity. The heart of this strategy is measurement (see Figure 10.1).

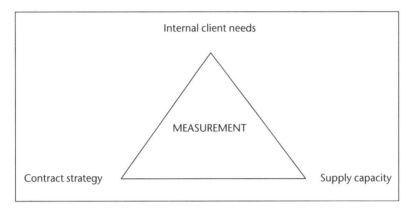

Figure 10.1   *Measurement at the heart of the overall strategic direction*

Purchasing has a number of stakeholders to consider when designing a measurement system. The first of these are internal (staff) resources. The second are other disciplines within the organization, and the third is the supply base. Such a measurement system works at three key interfaces:

1   the organization and management of the purchasing function
2   internal relations with other staff groups
3   the management of external relations in the supply network.

On the basis of such a measurement system, purchasing staff will be able to improve the quality of their decision making and build more effective relationships with key elements of the supply base. They will also be able to improve internal relationships as purchasing effectiveness becomes more visible to non-purchasing staff.

WHEN DO WE MEASURE?

There is some justice in the saying that 'measurement is just management that is too late'. As we noted in the criteria for successful measurement given in Box 10.2, measures need to be timely, usable and, if possible, predictive. There is little point in producing a measurement system for an FMCG (fast-moving consumer goods) production environment that samples once a year and tells you that your quality as described in defective parts per million is poor. Equally there is little point in measuring customer satisfaction every day, if your customers only use the service once per year.

Putting measures in place

Once you have designed your measurement system, the next step is to implement it. In this, there are a number of factors that you may need to consider. In many businesses insufficiently rigorous definition actively hampers the implementation of a measurement programme. Always remember that people generally will buy into outcomes and will only be interested in the processes that support those outcomes where the outcomes have proven validity. Purchasing may have the most highly skilled, well-trained staff possible. These staff may be integrated into sophisticated matrix-like organizational structures. Purchasing procedures may be well defined and explicit, but unless purchasing can deliver outcomes required by the different stakeholders within and outside the organization, there will be little point in measuring these processes.

Measuring purchasing key performance indicators

The three sets of strategic performance measures, which correspond to the key interfaces identified above, are:

1   Does purchasing employ its resources efficiently and effectively?
2   Does purchasing integrate efficiently and effectively with the organization as a whole?
3   Does purchasing manage the supply base/network so as to obtain the optimum performance for the organization?

MEASURING THE PURCHASING FUNCTION

Each measurement system is unique to the business that employs it, but all will have some common features. This is because the metrics used in measuring purchasing performance will be dictated by the objectives that are seen as critical. If reducing the cost of purchasing operations is an objective, metrics may well involve solely budgets and headcount. If improving purchasing positioning within the organization is an objective, metrics may well involve staff development.

This means that the first stage is to identify the objectives that you want to meet. These may include factors such as:

- *resource usage*, i.e. the amount of resources, staff, budget, and so on employed in purchasing activity, and how they are employed
- *purchasing positioning*, i.e. the degree to which purchasing was integrated with the company's other functions by both formal and informal methods
- *purchasing competence*, i.e. the degree to which the purchasing department had the skills to develop purchasing activity
- *stance on innovation*, i.e. the way in which the purchasing department wanted to carry out purchasing activity
- *competitive environment*, i.e. the contribution that increased competition makes to the use of supply management methods
- *internal performance management*, i.e. the overall exceptions to authorization procedures and so on.

In looking at the first of these objectives, we can identify problems. The simplest measure of purchasing performance is the ratio of net profitability to staff headcount. Clearly, if the company makes $50,000,000 net profit, and has 5,000 staff, it is easy to assess the profit per person.

The problem with this type of measure is its granularity. There is no way of tying down profits to particular departments, teams or sections. In more refined forms of budgetary management, it is possible to identify these figures, but calculating the profitability of an individual is difficult, as people shift responsibilities, and tasks and roles become unclear.

The other problem with this type of measure is purchasing's traditional role as a support function. In a world where marketing can prove its profitability by measuring the funds that it brings into the business, purchasing can rarely (and less often, credibly) argue that it generates profit. Whilst functions such as HRM can generate income from external consulting and training, purchasing rarely carries out this type of activity except through consortia purchasing, which has its own problems and benefits.

This means that purchasing often needs to demonstrate performance by setting cost reduction targets. Individuals may be organized into category or commodity managers and spend reduction strategies achieved through spend aggregation, or improving supply stability. Of course, many organizations have no information on spend analysis as a starting point. They need information such as:

- Who spends the budget?
- What is the budget spent on?
- Where, geographically, is it spent?
- Who is it spent with?
- How is the budget spent?
- And, more problematically, why is it spent in this way?

This is often difficult for many organizations to collate, which makes the setting of spend reduction targets difficult, and the measurement of purchasing performance using that metric impossible.

This means that each metric used should clearly link to an objective. In the case of multiple objectives, you will need to weight the objectives so that the metrics that you use correspond to the importance of the relative objectives. If staff development is more important than reducing operational costs, you might wish to give the former a higher weighting. This means that the first stage is to identify the objectives that you may wish to meet (see Box 10.3).

MEASURING THE WAY PURCHASING INTEGRATES WITHIN THE BUSINESS

Within the literature on purchasing and supply management very little attention seems to have been paid to purchasing connections with other disciplines and the users of purchasing services. Many purchasing practitioners consider it ridiculous to see themselves as service providers within the organization. Although, within the literature on quality, we can identify a recurring theme of 'next operation as customer', this idea appears to have faced real problems in being taken up within organizations. In addition, many purchasing staff can often find themselves trapped between the needs of internal users, such as production, and the capacity of the supplier. This can lead to production scapegoating purchasing for supplier failures. It is very difficult to occupy a service provider position in these circumstances.

Box 10.3 Internal performance metrics

1   Number of purchasing staff vs spend
2   Number of purchasing staff vs number of active suppliers
3   Number of purchasing staff vs number of contracts
4   Purchasing spend vs sales revenue
5   Purchasing operating expenses vs sales revenue
6   Number of suppliers vs total spend
7   Type of supplier communication vs frequency of supplier communication
8   Frequency of supplier visits
9   Number of suppliers vs proportion of spend
10   Percentage of spend handled by purchasing
11   Annual training hours per staff member
12   Qualified staff vs unqualified staff
13   Number of supplier-specific projects with milestones
14   Work initiated by purchasing vs work received by purchasing

---

The objectives of purchasing integration may include factors such as:

- *workflow management*, i.e. ensuring that workflow across different departments occurs with the minimum of mistakes and costs
- *task definition*, i.e. ensuring that responsibilities for task are clearly defined, and well communicated.
- *role definition*, i.e. ensuring that role responsibilities are clearly defined and well communicated
- *user evaluation skills*, i.e. how well users of the purchasing can evaluate the service that they receive in terms of contracting, supplier relationship management, and so on.
- *user expectation management*, i.e. the type of expectations that a user may have of purchasing. Do they expect a fire fighter, an expert, or an administrator?
- *user perceptions of risk*, i.e. where responsibility for the execution of the end product lies – is it with engineering, production, design, quality or purchasing?
- *user perceptions of benefit*, i.e. what sort of outcomes do the users require from purchasing?

At the internal relational level, we can also suggest that in a decentralized purchasing environment, information is required with regard to the relationship between the central purchasing function and decentralized units. There is a great deal to be learned from understanding the reasons that decentralized units buy from their suppliers, and the type of performance profile they obtain. It should be stressed that this information does not describe the relations between central departments and decentralized units *per se* but rather decentralized units and their suppliers.

Many purchasing departments tend to use service-level agreements (SLAs) to regulate their relationships with other departments. Purchasing departments are, in many cases, beginning to perceive the importance of service user satisfaction. Fewer organizations are trying to assess and manage service user satisfaction properly. The effective assessment and management of service user satisfaction offers many benefits in terms of profitability, staff satisfaction, reduced marketing costs, and the like.

Assessing – measuring – and managing service user satisfaction is much more than merely sending out a service user satisfaction survey twice a year, or adopting slogans such as '100 per cent service user delight every time'. Because service user satisfaction is intensely difficult – and even frustrating – to manage, managers and staff need to recognize and understand satisfaction before they attempt to manage it.

Introducing a service quality programme need not be difficult if you follow some guiding principles.

Principle 1   Understand your service user as part of a target market. Understand how your service interacts with service users and how service users interact with each other. Understand how service user perceptions of need, skills and perceptions of risk affect your service. Understand that the 'service user' can often be made up of several different people – those who use the service, those who acquire the service and those who evaluate the service.

Principle 2   Design your service. Do not think that your user understands what purchasing does, just because they use your service. Describe what you do in terms that your service user can understand. Understand what your service offers that other services, such as logistics, don't. Consider how you can work with the service user to reduce risk and enhance benefit.

Principle 3   Understand your objectives. Understand how your objectives line up with service user and staff perceptions of value (see Box 10.4). Recognize that objectives need to be realistic from the viewpoint of colleagues, staff and service users.

Box 10.4 Service outcome measures

We saw earlier that users value outcomes. One of the classic measures of service quality is the Servqual scale devised by Parasuraman, Zeithaml and Berry (1990). This identifies a range of service dimensions that seem to be important to users:

- *Reliability* – will the service deliver on time, and to promise?
- *Responsiveness* – will the service adapt itself to users' needs?
- *Competence* – is the service able to deliver on its promise?
- *Empathy* – do the service providers understand the needs and position of the user?
- *Accessibility* – can the service be reached when the user needs it?
- *Courtesy* – do the providers seem to value the users?
- *Communication* – are users kept informed of the progress of the service?
- *Credibility* – do the service providers seem to know their job?
- *Security* – is risk managed effectively when using the service?
- *Tangibles* – do the premises and staff appearance communicate the desired effect?

Principle 4   Understand the critical challenges. Understand how the nature of the service design will help you in managing the challenges of demand, measurement and quality.

Principle 5   Understand the nature of the systems that you use. In managing services, the way in which people and systems interact is critical. The 'architecture' of services needs to be flexible, and this flexibility will only come from effective integration.

Principle 6   Look for improvement opportunities so that you can maintain the competitive edge. Successful service businesses constantly look for ways in which they can improve their service, both to help the service user structure their needs and to fulfil those needs.

Service quality management is difficult for a number of reasons. Purchasing is, more often than not:

- *Intangible*: most service activity is intangible. Service users cannot perceive the service before it is used. This means that they will assess the service provision differently to the way in which they assess products. The service provider therefore needs to find ways in which the service can be made more tangible, and risk in use can be minimized. This may range from improving the quality of supporting materials through to improving point-of-service staff motivation through shifts in reward policies, training and systems development.
- *Perishable*: much service is literally 'consumed' at the point of delivery. Service cannot be kept in a store. This means that managing supply and demand in service provision can be more difficult than managing production supply and demand. Managing supply and demand more effectively may involve improving staff flexibility through increased use of short-term contracts or through multi-skilling.
- *Co-created*: services are not really something you do 'to' the service user. They should always be something you do 'with' the service user. Service production and service consumption are linked at the point of delivery. Again, because the service is co-created by the producer and consumer, it cannot be stored. Because the service is co-created, it is also transparent at the delivery point – the service user can see it being 'made' and failures are hard to hide. This again has an impact upon demand and staff availability. It also has an impact upon service user evaluation because delivery failures are obvious. Meeting these challenges may involve educating the service user in how to use the service more efficiently.
- *Variable*: because service delivery is co-created, it depends on the interaction between the service user and the staff member. Different levels of energy and different mind sets within both these groups can cause the quality of service to vary widely. Variability can be managed by ensuring that your staff recruitment, selection and motivation are excellent, and also by ensuring that the systems are in place to support consistent levels of quality.

Once you have developed purchasing service quality, you can go on to consider how to measure purchasing's core function.

MEASURING HOW PURCHASING MANAGES THE SUPPLY NETWORK

Every joint activity involves some form of cost and therefore some type of risk. The costs may be in finding a supplier, assessing a supplier, writing specifications, writing requests for proposals or tenders, issuing and selecting on the basis of tender returns, arranging delivery, inspecting goods when delivered and so on. The risks are of finding the wrong type of supplier, writing a poorly thought-out specification or miscommunication.

In managing the supply base, the strategic objective of the purchasing department is initially to prevent supplier failure (see Box 10.5). This may seem a limited objective, but it is often beyond the capacity of the purchasing function. Once the purchasing function has

Box 10.5 External measures

- **Cost** – price against previous contract, price against competing bidders
- **Delivery** – delivery accuracy to specified times plus or minus a percentage. Lead time reduction
- **Quality as reliability** – conformance to specification
- **Quality as consistency** – number of defective parts per million (or billion) received
- **Agility** – Number or frequency of changes to product line or service in time period A
- **Service** – degree of customer satisfaction with regard to accessibility, courtesy and so on as measured against expectations
- **Innovation** – number of innovative suggestions. Savings from innovative suggestions

eliminated supplier failures, it can then look to develop and achieve optimum supplier performance.

In eliminating supplier failures, measures therefore need to use a very broad approach in defining failure. Failure would here be not having the lowest possible costs in the marketplace, not having completely accurate delivery times, not coming up with value-adding solutions when they were available and so on.

Of course, when we talk of 'purchasing' we are describing a whole range of activities, each of which may need its own tactical objectives. These activities may include:

- *sourcing* – finding the right sources of supply
- *market and network analysis* – ensuring that the supplier can be optimized by understanding the market that the supplier operates in and the way in which they interact with other suppliers at lower tiers
- *communication* – communicating with the supplier through invitations to tender, requests for proposals, assessing the supplier's or vendor's capacity, problem solving with the supplier, and so on.
- *motivation* – making sure that the supplier is properly motivated by efficient use of contracts, award programmes, selective disclosure of market knowledge
- *standards development* – making sure that the supplier is aware of their task, and that the correct processes that support this task are properly described and audited.
- *supplier development* – making sure that the supplier's processes are integrated effectively, and that their skills are adequate for delivering the required performance in fast-changing environments.

Within the field of supplier measurement, we can identify two common approaches. The first is to measure supplier *outcomes*. Metrics here may be used to describe supplier outcomes in terms of critical service user value dimensions such as cost (price), delivery, reliability, consistency, service, innovation and flexibility. The problem with measuring outcomes alone is that the purchasing manager or other user will not know what actually causes these. Unless you understand what causes them, you can't replicate them when they are right or 'fix' them when they go wrong.

The second approach is to measure supplier *processes* in some form of supplier or vendor assessment. Metrics here may include process certification such as ISO 9000 or ISO 1400, or the assessment of management quality and track record, team working structure, or service user history and so on. The problem with measuring processes is how to select the right processes that invariably lead to the outcomes required. ISO 9000, for instance, once valued as a method of quality assurance, is now less useful because of some flaws (from the point of view of purchasing) in the assessment process.

A more useful form of measurement is to marry these two approaches and look at the way in which different processes correlate with the outcomes required from the supplier (see Box 10.6). In the case of cost management in a manufacturing setting it is likely that a supplier will only be able to manage costs if they can identify them. It is also likely that they will need to be familiar with the philosophy of cost management. In addition they will need a range of cost management tools to be able to reduce costs with the full involvement of the supplier in the process.

Box 10.6 Linking outcomes and processes in assessment

Outcome	Process
	Activity-based costing
	Value analysis
	Value engineering
Reduced costs	History of cost reduction programmes
	Devolved budget
	FLS budget training
	Team-based communication
	And so on.

Summary

Measurement is, as we have seen, a difficult and complex business. This does not mean that we should ignore its power. Just copying another business's measurement system is not the answer, because we are unlikely to have the same objectives as that business. Equally, throwing together an *ad hoc* measurement system is likely to lead to problems – within the purchasing department, within the supply base or within the business.

Measurement is a way of helping us make sense and make use of information. In one sense, measures add value to information. The more valuable the information available to the purchaser, the higher their standing within the organization and within the business network. This means that managing measurement is a critical activity for purchasing. Without an adequate measurement system, purchasing is 'flying blind' with no understanding of what is happening within the supply network, or of why it is happening. Without such an understanding, purchasing cannot craft the strategies needed to manage within supply networks.

Care and forethought need to be taken in designing and implementing a measurement strategy and system. Such a system needs to have clear objectives and also needs to meet a range of criteria with regard to usefulness, accuracy, and so on.

At a strategic level, purchasing needs three sets of measures. The first assesses its effectiveness and efficiency as a stand-alone function. The second assesses the way in which it integrates into the business as a corporate function. The third assesses the way in which purchasing manages the supply base. All of these will have different objectives, and these objectives need to be reconciled.

Effective measurement leads to effective decision making. This should, in turn, lead to effective purchasing. Poor measurement leads to exactly the opposite.

References

Crosby, Alfred W. (1990), *The Measure of Reality*, Cambridge: Cambridge University Press.

Nohria, Nitin and Eccles, Robert G. (eds) (1992), *Networks and Organizations*, Harvard, MA: Harvard Business School Press.

Stannack, Peter and Osborn, Martyn (1997), *Beyond Quality in Supply Management*, Proceedings of the 82nd Annual International Purchasing Conference, NAPM.

Stannack, Peter and Osborn, Martyn (1998), *Supplier Assessment – A Joke That's Gone Too Far*, Proceedings of the 83rd Annual International Purchasing Conference, NAPM.

Zeithaml, Valarie A. Parasuraman, A. and Berry, Leonard L.(1990), *Delivering Quality Service – Balancing Customer Perceptions and Expectations*, New York: Free Press.

11 Business process management: opportunities and caveats

Chris Harty and Marc Day

Introduction

This chapter will give a balanced overview of the ideas that form the foundations of business process management. We use a review-based approach to consider organizational activity as a set of processes. This perspective has become important for purchasing, as many practitioners are attempting, on a continual basis, to understand and change their business processes to accommodate change.

A number of commentators have argued that more enlightened purchasing teams, as part of their appraisal of electronic tools, appear to have an understanding of what they define as the processes that run through the procurement function. They use this knowledge as a starting point for appraising whether process change, or the use of a software or hardware solution, will deliver benefit for the organization. This value judgement is based on a continual reassessment of how the organization manages purchasing, and how it can improve. It is with this thinking in mind that a series of insights have been brought together that identify what this reorganization activity comprises, how we can conceptualize the 'how to' of business process change, and a critique of business process management.

We first examine one of the landmark articles in this area by the business process reengineering (BPR) 'guru' Michael Hammer. The review critically assesses Hammer's contribution which appeared originally in the *Harvard Business Review*. The main elements of Hammer's philosophy and method are examined, and some examples of the work he has done with it are provided. The review concludes that BPR may be a fad, and could be criticized for being too flimsy for consideration as a useful business strategy.

Taking this critique further, we consider the caveats identified by Grint (1994), who provides us with an academic interpretation of what BPR (or reengineering, to be consistent with Grint) was all about and how it fitted into its particular organizational, cultural and historical context. Business process 'hype' is subjected to some deeper analysis, and some learning is extracted to show the worth of Hammer's method of organizational reconfiguration.

We finally review business process management and socio-technical design (STD) with the assistance of Mumford (1994), who adopts a 'BPR is not particularly new' position. She argues that STD (a method of reorganizing the workplace which tries to provide efficiency and productivity gains) is better positioned to keep a healthy balance between technology-led drives for efficiency and the quality of work for human employees.

Sparking interest in business process management

Business process reengineering (BPR), delivered in part by Michael Hammer, came into vogue in the early 1990s. In the article entitled 'Reengineering Work: Don't Automate, Obliterate', the main elements of Hammer's philosophy and method were outlined, as well as some examples of the work he had done with it.

Hammer, an IT consultant, spotted an apparent problem with the way the newly emerging information technologies (ITs) of the late 1980s were being adopted, utilized and embedded in corporate organization. BPR was Hammer's revolutionary strategy to rethink the way technology was (and is) being employed in firms: reconfiguring business practice and process, rather than using technology to speed up old ones. He says:

> Instead of embedding outdated processes in silicon and software, we should obliterate them and start over. We should 'reengineer' our businesses: use the power of modern information technology to radically re-design our business processes in order to achieve dramatic improvements in their performance. (Hammer, 1990, p. 104)

History shows us that some American corporations had suffered from an inability to react to the new corporate climate and markets of the 1980s and early 1990s. Hammer addresses his article directly to these firms, and, like the concerned parent, gently reminds them of what the competition is capable of: 'Japanese competitors and young entrepreneurial ventures prove everyday that drastically better levels of process performance are possible' (Hammer, 1990, p. 105).

BPR rests heavily on this idea that there has been a change in the way business operates: times have changed and business needs to change with it. Hammer tells us that too many firms are still clinging on to 'assumptions about technology, people and organisational goals that no longer hold' (Hammer, 1990, p. 107). These assumptions and goals are directed at managing cost, growth and control. Business now needs to be focused on quality, innovation and service. He opposes the past with his present, and argues that past attempts to fragment, mechanize and supervise work now need to be reintegrated. Narrow goals (of department, line or division) need to be rethought in terms of overall organizational goals, we need to 'see the big picture' (ibid., p. 108). It is no good merely attempting to speed up processes; they have been developed in the past and are no longer applicable to the present.

On inspection, much of what Hammer is saying sounds familiar. There is a large academic (and not just business- or managerial-based), 'authenticated' literature about the apparent changes that society has experienced sometime between the 1970s and the present. The concepts of 'post-Fordism' and the 'post-industrial society' are widely deployed; the premises on which they are based are similar to the changes that BRP is trying to respond to. Where Fordism (a method of organizing production closely associated with the early practices of the Ford Motor Company) relied on fragmentation, automation, routinization and supervision of unskilled work by management, post-Fordism introduces flexibility, more complex tasks and less direct supervision. Post-industrial society (a term first used in the late 1960s) refers to the decline of manufacturing as the main form of economic activity, replaced by the provision of services. This refers both to the growth of industries such as sales, and to the rise of new types of flexible, multi-skilled workers, fluent in IT use and able to perform a multiplicity of tasks, a response to the new division of labour under less rigid management control. The fragmented and unskilled work of mass production is no longer appropriate; flexibility in terms of product and worker is required, with an emphasis on quick lifecycles and innovative products. Business needs to respond to the whims and vagaries of the customers who demand choice, rather than mass-produced standardized products or services.

So, perhaps there is more to Hammer's call for changes than just buzzwords. Hammer doesn't actually refer to any other literature, or use any 'post' terms himself, but that doesn't prove (or disprove) that he wasn't aware of them. Having discovered some of the undercurrents running beneath BPR, we can look at the actual principles or sets of tasks that the BPR process itself requires.

Hammer pulls no punches when he states that undertaking BPR is not easy, or quick, nor a particularly pleasant experience for those involved: 'reengineering is a tremendous effort that mandates change in many areas of the organisation' (Hammer, 1990, p. 112). However, it's worth it; it stops you losing out to youth or East Asian firms, making your company successful in the 1990s.

Hammer provides several catchphrases which set out the methodology of BPR. All of these can be concisely summarized. They tell you to do the same thing several times: integrate processes; get workers to do more complete tasks, following a whole process through from start to finish, trust them with responsibility and self-management, and use IT to aid this process, through electronic capturing, storing and transmission of data. Put this way, it seems sensible, but hardly revolutionary.

Hammer provides us with some case studies where BPR has produced large cost savings and productivity gains. One of these studies describes how Ford reengineered the way its accounts payable department worked, allowing a 75 per cent reduction in head count, an exercise originally intended to save 20 per cent. Rather than have workers aligning purchase orders (POs) from the purchasing department, goods received notes (GRNs) from the stock-room and invoices from the supplier before making payment, the 'BPRed' process input POs and GSNs into a database that cross-referenced them and told the accounts payable worker to send payment to the supplier. This is a highly simplified system, allowing IT to take over the simple process of checking that the PO and GSN match before giving the go-ahead for payment. It completely dispenses with invoices, instead paying as soon as the goods are received.

However, Ford's accounts payable department had some specific features that made it a very good candidate for 'BPRing'. First, it was a process that used people to do a job that IT is particularly good at: checking numbers. The technology was therefore able directly to replace the people; there is no redesign or reengineering involved here. Second, Ford cheated by lopping off a part of the process (waiting for the invoices from the supplier). Had this not been done, workers would still have been required, if only to key in the information from the invoice into the database. As before, the process would have been dependent on the punctuality with which the suppliers got their invoices out. So this exclusion created a lot of the value of implementing the 'BPRed' process.

However, this had severe, and probably unexpected, problems. Hammer tells us that 'there are no invoices to worry about, as Ford asked their vendors not to send them' (Hammer, 1990, p. 105). Later, though, he adds, 'vendors had to adjust. In many cases invoices formed the basis of their accounting systems' (Hammer, 1990, p. 112). This rather innocuous comment glosses over some wide-ranging consequences. Ford wanted to save a few dollars by getting rid of clerical workers and getting a computer to do the same job, to make it useful, while the omission of invoicing left Ford's suppliers needing to change the way they did business. They worked by supplying products and invoicing customers. This is no small adjustment, but a total redesign of BPR proportions. If vendors wanted to keep selling to Ford they would have to configure a system that allowed payments to be received without raising and referring to an invoice. Assuming they want to continue supplying for Ford, the vendor has two choices: have a more complicated accounting system that sometimes doesn't use invoices (for Ford transactions) and which sometimes does (for all of the vendor's other customers), or move wholly towards invoiceless transactions. This would then have consequences for their other customers, who may need an invoice to reconcile POs, GRNs and invoices in exactly the way Ford used to work.

There are issues of power and dependency when examining these sorts of systemic effects, where a change by one firm affects others connected to it. Ford presumably had the power to tell their suppliers, 'Sorry, we don't do invoices any more; deal with it'. But if a firm couldn't cope with this change, it was out. A firm dependent on Ford for its income would have to adjust or die, all because Ford wanted to lose a few administrators.

There are also questions to be asked about how easy it is to transfer a specific technology or process from one place to another: just because it worked for Ford doesn't mean it will be a success for Chrysler. The subtleties of how processes are performed in different locations involving different people has an impact on how easily these processes can be changed. This is of course, dependent on how well IT (a pattern of systemized activities) can take over or manage parts of the process.

Hammer has shown us so far that there may be a place for business process thinking, but we do need to take care when considering organizations as automated functions that can change swiftly as a result of managerial intervention. We will now move to a more fundamental critique of BPR in order to gain a more contextual understanding of organizational structure and dynamics.

Sceptical responses

As would be expected, the popularity of Hammer's technique of business process reengineering (BPR) in the business world also caused a stir within the academic community. Academic attention gave us a chance to see whether BPR could withstand the rigours of intellectual critique, see if it was professing anything new, see what its inherent values were, but mainly to see why it became so popular in a short space of time. It also allows practitioners to evaluate the foundations of a 'new' method of working before adopting it and making potentially significant changes to their workplace management and organization. One of the key critiques to emerge about BPR was published in 1994 by Keith Grint. The aim of this particular article was to provide an academic interpretation of BPR (or reengineering to be consistent with Grint) and how it fitted into its particular organizational, cultural and historical context; and to examine the hype and extract the true worth (if it existed) of Hammer's method of organizational reconfiguration.

REENGINEERING HISTORY

Grint (1994) divides his article into three chunks. He first looks at the claims made by re-engineering and its supporters, then at ten specific organizational practices heralded by Hammer and Champey as those most central to the reengineering process. Finally he provides his own arguments about why reengineering captured so many people's (well, managers') imaginations. The claims are familiar: there was a spectrum of support from the slightly sceptical in tone: 'the management world's most fashionable fad' (*Financial Times*, 22 June 1993) via the more trusting: 'a radically new process of organizational change that may companies are using to renew their commitment to customer service' (Janson, 1992) to the extremities of faith prophesied by the man himself: 'a reversal of the industrial revolution' (Hammer and Champey, 1993a). We were told by various sources that reengineering saves time and money, makes the workforce happy and loyal and allows the USA to compete again with Eastern methods of organization. One enthusiast wrote:

> the following changes are possible: 30–35% reduction in the cost of sales; 75–80% reduction in delivery time; 60–80% reduction in inventories; 65–70% reduction in the cost of quality; and an unpredictable but substantial increase in market share (Ligus, 1993)

and this constituted a rather large carrot for management consultants.

But what did the reengineering process actually entail? Essentially, it was about reversing the functional divisions and dismantling the hierarchies that characterize production under the rules of insatiable mass demand. Why? Because basically, times have changed, and so have the wants of the customer. Methods of mass production no longer ensured the sales, profits and retention of an organization's market share. Functional barriers needed to be broken down, focus needed to move to the customer, not the boss; to business processes that fulfil customer desire, not the functions that make up those processes. In short, a new way of thinking about your business, where the customer is king, and where organization is horizontal, with teamwork, joint decision making and goal setting as the basis for doing work. This replaced vertical organization, with differentiated work tasks integrated through management control and monitoring.

That's all fine, but, as Grint quickly points out, 'unfortunately, it ... appears that the majority of reengineering projects fail: 70 percent' (Grint, 1994, p. 181), according to industry consultants. Why do they fail? Why does reengineering retain such support if it is likely, in seven out of ten cases, to result in zero gain? Perhaps because if it is successful, reengineering does seem to produce results. Examples of its successes may be few and far between, but they do represent impressive changes. For instance, lead-times for dealing with new customers falling from three months to one month and for existing customers from two weeks to 15 minutes! Again, a carrot of jaw-dropping proportions with which to tempt managers trying to solve the problems of reduced sales, growing administration cost and time and market shares being reduced by leaner, younger outfits.

After rehearsing the supposed generic benefits, Grint looks at ten specific reengineering practices to achieve a new, competitive, streamlined organization, that Hammer himself outlined (in Hammer and Champey, 1993a). These are:

- a switch from functional departments to process teams
- a move from simple tasks to multidimensional work
- a reversal of the power relationship: from the superordinate to subordinate empowerment
- a shift from training to education
- the development of reward systems that drop payment for attendance in favour of payment for value added

- a division into two branches of the link between reward for current performance and advancement through assessment of ability
- the overturning of employee focus: from concerns for the boss to concern for the customer
- changes in management behaviour: from supervisors to coaches
- the flattening of hierarchies
- changes in executive behaviour: from 'scorekeepers' to leaders.

Some of these points are self-explanatory. Further discussion of these practices by Hammer himself can be found in Table 11.1.

Table 11.1 *Michael says ... Hammer and Champey's explanations of why companies should reengineer and what reengineering these processes results in.*

- **A switch from functional departments to process teams**
  'Most companies today – no matter what business they are in, how technologically sophisticated their products or services, or what their national origin – can trace their work styles and organizational roots back to the prototypical pin factory that Adam Smith described in the *Wealth of Nations* published in 1776.'
- **A move from simple tasks to multidimensional work**
  'As a result, after reengineering, work becomes more satisfying, since workers achieve a greater sense of completion, closure and accomplishment from their jobs. The actually perform a whole job – a process or sub-process – that by definition produces a result that somebody cares about.'
- **A reversal of the power relationship: from the superordinate to subordinate empowerment**
  'A task oriented, traditional company hires people and expects them to follow rules. Companies that have reengineered don't want employees who can follow rules... within the boundaries of their obligation to the organization – agreed upon deadlines, productivity goals, quality standards, and so forth – they decide how and when work will get done.'
- **A shift from training to education**
  'Traditional companies typically stress employee *training* – teaching workers how to perform a particular job or how to handle one specific situation or another. In companies that have reengineered, the emphasis shifts from training to *education* – or to hire the educated . . . people who already know how to learn.'
- **The development of reward systems that drop payment for attendance in favour of payment for value added**
  'Worker compensation in traditional companies is relatively straightforward; people are paid for their time . . . Paying people based on their position in the organization – the higher up you are the more money you make – is inconsistent with the principles of reengineering . . . [in which] performance is measured by value created, and compensation should be set accordingly . . . [and] substantial rewards for outstanding performance take the form of bonuses, not pay raises.'
- **A bifurcation of the link between reward for current performance and advancement through assessment of ability**
  'A bonus is the appropriate reward for a job well done. Advancement to a new job is not. In the aftermath of reengineering, the distinction between advancement and performance is firmly drawn. Advancement to another job within the organization is a function of ability, not of performance. It is a change not a reward.'
- **The overturning of employee focus: from concern for the boss to concern for the customers**
  'Reengineering entails as great a shift in the culture of an organization as in its structural configuration. Reengineering demands that employees deeply believe, for instance, that they work for their customers, not their bosses. They will understand this concept only to the extent that the company's practices of reward and punishment reinforce it.'
- **Changes in management behaviour: from supervisors to coaches**
  'Work teams, consisting of one person or many, don't need bosses; they need coaches. Teams ask coaches

for advice. Coaches help teams solve problems . . . This is a different role than the one most managers have traditionally played.'

- **The flattening of hierarchies**
  'When an entire process becomes the work of a team, process management becomes part of the team's job. Decisions and interdepartmental issues that used to require the meetings of managers and managers' managers now get made and resolved by teams during the course if their normal work . . . With fewer managers, there also exists fewer management layers.'
- **Changes in executive behaviour: from 'scorekeepers' to leaders**
  'Leaders who can influence and reinforce employees' values and beliefs by their words and their deeds make the most effective executives. Executives have overall responsibility for the reengineered process performance without having direct control over the people performing them... Executives fulfil their responsibilities by ensuring that processes are designed in such a way that workers can do the job required and are motivated by the company's management systems – the performance measurements and the compensation systems, for instance – to do it.'

Source: Hammer and Champey (1993a).

Grint looks at each of these in turn, assessing the 'substance and historical antecedents' of each. Many revolve around the general problems of reengineering discussed in the Hammer review, and so needn't be repeated. Grint does, however, employ some interesting material to demonstrate reengineering more as repackaging than new ideas, including the team-oriented approach to organization used by German and American shipyards in the nineteenth century, Durham miners during the 1940s and 1950s and Volvo in the 1970s. He also reminds us that research into worker empowerment since the 1960s has produced inconclusive results regarding increasing efficiency, so it is wrong to assume that multitask or multidimensional work equates to happy and productive workers. He adds that debates over differentiating between training given to do a specific task and general education to produce individuals who can apply their own knowledge to a range of problems has a long history. This debate goes back to Cardinal Newman in the mid-nineteenth century, who bemoaned the lack of 'general education' whose absence was supposedly 'dumbing down' the expanding numbers of industrial working classes.

Grint also picks up on a couple of deeper-seated problems for the reengineering approach. A key issue is the way in which power is treated. Hammer's approach assumes power is a 'thing' that people can possess, and that in a hierarchy, the higher up you go the more power you get. This seems plausible, but he asks us to consider it in a different way. It has been suggested that the power in hierarchies actually comes from the bottom, and that the reason the boss 'has power' is because his or her subordinates have chosen to do what he or she tells them to do. If they decide to ignore the boss's wishes, then his or her power disappears. Neither of these positions is right or wrong, but it is important to see how reengineering assumes one position and assumes it to be true, without looking critically at how power is working in different organizations. A second problem is the simplistic way the transition from automated or docile worker carrying out simple, repetitive tasks to a multiskilled, team-playing, go-getter is presented. The lack of evidence to link work 'quality' and worker productivity has been mentioned above, but this is perhaps a more difficult question. If the type of work predominant in US organizations forces people to switch off and go through repetitive motions, then how do you 'reengineer' them to switch back on? This problem is not seriously addressed in any of the literature advocating reengineering.

It is also worth making the general point here that the problems of industrial work, to which reengineering is a response, are the very problems that have been endlessly debated for a good 150 years or more. The historical and social implications of the industrialization process, the very problem at the heart of why reengineering should be attempted, was and still is a fundamental problem for social science. Claims to have solved the alienation of the worker by applying this 'ten steps for success' type method to organization are likely to provoke immediate scepticism. It is little wonder then that Grint systematically reveals reengineering as little more than rehashed ideas with some quite serious flaws.

THE NOVELTY VALUE OF REENGINEERING

Having dealt with and dismissed the academic worth of the reengineering approach, Grint then sets off on the real issue in the paper. He sets out to examine why something he has revealed to have no real novelty or demonstrable academic value became so popular:

> some of the 10 aspects involved in reengineering are more novel than others ... few, if any are actually innovations, least of all radical innovations that would support the hype ... why should an amalgam of relatively unremarkable ideas prove to be such a winner? (Grint, 1994, p. 191)

This is also where much of the interest in his critique lies.

Grint differentiates between two different types of appeal that he calls internalist and externalist. Internalist accounts justify success (or failure) based on the inherent qualities of whatever it is that is so popular (or unpopular). This clearly is not the case with reengineering according to Grint so far, so its popularity must be explained through an externalist account. This examines how success is achieved through the ability of advocates to construct a series of 'sympathetic resonances'. Basically make it sound as if, its good, and is the answer to current and contemporary problems, regardless of what it really offers and what it can actually do. Grint tells us that he wants to:

> argue here that the persuasive utility of reengineering, the reason for its popularity, rests not in the objective validity of the constitutive elements of the whole, the internal novelty and validity of reengineering as it were, but in the way the rendering of the problem and the solution provided by reengineering generates a resonance with popular opinion about related events. (Grint 1994, p. 192)

So, how does Grint set about this task? He looks at three different types of 'resonance'. We shall mirror this format, looking first at the 'cultural and symbolic'. He argues that reengineering is a set of ideas or texts that explain and frame contemporary problems in a specific way. There is an emphasis on a gap between 'old' and 'new' (note how many times the word 'traditional' is used in Table 11.1) and also at the way Hammer uses the idea of 'youthful entrepreneurship' as a threat and positions the East as competition in his review. This centres the target for reengineering as 'traditional' American organizations and positions as solving problems regarding new competition from the East and from younger companies.

This is a strange appeal when we dig a little deeper: the 'American dream' is founded on qualities such as individualism and self-reliance. Precisely the opposite of the team-playing and responsibility-sharing characteristics of the ideal reengineered worker! However, the texts produced by Hammer rhetorically merge these two opposites together with a healthy dose of old-fashioned positive spin:

> Reengineering capitalises on the same characteristics that made Americans such great business innovators: individualism, self-reliance, a willingness to accept risk and a propensity for change ... it takes advantage of American talents and unleashes American ingenuity. (Hammer and Champey, 1993b)

Does reengineering utilize self-reliance or teamwork? It is about taking on risk or sharing it with others? So, is it compatible with American individualism? Certainly, it is being offered as a way to adjust the American 'natural tendencies' for, and history of, business success in such a way as to bring it in line with the corporate climates of the 1990s. Reengineering is not just advocating the relearning of skills and talents that 'traditional American' firms and individuals already possess. It is a particular interpretation (or definition) of what those skills are, and the techniques of how best to use them.

A plausible argument is being constructed here. The reengineer is telling the firm that it is not that they don't possess the abilities to compete and that he or she can provide them with those skills, but that they already have them. They just need to be shown how best to apply them to current situations. This builds reengineering into a history of American success, from the past (industrialization, development of the production line and advanced Taylorist work practices) through the present (a slight dip on the world stage as Japanese and other more flexible methods of production adapt more quickly to changing customer demand) and into a future. Here, traditional (but reengineered) companies take back their market share and relive the levels of success of the past. This sort of simple narrative with a happy ending can be very persuasive.

The next set of resonances are 'economic and spatial'. Here, Grint (1994) looks at the increasing power of the transnational corporation (TNC) and how the influence and power of these are exceeding those of some nation states. He outlines a form of neo-Machiavellianism, where 'the princes' are these TNCs: highly influential in a global arena and commanding total worker loyalty. The argument here is that reengineering appeals to this trend. The reengineered firm empowers the employee, giving them more fulfilling work and more autonomy, clear rewards and good advice. For this, the employee is loyal as well as productive. The might of TNCs such as oil and automotive producers appeals to the organization that is perhaps suffering from increased competition and lessening market share. The successes of TNCs are highly visible; redirecting the goals of the firm to align with those employed by TNCs can be seen as a recipe for increased success.

The final set of resonances are 'political and temporal'. Reengineering appears at a particular historical period where the boom time lasting from the end of the Second World War to the mid-1970s are over. Crises and foreign competition threaten success; America's power on the world stage seems to be diminishing. So, it juxtaposes the good old times, the all-American qualities discussed above, with the politically turbulent contemporary times and comes up with a picture of reengineering as a reactionary doctrine of return to the 'good old days' at this time of uncertainty and radical change. There is safety in the past, and attempts to return to it in difficult times are littered throughout world history. Grint calls this a 'radical return to tradition' (Grint, 1994, p. 197). He links it to Weber's argument that one of the reasons for the success of Christ's apparently radical doctrine was that it was deeply embedded within Jewish culture and also resonated with popular issues and problems at the time: 'radical innovations prosper best when they are marketed as methods to return to former glories' (ibid., p. 198).

This matrix of resonances interlocks and creates a strong appeal for particular types of person, or organization, at a particular time. Grint, by teasing apart different strands of the technique's appeal, argues that British or Japanese firms would not react as well to re-engineering's strategy as the Americans did. This is quite possibly the case. The target is persuaded that reengineering holds particular properties that will solve historically, politically and culturally specific problems. However, Grint takes his critique about BPR not being 'new' quite far enough. We need to look at the historical antecedents of business process management in more detail to assess its transformative impact on business and management.

Contrasting business process management with socio-technical design

We should now feel more comfortable with the ideas behind business process reengineering as well as some of the criticisms it encountered from the academic community, plus also why it provoked them. But what about other organizational redesign methodologies? Is business process management truly innovative?

Mumford (1994), in an effort to position BPR, argues that socio-technical design (STD) (emanating from work undertaken in the 1950s) seems to be quite familiar to the lists of 'things to do' that Hammer gave us, and given that Grint (1994) warned us to be careful of the hype of BRP, it is worth applying the same rationale to STD as well.

Mumford argues that STD developed a great many of the principles that BPR claims to be original and its own. Several are listed, such as the principle of multiskilling, the principle of information flow, ensuring that the organization is in place so that it can travel efficiently from source to where it is needed, and the principle of boundary management, to look for possible problems or upsets, especially prevalent with sequentially ordered practices. It has to be agreed that much of this sounds like BPR. In fact, STD in general has much in common with BPR, sadly including one fundamental problem. Mumford criticizes BPR, citing the same problems that Grint highlighted regarding a high failure rate for BPR projects. However, although the coal mining and Volvo STD experiments are looked at, these were both failures, and so STD seems to share the flaw of not being particularly workable in specific situations.

Mumford is also rightly critical of the hype that surrounded BPR in terms of the apparent magical improvements in performance that IT was going to bring to all business. The idea that the black box of IT could be plugged into your business and generate huge speed gains and cost savings is simply false. One difference is in orientation. Where BPR is concerned with improving performance and productivity, and is oriented towards managers, STD is concerned with the problems experienced by workers, and how to alleviate them. Although step eight of the STD process demands improvements to both the workers' morale and the production process, the whole article is woolly regarding the possible productivity gains STD can provide. This suggests that either STD is not the thing to try if you want your firm to be more productive, or that STD is assuming that a happy worker is a more productive one. The problem with this is that only the nicest boss would be prepared to reorganize just to make the workers happier with no gain. If productivity gain is desired, Grint (1994) has already let us know that the connection between happy worker and increased productivity is tenuous (see the Grint review for more details).

Mumford also goes on to argue that other organizational methodologies such as just-in-time (JIT) and lean production swing too much towards the performance and efficiency benefits of automation and IT without looking at the more humanistic problems these techniques can cause. The well-known arguments about the suitability of Japanese culture to their efficient and obedient forms of work, countered by emerging criticism from Japanese trade unions, are rehearsed. She advocates a middle ground, with the emphasis on efficiency of BPR or JIT, but with consideration of social or human factors. She advocates demonstrating some caution in the implementation of new improved technologies, looking at how they might affect the workforce as the 'tightness' of these efficient technology-based approaches 'places workers under too much stress' (Mumford, 1994, p. 323).

It is difficult, though, to see how Mumford's 'middle way' would work. She makes no suggestions, and the problem may be that top-tier management implement radical reorganization like BPR or JIT for efficiency gain, and generally in times of particular crisis. Remember how Grint justifies BPR's whole existence and popularity as a reactionary response to the hard times of the early 1990s US economy? This suggests that there wouldn't be a lot of room for concern for the psychological well-being of workers if the company were fighting for survival. The Volvo experiments perhaps demonstrate that, in times of economic crisis, STD is perhaps not the best way to organize your work.

Conclusion

Where are we left with BPR? It does seem to exist in response to changes in the corporate environment that are backed up by many other sources. However, after this plausible start BPR starts to look a little insubstantial when the rules for its implementation are unveiled. They make similar generalized statements: integrate fragmented processes, utilize the abilities of new multiskilled workers by giving them responsibility and accountability, and use IT to support them, taking over routine and clerical tasks. Too many assumptions are made about workers, about IT and the abilities of 'expert systems', and about the consequences within the entire system that specific and particular changes can have.

In general, the statements made by Hammer (1990) are reasonable: increase flexibility by providing more autonomy to workers; this will allow you to respond to changes in market or customer demand. Cut costs by replacing expensive people with cheap technology. Above all, BPR deserves credit for announcing that often changes are needed, but IT is not the answer to all the problems an organization experiences. IT must be tailored to its environment, and its environment must meet it halfway. One of the main reasons that IT is sometimes less successful than expected is because the changes required to accommodate it are not understood and not attempted.

Looking at BPR teaches us a useful lesson. The redesign or reengineering of business processes is not something that can be reduced to some catchy phrases or a list of 'things to do'. The 'guru' style approach to management can ignore crucial and complex factors, and therefore confine our own appreciation of them in a simplistic manner. The interactions between the firm, its workers, its customers (both upstream and downstream), and the technologies, both old and new, that it utilizes create a highly complex and interrelated network. Such complexity cannot be wholly captured within, let alone altered, according to a set of simple rules or guidelines. Practitioners and academics appreciate that it's all too complicated for that. However, the very fact that trying to assess the use of BPR shows us the complexity of introducing and embedding new information technologies and new working practices is something of positive use.

In attempting to analyse BPR, Grint (1994) makes his own position very explicit throughout. Reengineering is best seen as a particularly clever set of texts that managed to persuade many people into adopting or at least accepting it even though it was based on tentatively grounded principles. The skill of reengineering lay not in what it did and how it was applied, but in how it constructed itself as a reflection of a successful past, turbulent present and uncertain future of the American corporate world of the late 1980s and 1990s. This is a plausible academic critique of a set of principles that lacked a sense of academic rigour (after all, Hammer himself was not an academic, but a consultant). However, although examples of success were few and far between, reengineering, when it worked, created huge productivity increases and cost cuts. In light of this, even though Grint's argument is useful and deserves to be considered, whether reengineering's success can be explained away as purely circumstantial is not an easy claim to uphold.

When contrasting BPR with socio-technical design, Mumford (1994) places BPR into a historical context. Although quite critical of the originality claimed by Hammer (1990) for BPR, Mumford offers us a good insight into the key issues involved in a systems view of business activity. There is a balance between what can be achieved through automation and what needs to remain more flexible in all work. Long-run manufacture achieves the economies of scale to make the initial high costs of automation the best option. More customer-oriented work has to deal with many different people and problems, and so only be automated to a certain limited degree. In these cases, making small teams jointly responsible and accountable for particular processes seems to work. In different circumstances things happen differently. Nobody can hold up a model for business organization and herald it as universal, the one-size-fits-all solution for work and production doesn't work here.

References

Grint, K. (1994), 'Reengineering History: Social Resonances and Business Process Reengineering, *Organization*, Vol. 1, No. 1, pp. 179–201.

Hammer, M. (1990), 'Reengineering Work: Don't Automate, Obliterate', *Harvard Business Review*, July/August.

Hammer, M. and Champey, J. (1993a), 'Reengineering the Corporation', *Insights Quarterly*, Summer, pp. 3–19.

Hammer, M. and Champey, J. (1993b), *Reengineering the Corporation: A Manifesto for Business Revolution*, London: Nicholas Brealey.

Janson, R. (1992), 'How Reengineering Transforms Organizations to Satisfy Customers', *National Productivity Review*, Winter, pp. 45–53.

Ligus, R.G. (1993), 'Methods to Help Reengineer your Company for Improved Agility', *Industrial Engineer*, January.

Mumford, E. (1994), 'New Treatments for Old Remedies: Is Business Process Reengineering Really Sociotechnical Design?', *Journal of Strategic Information Systems*, Vol. 3, No. 4, pp. 313–26.

12 Purchasing IS/IT software: the impact of e-business on procurement and supply management

Andrew Cox, Lorna Chicksand and Paul Ireland

Introduction

There have been significant increases in the scale and pace of change in the structure and nature of various industrial and commercial markets in recent years. Rapid changes in technology, legislation and market conditions have dramatically altered the nature of competition. As a direct result of these changes, many companies have been forced to either create new strategies that are aligned to this dynamic environment or, alternatively, to accept decline and the subsequent failure of their businesses.

The most significant changes are a result of the increasing role that information technology is playing in the business world. In particular, the advent of the Internet has provided the medium for the efficient and effective transfer of information between buyers and suppliers.[1] Business strategies have had to be redesigned to meet the challenges and opportunities presented by this new technology. At the same time, the technology generates real-time management information that has the potential to enable practitioners to develop more appropriate strategies.

However, whilst the impact of the Internet on business is certain to be profound, it may not necessarily be universal. With procurement professionals being inundated with different Internet applications for procurement and supply chain management, it is not surprising that organizations are finding it difficult to understand the complexity (and confusion) that surrounds the adoption of this technology. This confusion is fuelled by the hype from the media, service providers and consultancy organizations. Therefore, procurement professionals need to understand the impact that these Internet applications will have on current supply strategies and operational practices. Rather than adopting these applications in reaction to the hype, organizations need to have a way of thinking so that they can recognize and anticipate the key problems and potential opportunities that may present themselves.

This way of thinking will require the development of robust e-supply strategies.[2] However, current research undertaken by the authors[3] has indicated that, whilst early adopters do have e-supply strategies in place, these have not always been robustly developed. Indeed, only 11 per cent of our respondent organizations had an e-supply strategy that was well developed (that is, written, codified and being implemented). This lack of robust e-business strategies may mean that buyers are developing and implementing inappropriate e-business solutions for their particular business circumstances.

This chapter will discuss a number of issues that are fundamental to understanding the impact that the Internet will have on procurement and supply chain management. In the next section, we will discuss a number of important issues that need to be considered when developing an appropriate e-supply strategy. This includes a discussion of whether the pursuit of improved operational efficiencies is a first-order strategy. The following section will provide an overview of the Internet applications that are currently available and discuss the functionality of these different offerings.Then we will discuss what organizations are currently doing in the area of e-supply. This highlights that, whilst some organizations are achieving limited success, others are experiencing significant problems. These findings are based on evidence from a major survey of current Internet usage by business.

Developing an e-supply strategy

INTRODUCTION

There is much confusion as to the role of the purchasing or procurement function within the organization. Historically, the purchasing function has commanded a position of relatively low importance within the organization. This mainly stemmed from the fact that the function was traditionally a subset of manufacturing and operations involving only a basic responsibility for buying inputs to the firm. However, the recent focus on outsourcing to create leaner and more efficient operations and the increased pressure on costs has resulted in the purchasing/procurement function having a greater role (and influence) in the development of business strategies.

Whilst the status of the procurement function has been enhanced by senior management's recognition of the major impact it can have on bottom-line profitability,[4] its processes and procedures have the potential to be significantly transformed by the Internet. However, evidence from the authors' survey would seem to suggest that early adopters of Internet applications for procurement and supply chain management are having mixed results, with some organizations experiencing considerable problems. This is not to say that there are no benefits to be achieved by adopting Internet applications, rather we raise this point as a caution against mindlessly jumping on the Internet 'bandwagon'. As past management fads have shown, mindless imitation as a strategy for business success has had limited results. Therefore, procurement practitioners need to have a way of thinking that enables them to recognize and anticipate the key problems and potential opportunities that may present themselves.

Indeed, the Internet can impact upon procurement and supply chain management in two principal ways:

- *improve operational efficiencies so as to reduce transaction costs; and/or,*
- *alter the power structure between buyers and suppliers so as to improve quality and reduce input costs.*

OPERATIONAL EFFICIENCIES

Until recently, the media has focused on B2C (business-to-consumer) dot-coms and how the Internet provided a mechanism to transform the relationship between suppliers and consumers. However, it is now becoming apparent that the real benefits from Internet applications may well arise in the context of more efficient operational processes and practices *between* businesses (B2B). In particular, many companies are expecting to obtain significant benefits from the creation of a seamless order placement, fulfilment and payments process. This seamless web-enabled process offers a vision of a truly paperless office, with not only orders, fulfilment and payments automated, but also one in which companies can concentrate on the more effective management of all of their internal processes.

Figure 12.1 illustrates how the Internet has increased the potential to achieve significant operational efficiencies through the speeding up of the process and reduction of the paperwork involved. In particular, the procurement professional achieves lower transaction costs (the cost of each individual purchase) because of the more efficient and effective mechanism for information transfer between buyer and supplier and the simplified and standardized processes involved.

Although the actual changes in transaction costs from the introduction of Internet technologies may be difficult to quantify, it is useful for the purchaser to recognize the key elements of such costs. The major source is associated with the administrative burden of putting a transaction together and is 'related to the need to determine prices and other details of the transaction, to make the existence and location of potential buyers and suppliers known to one another, and to bring these parties together to transact'.[5] These costs are referred to as the coordination costs, and it is in the area of the reduction of search costs and efficiencies brought about by better-quality information about the supplier and their products and services that enables the largest reduction in transaction costs.

On the other hand, however, transaction costs may actually be increased by the use of the Internet. Created by informational incompleteness and asymmetries, costs may be increased 'when the parties to the transaction do not have all the relevant information needed to determine whether the terms of an agreement are acceptable and whether they are actually being met'.[6] Issues of adverse selection and buying a lemon may become more prevalent in online transactions. The net effect of these reductions and increases is uncertain and will vary significantly from one industrial sector to another.

In addition to the reduction in transaction costs, the simplification of the procedures also contributes to the increased control that exists over *ad hoc* and uncoordinated maverick purchasing. However, these process changes will tend to provide only short- to medium-term benefits, with many of these being quickly eroded by benchmarking and competitive replication of any new Internet applications.

ALTERING THE POWER POSITION

The Internet also has the potential to fundamentally alter the relationship between buyers and suppliers. Under certain circumstances, Internet applications may provide the buyer with an opportunity to lower the costs of inputs to their organization through increased supply leverage. As such, buyers need to be aware of the supply and demand characteristics of the markets in which they are operating in order to ascertain just what *is possible* from adopting an e-supply strategy. Furthermore, early adopters can create competitive advantage for

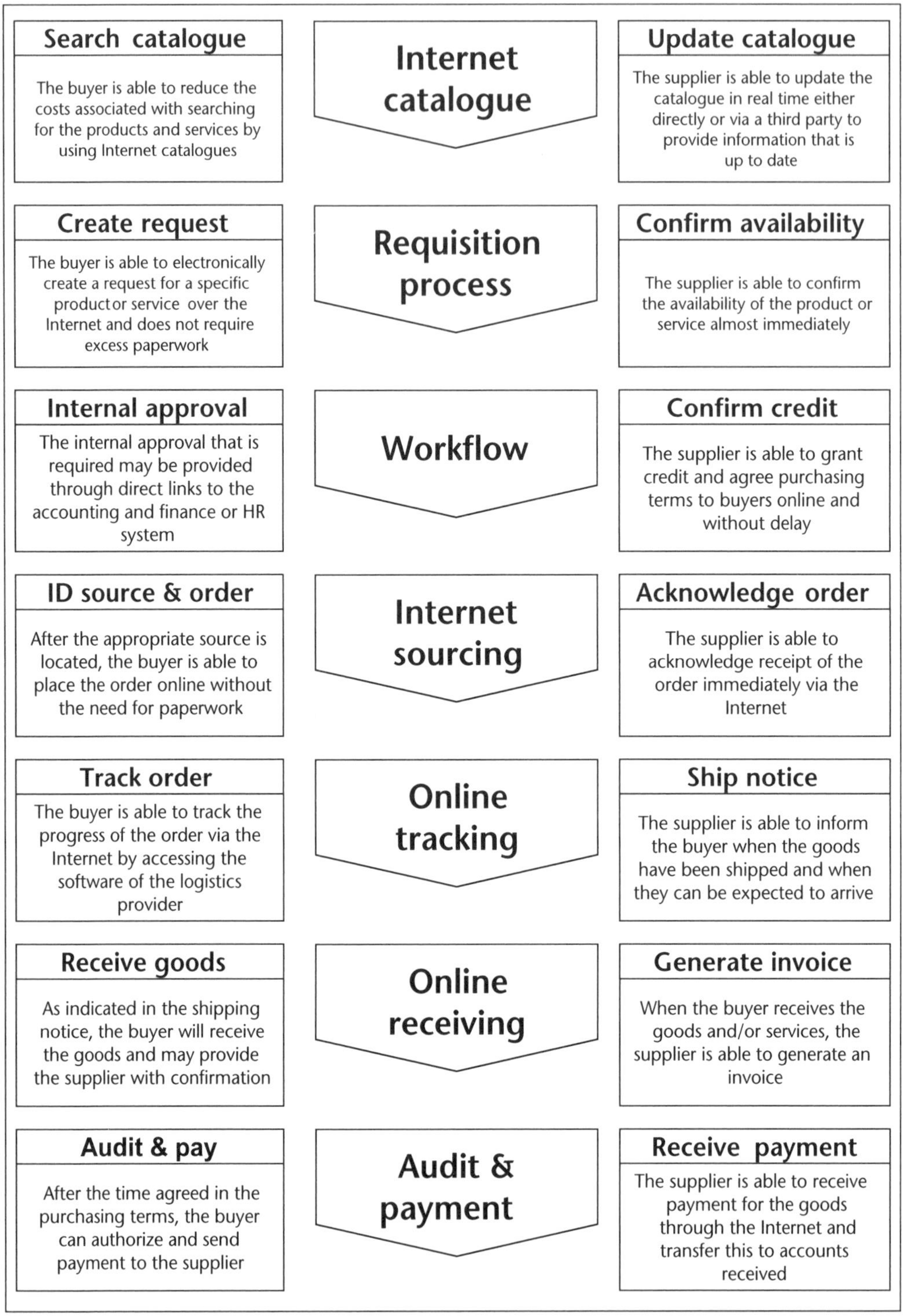

Search catalogue	Internet catalogue	Update catalogue
The buyer is able to reduce the costs associated with searching for the products and services by using Internet catalogues		The supplier is able to update the catalogue in real time either directly or via a third party to provide information that is up to date
Create request	**Requisition process**	**Confirm availability**
The buyer is able to electronically create a request for a specific product or service over the Internet and does not require excess paperwork		The supplier is able to confirm the availability of the product or service almost immediately
Internal approval	**Workflow**	**Confirm credit**
The internal approval that is required may be provided through direct links to the accounting and finance or HR system		The supplier is able to grant credit and agree purchasing terms to buyers online and without delay
ID source & order	**Internet sourcing**	**Acknowledge order**
After the appropriate source is located, the buyer is able to place the order online without the need for paperwork		The supplier is able to acknowledge receipt of the order immediately via the Internet
Track order	**Online tracking**	**Ship notice**
The buyer is able to track the progress of the order via the Internet by accessing the software of the logistics provider		The supplier is able to inform the buyer when the goods have been shipped and when they can be expected to arrive
Receive goods	**Online receiving**	**Generate invoice**
As indicated in the shipping notice, the buyer will receive the goods and may provide the supplier with confirmation		When the buyer receives the goods and/or services, the supplier is able to generate an invoice
Audit & pay	**Audit & payment**	**Receive payment**
After the time agreed in the purchasing terms, the buyer can authorize and send payment to the supplier		The supplier is able to receive payment for the goods through the Internet and transfer this to accounts received

Figure 12.1 *The Internet-enabled procurement process*

themselves by achieving cost reduction and quality improvements that their competitors cannot quickly replicate, thus giving a sustained procurement advantage.

When assessing the impact of the Internet on buyer–supplier relationships one needs to consider the effect on the relative power that each party has in the exchange. It is therefore important to start any thinking about procurement and supply management from what we have called the power perspective (Cox, 2001). This is for a number of reasons.

Recently, a consensus about what constitutes 'best practice' in procurement and supply management has developed. This involves the rejection of a historic focus on adversarial buyer–supplier relationships in favour of more collaborative long-term approaches based on trust. However, this growing belief seems contrary to the view that the best position for the buyer to be in (and one that ensures that suppliers innovate and pass value to buyers) is the maintenance of perfectly competitive supply markets, with low barriers to entry, low switching costs and limited information asymmetries.

Buyer–supplier relationships can only occur if both sides obtain some benefit from doing business – nobody would trade if they did not derive some benefit from the exchange. As a result, the buyer has choices over the level of adversarialism (conflict over the level of value appropriated) and how closely they will need to work with the supplier to achieve their profit-maximizing or -satisficing goals (collaborative or arm's-length way of working). To do what is appropriate in relationship management terms is key, and specific approaches will vary over time.

The power perspective has shown to be of utility in developing appropriate supply chain management strategies. According to this perspective, supply chains are analytical constructs; that is, they are structures of power. These structures are derived from the power resources that both buyers and suppliers bring to the process of exchange. Some resources are structural or regulatory, whilst others are critically influenced by the flow of information and knowledge management (see Cox et al., 1999a; 1999b; 2001b). It is, therefore, imperative that practitioners have a clear understanding of the power resources held by actors within the supply chains in which they operate, what is achievable under those particular circumstances and how the various Internet applications will impact upon the structures of power.

The Internet has the potential to transform the buyer–supplier relationship through:

- *aggregation with other buyers*
- *consolidation of spend*
- *greater contestation in the supply market*

Demand side

On the demand side, power within the supply chain is primarily a function of the utility of the resource in question. This is dependent upon a number of factors, including:

- the type of product – operating/secondary inputs or primary inputs
- frequency of purchase
- importance to business
- volume

- geographical focus
- substitutability.

Thus, for instance, an Internet application that allows for aggregation with other buyers and/or consolidation of external spend may alter the power structure in a number of ways. The buyer's purchasing power may be enhanced by the increase in the relative volume and salience of the spend to the supplier. Aggregation and consolidation may also enable the buyer to engineer a regular and predictable spend that can incentivize the supplier to offer improved purchasing terms.

Supply side

On the supply side, the nature of the supply market will have a direct bearing on what can be achieved through employing an e-supply strategy. The primary factor to be taken into consideration is the relative scarcity of supply. This, like utility, is dependent upon a number of factors[7] including:

- information asymmetry
- buyer switching costs
- reputation effects
- buyer search costs
- economies of scale.

The preferred position for the buyer is not only to have an external spend that is valued by suppliers (in terms of volume and regularity) but also to be sourcing these external resources from a highly contested supply market. The Internet can alter the dynamics of the supply market to the buyer's advantage by increasing the number of potential suppliers available to the buyer. In particular, the reduction of search costs and information asymmetry that is made possible by the Internet provide the buyer with a greater opportunity better to understand the supply market and select the supplier who provides the best value for money (defined in terms of quality and cost).

However, under certain circumstances, the power resources held by the supplier will mean that the adoption of an Internet application by a buying organization will have a very limited impact on the nature of the supply market. It is conceivable, for instance, that in situations where buyers are faced with having to deal with a monopoly supplier, Internet applications will have very little impact. Similarly, if a supplier's power relative to that of the buyer is based on intellectual property rights, it is difficult to envisage how the Internet will be able to change the balance of power.

Internet applications for e-supply

INTRODUCTION

There are a number of Internet applications currently available which form the basis of an e-supply strategy. However, many attempts to clarify the complexity are hindered by the mass of terminology that has been created. This section will, therefore, attempt to clarify the widespread misunderstanding of the terminology and the differences between the different B2B applications.

Before we address this complexity, it is important to understand which Internet applications are likely to have the largest impact on the management of the supply chain. The previous discussion highlighted the demand- and supply-side factors that practitioners need to consider when implementing an e-supply strategy. However, it is also important to understand the way in which certain 'applications' act as intermediaries and therefore appropriate value for themselves from the supply chain. Indeed, Internet applications that act as an intermediary between buyers and suppliers have a significant capacity to alter the balance of power within supply chains. These applications may also affect the ability of the firm to improve operational efficiencies.

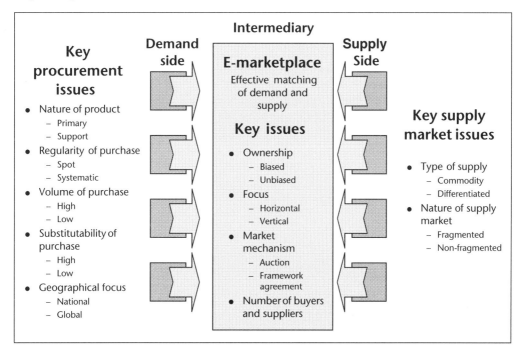

Figure 12.2   *The key supply chain issues*

The impact of the Internet on market and supply chain structures is the subject of considerable debate amongst academics. Analysts such as Evans and Wurster (1999) have argued that the 'new economics of information' will disrupt the traditional compromise faced by businesses between richness and reach. They argue that the Internet will break this trade-off, leading to the deconstruction of established value chains. Other commentators (Benjamin and Wigand, 1995; Daniel and Klimis, 1999; Gellman, 1996; Lewis, 1997) take this analysis one step further and argue that the medium of the Internet will totally reshape value chains, resulting in the 'disintermediation', that is to say elimination, of the traditional middle role. Countering these claims, some academics (Sarkar et al., 1996; Bailey and Bakos, 1997; Hagel and Rayport, 1997; Hagel and Singer, 1999) argue that the overabundance of information provided by the Internet will lead to 'new, Net-based forms of intermediation' (Vandermerwe, 1999, p. 598).

INTERMEDIARY BETWEEN BUYER AND SUPPLIER: E-MARKETPLACES

Often referred to in academic literature and the press as portals, hortals, vortals, hubs and exchanges, e-marketplaces are, in a nutshell, Internet sites where buyers and sellers can come together to trade. The e-marketplace landscape is very unstable at present, with a great deal of consolidation occurring. Several, well-documented e-marketplaces, such as Chemdex (which was itself the recipient of a take-over bid by Ventro), have ceased to trade. This could possibly explain why, despite the media hype surrounding the supposed benefits of e-marketplaces, our survey found that only one-third of organizations with e-supply strategies are using e-marketplaces.

What the future for e-marketplaces holds is unclear. However, if procurement practitioners are considering the use of e-marketplaces as part of their e-supply strategy, they need to appreciate that e-marketplaces vary significantly in their structure and focus. In effect, the generic term 'e-marketplace' masks the complexity of, and differences between, e-marketplaces.

E-marketplaces can be distinguished from each other by a number of features:

- industry focus
- number of buyers and sellers
- market mechanisms
- type of products traded
- ownership of the e-marketplace.

Industry focus

We have categorized e-marketplaces according to whether they involve the bringing together of buyers and suppliers from within the same industry or from different industries. The number of e-marketplaces has risen dramatically over recent years and now includes firms in almost every industry and country. According to *The Economist*, as of March 2000, there were more than 750 B2B markets around the world and at least 20 industry exchanges publicly trading at a combined value of more than $100 billion.[8] Other industry commentators put an even higher figure on the number of e-marketplaces currently in existence.[9]

E-marketplaces which have an intra-industry focus (often referred to as vertical marketplaces) are concentrated on specific industries (e.g. chemicals, automotive, plastics, food and beverage, or electronics) and tend to be set up in order to streamline the trade of direct goods and obtain the benefits of leverage from consolidated spend. For example, e-Steel is an e-marketplace that services the needs of the steel industry.

E-marketplaces which have an inter-industry focus (often referred to as horizontal marketplaces) concentrate on specific functions or business processes or involve the trade of similar indirect goods and services. These marketplaces are often set up by a number of large organizations that have recognized the potential to consolidate their expenditure to obtain increased value for money from suppliers.

Number of buyers and sellers

E-marketplaces can also be distinguished by the number of buyers and sellers that are brought together to use and trade on the site. Figure 12.3 illustrates that there are nine alternatives in the buyer–supplier interaction.

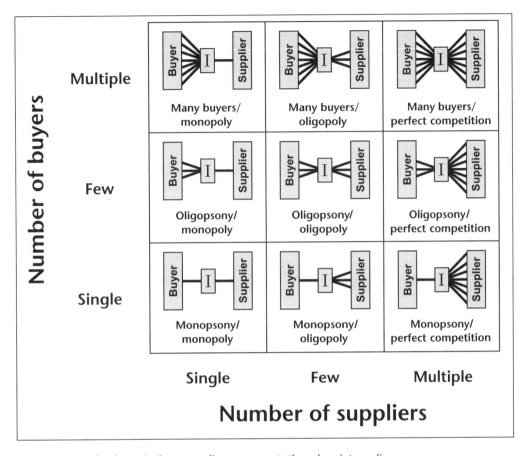

Figure 12.3 *The alternative buyer–supplier arrangements through an intermediary*

Market mechanisms

A number of market mechanisms are used by e-marketplaces. These include:

- auctions
- spot catalogues
- framework agreement catalogues.

Auctions

B2B auctions have been the subject of considerable media and academic speculation. According to some commentators, 'the dynamic pricing model of auctions will shake up the buyer–seller relationship across the economy'.[10] The auction mechanism allows multiple buyers to bid competitively for products from individual suppliers. This market mechanism is particularly suited to hard-to-move goods such as used capital equipment and surplus or excess inventory. Auctions are becoming a feature of many e-marketplaces, but some use auctions as their primary market mechanism, for example, AdAuction and TradeOut.com (used equipment).

Reverse auctions are also used on many e-marketplaces. With reverse auctions, buyers post their need for a product or service, then suppliers bid against each other for pre-specified

contracts. These auctions are based on detailed request for proposals (RFPs) where pre-quali-
fied suppliers are invited to take part in the auction. Unlike an auction, prices only move
down. FreeMarkets (industrial parts, raw materials) uses reverse auctions as its primary market mechanism. The primary benefits of using a reverse auction are the cost savings and the
reduction in time spent dealing with suppliers and negotiating prices and terms of transactions (instead of one-to-one negotiations with individual suppliers, Internet reverse auctions
allow multiple suppliers to engage in the process simultaneously). Organizations are reporting significant savings using reverse auctions. For instance, General Motors saved almost
$150 million in one single online auction for rubber parts. Similarly, Quaker Oats reported
saving over $8.5 million in online auctions for transportation services and raw ingredients.[11]

Spot catalogues

This market mechanism is single transaction-oriented and helps buyers to find the lowest
price by matching supply and demand. There is no ongoing relationship between buyer and
supplier and the sourcing decision is usually made solely on cost. Where purchases become
more regular it is important for the buyer to recognize the changing dynamics in the
buyer–supplier relationship.

Framework agreement catalogues

These catalogues are used when a pre-negotiated contract exists between the buyer (or
e-marketplace) and supplier. They tend to exist where the buyer has a long-term relationship
with the supplier because of the regularity of purchase or where the buyer wants to guarantee
supply. Where framework agreements exist, the e-marketplace may offer additional functionality by acting as a catalogue integrator and aggregating the products and services of
many suppliers.

However, despite the numerous alternatives available, many e-marketplaces are now
moving towards integrated, multi-market mechanisms. This mirrors the range of sourcing
arrangements that procurement professionals adopt.

Type of products traded

E-marketplaces are used to trade in primary products, support products or a combination of
both. By primary products we mean the raw materials/components used directly in the manufacturing process. By indirect goods/services we refer to those goods and services which are
required to maintain the functioning of a company, such as MRO (maintenance, repair and
operating) inputs.

When considering the nature of the products and/or services traded through the
e-marketplace it is also important to consider their strategic importance to the buyer and
supplier. While the goods may not be critical to the buyer (certainly the case for many MRO
items), they will almost always be more strategic to the supplier. Figure 12.4 illustrates the
two quite different supply chains that exist for products and services. The structures of power
within these supply chains have to be understood so that the appropriate relationship management strategies can be developed for products and services of differing criticalities.

Ownership of the e-marketplace

When describing e-marketplaces it is important to understand any bias that may exist.
The level of bias will depend on the parties that own and/or control the marketplace. These
are:

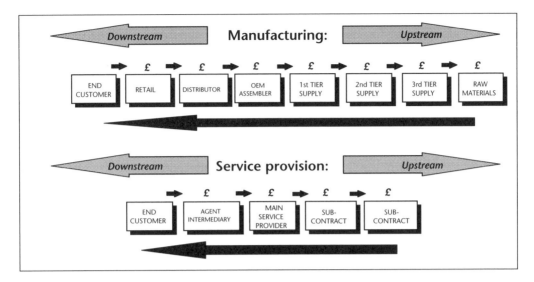

Figure 12.4   *The supply and value chains for products and services*

- neutral industry service provider
- technology firm
- technology firm and industry player(s) alliance
- single-industry player.

Neutral industry service provider

These are run by independent firms to bring buyers and sellers together in order to rationalize previously fragmented industries. As such, they tend to work as exchanges by matching supply with demand. Independence allows these e-marketplaces to offer a level playing field to all participants, ensuring that power is not biased towards one side of the transaction. These e-marketplaces tend to trade in industry-specific primary goods such as automotive parts, chemicals and metals, although some are focused on indirect goods and services, including MRO and office supplies.

However, a major problem for these e-marketplaces is gaining critical mass; liquidity is needed to overcome the constraints of buyers and sellers finding each other efficiently, which in turn determines the market price of goods and services. The technology used to run these e-marketplaces is either bought in or developed internally.

Neutral e-marketplaces tend to favour two market mechanisms in particular: spot catalogues and framework agreement catalogues. For example e-Steel and PaperExchange use spot catalogues, whereas Chemdex operates through framework agreement catalogues, having pulled together product catalogues from many companies.

Some e-marketplaces are biased by design and either work for the buyer or supplier. Biased hubs can act as both aggregators and matchers. When they favour buyers, they act as reverse aggregators or reverse auctioneers, and when they favour suppliers, they act as forward aggregators or forward auctioneers.

Technology firm

Most of these e-marketplaces were initially set up by e-procurement software vendors to connect buyers using their automated procurement software with supplier networks. For example, the Ariba.com Network provides buying organizations using Ariba's ORMS e-procurement software with access to more than 10.1 million items from 84,700 vertical-industry content suppliers. Thus buyers are given access to a wider supply market and yet can still download information regarding any transactions into an e-procurement application. Initially, they focused on the trade of indirect goods and services, although some have developed and are now trading in direct goods as well, for example Commerce One's MarketSite. Although the prevalent market mechanism used on these e-marketplaces is framework agreement catalogues, several sites have added other market mechanisms such as auction/reverse auction capabilities. There has also been a move away from a licensed model to a hosted model, whereby software and catalogues are hosted on central hub (see ASPs below).

Technology firm and industry player(s) alliance

There has been a rapid growth of trading communities driven by large industry players who have formed alliances/joint ventures with technology companies.[12] These e-marketplaces can be further differentiated according to whether they are open or closed. Open e-market-places include Commerce One's Global Trading Web. This consists of many e-marketplaces running on the Commerce One MarketSite portal solution. Each global trading portal is owned and managed by a third party – for example, BT in the UK, Commerce One in the USA and Deutsche Telecom in Germany.

Those that are closed limit participation in the e-marketplace to sponsor companies and their suppliers (i.e. few to many). They are generally set up by a major manufacturer or retailer in partnership with other manufacturers/retailers in a given industry in order to capture the majority of trading volume in that industry. Most claim that they will eventually operate as independent companies.

Box 12.1 Examples of e-marketplaces run by industry-specific consortia and technology firms

- *Covisint*

Set up by Ford, DaimlerChrysler, General Motors, Renault and Nissan in partnership with Commerce One and Oracle, Covisint will buy $240bn worth of parts from tens of thousands of suppliers.

- *PetroCosm*

Set up by Chevron and Ariba in January 2000, this e-marketplace is owned by buyers and sellers in the energy industry (including Chevron, Texaco, Crosspoint Venture and National Oilwell) and used to purchase drilling and electrical equipment, pipes, valves and fittings and professional engineering and construction services. It claims to have more than 565 suppliers and, during 2000, to have completed more than 1,300 transactions.

- *Energy and Petrochemical Exchange*

The founders of this e-marketplace include: Shell; BP–Amoco; Statoil; Mitsubishi; and Total Finaele. Based on Commerce One technology, the e-marketplace will have a

Continued

combined annual spend of $125 billion. Initially users will be charged a $1–$2 per transaction fee, although eventually it is envisaged that the marketplace will be financed by the services it offers.

- *GlobalNetXchange*

Launched by Sears Roebuck & Co. and the Carrefour Group, a France-based retailer in conjunction with Oracle Corp. This alliance will bring together approximately $80 billion in annual purchases from around 50,000 suppliers.

- *MyAircraft.com*

Set up as a joint venture between aerospace suppliers Honeywell and United Technologies and software company to sell spare aircraft parts and engines.

Single-industry player

In some cases, e-marketplaces have been formed by individual suppliers. Many suppliers have been wary of joining the other types of e-marketplaces for a number of compelling reasons:

- fear of diluting brand image
- worry that margins will have to be reduced as a result of price competition, especially for commodity-type products
- concerns with allowing an intermediary (who could appropriate the value flow within the supply chain) to come between themselves and their customers
- the inconvenience of creating multiple technology platforms to link with the various e-marketplaces with the concomitant inconvenience of having to update catalogue content on the differing platforms
- concerns with opening up their pricing and inventory information to competitors.

For example, TraneCo., an air-conditioning parts maker, after being approached by a number of construction industry e-marketplaces, decided to build its own private exchange. Their e-marketplace offers its 5,000 dealers the opportunity to buy equipment, schedule deliveries and process warranties.[13] Other examples include Staples and Travelocity.com, which offer their services through their e-marketplaces.

NO INTERMEDIARY

The Internet has enabled intermediaries to engineer a more efficient flow of products and services along the supply chain. However, there are numerous instances where IT has enabled the buyer and supplier to trade without the need for an intermediary to own, control and manage the transaction.

SUPPLY CHAIN SOFTWARE

Supply chain software helps buyers and sellers to collaboratively plan, forecast and replenish inventory, enabling firms to determine whether online customer orders can be fulfilled. Acting essentially as decision-support software packages, using mathematical principles to balance supply and demand, they provide the ability to make real-time, interactive decisions. The key vendors in this area are companies such as i2 and niche ERP vendors such as Manugistics, Oracle, SAP and JD Edwards.

Buy-side e-procurement software

E-procurement applications are web-enabled software systems that allow buying organizations to streamline and automate their procurement processes. The applications link a buying organization with its approved suppliers' catalogues electronically and allow the whole purchasing process, from initial requisition to delivery of goods, to be transacted via the desktop, over the web (although it must be noted that not all firms are using all these features). At present, e-procurement applications are generally being used for the procurement of non-production goods and services (often referred to as maintenance, repair and operating (MRO) supplies). Responsibility for purchasing is handed over to end users, who access the electronic catalogues of approved suppliers on their company intranet. Spending limits and approval routings can be automatically enforced according to buying rules set by purchasing management.

Buy-side e-procurement software has tended to be implemented for the purchase of indirect goods and services which have proven to be less streamlined and more inefficient than the purchase of direct goods/services. According to the Centre for Advanced Purchasing Studies, indirect goods account for over one-third of all costs to a business, rising to 60 per cent in service companies.

Although there are differences between the systems, they generally share the following features:

- They aggregate many supplier catalogues into a single 'universal' catalogue.
- They allow end-user requisitioning from the desktop.
- They purchases made can be linked to back-office ERP/accounting systems.
- They help manage workflow and administration involved in procurement with 'rules' built into the software to ensure automatic approval.
- They automate the requisition, ordering and tracking process.
- They log and analyse information re company spending.

Although these systems were initially targeted at the largest buyers, they are increasingly being hosted by ASPs (see below) to address the SME market.

The main vendors in this market include pure-play B2B application vendors such as Infobank, Ariba and Commerce One, as well as ERP vendors such as Oracle, SAP, JD Edwards and Peoplesoft. In addition, several supply chain software vendors have introduced e-procurement systems to their product line. Initially, many of the systems operated primarily through framework agreement catalogues. However, many of the e-procurement application vendors have bought or are building added functionality to their systems. For example, the Ariba system offers both auction and exchange functionality through its purchase of TradingDynamics and Tradex respectively.

One of the key differentiators between the e-procurement systems revolves around the issue of catalogue/content management. Three methods of catalogue management can be identified:

- buyer-maintained
- supplier-maintained
- hosted by third party.

Buyer-maintained catalogue

With a buyer-maintained catalogue, as its name suggests, the catalogue resides on a server at the buying organization, with the buying company responsible for maintaining updates and verifying the accuracy of the data. However, some buy-side catalogue systems allow suppliers to access and update the catalogue (see below).

Supplier-maintained catalogue

There are two main variants of supplier-managed catalogue systems. In the first, suppliers' catalogues are downloaded into the buyer's catalogue. Suppliers are then given access to their catalogue on a staging server, from which they can make any changes. Once these changes have been made, the buying organization publishes the changes in the catalogue from the staging server out to the production databases. The second way in which suppliers can maintain control over their own catalogues is through 'punch out' capability. Buyers can connect directly to suppliers' catalogues over the Internet but they see a personalized view of products and pricing. Data from the suppliers' catalogues are then pulled back into the buyer's application. For example, both IEC Enterprise from Intelisys and Ariba's Buyer software offer this 'punch out' option.

Third-party hosted catalogue (can be partly or fully hosted)

With third-party hosted catalogues, the hosting company is responsible for developing and maintaining a master catalogue of multiple suppliers, products and services. For example, the Ariba Network offers free tools and templates for suppliers to publish a hosted electronic catalogue which is then available to buyers on its network.

Increasingly, access to catalogues is carried out through a combination of the above: a buying organization which uses e-procurement software will increasingly 'punch out' to e-marketplaces and other catalogues held on industry-specific sites and then use the automated procurement tool as a management tool.

Application software providers (ASPs)

Application software providers (ASPs) offer network-based e-commerce applications as a service. The technology platform and software applications are owned and managed by the ASP in a centrally controlled location and then the applications are accessed via a browser over a wide area network (WAN). For example, Commerce One's CSF hosted buy-side solution (which is used with MarketSite, which hosts the supplier catalogues) is available as a browser-based service, giving customers access to the buy-side solution at a fraction of the cost of the licensed software. Similarly, Ariba offers its buy-side software in an ASP edition.

E-supply in practice

INTRODUCTION

At the outset of this chapter, we argued that the Internet can affect procurement and supply chain management in two principal ways: improve operational efficiencies, and/or alter the power structure between buyers and suppliers. However, the evidence from our survey would seem to suggest that the claims made by many business commentators in regard to the Internet transforming all aspects of supply chain management appear to be overblown (Cox et al., 2001a). Only 23 per cent of the organizations surveyed are currently using the Internet to improve aspects of their supply management activities. Indeed, the predominant use of the Internet is as an information-gathering and communication tool. The use of the Internet for procurement and logistics is still at an embryonic stage; it is not currently being used to its maximum potential for managing supply and demand.

In the rest of this chapter we will present some of the major findings from the survey in respect of supply management. In doing so, we will highlight: the current usage of B2B Internet applications; the impact of e-supply strategies on efficiency and/or effectiveness performance gains; and the major problems being faced by e-supply strategy developers.

CURRENT USAGE OF E-MARKETPLACES AND OTHER B2B APPLICATIONS FOR SUPPLY MANAGEMENT

As previously stated, despite the media hype surrounding the supposed benefits, e-marketplaces are not currently widely used. Our survey found that only a third of organizations with e-supply strategies are using them to improve aspects of their supply management activities. This innovation currently appears to be confined to larger organizations in the services and manufacturing sectors. Clearly larger organizations have the market power and entrenched position with suppliers that allows them to innovate with this type of application. It is apparent that small and medium-sized organizations are adopting a 'wait-and-see' attitude. This is not surprising, as it is the larger organizations that have the market power and entrenched position with suppliers that allows them to innovate with this type of application.

Although the usage/take-up of e-marketplaces is relatively low, other B2B applications, such as buy-side software and supply chain software, appear to be more popular. With buy-side software there appears to be a preference for supplier-maintained catalogues (see Figure 12.5).

THE IMPACT OF E-SUPPLY STRATEGIES ON PERFORMANCE

There are major performance benefits that early adopters claim arise from the use of B2B applications as part of an e-supply strategy. These benefits are discussed below under the headings of costs, supply chain efficiency, quality and revenue generation.

Costs

When considering the impact of e-supply strategies on the costs of transactions (Figure 12.6), the major benefits appear to result from the creation of *operational efficiencies*, rather than through an improvement in the relative power of the buyer to achieve reductions in the direct costs of purchases. The efficiencies that are being achieved stem mainly from reductions in the costs of search and from improvements in operational process management.

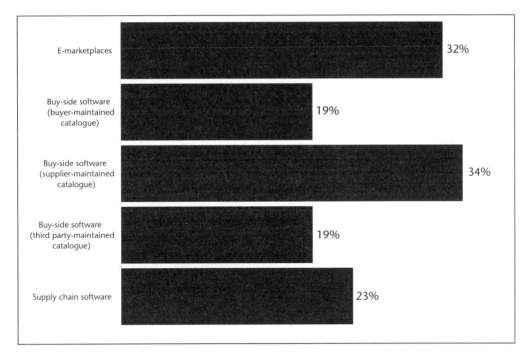

Figure 12.5   *The use of e-business applications by organizations with e-supply strategies*

This is an interesting finding. Despite the high profile of online reverse auction/bidding processes, which have captured the attention of many practitioners for their potential to offer reductions in the costs of purchasing inputs, it is the longer-term benefit of improving transactional processing (internally and externally) that practitioners expect to be most lasting.

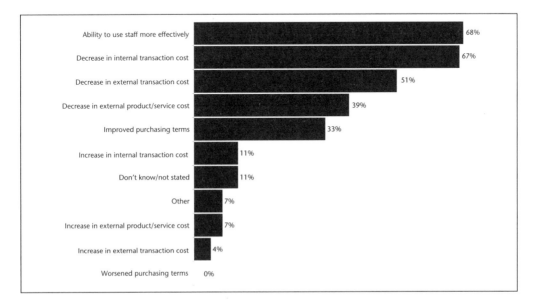

Figure 12.6   *The impact of e-supply strategies on cost*

For those practitioners pursuing 'bottom-line' quick wins, it is worth noting that, once these have been achieved, it is likely that *sustained* benefits will only flow from the full automation and integration of supply chain relationships. This is not to argue that all supply relationships should be developed this way, but that when it is appropriate to do so, this is where the major long-term benefits are likely to be achieved. Furthermore, that 11 per cent of organizations have found that their internal ownership costs have risen using B2B applications, whilst 5 per cent have found their external purchase costs rising, should provide grounds for practitioners to exercise caution in implementing e-supply strategies.

Supply chain efficiency

In terms of achieving supply chain efficiency, the major benefits appear to be increased speed of delivery, reductions in inventory levels, improvements in warehousing practices and improved information flow and demand forecasting (see Figure 12.7).

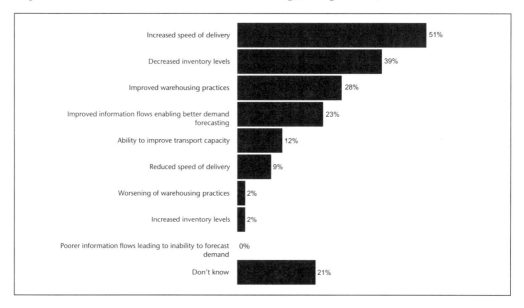

Figure 12.7   *The impact of e-supply strategies on supply chain efficiency*

Despite the obvious benefits being recorded in this area, there are still grounds for caution. Our survey found that 21 per cent of respondents were not able to specify any significant benefits in these areas, 9 per cent reported a decline in cycle time and 2 per cent recorded an increase in inventory levels after implementing e-supply strategies. This indicates that it is not enough to simply adopt this technology; it must be 'fit for purpose' if it is to work effectively.

Quality

In terms of quality improvements, the Internet has had the most marked impact in the areas of increased speed of delivery, access to product information and service innovations (see Figure 12.8).

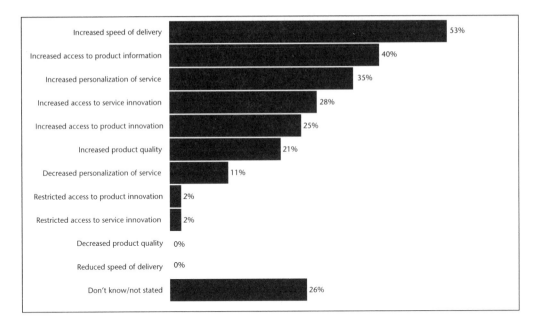

Figure 12.8   *The impact of e-supply strategies on quality*

Revenue generation

It would appear that most respondents are unaware of the direct benefits of the adoption of e-supply strategies for the generation of increased revenue. Indeed, fewer benefits are claimed in this area than in the other performance areas. The key impacts reported were increased access to new markets, increased customer retention and increased sales (see Figure 12.9).

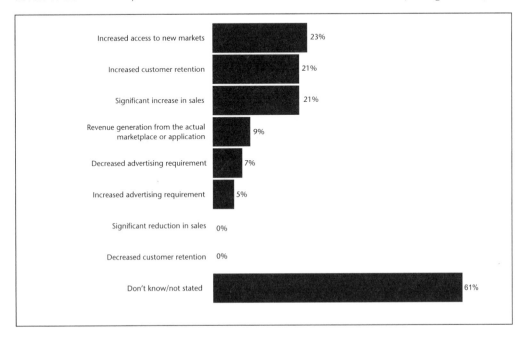

Figure 12.9   *The impact of e-supply strategies on revenue generation*

It is clear that, of the major areas of performance measurement, revenue generation is the least well understood or developed by practitioners on the supply side. Few respondents are aware of the revenue benefits – if any – that arise from the use of their e-supply strategies. At one level this is understandable. Practitioners developing upstream supply-side strategies are often not as closely involved in the downstream relationships in which their organization is involved. The problem is, however, that one of the major benefits claimed for the Internet is that it is supposed to provide the basis for practitioners to fully integrate all aspects of supply chain management – from raw materials to end customers.

THE MAJOR PROBLEMS IN IMPLEMENTING E-SUPPLY STRATEGIES

Despite the clear benefits for improved performance from the adoption of e-supply strategies, there are also a considerable number of difficulties that must be overcome before a successful strategy can be put in place. These include the following.

Systems integration

These include problems such as: connecting to multiple e-marketplaces; integration with legacy systems; more limited scope of use and benefits from the new applications than anticipated; management information more difficult to coordinate; and resistance to implementation for suppliers or trading partners.

Internal politics

These include problems such as: resistance from senior management; lack of understanding from senior management; and resistance to change from the workforce.

Cost constraints

These include problems such as significant additional expenditure being required for IT hardware and software upgrades.

Competence gaps

These include problems such as: an inability to attract or retain staff with the necessary e-business skills; and the need to incur significant costs to train and develop existing staff competencies.

Indeed, evidence from our survey appears to suggest that early adopters are facing many of the above problems, which are preventing them from achieving all the benefits they had anticipated from the adoption of Internet applications. In particular, organizations using e-supply strategies are encountering difficulties with integrating new software into existing IT legacy systems and a lack of clear understanding of the issues involved from senior management.

Conclusion

It is too early to tell whether many of the claims about the use of the Internet in supply management will achieve the benefits claimed for it, or whether it is really only marketing hype. There is evidence on both sides of the argument. We may be witnessing the early adopters' learning curve that will lead on to general and widespread use. Conversely, it could be that

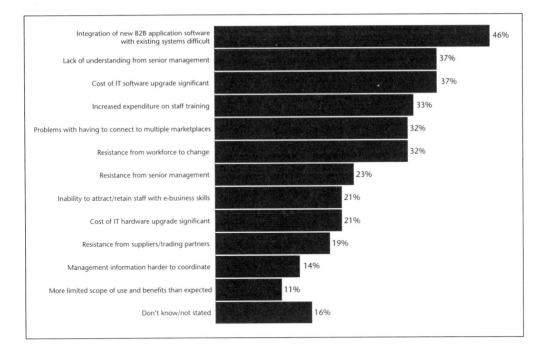

Figure 12.10   *The problems encountered when undertaking e-supply strategies*

many of the early adopters in B2B will eventually start to experience similar problems to those experienced by B2C early adopters, and the currently expected levels of take up in the future will not materialize.

There is also considerable evidence that many e-supply strategies do not appear to take account of the problems that occur when organizations buy credence goods in a marketplace with considerable scope for post-contractual lock-in of the buyer by the application provider. This implies that many e-supply strategies appear to be based on heroic assumptions by hard-pressed practitioners, who do not understand the economic concept of moral hazard, and who often lack truly independent external advice.

A further weakness is related to the problem that organizations do not appear to understand that they must develop an integrated supply chain management approach. Such an approach requires that an e-strategy for both demand and supply management be linked closely with organizational process transformation.

Practitioners must recognize the importance of understanding the power circumstances that they are in. Only when this is the case is it possible for appropriate sourcing strategies to be developed to change the current power circumstances to those that are more conducive to the buyer. When it is not possible to transform the power circumstances, it is essential that buyers manage those that prevail appropriately.

From the research, it is apparent that many practitioners do not fully understand the power circumstances they are in, and they fail therefore to manage exchange relationships appropriately. The discussion in this chapter will, it is hoped, have highlighted a number of important issues that will enable buyers to understand the power circumstances that they are in when using the Internet for procurement and supply management.

Notes

1. This is not a new phenomenon. Before the widespread introduction of Internet technologies, firms used EDI as a mechanism to transfer information and undertake business transactions electronically. However, the cost of obtaining the necessary technology, coupled with the uncertainty regarding standards, meant that EDI was not widely adopted. This contrasts sharply with transactions via the Internet, where these problems are not as significant.
2. Whenever an organization adopts an Internet software application to assist with the management of procurement or supply chain activities, the catch-all phrase 'e-supply strategy' is used to refer to this type of initiative.
3. The research is presented in Cox, A., Chicksand, L. Ireland, P., and Day, M. (2001), *The E-Business Report 2001*, Boston: Earlsgate Press.
4. The importance of effective procurement to the firm is widely overlooked. Whilst significant investments are provided to the sales and marketing function in the hope of attracting more customers and increasing revenues, the procurement function does not always receive equivalent resources. With sales of £100m and costs of £90m, the firm makes £10m profit. To double this profit figure the firm has either to double its turnover or reduce its costs to £80m (11 per cent reduction). These figures demonstrate that investment in the procurement may yield greater returns for the organization.
5. Milgrom, P. and Roberts, J. (1992), *Economics, Organisation and Management*, Englewood Cliffs, NJ: Prentice-Hall.
6. Ibid.
7. These factors are discussed within Cox, A., Sanderson, J. and Watson, G. (2000), *Power Regimes: Mapping the DNA of Business and Supply Chain Relationships*, Boston: Earlsgate Press.
8. Anon. (2000), 'Seller Beware', *The Economist*, 4 March, p. 85.
9. According to Deloitte Research, there are currently 1,400 e-marketplaces in existence. See Grubb, Arthur A. (2000), *B2B Darwinism: How e-Marketplaces Survive (and Succeed)*, London: Deloitte Research, p.1.
10. Schwartz, E., Neel, D. and Grygo, E. (2000), 'New World Economic Order: Internet Auctions, Exchanges Alter Business Landscape', *InfoWorld*, Vol. 22, No. 29, 17 July, pp.1 and 32.
11. King, Julia (2000), 'B-to-B Hard to Spell with XML: E-Commerce Growth May Stall Before Disparate Efforts Yield Concrete Standards', *Computerworld*, Vol. 34, No. 9, 28 February, p. 97.
12. According to Wyld, at least 60 of these consortia e-marketplaces have been announced, representing a combined $3 trillion in annual purchasing expenditure. See, Wyld, David C. (2000), 'The Auction Model: How the Public Sector Can Leverage the Power of E-Commerce Through Dynamic Pricing', Grant Report for the PricewaterhouseCoopers Endowment for the Business of Government, p. 25.
13. Idapta, (2001), *Using the Internet to Gain Strategic Advantage*, White Paper, Atlanta: Idapta Inc., p. 6.

References

Anon. (2000), 'Seller Beware', *The Economist*, 4 March, p. 85.
Bailey, J.P. and Bakos, J.Y. (1997), 'An Exploratory Study of the Emerging Role of Electronic Intermediaries', *International Journal of Electronic Commerce*, Vol. 1, No. 2, Spring, pp. 7–20.
Benjamin, R. and Wigand, R. (1995), 'Electronic Markets and Virtual Value Chains on the Information Highway', *Sloan Management Review*, Winter, pp. 62–72.
Cox, A. (1999a), 'Power, Value and Supply Chain Management', *Supply Chain Management*, Vol. 4, No. 4, pp. 167–75.
Cox, A. (1999b), 'Improving Procurement and Supply Competence', in Lamming, R. and Cox, A. (eds), *Strategic Procurement Management: Concepts and Cases*, Boston: Earlsgate Press.
Cox, A. (2001), 'The Power Perspective in Procurement and Supply Management', *Journal of Supply Chain Management*, Vol. 32, special edition.

Cox, A., Chicksand, L., Ireland, P. and Day, M. (2001a), *The E-Business Report 2001*, Boston: Earlsgate Press.

Cox, A. et al. (2001b), *Supply Chains, Markets and Power: Strategies for Appropriating Value*, London: Routledge.

Cox, A., Sanderson, J. and Watson, G. (2000), *Power Regimes: Mapping the DNA of Business and Supply Chain Relationships*, Boston: Earlsgate Press.

Daniel, E. and Klimis, G. (1999), 'The Impact of Electronic Commerce on Market Structure: An Evaluation of the Electronic Market Hypothesis', *European Management Journal*, Vol. 17, No. 3, pp. 318–25.

Evans, P. and Wurster, T. (1999), *Blown to Bits*, Boston, MA: Harvard Business School Press.

Gellman, R. (1996), 'Disintermediation and the Internet', *Government Information Quarterly*, Vol. 13, No. 1, pp. 1–8.

Grubb, A. (2000), *B2B Darwinism: How E-Marketplaces Survive (and Succeed)*, London: Deloitte Research.

Hagel, J. and Singer, M. (1999), *Net Worth: Shaping Markets when Customers Make the Rules*, Boston, MA: Harvard Business School Press.

Hagel, J. and Rayport, M. (1997), 'The New Infomediaries', *McKinsey Quarterly*, Vol. 4.

Kaplan, S. and Sawhney, M. (2000), 'E-Hubs: The New B2B Marketplaces', *Harvard Business Review*, May–June, pp. 97–103.

King, J. (2000), 'B-to-B Hard to Spell with XML: E-Commerce Growth May Stall Before Disparate Efforts Yield Concrete Standards', *Computerworld*, Vol. 34, No. 9, 28 February, p. 97.

Lewis, T. (1997), *The Friction-Free Economy: Marketing Strategies for a Wired World*, New York: Harper Business.

Milgrom, P. and Roberts, J. (1992), *Economics, Organisation and Management*, Englewood Cliffs, NJ: Prentice-Hall.

Sarkar, M. et al. (1996), 'Intermediaries and Cybermediaries: A Continuing Role For Mediating Players in the Electronic Marketplace', *Journal of Computer Mediated Communication*, Vol. 1, No. 3.

Schwartz, E., Neel, D. and Grygo, E. (2000), 'New World Economic Order: Internet Auctions, Exchanges Alter Business Landscape', *Infoworld*, Vol. 22, No. 29, 17 July.

Vandermerwe, S. (1999), 'The Electronic "Go-between Service Provider": A New "Middle" Role Taking Centre Stage', *European Management Journal*, Vol. 17, No. 6, pp. 598–608.

Wyld, D.C. (2000), 'The Auction Model: How the Public Sector Can Leverage the Power of E-Commerce Through Dynamic Pricing', Grant Report for the PricewaterhouseCoopers Endowment for the Business of Government.

13 *Purchasing and knowledge management*

Richard Hall

The nature and characteristics of knowledge

Knowledge management (KM) is a hot topic at the start of the third millennium not only because recent advances in information technology (IT) and information communication systems (ICS) allow us to process data and communicate information with increasing ease, but also because the knowledge content of the products and services which we produce and consume is increasingly significant. It is probable that the life span of the literature devoted to KM will be limited; the lifecycle will be defined by the time it takes for the language and perspective associated with the subject to be 'internalized', that is, to be widely accepted and incorporated implicitly in management practice.

What do we mean by data, information, knowledge and knowledge management? Data are facts, for example the number of fixed-line telephones in London. Information is data with added value, for example the fixed-line telephones in London categorized by private and business usage and arranged in the alphabetical sequence of the owners' names.

The rapid advances in IT and ICS in recent years has resulted in much attention being given to information management, to groupware, intranets, extranets, and so on. Whilst information management is a significant component of knowledge management, it will not be treated in depth in this chapter. Knowledge is more difficult to define than data and information; most authors suggest that it is a mixture of information and experience. In this chapter we define knowledge as including all the factors which have the potential to influence human thought and behaviour and which allow the explanation, prediction and sometimes control of physical phenomena. This is a very broad definition; it includes factors which range from skills and intuition to organizational culture and codified theory.

The KM literature has resulted in a widespread acceptance of two types of knowledge: tacit knowledge and explicit knowledge. The significance of the concept of tacit knowledge was first identified by Polanyi (1948). Tacit knowledge is acquired by experience, by learning by doing. It is the sort of knowledge a young child has of speech. Children learn to speak by copying their parents, siblings and friends; they become fluent without acquiring the knowledge of orthodox sentence construction and concepts such as subject, object, verb, and so on. Tacit knowledge is not codified, it cannot be communicated in a 'language', it is acquired by shared experiences, by observation and imitation. Before the early Middle Ages the knowledge of music could only be acquired by experience – one had to hear the tune. In the early Middle Ages the code, or language, of the bass and treble clef notation system was devised and after that the knowledge of music could be communicated easily to many people over large distances. Tacit knowledge may be held by an individual or it may be diffused throughout an organization. An organization's culture is an example of diffused tacit knowledge. When new employees join a firm they are not given a manual which codifies the organization's culture, which defines 'The way we do things around here', yet by observation and imitation they will rapidly assimilate the culture if they want to belong. This is an example of the rapid diffusion of tacit knowledge from a group to individuals.

Explicit knowledge, unlike tacit knowledge, can be embodied in a code, or a language, and as a consequence it can be communicated easily. The code may be words, numbers, or symbols such as those used in the notation system to capture the knowledge of music. There is not a dichotomy between tacit and explicit knowledge; rather there is a spectrum of knowledge types with tacit at one extreme and explicit at the other. In the natural science paradigm knowledge progresses from personal tacit knowledge, through generalizations and taxonomies, to models and metaphors and ultimately to theories which have the power to predict the outcome of previously unexperienced phenomena. Whilst this conceptualization implies that explicit knowledge is in some way superior to tacit knowledge, in contrast Polanyi (1948) claims that we know more than we can say, and Boisot (1995) agrees by suggesting that when tacit knowledge is 'externalized', that is, taken out of the person, the knowledge is compressed and something is lost. It is possible to argue that, whilst the former view applies to natural sciences, the latter applies to social sciences where the complex richness of human behaviour cannot be fully captured in code.

Knowledge which is new to an organization either has to be invented internally or acquired from external sources. This new knowledge may add to, complement or substitute the existing knowledge base. New knowledge may be categorized as being either *additive*, or *substitutive*. A child's new knowledge of long division in a decimal system adds to its existing knowledge of simple division, a trainee programmer's new knowledge of the binary system involves substituting the existing knowledge of the decimal system with a completely different knowledge system, a difficult and therefore potentially risky experience. The substitution of old knowledge with different new knowledge is described by Nooteboom (1996) as a process of discontinuous learning, a process of *learning to do better, that is, different, things* as opposed to the process of continuous learning, a process of *learning to do things better*.

Knowledge management has been defined by Davenport and Prusack (1998) as being to do with the creation, sharing and application of knowledge in a given context. Creating new knowledge may involve incremental innovation, which proceeds in small steps, or it may involve radical innovation, which involves significant changes in practice due to the new knowledge replacing the old. Sharing knowledge involves not only motivating the owners of the knowledge to divulge what they know, but also motivating the intended recipients of the new knowledge to accept it and apply it. Davenport and Prusack (1998) suggest that there are three reasons why a knowledge worker would share knowledge:

1   for reasons of esteem, i.e. to be well thought of
2   for reasons of exchange, i.e. in anticipation of reciprocation
3   for reasons of altruism.

Snowden (2000) suggests that, for new knowledge to be accepted and applied, the following conditions should, if possible, apply:

• The new knowledge should relate to previous experience.

- The new knowledge should legitimize previous experience but identify new potential by changing the recipient's perspective.
- The new knowledge should be presented in a descriptive, not prescriptive, form.

One of the key senior management roles in the knowledge company is to provide an environment which will facilitate both the giving and the receiving of knowledge. In the context of a single company this is not an easy task. When the context is moved to that of inter-company giving and receiving of knowledge it becomes even more difficult. We will see later that this task is made easier when the companies in question have a trusting partnership relationship.

It is appropriate to summarize the concepts introduced thus far:

- *Data* are facts.
- *Information* is facts with value added.
- *Knowledge* comes from information and experience.
- *Tacit knowledge* is uncodified and is acquired by experience.
- *Explicit knowledge* is codified and can be communicated quickly to large numbers of people over large distances – it is essentially the same as information.
- New knowledge may be *additive*, i.e. the same as existing knowledge.
- New knowledge may be *substitutive*, i.e. different to existing knowledge and necessitating the unlearning of the old knowledge base.
- Knowledge management is about *creating, sharing and applying* knowledge in a *given context*.

The resource-based view

It can be argued that KM is a natural extension of the 'resource-based view' (RBV) of the firm and it is therefore appropriate to digress briefly to introduce the concepts of the RBV. For many years the strategic literature was dominated by economists who took a 'top-down' or 'outside-in' view of the way firms and sectors behaved. The famous Boston Consulting Group Matrix analysis suggested that firms should try to achieve a dominant market share in high-growth sectors. This self-evident truth did not help practitioners who were not in those situations; these practitioners were concerned with doing the best they could with the resources at their disposal. Their challenge was to identify the resources which gave them an advantage today and the resources which might give them an advantage in the future. At the end of the 1980s and the start of the 1990s the 'outside-in' perspective was balanced by an 'inside-out' perspective; this is the RBV. It is not a case of the earlier perspective being wrong and the latter right; both are needed. The RBV may be neatly illustrated with the following story:

> In the 1970s the M.D. of a small British manufacturing company decided it was time to export to Europe. He called his management team together and asked 'Can anyone speak any language other than English?' One manager replied that he could speak Spanish. 'Right,' said the M.D. 'We're going into Spain.' (Anon.)

Prahalad and Hamel (1990) in a seminal article suggested that products which meet customers' requirements are the result of firms' competencies and that the ultimate competitive arena is concerned not with products but with competencies. They suggested that core competencies usually take a long time to acquire and that, if they are to be sustainable, they should be difficult for competitors to identify and copy. It can be argued that in an age when new technology can have a major impact on a firm's operations, a resource-based perspective is appropriate so that new technology may be recognized and harnessed as soon as it becomes available. It should also be noted that a collection of competencies is of little use if there is no 'background competence' which facilitates the integration of the individual competencies in order to add the required value.

The following quotation from Nooteboom (1996) captures the essence of the RBV perspective:

> the firm is made up from a number of competencies, based on resources, embodied in a configuration of various forms of capital (financial, human, social), which to a greater or lesser extent is idiosyncratic to the firm. It is such unique capabilities of firms that allow them a basis for profit.

It is often the case that the valuation which a stock market puts on a company's shares exceeds the net worth as stated on the balance sheet by a factor of four or five. This means that between three-quarters and four-fifths of the total value of a firm is due to factors which are off the balance sheet, we will call these factors 'intangible resources'. In earlier research Hall (1992) established that many chief executive officers (CEOs) believe that the three most important intangible resources are reputation, employee know-how and organizational culture. These key intangible resources are all knowledge-based: reputation is a mix of diffused tacit and explicit knowledge, know-how is clearly knowledge-based; and, as we have seen, organizational culture is diffused tacit knowledge. It follows therefore that knowledge, in one form or another, usually accounts for the bulk of the value of a firm. Grant (1997, p. 451) suggests that the 'resource-based view of the firm' can be reconceptualized as a 'knowledge-based view of the firm' which he describes as follows:

> If individuals must specialise in knowledge acquisition and if producing goods and services requires the application of many types of knowledge, production must be organised so as to assemble these many types of knowledge while preserving specialisation by individuals. The firm is an institution which exists to resolve this dilemma: it permits individuals to specialise in developing specialised expertise, while establishing mechanisms through which individuals co-ordinate to integrate their different knowledge bases in the transformation of inputs into outputs.

The integrating mechanisms which Grant refers to are similar to the 'background competence' described above.

KM analysis models

The definition of knowledge given earlier included factors such as skills, intuition, organizational culture, reputation and codified theory. All the factors contained within the definition may be placed on a spectrum of knowledge which runs from tacit (uncodified) knowledge at one extreme to explicit (codified) knowledge at the other (see Figure 13.1).

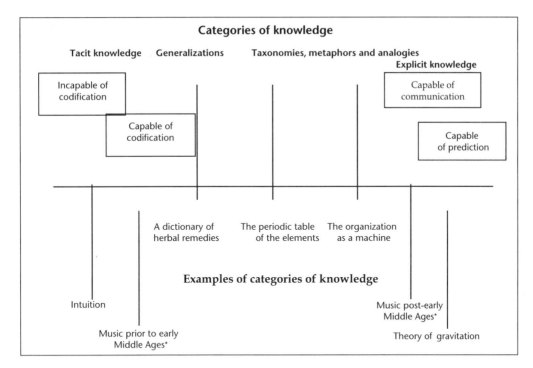

*Until the system of bass and treble clef notation was devised the knowledge of music could only be
  acquired by direct experience.

Figure 13.1   *The knowledge spectrum*

The historical development of many disciplines, such as medicine and engineering, can be
traced as a progression along the knowledge spectrum from tacit to explicit knowledge. Much
medical knowledge, especially that to do with alternative medicine, is still of a tacit nature: we
know that camomile tea is good for an upset stomach but we don't know why. This may not
matter until the camomile treatment is mixed with some other remedy with which it has an
adverse reaction. If we had known why the camomile tea treatment worked we might have
been able to predict the adverse reaction. Tacit knowledge, acquired by experience, allows the
prediction of previously experienced phenomena; whereas codified theory, as exemplified by
natural science, enables the prediction of previously unexperienced phenomena.

The disadvantages of tacit knowledge are clear and most organizations strive to make
explicit the bulk of the knowledge they possess so that:

- the organization is not vulnerable to knowledge being lost when employees leave and take
  their personal knowledge with them;
- the knowledge which the organization possesses can be disseminated to large numbers of
  employees over large distances and used in a wide range of applications;
- theory exists which allows the simulation and operation of 'what if' scenarios and which
  will indicate appropriate corrective action to be taken when things go wrong.

If a large explicit knowledge base is the source of competitive advantage, as it is with many
global companies, then there is a clear need to protect, where possible, that knowledge base
with intellectual property rights and other legal devices.

Notwithstanding the advantages of operating with a largely explicit knowledge base there are certain disadvantages associated with operating with the resultant small tacit knowledge base. Whilst a small tacit knowledge base renders the firm safe from employees walking away with their personal knowledge, the firm may be vulnerable due to the ease with which competitors can identify and copy the predominantly explicit knowledge base. We can describe two types of strategic vulnerability:

- *Internal vulnerability* exists when a large tacit knowledge/small explicit knowledge base renders the firm vulnerable to employees walking away with irreplaceable knowledge.
- *External vulnerability* exists when a large explicit/small tacit knowledge base renders the firm vulnerable to being copied by competitors.

It can be argued that the knowledge which underpins a sustainable distinctive competence will often have a high undiffused tacit knowledge content, because if it were diffused it would not be distinctive; if it were explicit it would have the potential to leak away and cease to be sustainable. We will see later on that this situation can explain why it is sensible to enter into a partnership relationship so that the tacit knowledge bases which underpin distinctive competencies can be shared and enhanced.

As with many management issues there is no right answer to the question of how much effort to invest in the codification of accumulated tacit knowledge; it all depends on circumstances. The R&D director of a leading manufacturer of powered garden equipment suggested that the issue of codification was a typical trade-off situation. Codification facilitated communication with geographically separated plants but at the expense of speed of action and flexibility within the R&D unit.

The model of knowledge space shown in Figure 13.2 is derived from Boisot (1995) and Nonaka (1994).

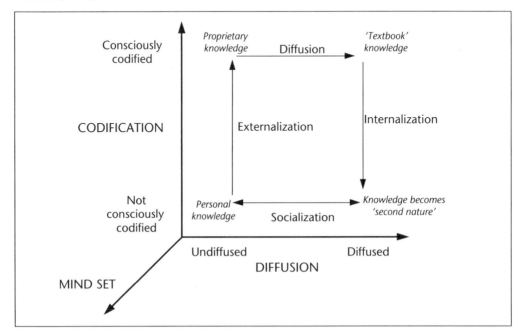

Figure 13.2   *Knowledge space*

Externalization describes the codification of tacit knowledge – the transformation of knowledge from tacit to explicit. Nonaka (1994, p. 20) describes the process of *externalization* as involving:

> the sophisticated use of metaphors ... used to enable team members to articulate their own perspectives, and thereby reveal hidden tacit knowledge that is otherwise hard to communicate.

In the case of music, externalization describes the process a composer goes through when she captures a tune on 'sheet music'. It should be noted that the musical codification system allows not only the easy communication of the knowledge 'at a distance', it also allows the composition of music which, without the codification system, could not be created – for example, a symphony.

Diffusion describes the process of disseminating codified knowledge by means of a code, or language. In the case of music, 'sheet music' not only allows rapid dissemination, it also allows musicians to coordinate the composer's knowledge of a symphony when they play together as an orchestra.

Internalization describes the learning by doing which embeds the explicit knowledge so that it becomes 'second nature' at which point one has lost the need to refer consciously to the explicit knowledge base – it has re-entered the tacit domain; this is what Polanyi (1948) called 'subsidiary knowledge'. A concert pianist internalizes both the conscious control of the fingers and the explicit knowledge contained in the code on the 'sheet music'.

Socialization describes the process of communicating and enhancing tacit knowledge. A child learning to speak its first language by imitation and observation is an example of 'one-to-one ' transmission of tacit knowledge. An individual assimilating an organization's culture is an example of 'many-to-one' transmission of tacit knowledge. The transmission of tacit knowledge is usually a time-consuming process requiring frequent physical proximity and the development of trust. Folk music has traditionally been transmitted, and enhanced, by shared experience; and some would argue that capturing the knowledge of folk music on 'sheet music' is to put it into a straitjacket which may inhibit further development.

Discontinuous learning, that is, moving along the 'mind set' axis will involve, at the least, new substitutive knowledge replacing old knowledge, and at the most a paradigm shift.

The model of knowledge space shown in Figure 13.2 can inform our understanding of why different trading relationships are appropriate in different circumstances. The circumstances are defined by the nature of the knowledge associated with the transaction.

The rationale for placing the four different relationships as shown in Figure 13.3 is as follows:

- *Partnership* Vollmann, Cordon and Raabe (1995) suggest that the prime candidates for partnership status are the companies which make the greatest contribution to the distinctive competencies of the purchasing organization. A fundamental reason therefore for a partnership relationship is that the partners can create a new joint capability due to their collaboration which they would not be able to create if they were not collaborating. If the new joint capability is to be developed from existing capabilities which are underpinned with tacit knowledge, then these tacit knowledge bases will be best shared and enhanced by a process of socialization involving frequent physical proximity, shared experiences and the development of trust – in other words, a partnership relationship.

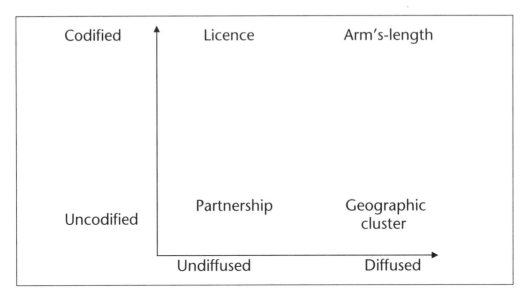

Figure 13.3   *Trading relationships placed in knowledge space*

- *Licence*   Explicit knowledge which is undiffused and held proprietarily, for example, protected by intellectual property rights, allows the owner of the property to license the knowledge to a licensee.
- *Arm's-length*   When the knowledge associated with a transaction is clearly specified and universally understood, for example buying steel pipe or foreign currency, then there is little point in operating on anything other than an arm's-length basis.
- *Geographic clustering*   Nooteboom (1996) suggests that the geographic clustering of expert firms may be explained by the need for the firms to exchange and enhance their tacit knowledge bases; they need to be geographically close so that frequent physical proximity is possible.

The management of external resources

Malone (1999) suggests that the impact of information communication technology in recent years has been to move the efficient boundary of the firm so that it is increasingly appropriate for many large firms to outsource non-core activities. Whilst in sales terms, firms which have outsourced have not become smaller, in terms of the operations which they carry out internally, they have become smaller. As a consequence there has been a reduction in the variety of operations carried out within the firm. If firms are considered as systems (Senge, 1990), then it can be argued that Ashby's Law of Requisite Variety (Ashby, 1956) will apply. Stacey (1993, p. 125) explains Ashby's Law as follows:

> the huge variety of disturbances presented by the environment must be neutralised by a huge number of responses such that the outcome can match the one desirable state selected in advance that will fit the environment. In order to be able to do this … the number of potential responses must match the number of potential disturbances so that they can cancel each other out and produce the desired outcome.

If the variety of a firm's internal operations has been reduced due to outsourcing and if the external variety of its supply markets and sales markets, that is, its environment, has increased, how is the resulting imbalance in variety to be corrected? Does the firm's network, not the firm, become the system which contains the requisite variety? If the network is to replace the firm as the unit of analysis, perhaps we should be concerned with a knowledge-based view of the network. In describing the functioning of the Toyota network of suppliers, Dyer and Nobeoka (2000, p. 365) suggest that:

> the notion of a dynamic learning capability that creates competitive advantage needs to be extended beyond firm boundaries. Indeed, if the network can create a strong identity and co-ordinating roles, then it will be superior to the firm as an organisational form at creating and re-combining knowledge owing to the diversity of knowledge that resides within a network.

Toyota's need to manage external sources of knowledge, to access the *diversity* of knowledge which resides within the network, resonates strongly with the Law of Requisite Variety argument given above. A major challenge which faces senior managers therefore concerns the management of the external resources, especially the resource of knowledge, which can affect all the firm's fundamental processes.

The management of network knowledge

It has been suggested that most important resources are knowledge-based; the challenge involved in managing network resources therefore is to manage all sources of relevant knowledge, external as well as internal. This will involve deciding what sort of knowledge is relevant, then locating, accessing, acquiring and applying it.

Research carried out by the author in the financial services and telecommunications sectors in the UK suggests that the approach outlined below can be productive.

With respect to relevance it is appropriate to ask 'Relevant to what?'. This question may be answered by identifying the processes which are key to the business and then giving nominated managers the job of identifying the sources of knowledge which can affect each process favourably. Examples of processes which might be identified as being fundamental to the business are:

- developing new products
- winning customers' orders
- fulfilling customers' orders
- after-sales service
- managing treasury
- strategizing
- and so on.

The organization's structure may be aligned with the processes outlined above and 'process owners' may be formally appointed, or the 'process owner' concept may overlay the traditional functional structure. Each 'process owner' (formally or informally appointed) may be given the job of locating, accessing, acquiring and applying the new knowledge which is relevant to his/her process. The purchasing professional should be ideally placed to be the process owner for the 'fulfilling customers' orders' process, which is essentially a definition of supply chain management; he or she should also be able to contribute to other processes, and indeed it can be argued that if the management of external resources is to be assigned to one person only, then the purchasing professional should be a strong contender.

Once a process for identifying the relevant sources of knowledge has been established, all concerned must understand the issues which need to be addressed with respect to the application of new knowledge. These are outlined below.

Applying new knowledge may be thought of as bridging a gap between the current 'platform' knowledge and the required 'target' knowledge. Bridging a knowledge gap may involve using knowledge from three sources; see Figure 13.4.

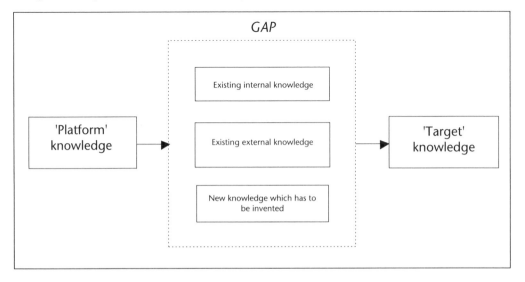

Figure 13.4   *Bridging a knowledge gap*

Bridging the gap with existing knowledge will involve identifying the communities which have the current knowledge and those which need the required knowledge. It will probably be necessary to modify existing knowledge in terms not only of who has it, but also in terms of its nature. Is it currently tacit? Does it need to be explicit? Managing the knowledge needed to bridge the gap will therefore involve the processes identified in an earlier section:

- *Externalization* (codifying tacit knowledge) may involve collecting data, creating information and creating new theory by establishing cause-and-effect relationships which allow simulation.
- *Diffusion* (spreading the 'word' to those who need it) can involve IT and ICS such as groupware, intranets and extranets.
- *Internalization* (making the knowledge second nature) is largely concerned with training and learning by doing.
- *Socialization* (communicating and enhancing tacit knowledge by means of shared experience usually involving the development of trust) means engaging in relevant shared experience. It can, in some circumstances, be the most important KM process.

If new knowledge needs to be acquired and applied, it is appropriate to ascertain the degree to which it is additive or substitutive. If a large amount of substitutive knowledge is required and the consequences of failing to unlearn the old and learn the new are serious, then a risk 'hot spot' has been identified.

The basic arguments which have been presented in this chapter may be summarized as follows. As new technologies appear with bewildering frequency, a resource-based view is needed so that all the knowledge and technology which can deliver benefits to customers in the future can be identified and harnessed wherever it is held; managers will be required to determine how developing technologies can affect all the business's processes. This may require new relationships between the marketing function and other functions, or between the different 'process owners'. Whatever organizational form the firm implements, the purchasing professional will be a strong candidate for the role of 'manager of external resources' by virtue of his/her skill at identifying new sources of supply and managing ongoing relationships. If the purchasing professional is to hold down this new role he/she will need to be conversant with the concepts and techniques of KM so that the fundamental resource of knowledge can be effectively managed.

References

Ashby, W.R. (1956), *Introduction to Cybernetics*, New York: John Wiley.

Boisot, M.H. (1995), *Information Space: A Framework for Learning in Organisations, Institutions and Culture*, London: Routledge.

Davenport, T.H. and Prusack, L. (1998), *Working Knowledge*, Harvard, MA: Harvard Business School Press.

Dyer, J.H. and Nobeoka, K. (2000), 'Creating and Managing a High-performance Knowledge Sharing Network: The Toyota Case', *Strategic Management Journal*, Vol. 21, pp. 345–67.

Grant, R.M. (1997), 'The Knowledge Based View of the Firm: Implications for Management Practice', *Long Range Planning*, June, p. 451.

Hall, R. (1992). 'The Strategic Analysis of Intangible Resources', *The Strategic Management Journal*, Vol. 13, pp. 135–44.

Malone, T.W. (1999), 'Mastering Information Management', *Financial Times*, 1 March.

Nonaka, I. (1994). 'A Dynamic Theory of Organisational Knowledge Creation', *Organisation Science*, Vol. 5, No. 1, pp. 14–37.

Nooteboom, B. (1996), 'Globalisation, Learning and Strategy', *EMOT Workshop*, Durham University, 28–30 June.

Polanyi, M. (1948), *Personal Knowledge: Towards a Post-Critical Philosophy*, Chicago: University of Chicago Press.

Porter, M.E. (1985), *Competitive Advantage*, New York: Free Press.

Prahalad, C.K. and Hamel, G. (1990), 'The Core Competence of the Corporation', *Harvard Business Review*, May–June, pp. 79–90.

Senge, P.M. (1990), *The Fifth Discipline: the Art & Practice of the Learning Organization*, New York: Doubleday.

Snowden, D. (2000), Workshop on 'Organisational Networks as Distributed Systems of Knowledge', ISUFI, University of Lecce, Italy, 2–5 July.

Stacey, R.D. (1993), *Strategic Management and Organisational Dynamics*, London: Pitman Publishing.

Vollmann, T.E., Cordon, C. and Raabe, H. (1995), 'Supply Chain Management', *Financial Times Supplement*, 29 December, pp. 13–14.

14 *Purchasing and 'green' issues*

Barbara Morton

Introduction

The profile of purchasing and supply management within organizations has been raised in recent years (Gattorna and Walters, 1996; van Weele, 1994) and purchasing is increasingly regarded as a strategic function within organizations. The traditional model of purchasing has been replaced by one in which purchasing and supply managers are recognized as having a wider and more significant role in delivering strategic objectives.

In parallel with this development in purchasing there has been a growth in concern for the environment in which corporations operate (New et al., 2000). Organizations have begun to address their own environmental performance and, increasingly, to examine the impacts associated with both bought-in goods and services and the environmental performance of their suppliers. As corporations become more concerned with sustainability and the 'triple bottom line', the potential influence of purchasing and supply management is likely to increase.

Is environment relevant to purchasing and supply management?

Environmental management is now firmly on the corporate agenda as well as being reflected in the policies and practices of governments at both national and local level. In response to key drivers such as environmental regulation at a global and local scale, organizations have begun to address their environmental responsibilities. This trend can be traced through the growth of certification to environmental management systems – notably ISO 14001, the International Standard and the European Eco-Management and Auditing Scheme (EMAS). Even without such standards, organizations increasingly recognize that their own environmental performance is closely linked to that of their suppliers.

For some, purchasing follows the lead set by environmental specialists and, in other cases, purchasing and supply managers have been proactive in seizing the opportunities offered by adoption of good environmental practices. In the absence of clearly defined and accepted methodologies, those organizations that led the way in environmental purchasing had to develop their own policies and practices. Early adopters of environmental supply chain management included those companies for whom bought-in goods and services accounted for a very large proportion of expenditure (BT, 1993; Gillett, 1993; IBM, 1995). Since then, a number of companies have developed approaches to the management of environmental performance from a supply chain perspective (B&Q, 1995, 1998; Green et al., 1996, 1998; Lamming et al., 1996).

Environmental purchasing is now being adopted throughout the world, across many industrial and commercial sectors and at a variety of scales (Russel, 1998). In the UK, Business in the Environment (BiE) and the Chartered Institute of Purchasing and Supply (CIPS) have published material which highlights the shift that has taken place in environmental supply chain management from a novelty in the early 1990s to a mainstream activity today (CIPS/BiE, 1993; CIPS, 1995; CIPS/BiE, 1997; BiE, 2000a). This guidance can assist those looking to develop tools and techniques for their own organizations. Corporate approaches to key elements of environmental purchasing have been discussed and developed over recent years (Noci, 1997; Lamming et al., 2000).

In the USA, the Environmentally Preferable Purchasing Program provides evidence of recent corporate activity (http://www.epa.gov/oppintr). The green supply chain work of the United States–Asia Environmental Partnership demonstrates how environmental supply chain management is now on the agenda of corporations worldwide (http://www.usaep.org).

In the UK, where the Greening Government initiative is under way, the Department of the Environment, Transport and the Regions (DETR) has produced a *Green Guide for Buyers* which outlines the rationale and provides guidance on environmental purchasing practice. (http://www.environment.detr.gov.uk/greening/greenpro/ggbp1.htm).

There are now many examples of good practice in public authorities and municipalities such as that of Santa Monica, California (http://www.epa.gov/oppintr/epp/santa.pdf) and those participating in BIG-NET – a network of municipal purchasers in Europe (http://www.iclei.org). The activity of UK local authorities is also well documented (Warner and Ryall, 2001), with Belfast City Council being especially proactive in the field (Murray, 2000). In the education sector the environmental purchasing activity at Rutgers University has recently been documented and illustrates an effective approach (Lyons, 2000).

Environmental purchasing is not without difficulties of a very practical nature, however. Purchasers have often found themselves wrestling with questions such as:

• What is a 'greener' product or service?
• How can we determine 'greener' alternatives?
• What information is available on 'greener' products and services?
• Are these products and services independently certified?
• Should we aim to buy from 'greener' suppliers?
• What techniques can be used to assess environmental probity in the supply chain?
• Does 'greener' purchasing conflict with achieving cost reduction targets?
• Does greener purchasing imply reduced quality standards?

The relevance and validity of these concerns vary between organizations. Individual environmental purchasing initiatives such as a 'buy recycled' programme may satisfy one organization's requirements, while others need to implement a comprehensive set of environmental practices to deal with everything from the hazardous material content of specific products to continuous environmental improvement throughout the supply chain.

Effective environmental purchasing therefore requires that companies and organizations should be clear as to their own environmental management priorities and how these relate to both goods and services bought in and the environmental performance of suppliers. For this an environmental purchasing strategy is required. This in turn will be most effective and most meaningful when formulated and operated as part of an organization-wide environmental strategy.

Why have an environmental strategy?

Environmental purchasing strategies are in many cases part of a wider environmental strategy developed to address a range of activities and operations. The major drivers of environmental activity within companies and organizations include:

- *Environmental regulation and legislation*   Legislation covers diverse aspects of operations, including emissions to the atmosphere, discharges to water, noise, waste and waste management. Recent European Union (EU) Environmental Action Plans, for example, have reflected a move towards greater use of market and financial instruments, such as landfill taxes.
- *Customer pressure*   Companies increasingly need to respond to customers' environmental demands – often communicated through supplier selection and appraisal systems. The threat of de-listing and consequent loss of business represents a major driver.
- *Investors*   Major investors are beginning to take account of the environmental performance of companies, mirroring the move towards corporate responsibility and 'sustainability' reporting.
- *Insurers*   Companies with good environmental track records will be able to secure insurance more easily and at lower cost by reducing their potential liabilities from spillages, leaks and other uncontrolled events and the costs of contaminated land remediation.
- *Competitors*   Customer demands for environmentally 'preferred' good and services result in competitive advantage for companies able to meet these needs. The effect of environmental benchmarking and perceptions of environmental performance among competitors can be traced in initiatives such as Business in the Environment's *Index of Corporate Environmental Engagement* in the UK which began in the mid-1990s (BiE,1996; BiE, 2000b).
- *Community and other stakeholders*   The general public and other stakeholders are increasingly concerned with the impact of corporate activity on the environment at a global as well as a local scale.

Developing environmental management systems

The response of many companies has been to adopt an environmental management system (such as ISO 14001 or EMAS) which places on them a responsibility to address the environmental probity of their suppliers, although this requirement has been interpreted in many different ways. Hence we can trace a variety of approaches amongst organizations.

The most effective approaches to environmental purchasing are likely to be:

- integrated with the organization-wide environmental strategy
- backed by senior level commitment and the allocation of responsibilities
- well communicated throughout the organization
- supported by clear objectives and targets
- 'owned' by those responsible for delivering them.

In addition, in the more successful cases:

- the roles of internal customers as well as purchasers are defined and understood
- results are included in reports
- savings are used to stimulate further actions.

Developing an environmental purchasing strategy

Purchasing and supply management professionals who are members of The Chartered Institute of Purchasing and Supply (of which there are 30,000 worldwide) have recently been provided with an environmental policy document which urges them to recognize and embrace the lead role they can play in the process (CIPS, 2000).

The content of an organization's environmental purchasing strategy should reflect the organization's overall environmental strategy and objectives. These objectives will vary according to the nature of the business, its supply chain relationships and the environmental pressures and opportunities affecting the business. Those developing strategies and polices for purchasing need to bear in mind factors such as:

- organizational arrangements for purchasing – centralized or devolved, for example
- the size and buying power of the organization
- the degree of influence of the organization in its major markets
- public sector constraints on purchasing – where these are relevant.

Where an environmental purchasing policy does not exist (or where an overall environmental policy and strategy are absent) purchasing professionals and others may need to make a case for adopting such a policy. Environmental purchasing is a mainstream issue because it is associated with the following.

SECURING SUPPLY OF GOODS AND SERVICES

Figure 14.1 shows the potential impact of various pressures on the purchasing process and on security of supply. Threats can be posed from the elimination of certain substances through regulation, for example. Purchasers must know of the potential implications for supply in time to source alternative materials or to ensure that existing suppliers can continue to meet their needs.

Suppliers can be affected by regulation and they may also come under pressure from customers to improve their environmental performance. Failure to make the necessary improvements may result in loss of business or even business failure. Thus environmental pressure in one part of the supply chain has ramifications for suppliers and customers elsewhere.

MINIMIZING BUSINESS RISK

Business risks are posed to companies through the operations of their suppliers and contractors – where contractors are in breach of environmental regulations, for example. Poor performance on the part of suppliers can result in unwelcome media coverage for major corporations. Organizations cannot outsource their environmental responsibilities, so

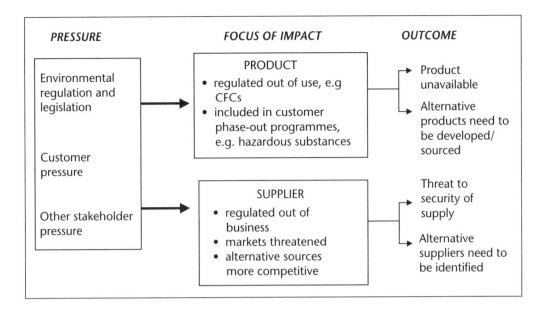

Figure 14.1 *Securing supply of good and services*

purchasers need to understand the environmental risks associated with procured goods and services in order to be able to negotiate effectively.

COST SAVING

Cost saving remains high on the list of priorities for many purchasing professionals since their incentives and rewards are often linked to savings achieved. As the quality of 'greener' products has improved, organizations have been able to source products with better environmental characteristics, using a whole-life costing approach, and have demonstrated the cost savings that can be achieved. Examples are to be found in the BiE/CIPS publication *Buying into a Green Future* (1997).

ADDING VALUE

Purchasing and supply managers can use the enhanced environmental performance of the goods and services they buy to deliver 'added value' to their organizations. When total cost (rather than simply purchase price) is taken into account, the benefits become apparent – waste management costs are reduced, liabilities are minimized, consumption is appropriate to the needs of the organization and all parties are engaged in delivering effective solutions.

ENHANCING CORPORATE IMAGE

Corporate image is enhanced through environmental purchasing strategies since they demonstrate to a wide audience, including suppliers, customers and the public at large, that the organization is concerned with all the consequences of its operations and activities.

CREATING MARKETS

Those purchasers with significant buying power in particular markets can, for example:

- encourage suppliers to invest in new technologies
- encourage suppliers to develop new products with higher environmental specifications
- stimulate markets for recycled products or those with a high recycled material content
- stimulate markets for services delivering the function of products at lower environmental cost.

RAISING THE PROFILE OF PURCHASING

By addressing each of these opportunities for action, purchasers can help to raise the profile of purchasing within their own organizations. They can demonstrate the key role for purchasing in:

- forming cross-functional teams to address total consumption and the development of specifications
- collecting, analysing and sharing information on products, services and suppliers
- sending signals to the market about priorities for environmental improvement.

UK government views on modernizing local government, for example, highlight the importance of delivering environmental stewardship and best value, suggesting a new role for local government purchasing – one that embraces 'greening' (Murray, 2000).

Implementing an environmental purchasing strategy and policy

PURCHASING'S OWN ACTIVITY

While being concerned to address the impact of supply chain activity, purchasers should not overlook the impact of their own activities on the environmental performance of their organizations. The potential impact of e-procurement on environmental performance is currently being debated. Purchasers should look to adopt means of transacting business that reduce environmental impact:

- by maximizing the use of electronic forms of communication with colleagues and suppliers
- by using waste exchanges and other Internet-based resources.

SUPPLY CHAIN ACTIVITY

Companies commonly purchase thousands of items from hundreds of suppliers, making it difficult to tackle every potential impact at once. Some means of establishing priorities and of focusing resources is usually essential.

Effective environmental purchasing must take account of a combination of factors, including:

- concern for the impact of products and services purchased
- concern for the impact of suppliers and contractors.

The risk-based approach to environmental management in the supply chain adopted by many companies is linked to familiar purchasing practice (Steele and Court, 1996) and ensures that 'the environment' is treated as simply another facet of commercial risk.

Such approaches generally focus on identifying sources of high environmental risk in the supply chain and mapping them on to existing methods of categorizing supply, as illustrated by Lamming and Hampson (in Lamming et al., 1996). Increasing attention is being given to the complex relationship between environmental impacts, costs and risks (Lamming et al., 2000). The organization can then determine which purchases should be given most attention and which approaches and techniques are most appropriate for use in the acquisition process.

As Figure 14.2 indicates, there are a number of stages at which purchasers can take action based on this assessment and a number of techniques they can use to deliver improvement.

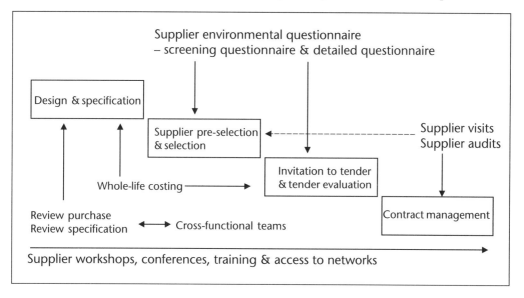

Figure 14.2   *Addressing environmental management through the purchasing process*

STAGES IN THE PURCHASING PROCESS

Purchasers should be aware of their own organizational circumstances and aim to introduce environmental criteria as early as possible into purchasing decision making. The earlier in the process environmental factors are introduced, the greater the potential benefit. For example, waste management costs can be reduced considerably by changing packaging and product requirements. Although many organizations begin to address their impacts at use and disposal or end-of-life phase, the maximum impact is likely to result from action taken at the early stages in the 'acquisition' process.

Purchasers and those responsible for 'acquisition' can usefully apply the same principles as in the familiar waste hierarchy:

- Eliminate
- Reduce
- Reuse
- Recycle
- Dispose (or 'end-of-life management')

Stages of the purchasing process at which environmental criteria can be introduced are illustrated in Figure 14.2:

1 identification of need and alternative solutions
2 supplier pre-selection and qualification
3 invitation to tender/tender evaluation/contract award
4 contract management.

Effective environmental purchasing takes account of the environmental opportunities and threats presented at each of these stages, although in many organizations purchasing professionals do not have direct responsibility at each stage – hence the need for internal collaboration.

Figure 14.2 also illustrates a number of approaches and techniques that may be adopted at various stages in the purchasing process – several of which are applicable at more than one stage.

Stage 1   Identification of need and alternative solutions

Effective environmental purchasing requires purchasers and their colleagues – internal customers, technical staff, other users and specifiers – to consider the needs of the organization being satisfied by the products and services they demand. These issues generate related approaches that can be used by purchasers at an early stage in the purchasing decision-making process. These include:

Approach 1   Reducing consumption

Reducing overall consumption is an effective means of reducing environmental impact and of reducing costs. The opportunity to address total consumption should not be overlooked, particularly in relation to the use of non-renewable resources and hazardous or dangerous materials, where alternatives exist. This needs to be done in collaboration with internal customers since their operational activities largely determine overall levels of consumption, as well as with suppliers where appropriate. Consumption should be examined with a view to achieving the optimum balance between resource consumption and operational effectiveness.

Closer working with suppliers assists in:

- reviewing order quantities and frequencies – revealing opportunities to reduce overall consumption; and
- reducing excessive stockholding and wastage – this leads to reduced waste charges.

Examples can be found in *Buying into a Green Future* (CIPS/BiE, 1997).

Approach 2   Challenging repeat purchases

Identifying the need for a purchase can involve challenging repeat purchases. Purchasers and users have an opportunity to examine previous purchases, to question the need for a particular purchase and to investigate alternative means of delivering the 'function' required.

Approach 3   Identifying alternative solutions

This includes purchasing of services to deliver function, rather than purchasing of products. An example includes the payment of a flat fee to chemicals suppliers, providing an incentive for the supplier to develop ways of achieving the same level of service – or function – with a reduced volume of chemicals. This type of 'shared savings' approach has multiple benefits – it reduces overall environmental impact as well as reducing costs in the supply chain (*ENDS Report*, 1997).

As supplier rationalization continues, purchasers are focusing attention on those suppliers who can develop and deliver alternative solutions, offering environmental and cost benefits. Purchasers have a role to play in the search for environmentally preferable solutions, but they should not attempt to 'police' the process. Rather, they should act as catalysts, stimulating discussions both internally – with users and specifiers – and with suppliers.

Approach 4   Specifying 'greener' products

Product-specific approaches can be used by organizations wishing to address specific issues of concern to them, including reductions in the use of hazardous substances, for example. While many purchasers are buying finished goods and have limited scope to influence the specification of goods purchased, some have more control over product content. Volvo's 'black' list covers 'chemical substances which must not be used within the Volvo Group' while the 'grey' list identifies substances for which the company wishes to find alternatives (http://www.volvo.com).

Specifying recycled materials is an option for some organizations and many now set down requirements for minimum recycled content of packaging material, for example.
Public sector bodies can use the specification process as part of their strategy to 'close the loop' in recycled materials – as well as encouraging business and industry to adopt recycling practices, by specifying recycled materials in the products they source, they can help to stimulate markets. This illustrates the key role of public sector purchasers in the process known as 'market transformation' (see http://www.mtprog.com).

Under European Community (EC) Procurement Rules, government departments and other contracting authorities are free to specify their requirements in 'green' terms. Purchasers in the public sector need to work within the requirements of these rules and need to keep up to date with any changes to the rules that can and do affect the potential scope for environmental purchasing activity.

Examples of the development of 'greener' specifications continue to increase as more organizations become involved. Information is now available on a vast range of individual items – the UK DETR's *Green Guide for Buyers* gives advice in the form of checklists on a number of issues to assist in purchasing. These include:

- ozone-depleting substances
- vehicle exhaust gases
- procuring greener vehicles
- hazardous substances – the UK Red List

- batteries
- products using environmentally preferable refrigerants
- certification schemes for forest products.

Many other 'green' purchasing initiatives now cover similar purchased goods and, increasingly, services. These include: Canada's Environmental Choice initiative (http://www.environmentalchoice.com) and Green Seal (http://www.greenseal.org).

Useful guidance has been produced for specific sectors, such as the UK Building Research Establishment's *The Green Guide to Specification* (Building Research Establishment, 1998) and for specific issues such as energy, as illustrated by the UK's Energy Efficiency Best Practice Programme (http://www.eebpp.org).

Most purchasing guidance makes some reference to the use of eco-labels (or equivalent specifications) in purchasing practice. However, the number of products for which eco-labels have been developed is small and purchasers in Europe may benefit from referring to criteria developed elsewhere.

In considering the development of specifications for goods and services, purchasers need to be aware of the increasing number of certification schemes for products. The International Standards Organization (ISO) has developed standards for three types of environmental product claim, termed ISO Type I, Type II and Type III:

- Type I (ISO 14024) claims are based on criteria set by a third party and are multi-issue, being based on the product's lifecycle impacts. The awarding body may be either a governmental organization or a private non-commercial entity. Examples include the EC Eco-label, the Nordic Swan and the German Blue Angel.
- Type II (ISO 14021) claims are based on self-declaration by manufacturers or suppliers – for example 'made from x per cent of recycled material'.
- Type III (ISO 14025) claims use life cycle analysis to generate quantified product information – for example Volvo's product profile for its S80 motor car.

Single-issue labelling schemes such as that of the Forest Stewardship Council (FSC) and organic food labels are partially covered by ISO 14020 – General Guidelines for Environmental Claims and Declarations (Bendell, 2000). A recent development is the Marine Stewardship Council label (*ENDS Report*, 2001).

One of the difficulties facing purchasers seeking to buy more environmentally sound products and services is how best to assess the validity of competing claims made by manufacturers and suppliers. The UK's DETR has produced a useful Green Claims Code which offers a code of conduct for the use of Type II claims at http://www.environment.detr.gov.uk/greening/greenpro/gcode.htm

Examples of the development of specifications with the environment in mind can be found in *Buying into Greener Transport* – a guide to asking the right questions (CIPS/BiE, 1999).

Approach 5   Product design and development

Purchasers and their colleagues can encourage the use of techniques such as design for the environment – including design for disassembly and remanufacture – by suppliers. Manufacturers in certain sectors are leading the way, particularly those most directly affected by forthcoming European Directives on Waste Electrical and Electronic Equipment and End-of-Life Vehicles. Purchasers should ensure that they are able to exploit the commercial opportunities available to them to require take-back of products by suppliers, for example.

THE ROLE OF PURCHASING IN DELIVERING ALTERNATIVE SOLUTIONS

Increasingly, purchasers are responsible for specifying services rather than products. They need to be able to negotiate contracts that reflect their knowledge of the environmental and other risks associated with outsourcing.

Purchasing and supply chain managers are uniquely placed to bring together the expertise required to deliver new solutions. Cross-functional teams can be used and include, for example:

- internal customers, including budget-holders
- technical staff
- environmental managers
- purchasing and supply chain managers
- existing and potential suppliers.

Stage 2   Supplier pre-selection and supplier selection

The process of supplier selection (and pre-selection, where this is undertaken by organizations) is frequently driven by several factors, including the need for the customer company to rationalize its supply base and a desire to assure itself of the supplier's ability to meet requirements. Linked to these drivers in recent years has been the need to ensure the environmental probity of suppliers.

A range of techniques can be used at the supplier (pre-)selection stage and it is important that the system adopted by the organization determines the appropriate technique to be used. Techniques employed at supplier selection (and at other stages – as outlined later) include:

- supplier questionnaires
- supplier audits – by internal staff or by third parties
- supplier visits.

Many organizations have devised a questionnaire system that starts with a standard 'screening' questionnaire which allows quick assessment for the supplier firm as a whole in their pre-selection systems. Here questions usually relate to issues such as:

- policy
- accountability
- reporting.

More detailed questionnaires are used at subsequent stages of the selection process, so that the quality and quantity of information required increases as the number of potential suppliers is reduced.

In (pre-)selecting suppliers therefore, it can be useful to analyse the products and services supplied and the suppliers concerned using an approach based on risk or 'engagement'.

The potential for environmental performance to be used as a tool in supplier rationalization is well illustrated in the automotive sector, where targets have been set down by major manufacturers including Ford and General Motors, for their suppliers to achieve ISO 14001. In many supply chains, however, customer influence is much less.

Those organizations subject to EC Procurement Rules must comply with certain conditions regarding pre-selection of suppliers. UK government departments and agencies can again make reference to the information contained in the Treasury and DETR guidance note *Environmental Issues in Purchasing* which makes reference to the requirement that all public procurement of goods and services is to be based on value for money, defined as 'the optimum combination of whole life cost and quality (or fitness for purpose) to meet the customer's requirement' – guidelines are set out at: http://www.hm-treasury.gov.uk/guid.html.

Technique – supplier environmental questionnaires

Figure 14.2 shows that questionnaires are widely used in addressing environmental issues in the supply chain. Purchasers routinely use questionnaires in many aspects of their activity, but supplier environmental questionnaires have not always been used appropriately. They can be a resource-efficient way of collecting large quantities of information, but they can also confuse and mislead if designed and used inappropriately (Mackenzie, 1998).

Some key points should be borne in mind when using questionnaires:

- They should be clear and unambiguous.
- They should be integrated into the purchasing process.
- Their use should be explained to suppliers.
- Feedback on the results should be conveyed to suppliers.
- Their content should relate to the stage at which they are used.

The content of a supplier environmental questionnaire is particularly relevant to public sector organizations since EC Procurement Rules govern the criteria to be used in tender evaluation (see CIPS, 2000).

Stage 3   Tender evaluation/contract award

When evaluating tenders, purchasers and their colleagues weigh the relative merits of competing bids against criteria set down at the beginning of the contracting process. These criteria – including environmental factors – may be weighted in advance, often by a cross-functional group, to reflect the level of importance assigned to various attributes.

Technique – Whole life-costing

Whole-life costing provides the means of determining if it is cost-effective to invest in a more expensive product initially to reduce costs in the long run, and is familiar to many purchasers. The approach adopted by United Utilities plc for the purchase of tyres is a good example (CIPS/BiE, 1997). The significance of whole-life costing in the context of 'green' purchasing is that it demands a holistic view (New et al., 1995). For example, UK DETR guidance makes reference to the need to think about whole-life costs before the invitation to tender stage. There is a requirement on UK government departments and agencies to award their contracts on the basis of whole-life costs and quality, and DETR guidance indicates the types of cost to be taken into account:

- *Direct running costs*, e.g. energy, water and other resources used over the lifetime of the product or service.

- *Indirect costs*, e.g. less energy-efficient IT equipment will produce more heat, causing plant in air-conditioned buildings to work harder to remove it, so adding to electricity bill.
- *Administration costs*, e.g. the use of a more expensive product which is less harmful to the environment and people's health may reduce the time spent by staff in complying with the Control Of Substances Hazardous to Health (COSHH) Regulations.
- *Investing to save revenue costs* – 'spend and save' – e.g. specifying higher levels of insulation where the extra expenditure can be recouped from lower energy costs.
- *Training*, e.g. if the product is not user-friendly it may entail time, money and effort being expended in training staff to operate it.
- *Specifying refurbished products*, e.g. not generally insisting on new items when refurbished parts or products could be used.
- *Recyclability*, e.g. purchasers can create markets for their own waste such as paper, toner cartridges etc. by buying products containing recycled materials. Purchasers should, however, look first to reduce waste at source.
- *Cost of disposal*, e.g. it may be worth paying a premium to a supplier giving an undertaking to remove the product or a hazardous substance at the end of its useful life. For more information see http://www.environment.detr.gov.uk/greening/greenpro/greenbuy/09.htm.

Stage 4   Contract management

Contract management includes managing performance over the lifetime of a contract or ongoing relationship with a supplier and for many companies now includes environmental criteria reflecting customer requirements. Purchasers can, for example, agree targets for improvement with suppliers as part of a continuous improvement programme and can use contract review meetings to discuss progress.

Technique – supplier environmental audit

Supplier auditing is a familiar mechanism in purchasing and supply chain management and one that has been extended by many organizations into the area of environmental management. Again, the nature of the purchase and the source of supply help to determine the extent to which supplier auditing is carried out. With limited resources, most organizations have to focus attention on those areas in which commercial and environmental risk is greatest.

Supplier audits may be carried out by internal staff or by third parties and many companies opt to link their environmental auditing of suppliers to existing audit processes, including quality audit. This optimizes the use of limited resources.

Technique – supplier visit

Supplier visits are also routinely used and can yield particularly valuable information since they allow customers to verify suppliers' environmental claims and to see evidence of their environmental performance at first hand. This can help to develop understanding between customers and suppliers as well as revealing opportunities for improving performance and identifying solutions to problems. Supplier visits can be useful in developing cross-functional teams, therefore.

Technique – supplier workshops and conferences

These can help companies put 'the environment' on to their suppliers' agenda more effectively than by using written communication, for example. In a workshop situation, suppliers can ask questions, air concerns and offer their own ideas about performance improvement, building on the day-to-day dialogue between purchasers and suppliers.

Technique – supplier environmental training

While a few large companies (for example, Ford) now offer training to suppliers, most prefer and are able only to point suppliers in the direction of suitable training to improve their environmental performance. The European Union supports some training for suppliers, but mainly those in the small and medium-sized enterprise (SME) category. Corporate customers should not overlook the need to address improvement by the rest of their supply base, bearing in mind the risks associated with larger suppliers.

The role of networks

Purchasers and their colleagues can benefit from becoming involved in the environmental purchasing networks that are beginning to develop locally, nationally and internationally.

Summary of good practice

Elements of good practice in environmental purchasing and supply include:

- use of cross-functional teams:
  - to examine and review purchases
  - to seek alternative solutions
  - to develop new specifications
  - to identify opportunities for improved management practices
  - to identify opportunities for shared savings
  - to stimulate new product development
  - to stimulate investment in resource-efficient technologies
- appropriate use of techniques for environmental information-gathering
- dialogue with suppliers throughout the purchasing process using relevant formats:
  - supplier workshops
  - contract review meetings
  - supplier visits and audits
  - supplier conferences to include feedback on environmental performance
- identification of training opportunities for suppliers where appropriate
- development of a programme of continuous improvement in purchasing to include negotiated environmental improvement, identifying opportunities for resource reduction and cost savings.

References

B&Q (1995), *How Green is my Front Door? B&Q's Second Environmental Report*, Eastleigh: B&Q plc.
B&Q (1998), *How Green is my Patio? B&Q's Third Environmental Report*, Eastleigh: B&Q plc.
Bendell, J. (ed.) (2000), *Terms for Endearment: Business, NGOs and Sustainable Development*, Sheffield: Greenleaf Publishing.

BT (1993), *BT and the Environment, Environmental Performance Report 1993*, London: BT.

Building Research Establishment (1988), *The Green Guide to Specification, BRE BR351*, Garston: BRE.

BiE (Business in the Environment) (1996), *Index of Corporate Environmental Engagement*, London: BiE.

BiE (Business in the Environment) (2000a), *Buying into the Environment, CD-ROM*, London: BiE.

BiE (Business in the Environment) (2000b), *Performance – Sustaining the Business Revolution – BiE's 4th Index of Corporate Environmental Engagement and Performance*, London: BiE.

CIPS (Chartered Institute of Purchasing and Supply) (2000), *The CIPS Environmental Policy Statement*, Stamford: CIPS.

CIPS/BiE (Business in the Environment/Chartered Institute of Purchasing and Supply) (1993), *Buying into the Environment*, London: CIPS / BiE.

CIPS (Chartered Institute of Purchasing and Supply) (1995), *Supply Chain – the Environmental Challenge*, London: HMSO.

CIPS/BiE (Chartered Institute of Purchasing and Supply/Business in the Environment) (1997), *Buying into a Green Future: Partnerships for Change*, London: CIPS/BiE.

CIPS/BiE (Chartered Institute of Purchasing and Supply/Business in the Environment) (1999), *Buying into Greener Transport*, London: CIPS/BiE.

ENDS Report (1997), 'Nortel: Shared Savings for Chemicals and Waste Reduction', *ENDS Report No. 267*, April.

ENDS Report (2001), 'Marine Stewardship Eco-label Poised to Catch Big Fish', *ENDS Report No. 312*, January.

Gattorna, J.L. and Walters, D.W. (1996), *Managing the Supply Chain: A Strategic Perspective*, London: Macmillan.

Gillett, J. (1993), 'Ensuring Suppliers' Environmental Performance', *Purchasing and Supply Management*, October.

Green, K., New, S. and Morton, B. (1996), 'Purchasing and Environmental Management: Interaction, Policies and Opportunities', *Business Strategy and the Environment*, Vol. 5.

Green, K., New, S. and Morton, B. (1998), 'Green Purchasing and Supply Policies: Do They Improve Companies' Environmental Performance?', *Supply Chain Management: An International Journal*, Vol. 3, No. 2.

IBM (1995), *Consulting the Stakeholder – A Profile of IBM's Environmental Performance*, London: IBM.

Lamming, R. and Hampson, J. (1996), 'The Environment: Issues and Implications for Purchasing', in R. Lamming, A. Warhurst and J. Hampson (eds) (1996), *The Environment and Purchasing: Problem or Opportunity?*, Stamford: CIPS.

Lamming, R., Warhurst, A. and Hampson, J. (eds) (1996), *The Environment and Purchasing: Problem or Opportunity?*, Stamford: CIPS.

Lamming, R., Cousins, P., Bowen, F. and Faruk, A. (2000), 'A Comprehensive Conceptual Model for Managing Environmental Impacts, Costs and Risks in Supply Chains' in A. Erridge, R. Fee and J. McIlroy (eds), *Perspectives on Best Practice Procurement*, Aldershot: Gower.

Lyons, K. (2000), *Buying for the Future*, London: Pluto Press.

Mackenzie, N. (1998), 'Questionnaires Disease', *Supply Management*, 24 September.

Murray, J.G. (2000), 'Effects of a Green Purchasing Strategy: The Case of Belfast City Council', *Supply Chain Management: An International Journal*, Vol. 5, No. 1.

New, S., Green, K. and Morton, B. (1995), 'Green Supply: Getting a Grip with Whole Life Costs', *Purchasing and Supply Management*, November.

New, S., Green, K., and Morton, B. (2000), 'Buying the Environment, the Multiple Meanings of Green Supply', in S. Fineman (ed.) (2000), *The Business of Greening*, London: Routledge.

Noci, G. (1997), 'Designing "Green" Vendor Rating Systems for the Assessment of a Supplier's Environmental Performance', *European Journal of Purchasing and Supply Management* Vol. 3, No. 2, pp. 103–14.

Russel, T. (ed.) (1998), *Greener Purchasing: Opportunities and Innovations*, Sheffield: Greenleaf Publishing.

Steele, P. and Court, B. (1996), *Profitable Purchasing Strategies*, London: McGraw-Hill.

United Utilities plc. (1997), *Environment Report 1997*, Warrington, UK: United Utilities plc.

Warner, K.E. and Ryall, C. (2001), 'Greener Purchasing Activities within UK Local Authorities', *Eco-Management and Auditing*, Vol. 8, pp. 36–45.

Weele, van A.J. (1994), *Purchasing Management*, London: Chapman and Hall.

15 *Ethical issues in purchasing*

Christopher J. Cowton and Christopher J. Low

Introduction

The significance of purchasing to overall company success has become more widely appreciated in recent years. Product quality and cost control are two core benefits which can be delivered by efficient and effective purchasing. However, developments over the last few years mean that purchasing and supply management must also deliver on new fronts. In this chapter we wish to demonstrate that ethics deserves to be taken seriously in purchasing. Major trends such as globalization, changes in approaches to sourcing and new modes of corporate accountability throw up significant ethical issues. Experience and some recent high-profile cases suggest that ethical standards are important for effective management of purchasing and supply.

Ethics challenges business at both the corporate and individual level. It can also have an important professional dimension. Yet business ethics is frequently dismissed, somewhat flippantly, as an oxymoron – a contradiction in terms. It is often supposed that business operates according to some crude 'law of the jungle', with greed and competition ensuring that there is no space for morally admirable behaviour. While business is certainly not all 'sweetness and light', such simple generalizations ignore much of actual business practice. Business can be tough, but that does not mean that there is no room for ethics. The aim of the chapter is not to preach some idealistic message but rather to establish the importance of ethics, to highlight some of the major issues involved, and to suggest ways in which they can be addressed. We pay particular attention to formal written policies or codes of ethics, which are an increasingly common feature of business.

The public face: supply chain ethics

Unprecedented levels of attention have recently been devoted to the purchasing and supply activities of companies by the media, consumers and campaigning groups. In some industries regulators are also taking a keen interest. Issues such as the presence of child labour in the factories of suppliers to major sportswear manufacturers have become front-page news. In other words, as companies like Reebok know only too well (see Box 15.1), the process of how a product is made has come under the microscope, not simply the final product attributes enjoyed by the consumer. Putting it simply, it seems that you can outsource production, but you can't outsource ethics.

Box 15.1   Reebok case study

In 1995 Reebok was criticized when children under ten years old were found to be involved in the manufacture of their footballs in Pakistan. After extensive media coverage of this in the run-up to the Euro '96 football tournament, Reebok decided to take action. They began a shift away from small-scale producers, which are difficult to monitor, and moved to help develop much larger production facilities, which could be closely monitored. They are now one of the leading actors in addressing labour conditions in the supply chain and are the only brand that markets 'Child Free' footballs.

Source: *Helping Business to Help Stop Child Labour: A Report by Anti-slavery International*, 1996.

Reebok is a major consumer brand name. Learning from each successive example and using the Internet to good effect, campaigning groups are increasingly effective in influencing consumers through the media, gaining leverage on business-to-consumer (B2C) companies through threatening their reputation and brand value. This should be enough to put the issue of supply chain ethics on many senior managers' agenda, but the whole topic has been given extra impetus in the UK through the publication of the Combined Code, which incorporates the recommendations of the 1999 Turnbull Report on corporate governance. With a focus on risk, the Turnbull Report has raised expectations that companies should have sound systems of internal controls in place to safeguard their shareholders' investments. As the supply chain is now one such risk area, companies will increasingly find themselves being forced to account for the activities of their suppliers. The reputational risk points will depend on the situation, but several of the more public ones of recent times involve the Third World, with environmental, child labour or health and safety issues to the fore.

If all this sounds rather negative, ethics can affect reputation in a second way. Instead of just guarding against downside risk, it may be possible to build a brand where ethics is at the core of the proposition. A conspicuous example is The Body Shop, where certain standpoints are central to its product offering. Whatever one thinks of its ethical vision and commercial success – particularly as others copy other elements of its offering – there is no denying that a substantial business has been created around a particular set of values. Other examples would include businesses where consumer trust is vital (for example, pharmaceuticals, household remedies); the behaviour of the organization can have an effect on perceptions of its products.

Whether such organizations pursue a positive ethical strategy, with its implications for purchasing, for its own sake (principled) or for commercial reasons (pragmatic) is beside the point here; the important lesson is that it is possible to run a successful business with avowedly high ethical standards. Even someone who follows Milton Friedman's dictum that the only social responsibility of big business is to increase profits while staying within the rules of the game wouldn't object to a large extra dose of ethics – if consumers value it sufficiently. Perhaps those who do so most highly – ethical consumers who actively research the products they buy – are in a minority. But they are a growing minority, they have greater than average buying power and, as pioneers, they can have an impact on the extent to which the general mass of consumers take ethical issues into account when they are shopping.

So far our discussion has focused on relatively large companies, building a reputation based on ethics or, at least, seeking to protect their brand value through controlling behaviour in the supply chain. These are the kinds of case that have raised public awareness of the importance of ethics in purchasing. They might also, though, be taken to imply that the scope of ethics is limited to big, high-profile companies which not only have much to lose but also have the power to influence behaviour in desirable ways.

However, the same basic logic can apply to not-for-profit organizations too. Indeed, for those that operate in the political or charitable domain, supply chain ethics may be crucial to their public legitimacy. Meeting the legal minimum will not be enough to protect themselves from criticism.

Furthermore, beyond the public face of B2C supply chain ethics there is a set of issues which applies to all organizations, high consumer profile or not. For wherever goods and services are purchased from another business (B2B) there arise issues which we will refer to as falling within the domain of 'professional ethics'.

The professional core: key issues

As befits a professional body, the Chartered Institute of Purchasing and Supply (CIPS) has published a code, updated in 1999, which provides useful help, especially in the Guidance section, where it identifies areas in which the general principles set out earlier are likely to be important. The full Code is reproduced in Box 15.2.

Box 15.2   The CIPS Code of Ethics

Introduction
1. Members of the Institute undertake to work to exceed the expectations of the following Code and will regard the Code as the basis of best conduct in the Purchasing and Supply profession.

2. Members should seek the commitment of their employer to the Code and seek to achieve widespread acceptance of it amongst their fellow employees.

3. Members should raise any matter of concern of an ethical nature with their immediate supervisor or another senior colleague if appropriate, irrespective of whether it is explicitly addressed in the Code.

Principles
4. Members shall always seek to uphold and enhance the standing of the Purchasing and Supply profession and will always act professionally and selflessly by:
a. maintaining the highest possible standard of integrity in all their business relationships both inside and outside the organizations where they work;
b. rejecting any business practice which might reasonably be deemed improper and never using their authority for personal gain;
c. enhancing the proficiency and stature of the profession by acquiring and maintaining current technical knowledge and the highest standards of ethical behaviour;
d. fostering the highest possible standards of professional competence amongst those for whom they are responsible;

Continued

e. optimizing the use of resources which they influence and for which they are responsible to provide the maximum benefit to their employing organization;

f. complying both with the letter and the spirit of:

i. the law of the country in which they practise;

ii. Institute guidance on professional practice;

iii. contractual obligations.

5. Members should never allow themselves to be deflected from these principles.

Guidance

6. In applying these principles, members should follow the guidance set out below:

1. Declaration of interest – Any personal interest which may affect or be seen by others to affect a member's impartiality in any matter relevant to his or her duties should be declared.

2. Confidentiality and accuracy of information – The confidentiality of information received in the course of duty should be respected and should never be used for personal gain. Information given in the course of duty should be honest and clear.

3. Competition – The nature and length of contracts and business relationships with suppliers can vary according to circumstances. These should always be constructed to ensure deliverables and benefits. Arrangements which might in the long term prevent the effective operation of fair competition should be avoided.

4. Business gifts – Business gifts, other than items of very small intrinsic value such as business diaries or calendars, should not be accepted.

5. Hospitality – The recipient should not allow him or herself to be influenced or be perceived by others to have been influenced in making a business decision as a consequence of accepting hospitality. The frequency and scale of hospitality accepted should be managed openly and with care and should not be greater than the member's employer is able to reciprocate.

Decisions and Advice

7. When it is not easy to decide between what is and is not acceptable, advice should be sought from the member's supervisor, another senior colleague or the Institute as appropriate. Advice on any aspect of the Code is available from the Institute.

Approved by the Council of CIPS on 16 October 1999.

Perusal of the Code reveals two types of ethical issue. The first – the treatment of suppliers – is discussed below.

TREATMENT OF SUPPLIERS

There are moral arguments for the ethical treatment of suppliers, perhaps based on their status as 'stakeholders' – sometimes relatively vulnerable ones if they are much smaller that the purchasing concern. But there are also pragmatic, commercial reasons for treating suppliers ethically. For example, there might be reputational repercussions: cause-related stakeholders such as ethical investors and ethical consumers might boycott a company known to treat its suppliers badly; or other potential suppliers might be reluctant to offer attractive terms. Perhaps of greater importance, though, is that if supplier and purchaser act ethically towards one another, one probable outcome is mutual trust, which is likely to provide a basis for lower transactions costs – the costs of doing business, broadly conceived. Indeed, it could be argued that trust is an important means of turning a succession of transactions into a relationship or partnership – which is in line with much contemporary thinking on purchasing. This is not to say that the only reason for being ethical is that it pays commercially. Rather, as in the section on supply chain ethics, the point is that ethics and profit are not always in conflict.

There are several ethical issues which arise at various stages of the purchaser–supplier relationship. Many of them come down to a question of honesty, and whether the rules regarding truth-telling in business are less stringent than in everyday life. A familiar setting for such questions is commercial negotiations. For example, is it wrong to bluff, perhaps initially claiming that it would not be possible to pay more than £10 per item, but actually having a ceiling of £12? Some (for example, Carr, 1968) would say that this is morally acceptable because participants are acting according to the known rules of the game. Others would say that bluffing is lying or deception by another name, and the fact that the practice is generally accepted is insufficient justification. Some members of the purchasing function might believe that, through experience, they are able to recognize a dividing line between acceptable bluffing and unacceptable lying. However, it is interesting that the CIPS Code states that information given in the course of duty 'should be honest and clear', and there is no indication in the Code that commercial negotiations are excluded from this provision. Perhaps it is unrealistic to expect all bluffing to be eradicated, but we would recommend taking a step back to ask whether the process can be set on a different footing, particularly if the negotiations take place in the context of what is intended to be a longer-term commercial relationship.

A further area in which practices can be less than honest is in the tendering and bidding process. For example, quotations are sometimes solicited with no intention of proceeding to order or even negotiation, which seems very unfair on the would-be suppliers whose time is wasted. Sometimes it is done simply to keep existing suppliers competitive on price. On other occasions the ideas of one bidder are taken and given to another, probably cheaper supplier. This is a particular problem where creativity is central to the product or service being supplied, for example in the running of an advertising campaign.

Even when everything has been agreed and the product delivered, there still remains one area where much practice is ethically dubious – payment. Although payment terms will be contractually specified and could, in theory, be legally enforced, it is common to keep suppliers waiting for their money for much longer than agreed. From an ethical point of view this involves the breaking of a promise, the 'theft' of interest on funds which have not been paid over on time and, on many occasions, a dose of lying too ('the cheque's in the post', 'we've mislaid the invoice' and so on). Delaying payment can also have serious business consequences, particularly for small firms which may be highly dependent for their very survival on the prompt settlement of what is, for them, a large invoice. Because of this the UK government has brought in regulations which oblige large companies to make statements about their payment policy and to report their performance in terms of average days to settlement. It is hoped that this will induce more transparent and improved behaviour in the corporate sector.

Justification for the above practices might be sought by arguing that they are in the employing organization's commercial interests, although whether that is the case in anything other than the short term is a moot point. But there exists a second area of professional ethics where there is high probability that the employer's interests are definitely *not* being served – bribery.

BRIBERY

Members of staff responsible for purchasing are in an influential position, for they are able to decide on the destination of large sums of company money. It is a major responsibility and, as the CIPS Code says, they should carry it out 'to provide the maximum benefit to their employer organization'. Suppliers are keen to obtain business, and it is not surprising that some seek to gain an advantage by offering inducements to buyers, thus threatening to drive a wedge between buyers' personal interests and those of their employer. Sometimes the bribes involved, while small in the context of the total deal, can be very large for the individuals concerned. Not many people have much trouble in recognizing that such payments, and their acceptance, are wrong.

The complications come when people try to distinguish between bribes and some other thing, such as a 'gift'. Gifts made in the context of a business relationship can range from the relatively minor, such as an inexpensive bottle of wine, through quite generous hospitality, perhaps at a major sporting event, to 'conferences' (holidays) in expensive locations. However, as an unnecessary transfer of value to a company official, presumably in the belief that it will increase the probability of business or induce more favourable terms, it is difficult to see such gifts as anything other than a form of bribery, albeit not on the same scale as the handing over of a large suitcase of money.

If a gift is accepted and not reported, the member of staff concerned is in danger of being compromised. The CIPS Code wisely makes it clear that no business gifts other than items of very small intrinsic value, such as diaries or calendars, should be accepted. In some cultures this can cause offence, in which case a choice has to be made – still to refuse, to receive but then donate, or to accept and declare. Refusal is probably the best course of action, if the buyer can prove that he or she is not permitted to receive such gifts. Hospitality can be more tricky, for it is natural to try to establish a good atmosphere and rapport, to the benefit of all parties to the discussions. Perhaps the key advice in the CIPS Code is not only that the hospitality should not be excessive, but that it should be managed with transparency. If you don't want people to know about it, is it right?

When it comes down to it, it is hard to justify accepting any gift, certainly beyond the most trivial. It is always likely to arouse suspicion that the buyer is not seeking his or her employer's best interest – otherwise why would the supplying organization make the gift? It might be argued that in some cultures it would cause genuine offence to refuse a gift – but that can often be dealt with, particularly if there is a formal written policy or code to which the buyer can make reference. The development and use of such policies is discussed in the next section.

Policies and codes

CIPS members are required by their own code to encourage their employer and colleagues to adhere to its provisions, which should help promote ethical behaviour in purchasing. Given its wide potential coverage, though, the CIPS Code cannot address all the possible issues in the degree of practical detail that might be desired. Different industries and countries entail different risks and challenges. However, many companies are producing their own formal, tailored policies on how to conduct business ethically. Whatever they are called (codes of conduct, codes of ethics and so on), the development of these explicit statements appears to offer the possibility of regulating behaviour in the purchasing and supply function.

A code can be used as a basis for guiding and controlling your own people responsible for purchasing. If you have one, it should feature in training and be a part of any formal manuals or guidance issued to staff. It can be particularly useful when working across cultures, when difficult situations, misunderstandings and temptations are much more likely to occur; Severn Trent introduced a code when its business became more international. A code can make expectations explicit, thus providing guidance to buyers. It can also make standards clear to suppliers. This can be helpful to buyers who risk causing offence when they refuse a 'gift'. Being able to point to a code provides authority for, indeed an obligation to do, what they are doing, thus reducing the likelihood that the refusal is taken as a personal affront.

However, although codes have become widespread amongst large companies in recent years, some commentators remain unconvinced by them. Warren (1993, p. 186), for example, condemns them as 'superficial and distracting answers to the question of how to promote ethical behaviour in corporate life'. The jury is still out on whether they make a real difference in many areas of business (Cowton and Thompson, 2000). Perhaps it would be fair to say that some codes are better than others. Not all codes are the same, and it might be unwise to lump them all together when judging them – or to expect too much of them.

There are several factors which influence whether a code is likely to have a real impact on behaviour. The following points provide guidance for developing a new code or for judging the likely effectiveness of an existing one. (The same points would tend to apply if a written policy covering only the purchasing function were being considered.)

AIMS

First, how ambitious is the code? Codes differ considerably in the aims accorded to them, and while researchers would like to discover whether codes have any impact on behaviour, it should be acknowledged that some do not have such lofty ambitions. It is not unusual to encounter the view that they are merely an exercise in public relations (PR). If a code is produced in response to public criticism, management might be content if it simply appeases external parties.

It is this kind of tactical (some might say cynical) use of codes that can undermine their credibility. However, while there may be some short-term benefits, the move might backfire on the companies concerned. Campaigning organizations will be back, and journalists and the public are unlikely to be impressed by codes that aren't worth the paper they're written on – or considerably less than the website they're posted on. Given the commitments that they imply, not taking codes seriously can be a risky business.

Of course, some organizations do take their codes seriously. While perhaps conscious of the possible PR benefits, they will seek to promote or safeguard certain standards of behaviour. But how ambitious should they be? Should they simply try to distil current values and practices to prevent poorer than expected behaviour – which can be particularly helpful when dealing with new purchasing personnel and suppliers? Or should the code aim to raise practice above previously accepted standards? This is a much more difficult task because, rather than expressing existing corporate norms, the code is pitched against them. Without an effective wider process and considerable support from management it is likely to fail.

Whether or not a code proves to be successful in terms of the aims held for it will depend on several further factors.

CONTENT

A critical factor will be the coverage of the code. First and foremost, given our interests in this chapter, does it even mention purchasing? Not all general codes do. If it does, it should probably pronounce on the key issues identified in the previous 'professional ethics' section, but the precise coverage and the way in which those issues are treated will depend to a large extent on the context in which purchasing takes place. Particular care should be taken to anticipate the likely risk points in the business. Thus a code needs to be more than just vague moral exhortation, which is of little practical value and likely to be viewed with scepticism by both insiders and outsiders.

The key to drawing up a code is to get the right balance between the general and the particular. Without claiming to be exhaustive, a code should identify major issues likely to be relevant to the particular business. It should give practical help to employees in doing their jobs. However, there are dangers in focusing exclusively on detailed rules. For example, it runs the risk of 'legalism' and a kind of moral 'dumbing down', where those who are so inclined look for loopholes ('where did it say I can't do that?') or treat the code as a ceiling rather than a floor (note that the CIPS Code says that members should work to *exceed* its provisions). General standards or statements of principle are needed to provide breadth of coverage and to indicate aspirations, while the detailed guidance should be seen as the most pertinent examples of the working out of those principles. Professionals are expected to be more than mere rule-followers.

This mix of general principles and more specific guidance can be seen in the CIPS Code. While an individual organization will be able to provide more detailed guidance than that Code, taking account of its own circumstances and risk points, it is wise not to lose sight of the desirability of the more general principles of ethical behaviour. Such statements of principle can include something of the reasoning and process of development which underpin the code.

DEVELOPMENT

The process of developing a code can be approached in a number of ways, and it is likely to influence the success of the code finally produced. The simplest method is just to 'lift' a code from somewhere else. It is also likely to be the least successful, unless it is merely a PR exercise. Nevertheless, it is certainly worth having a good look at codes produced by other organizations. Their efforts can be a rich source of ideas. An excellent resource is the 'Codes Online' website (address in 'Further Reading'), which provides a wide variety of examples.

However, a code is developed by and for an organization, which should usually mean more than being written by just one person, however well informed about other codes. Many commentators would recommend involving employees, at least in some consultative way, once a draft has been developed. This can help establish legitimacy and generate commitment. It can also improve the content, because employees can contribute their own concerns and experiences. It might be worth setting up task forces to deal with particular elements of the code. Thus purchasing people would be asked to pay particular attention to supply issues, perhaps even involving suppliers themselves.

At the end of the initial development process a code will be promulgated, but that is not the end of the matter. It is important to keep it under review, taking into account emerging issues and experiences.

IMPLEMENTATION

Ultimately, whether or not a code makes a difference depends on how it is implemented.

First, a code must be communicated adequately to the various parties – employees, and perhaps suppliers – who are to be bound by it. When it is introduced there is likely to be a flurry of activity via normal corporate communication channels. (If people aren't told about it, draw your own conclusions about why it is being introduced.) But telling people once isn't enough. They need to be reminded about it periodically, with the code becoming part of operating manuals and the like. And as with any important message, top management commitment and example-setting are important. Do they 'walk the talk'? Indeed, do they even mention the code once it's been in place for a while?

The code also needs to feature in training. This might include the training of suppliers if the code covers not just the relationship between them and purchasing officers (professional ethics) but also what suppliers do within their own businesses (supply chain ethics). This is something that the Pentland Group has been addressing (see Box 15.3).

Box 15.3   Pentland Group case study

The UK company, Pentland Group, which makes a number of major brands including Berghaus outdoor wear, Kickers shoes and Mitre footballs, has been prominent in labour standards reform efforts. They source extensively from South East Asia, including Vietnam. A particular problem in their supplier facilities is the management of hazardous chemicals. The company has in the last few years created a 'Business Standards' department whose brief covers the full range of labour issues including safety issues. The department provides training to both suppliers and buyers and one of its courses is the 'Risk Management of Chemicals in Production'. Buyers require this training in order to be able to detect problems. This is outside of their normal duties which tends to focus only on assessing product quality.

Source: www.ethicaltrade.org/_html/publications/ann-rep_2000/framesets/f_page.shtml

As already explained, no code of reasonable length can be expected to deal conclusively with every possible issue and situation that might arise in purchasing. Judgement will be needed on the part of those bound by it, and it might be wise to get a second opinion on occasions. The final paragraph of the CIPS Code mentions that advice on any aspect of it is available from the Institute. It also suggests that advice can be sought from a member's supervisor. In some cases, though, they might not be capable of resolving the issue, and the boss could even be part of the problem. A company with its own code should therefore consider setting up an advice point or 'hotline'.

Finally, although systematic evidence on the effectiveness of codes is limited, enforcement mechanisms have been identified as a crucial element by some researchers – which accords with common sense. If management isn't serious about the code, why would it be taken seriously by the very people whose behaviour it is intended to influence? This goes for both individual organizations and professional bodies. Sanctions can sometimes be serious. For example, Shell have a stated policy of 'No bribes' as Principle 4 Business Integrity (The Shell Report, 1999, p.17) – and dismissed three employees found to be soliciting or accepting bribes.

Some contraventions of a code will be discovered fortuitously or reported on an *ad hoc* basis, but companies taking the issues seriously will also wish to monitor compliance on a more systematic basis. Box 15.4 outlines how C&A has gone about the implementation and auditing of a code of conduct for suppliers.

Box 15.4   C&A case study

The Dutch retailer C&A has taken significant steps in order to eradicate the labour issues in its supply chain that campaign groups have highlighted. Particular problems have emerged in South East Asia, from where the company sources significant volumes of its garments. A code of conduct has been developed that includes provisions on child labour, forced labour, and safety standards. For example, if child labour is discovered in a factory, then the factory fails the inspection and is rated 'unacceptable'. Not only has a code of conduct been developed for suppliers but the company has also set up an entirely new and separate division known as Service Organization for Compliance Audit Management (SOCAM) in order to monitor compliance to the new code.

The setting up of a separate department reflects the problem for purchasing staff when faced with reconciling the twin and competing demands of keeping supply costs down while making sure that suppliers are maintaining high ethical standards. The clear temptation for purchasing staff is to 'overlook' lack of compliance if it keeps costs down (e.g. not paying workers overtime rates). In addition, buyers have to give advance notice of visits to factories to ensure that they meet the people with whom they normally do business. Auditing employment conditions, detecting problems of harassment, for example, is also a highly specialist task which normally has state professionals doing it. Therefore specialist staff are needed outside of the purchasing specialism. A huge effort is also required to actually trace the production facility. Many companies report that suppliers get a contract and then subcontract to facilities that the buying company has never seen and which may be the scene of labour problems.

Source: www.fashion-lifestyle.com/media/intl_print/socam98.pdf.

In conclusion, while the jury is out on the effectiveness of codes, there are some sensible points to bear in mind, as discussed above. Molander (1987, p. 631) provides a fair summary:

A well written ethical code, reliably and fairly enforced, can eliminate unethical practices, relieve ethical dilemmas and throughout the process demonstrate a firm's or industry's commitment to ethical conduct. If poorly designed and implemented, the code will not only be ineffectual but could further reduce business's credibility with the general public and important opinion-forming institutions in the society.

Getting personal

Many people try to avoid discussion of ethics by claiming that it is a personal matter which differs between individuals, especially when they are from different cultural backgrounds. However, to engage in commerce with others entails some responsibility for their treatment, and even if there are intractable moral differences within or between societies, over many business issues there is much common ground. Ethical issues cannot be avoided by closing one's eyes to them and, as we have argued, there are plenty of people keen to observe and judge the ethics of business, whether or not business people are happy with that.

Codes of ethics and other written policies can have an important role to play in guiding or controlling people whose moral sensitivities and commitment are not well developed. They can also provide useful guidance and support for business people who want to make sure that they do a *good* job, in the fullest sense of the word. Such people might find that the guidance they receive needs significant interpretation or does not cover issues that concern them; they might work in an organization without a formal policy or code; or, of course, they might wish to evaluate, contribute to or develop policies. How might they (you?) think through ethical questions? We stated at the outset of this chapter that we did not wish to preach, but we would like to suggest a few ideas or resources that might be of help.

First, moral philosophers have thought long and hard about how to make ethical decisions – which is probably why they've managed to find problems with the approaches they have come up with. We will mention three main strands. Academics might like to argue for the merits of one over the others, but in practice it is often found helpful to employ all three and see in which direction they point.

- *Deontology*   This is concerned with doing the right thing, in the sense that the action is in accordance with certain principles or rules. The rules might be positive (for example 'treat others as you would like them to treat you') or negative (for example 'do not steal'). Are there any rules that you believe are good in themselves? How might they apply to the situation you're facing?
- *Consequentialism*   As the term implies, this assesses actions by their consequences rather than portraying them as right or wrong in themselves. It's a kind of moral 'profit and loss', if you like. The real skill is not so much in the evaluation of the consequences – though that is difficult enough – but in being able to anticipate what kind of impact a particular action will have, particularly in its knock-on or ripple effects.
- *Virtue ethics*   This moves the focus from the actions and their consequences to the person. A virtue might be thought of as a positive disposition to act in a certain way. One way to put this perspective into practice is to ask yourself: if I repeat this behaviour, what does it say about me, and is this the kind of person I want to be?

Moral philosophers aren't the only people who try to help us to think through ethical issues. If you belong to some form of faith community, what teachings does it have that shed light on your problem? If its teachings seem difficult to relate to modern business practices, are there books or groups which have thought things through further than you feel able to do on your own? It can often be a good idea to work on this, to develop your thinking, *before* a problem comes up.

On a more prosaic level, another method is to ask yourself how you would feel if the newspapers reported your behaviour, or someone whose opinion you value came to know of it. Could you explain your actions to your husband, wife or whoever without shame and embarrassment?

Finally, decisions imply the existence of choice – otherwise there is no decision to be made. Moral philosophers sometimes express this as '*ought* implies *can*'. This is not saying that all ethically desirable actions (*ought*) are possible (*can*). Rather, the phrase is indicating that you should not ask others, or yourself, to do the impossible. This is sensible advice – but don't be too quick to invoke it! Habits of mind and customary practice can easily lead to myopia. Much depends on the nature of the problem, but perhaps we need to educate ourselves more about the situation (for example, how to deal with 'gifts' in that culture). With a bit of imagination or help we often discover alternatives that we did not perceive at first. Business ethics an oxymoron? Perhaps that's just said by people who haven't really thought about it.

Conclusion

In this chapter we have argued the case for paying proper attention to ethics in the purchasing function. Ethical issues need to be recognized and faced – increasingly so in an ever more visible business world. Sometimes the complexities and constraints are such that idealism has to be tempered with pragmatism, but it is our firm belief that managers who run headlong into decisions without considering the ethical implications of what they are doing are not only likely to make some morally regrettable decisions; they are also likely to make some commercially inept ones, perhaps missing opportunities to build revenues or risking the company's reputational capital – not to mention their own career and self-respect.

We have picked out some of the major issues which are likely to arise in purchasing, distinguishing between the traditional concerns of professional ethics and the more recently prominent area of supply chain ethics. Identifying ethical issues is an important managerial skill, but the issues then have to be addressed, and we have provided some advice on how this might be done. Written policies, perhaps as part of some broader code of business conduct, are one of the more obvious tools available. The material provided in this chapter, and the references to literature and websites at the end of it, provide resources which we hope will prove to be of help in understanding and resolving the ethical challenges that lie ahead.

References

Carr, A. (1968), 'Is Business Bluffing Ethical?', *Harvard Business Review*, Vol. 46, No. 1, pp. 143–53.

Cowton, C.J. and Thompson, P. (2000), 'Do Codes Make a Difference? The Case of Bank Lending and the Environment', *Journal of Business Ethics*, Vol. 24, No. 2, pp. 165–78.

Molander, E.A. (1987), 'A Paradigm for Design, Promulgation and Enforcement of Ethical Codes', *Journal of Business Ethics*, Vol. 6, No. 8, pp. 619–31.

Warren, R.C. (1993), 'Codes of Ethics: Bricks without Straw', *Business Ethics: A European Review*, Vol. 2, No. 4, pp. 185–91.

Further information

LITERATURE

Chryssides, G. and Kaler, J. (1996), *Essentials of Business Ethics*, Maidenhead: McGraw-Hill. (A useful introduction to general business ethics.)

Ethical Performance, a monthly independent newsletter for socially responsible business (see www.ethicalperformance.com).

Hurst, R. and Arnesen, M. (2000), *Where Did That Come From? A Study of Ethical Issues in the Supply Chain*, London, Institute of Business Ethics.

Le Jeune, M. and Webley, S. (1999), *Company Use of Codes of Business Conduct*, London, Institute of Business Ethics.

WEBSITES

There is a rapidly growing amount of material available on the Internet relating to business ethics. Although individual websites can disappear altogether, they have the advantage over printed material that good ones are regularly updated – including the addition of hyperlinks to new sites. The following are worth looking at:

http://www.cips.org, the Chartered Institute of Purchasing and Supply, including its Code of Ethics.

http://csep.iit.edu/codes/, Codes Online, for plenty of examples of business and other codes of conduct.

http://www.transparency.de, Transparency International, the global coalition against corruption, including bribery.

http://ecampus.bentley.edu/dept/cbe/, the Center for Business Ethics at Bentley College in the USA, which has strong ties with the Ethics Officer Association.

16 *Purchasing research*

Kenneth Lysons

There are numerous definitions of research, of which three typical examples may be quoted:

- an investigation directed to the discovery of some fact by careful study of a subject; a course of critical or scientific inquiry;[1]
- systematic investigation towards increasing the sum of knowledge;[2]
- the systematic investigation into and study of materials, sources etc. in order to establish facts and reach new conclusions.[3]

Purchasing research is, therefore, the application of research methods to the specific field of procurement. Possibly the best-known definition of purchasing research is that of Fearon (4):

> Purchasing research is the systematic collection, classification and analysis of data as a basis for better purchasing decisions.

An alternative definition adapted from market research is:

> The systematic gathering, recording and analysing of data about problems relating to the purchasing of goods and services[5]

Purchasing research can vary in scope from a simple 'searching' exercise to obtain better prices for a specific application to a large-scale exercise such as how best to coordinate central or local government procurement to obtain best value. Irrespective of the size and scope of the research project, however, the general aim is to carry out an investigation in some depth which will improve the efficiency or effectiveness of purchasing performance and thereby make a contribution to competitive advantage.

This chapter covers the following aspects of purchasing research: (1) classifications; (2) design and methodology; (3) areas; (4) organization and agencies and (5) dissemination.

Classifications

There are many ways in which research in general and purchasing research in particular can be classified. The following classification is by no means exhaustive:

(i) *Pure research*, involving the proving or disproving of theories of little apparent direct relevance to human concerns. This applies mainly to the physical sciences.

(ii)   *Applied research* starts from questions formulated to produce information on which future decisions can be based; questions about how well things are being done (evaluation) or questions designed to establish what would be the consequences of new or changed policies. Practically all purchasing research is applied research.

(iii)   *Secondary or 'desk' research* is concerned with the discovery and use of data (i.e. facts, figures or symbols which, when interpreted or processed, become information) which has already been researched for another purpose. Such data are, therefore, available much more rapidly and more cheaply than by doing the research for the first time. Thus, in researching possible suppliers of a product or component, sources of information include :
- Catalogues, including electronic catalogues
- Trade directories, e.g. *Kompass, Rylands, Buyer's Guides*
- *Yellow Pages*
- Databases – these can provide up-to-date information and may be space-saving substitutes for large reference collections. Details of how access may be obtained for various databases can be obtained from the Directory of On-line Databases, Britline; Directory of British Databases (EDIP Ltd).
- Logistics Pulse (www.logistics pulse.com) links purchasers with more than 23,000 suppliers.
- The Business Internet
- Trade journals
- Chambers of Commerce
- Government sources, e.g. the Department of Trade and Industry.

(iv)   *Primary or field research* is the obtaining of hitherto unavailable data for use in relation to a specific purpose. Such data can be obtained in a wide variety of ways, including observation, analysis of internal records, e.g. purchase orders, visits to suppliers and questionnaires. When visiting suppliers, data regarding their potential and suitability should be obtained, processed and stored in a systematic way. Supplier appraisal usually involves a combination of both desk and field research.

(v)   *Quantitative research* involves the numerical counting or measurement of data or the exposure of collected data to statistical tests and the expression of the resultant information in the form of tables, figures, graphs, bar charts etc. A quantitative approach could be used, for example, in research relating to supplier performance.

(vi)   *Qualitative research* is usually based on data obtained from interviews by which people's views or experiences relating to a specific matter are obtained and checked regarding their value, reliability, meaningfulness and applicability. Thus research into the status of the purchasing function in a sample of organizations could be based on interviews with purchasing staff and those using their services. Since all research contains some verbal description and most involves some counting, the difference between quantitative and qualitative research is often a matter of degree.

(vii)   *Macroeconomic research* is concerned with the study of whole economies or systems such as the economic environment of a particular country or taxation, wage rates, inflation etc. Such research has significance for all purchasing activities, but is especially important to the purchasers of sensitive commodities, e.g. raw materials such as copper, lead, zinc, rubber, where the prices fluctuate daily and where futures dealings are undertaken to reduce uncertainty arising from price fluctuations due to supply and demand changes.

(viii)   *Microeconomic research* is concerned with the study of individual producers, suppliers, consumers or markets. Such research may be essential before deciding whether to purchase from an overseas supplier or in relation to make-or-buy decisions.

(ix)   *Mesoeconomic research* is concerned with a specific industry sector, e.g. steel, castings or car manufacture.

There are numerous sources from which information relevant to macro-, micro- or mesoeconomic research may be obtained. These include:

- Government departments – information on appropriate departments may be obtained from the Central Office of Information. Of special importance is the Office for National Statistics.
- Research councils, e.g. the Economic and Social Research Council.
- Research centres – A full list of these can be obtained from a current issue of *Whitaker's Almanack*.
- Chambers of commerce, especially the London Chamber of Commerce, Information Department.
- *The Journal of the European Union*
- Banks
- Importers
- Trade associations – again, a list is provided by *Whitaker's Almanack*.
- Specialist enquiry agents, e.g. Dunn and Bradstreet offer a product funding service and can undertake credit checks on prospective suppliers.
- Directories e.g. *Kompass, Jaeger* and *Waldman* and the English-language edition of *Wer Liefert (Who Supplies What)*
- The Internet.
- Journals e.g. the *Economist* and the *Financial Times*; the latter provides a first-rate reference service.

As a general rule, secondary or desk research should precede primary research. This is because:

- desk research provides a 'feel' for the topic being investigated and reveals gaps that need to be filled by primary or field research, and
- secondary data searches can be rapidly and cheaply undertaken.

Design and methodology

The first step in purchasing, as with all other research, is to adopt a plan or model of the research from inception to completion. Sarantakos[6] states that the general assumption made by researchers who employ a research model in their work rests on the beliefs that:

- research can be perceived as evolving in a sequence of steps, which are closely interrelated, and in which the success of one depends on the successful completion of the preceding step;
- the steps must be executed in the given order;
- planning and execution of the research is more successful if a research model is employed. A typical model is shown in Figure 16.1.

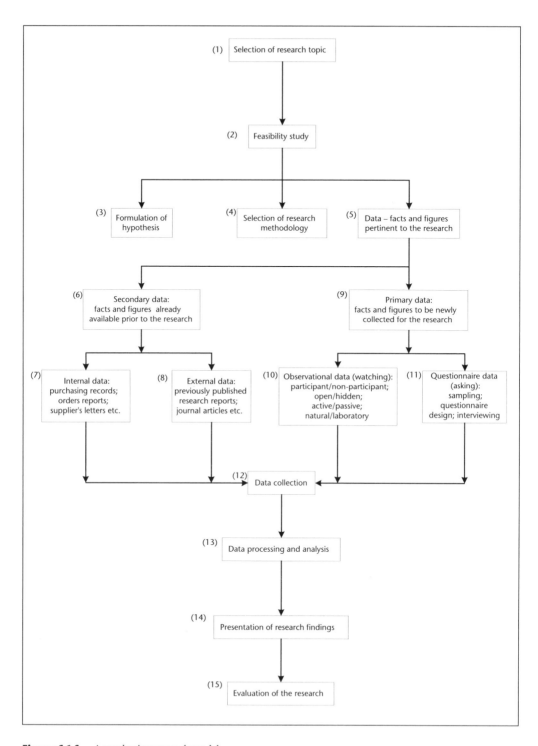

Figure 16.1 *A purchasing research model*

1 *Selection of research topic.* The topic selected can result from a problem encountered by an organization, e.g. would the organization derive competitive advantage from outsourcing the purchasing function or buying complete assemblies rather than components? It may also derive from the interests of the individual researcher, e.g. the measurement of supplier performance in a sample of medium-sized manufacturing companies. When selected, the words in the title of the research topic should be precisely defined, e.g. in the latter example the terms 'measurement', 'supplier performance', 'medium-sized' and 'manufacturing' should be defined in the context of the research and the size of the proposed sample indicated.

2 *The feasibility study* should indicate whether the proposed research can be successfully undertaken within a prescribed time at a cost not exceeding an agreed amount and with the resources available. The feasibility study may also include a cost/benefit analysis of whether the expected benefits of the research will justify its cost.

3 *Formulation of hypothesis.* A hypothesis is a tentative theory which may be proved or disproved by the research. Thus, the hypothesis may be that 'Outsourcing of the purchasing function will provide competitive advantage to our organization'.

4 *Selection of research methodology.* This involves a decision on whether the methodology of the proposed research shall be primarily quantitative or qualitative. Some further differences between the two methodologies are summarized below :

Quantitative	Qualitative
Provides answers to who? where? when? and how? questions	Is concerned with what happens? how? and why does it happen?
Counts numbers	Evaluates purpose
Records events	Predicts behaviour

It is important to note that neither methodology is best. The best method is the one most appropriate to the specific research. Often quantitative and qualitative methodologies can be combined and regarded as complementary rather than exclusive.

5 *Data.* Data requirements are ascertained by asking such questions as 'What do I need to know?', 'How precise an answer is required?' As shown, data can be secondary or primary.

6 *Secondary data*, as shown, can be subdivided into internal and external sources. These should be studied both before and during the collection of primary data. Secondary data will indicate what has already been done in the field of the proposed investigation, suggest further sources of inquiry, provide a 'feel' for the problem and may even eliminate the need for further research. Databases can greatly facilitate the location of secondary data. These include:

- BLAISE (British Library Automated Information System), which covers mainly British book material in all subjects and also conference reports and theses
- DIALOG, an American system holding over 300 databases, which concentrate on journal articles in all subject areas
- EUROBASES, a series of databases held by the European Commission, including a database called Cellex, which covers information on European law.

7   *Primary data.* Decisions regarding primary data will be made after consideration of such factors as (1) what data required for the research are not available from secondary sources; (2) whether the research methodology is primarily quantitative or qualitative; and (3) what constraints arising from cost and time are placed upon the research. Primary data are most commonly obtained from observations and surveys.

8   *Data collection.* Decisions regarding the methods(s) of data collection will be influenced by many factors, of which the research methodology is probably the most important. Thus research into the competitive advantage or otherwise of outsourcing the purchasing function will include quantitative research into costs and savings and qualitative research into the problems experienced by other organizations which have outsourced a function. Such problems may include the possible adverse effects on competitive advantage through the loss of skills and expertise of staff.

9   *Data processing and analysis* involves turning the collected raw data into information that can be analysed. Inductive and deductive analysis are associated with quantitative and qualitative research respectively.

10 *Research presentation.* Presentation of the results of the research usually includes conclusions or recommendations derived from the investigation.

11 *Evaluation.* Questions asked at the evaluation stage include: (1) have the research objectives been achieved?; (2) are the results valid and reliable? and (3) how might the research have been improved?

Areas of purchasing research

In selecting topics or areas for purchasing research, it should be remembered that the greater the area of expenditure, the greater is the potential for significant cost savings. Fearon states that the broad subject of purchasing research can be broken down into four major research areas:

- purchased materials, products or services
- major purchased commodities
- vendors
- the purchasing system.

Another writer, Van Weele, distinguishes between purchasing research and purchasing market research.[7] The former refers to subjects concerning the internal organization (such as research on the composition of the purchasing assortment, its pricing, research on buyers' workload and internal efficiency). The latter is concerned with analysis of macroeconomic developments in supplier countries, analysis of supply and demand of important raw materials and assessments of the (financial) strengths and weaknesses of the individual supplier organization.

There is, however, no aspect of purchasing that is not a potential field of purchasing research. It is only possible to indicate a small sample of possible topics under the following headings.

MATERIALS, COMMODITIES AND SERVICES

Fearon observes 'that most research under this heading falls into the category of *value analysis* which was the area of purchasing research that first received attention.[8] *Techniques of Value Analysis and Engineering*, by Lawrence D. Miles (McGraw-Hill, 1972) is still the classic on the subject. Areas of research include:

- Substitute materials or items
- Alternative production methods, e.g. purchasing complete assemblies rather than components
- Lifecycle considerations in the purchase of capital items
- Variety reduction
- Standardization and specifications.

PURCHASING POLICIES AND PROCEDURES

- Comparative studies of purchasing policies
- Make-or-buy decisions
- Outsourcing of services, e.g. cleaning, catering, waste disposal
- Global purchasing
- Ethical policies relating to the environment, suppliers etc.

ECONOMIC ASPECTS OF PURCHASING

- Economic trends affecting the requirements of an undertaking for specific materials, e.g. currencies, interest rates inflation
- Supply and demand analysis
- Price analysis
- Factors relating to buyers' and sellers' markets
- The contribution of purchasing to profitability and competitive advantage.

PURCHASING ORGANIZATION

- Factors affecting the status of purchasing in differing organizations
- Purchasing organizations in private/public, manufacturing/retail organizations
- Supply chain management
- Purchasing and its functional interfaces, e.g. production, finance, marketing
- Possible applications of materials and logistics management.

HUMAN RESOURCE ASPECTS OF PURCHASING

- Recruitment, training and appraisal of purchasing staff
- Comparative studies of purchasing staff titles, job specifications and remuneration.

SUPPLIERS

- Supplier appraisal and assessment
- Supplier performance rating methods

- Social responsibilities to suppliers
- Quality assurance and control
- Buying centres and sourcing decisions.

INVENTORY

- Inventory management in relation to independent and dependent demand
- The economics of stock management
- Variety reduction
- Economic order quantities
- Just-in-time purchasing.

NEGOTIATION

- Purchasing factors relating to negotiation
- Adversarial and partnership purchasing strategies
- Comparative studies of negotiating processes in different environments, e.g. purchasing, politics and industrial relations.

SUPPORT TOOLS APPLICABLE TO PURCHASING

Under this heading come, for example, purchasing applications of:

- information technology, learning curves, network analysis, operational research and management accounting approaches, including absorption, activity, lifecycle, marginal, standard and target costing.

PURCHASING PERFORMANCE

This is as measured by audits, benchmarking, ratio analysis, management by objectives etc.

Research organizations and agencies relating to purchasing

Some research is undertaken by all purchasing functions, even though this may be only rudimentary such as consulting a database or directory to locate possible suppliers of a 'new-buy' item. Some willingness to initiate research is essential if the status of purchasing is to receive due recognition. Unless such an initiative is taken by purchasing, the research role will be undertaken by other functions such as design and production. Ideally purchasing research should be collaborative.

Systematic research requires time and freedom from other distractions. These conditions can be satisfied by providing a special purchasing research section as a centralized staff activity providing assistance to line members of the purchasing function. There is evidence that undertakings with formal purchasing research arrangements engage in more research projects at greater depth and gain significant benefits in competitive advantage and profitability.

When, as in smaller organizations, the establishment of a specialized research section is not feasible, formalized purchasing research may be undertaken by:

- project teams, e.g. value analysis teams concerned with a specific problem and including staff from outside the purchasing function
- specialized outside research facilities, e.g. universities or research units – useful lists of research councils and research and technology organizations are provided in *Whitaker's Almanack*
- membership of a research consortium
- consultants
- research facilities provided by suppliers.

The above refers to internal research. Much external research is also undertaken by:

- Central and local government, e.g. The Procurement Group of the Office of Government Commerce, which facilitates collaboration between the purchasing units of government departments, and The Central Buying Consortium, the largest procurement group in local government with 17 major local authority members, which takes a leading role in the drive towards best value and the development of professional procurement in local government.
- Universities. The CBI has pointed out the numerous benefits that can result from research partnerships between industry and universities.[9] Apart from consultancy, such research can be 'contract', 'collaborative' or through 'clubs' and 'networks'. In 'contract research' the agenda for a project is set by the industrial partner with the university providing a service at a commercial price on the same basis as any other supplier.

  Collaborative research differs from contract research in that the research goals are jointly defined by both industry and the university. 'Clubs' or 'networks' are often set up by an individual university or consortium of universities to focus on a particular research aspect. Companies wishing to become members usually pay an agreed annual subscription.

  Currently, 12 British universities provide courses leading to MBA or MSc degrees which include a purchasing option. These universities are Bath, Birmingham, Cardiff, Cranfield, Glamorgan, Leicester, Salford, Staffordshire, Strathclyde and Ulster. All work closely with industry. Thus the Centre for Research in Strategic Purchasing and Supply at Bath claims to work at any time with over 100 companies often organized into 'project clubs'. Universities other than those above, including Durham, Warwick and the London and Manchester Business Schools, also provide facilities for contract and collaborative research and the supervision of individual projects up to PhD level.
- Professional institutions, e.g. the Chartered Institute of Purchasing and Supply and the Institute of Logistics and Transport. The CIPS inaugurated the first Chair in Purchasing and Supply Management at Bath University in 1995. The Institute of Logistics also supports university research and makes annual awards for the BSc, MSc and PhD dissertation or thesis of the year. It also maintains the Logistics Research Network, a special interest group of academics with some interested practitioner members. The Network organizes conferences and produces the *International Journal of Logistics Research and Applications*.
- Consultants. Some large consultancies undertake independent research which is made available to industry at a cost. One example is the Purcon Index,[10] a specialized survey of the salaries and total remuneration packages of purchasing and supplies staff throughout Britain, which is updated in March and September of each year.

Dissemination

An important aspect of research is how to make the considerable body of academic research into purchasing and related topics availble to practitioners. Universities such as Bath, Cardiff and Cranfield issue 'Publications Lists' of books and papers produced by staff members with interests in the fields of purchasing and logistics, but these have to be requested. Some research is reported in journals, including *Supply Management*, issued by the CIPS, *Logistics Management*, the *European Journal of Purchasing and Supply Management* and the *International Journal of Logistics* issued by the Institute of Logistics and Transport, and the *Journal of Supply Chain Management* of the US Institute of Supply Management. The availability of research findings in purchasing, as in all other areas, will, of course, be dramatically increased by the numerous databases now available. The problem, naturally, is locating appropriate databases; a useful first step is the British Library Automated Information Service. Details of academic theses on purchasing and supply subjects can be obtained by trawling through the Aslib Index to Theses with Abstracts. One of the best guides to research sources is *Research for Writers*[11]. 0ther useful aids are *The Internet, A Writer's Guide*+[12] and the Hutchinson *Directory of Web Sites*.[13]

Hard-pressed purchasing staff frequently object that they have neither the time nor the facilities to keep abreast of purchasing research or to prosecute it themselves. Both they and their employers often need to be educated into the importance of purchasing research both as an aspect of staff development and enhanced purchasing professionalism and a source of competitive advantage to organizations aware of its potential.

Notes

1. *Shorter Oxford Dictionary*.
2. *Chambers English Dictionary*.
3. *Oxford Compact English Dictionary*.
4. Fearon, H. (1976), *Purchasing Research Concepts and Current Practice*, American Management Association, p. 5.
5 Adapted from a definition by the American Marketing Association.
6 Sarantakos, S. (1993), *Social Research*. Macmillan Education, Ch. 4, p. 91.
7 Van Weele, A.J. (1994), *Purchasing Management*. London: Chapman and Hall, Ch. 6. p. 98.
8 Fearon, *Purchasing Research Concepts and Current Practice*.
9 *Research Partnerships between Industry and Universities*, CBI Publications, 1997.
10 Published by Purcon Consultants Ltd, Prospect House, Repton Place, Amersham, Bucks, HP7 9LP.
11 Ann Hoffman (n.d.), *Research for Writers, London:* A & C Black.
12 Jane Dorner (2000). *The Internet, A Writer's Guide. London:* A & C Black.
13 *The Hutchinson Directory of Web Sites,* Helicon Publishing, 1999.

17 *Purchasing and international legal issues*[1]

Paul Abbiati

Introduction: e-procurement equals e-procurement law

The new millennium sees the rise of electronic procurement (e-procurement) and electronic tendering (e-tendering). Some buyers perceive that there is no law in cyberspace, that it is 'the wild west'. This is a misconception. Most states have either e-business laws in force or are drafting them.

E-procurement, like any other method of national or international procurement, demands that buyers know not just their national e-procurement law, but other states' e-procurement law and international e-procurement law. The sections at the end of this chapter will identify some of the legal issues raised in procurement by the new technology.

Box 17.1   Purchy case study

Purchasing manager Purchy recently closed an attractive computer software contract with a supplier from Australia. Amongst the impressive contractual conditions were two penalty clauses. One related to the consequences of late delivery; the other to the performance of the computer program. Notwithstanding these arrangements the supplier performed badly, delivering the program at a later date than agreed. Furthermore, the program did not perform as expected. As a result Purchy decided to act in accordance with the contract clauses. As a first step, he informed the supplier that the last invoice would not be paid.

In response the supplier informed Purchy that he would make every possible effort to correct the faults in the program. However, before taking action on this, he required Purchy to pay the amount outstanding. Without that payment the supplier was not willing to conduct any rework. Purchy called his solicitor to ask for legal advice. The solicitor, an expert in common law, told Purchy that, according to Australian law, penalty clauses are not allowed. Furthermore, if Purchy wished to take the matter to court, he would have to appear before a court in Australia and, without doubt, the court would decide that both penalty clauses were invalid.

As the reader will have perceived from the cast study in Box 17.1, Purchy operates within a particular legal system in Europe. The concept of 'penalty' in a contract is a valid measure, which a party might take in order to reduce the risks and damage which might be caused by poor contract compliance by the supplier. In the case that the seller would not be able to live

up to his promises, as laid down in the contact, the buyer would be able to invoke the relevant clauses in the contract. This concept of 'penalty' is related to the concept of 'liquidated
damages' in the law system of Anglo-Saxon countries. However, in other countries the concept of 'penalty' is considered primarily as a sanction, which could lead to a situation in
which the buyer exerts an unwarranted power position *vis-à-vis* his supplier.

In international business many conflicts between parties, operating in different countries, are related to differences in national law. These differences, in their turn, are related to
differences in opinion with regard to:

* the role and value of the economic system which is prevalent in the respective countries
* the role of the government with regard to agriculture, industry and trade
* those matters, which according to national law and local customs, are to be accepted or
  need to be rejected.

This chapter describes the principles underlying socio-economic policy in some Western
countries. As will become clear, the opinions expressed in the West regarding culture and
ethics do not apply everywhere. The Commandment 'Thou shall not steal' underlines the
principle that citizens can have title to property. However, in a country where the concept of
private ownership simply does not exist, such as in former communist countries, all goods
belong to the state. In such circumstances it is impossible to steal. However, citizens may take
advantage of circumstances, and this is considered to be something entirely different from
stealing.

In such a system the buyer does not acquire the ownership of the goods from the seller.
In fact, what the buyer gets is the possession from the seller over the state-owned goods,
which were up to that time under his control. It will be clear that this will influence the
characteristics of the buying–selling arrangement and contract. In these circumstances the
price does not necessarily result from the laws of supply and demand, as this would be unacceptable in that the ownership of the goods resides with the state. Hence, the state will decide
what price to charge and to pay for the goods concerned. On the other hand, the state will
also fix the price which it considers to be right. It is important that all kinds of arrangement,
aimed at increasing security for the buyer in case of prepayments, are considered not to be
valid in legal systems which do not acknowledge private ownership of capital and goods.

In this chapter I describe four known legal systems and discuss the most important differences between them. From the point of view of the purchasing manager it is important to
be aware of these differences, for doing business within the context of different legal systems
can lead to practical problems. I illustrate the frustrations which may arise when managers,
against the background of their own culture, need to develop some form of judgement with
regard to opinions and values which exist in other parts of the world.

However, it should be noted that, even within similar legal systems, problems may occur
between two countries because of differences in interpretation of some regulations and
arrangements in business law. Some examples are presented to illustrate this point.

Finally, the question whether it is possible for any purchasing manager to have a good
understanding of all legal aspects of international business is discussed. I believe that, given
its complexity, this is not possible. However, as will be argued, in-depth legal knowledge is
not a prerequisite for success in an international business context. Of course, purchasing
managers should call on appropriate experts for advice in order to reduce business risk in an
international context. None the less, awareness of key legal issues will enable the purchasing

manager to judge when to ask for advice, and what fundamental risks are associated with international contracting in particular countries.

Principles of socio-economic policies in Western economies[2]

The socio-economic environment in which a buyer operates may significantly influence the legal framework of the contractual agreements between buyer and seller. Freedom of trade is one of the basic cornerstones of Western economies. Free trade and free competition are highly valued. This means, among other things, that private persons and companies may decide either to buy or not to buy, what, where, how and from whom.

Most Western economies do not specify how buyers and sellers should proceed in dealing with each other. Nevertheless legal arrangements do exist regarding the conduct of business transactions. In the buying and selling of goods there is a detailed framework of legal arrangements and laws. However, in most cases the buyer is free to decide whether to adhere to these laws or not. He may decide not to follow them. However, for those matters not covered in the contract, should there be a dispute, the law will determine how to solve the problems involved.

The legal frameworks in most Western countries are based upon the following principles:

- maximum contractual freedom
- anyone is free to choose the party with whom they wish to do business
- parties are autonomous in the sense that they come to their own contractual arrangements
- very few formal arrangements (contracts may be verbal, written, with or without seal implicit acceptance is possible, sometimes to be acknowledged by a solicitor or a public notary)[3]
- free delivery of goods;[4] no permission of public authorities is required
- private ownership is possible; citizens and companies are free to transfer this also to other parties.[5]

Of course, transactions between buyers and sellers should meet some essential requirements:

- Transactions may not conflict with public order and decency.[6]
- Parties which are economically vulnerable are protected. This principle in general leads to detailed regulations, also in the case of commercial transactions. In most Western legal systems the consumer is protected in a profound way.[7]

Commercial law with regard to buying–selling transactions is derived from the fundamental rights of Western democracies, namely that the people are the highest power of the governmental organizations and that all people are equal in the eyes of the law. A legal system based upon different principles will result in a different commercial law. Consequently, buyers who do business with sellers from countries with a different economic system should be prepared to face some problems.

Four different concepts of the law of contract

Taylor (1985)[8] has explained the conflicts that may arise in contractual arrangements between parties from different economic legal systems by grouping these into four different categories: common or Anglo-Saxon law; Romano-Germanic law; socialist law; and law based on philosophy or religion. Although his analysis dates back to 1985, we feel it is still relevant for buyers operating in the new millennium. The following descriptions of each legal system and general explanation of the difficulties arising from legal concepts rely heavily on Taylor's original 1985 analysis but put more specific emphasis on the influence of these four different legal systems on the law of contract and on the specific legal differences underlying contractual terminology under common and Romano-Germanic law.

COMMON OR ANGLO-SAXON LAW

In England the law of contract developed under the system known as common law, the basis of which is to use judicial decisions rather than legislation to settle disputes. Common law is dispensed by trial judges using the experience of their predecessors. Distinguishing features of contract law under this system are amongst others: unequivocal offer and acceptance, consideration and agreement on essential terms and willingness to be bound at law.

The British have brought these concepts to many other countries which have political links with England: the USA, Canada, Australia, New Zealand, some Middle Eastern countries, parts of South-East Asia and parts of Africa. In some of these countries common law has been accepted only in part, for example in Muslim states and in India, where it has stood alongside traditions of other civilizations.

ROMANO-GERMANIC LAW

The basic idea within Romano-Germanic law is the codification of existing legal rules. The historically most complete codification is the *Corpus Iuris civilis of Justinianus* (AD 527–565) and has been updated by later emperors (such as the German emperor Friederich II). The system was in uninterrupted use in Eastern Europe until the Russian October Revolution in 1917. In Italy during the eleventh-century Reception the forgotten rules were revived; the system was again applied by all countries in Western Europe, except England. At the beginning of the nineteenth century it was replaced by the French codification of Napoleon for those countries occupied by the French. In Germany in 1900 the *Corpus Iuris* was replaced by a German Code. The latest national codification is the New Civil Code of the Netherlands, in force in 1970, 1976 and, for the law of contract, in 1992.[9]

Romano-Germanic law has extended its influence to former colonial empires of European origin, to Latin America, to parts of Africa (South Africa, for instance) and the Middle East and in part to South-East Asia and Japan.

SOCIALIST LAW

The substance of socialist law differs tremendously from common law and coded law. Contract law is one of the various instruments used to create conditions for a certain social order in which state and law are synonymous. Under this system, the law of contract, as it is understood in the West, has been extinguished. It is subordinate to economic and political purposes and is thus an aspect of state policy.[10]

Much more important than differences in contract law are the enormous differences which exist in the meaning of such words as 'freedom' and 'property' between socialist legal systems and the systems in the West. Freedom of contract and autonomy of parties (described above) are not understood by socialist lawyers, because that kind of freedom with respect to property is considered as a power of the bourgeoisie over the working class.[11]

As economic circumstances change, contract law has to be as flexible as needed. In common law, as well as in coded legal systems, failure to execute undertakings or obligations carries redress. The one who fails is in default. *Force majeure* is no argument in the event that the raw materials needed for the production are late. However, under socialist law a default incurs penal sanctions, or has political consequences since if the materials needed for production are late, in this legal system it might indicate a failure in the state's planning system. Contracts are a tool of economic development.

Because the rule of law is still conceived by terminology which has its roots in the old Romano-Germanic legal system, the legal terms applied by commercial people and lawyers in socialist countries may be understood by purchasers. But the true meaning of the terms differs enormously from their meaning in the West.[12]

The liberation of the countries in Eastern Europe and the fall of the communist system has had no effect on the legal system, since a new system can only be introduced once all the independent countries have established a new state. It does not alter anything as far as this phenomenon is concerned as long as no other legal system has been introduced. This will not be possible before all of the independent countries have established a new state order. For the time being the ex-communist countries are condemned to use a legal system which does not fit their new economic ideology.

LAW BASED ON PHILOSOPHY OR RELIGION

The various legal systems in this category are independent of one another, but they do have some common characteristics. Under these legal systems men have religious and ethical duties and are not equal. In this respect they differ from democratic and socialist systems which, at least on paper, reserve the same rights to all individuals and companies. As persons are not equal it is impossible to establish general rules of law of contract which can be applicable in all contractual situations. More often, in the event of disputes, persons (wise men, judges) appointed by the head of the state decide case by case. Unlike common law, decisions taken by these judges are not always based on those of their predecessors. For purchasers it is not easy to distinguish assumed contractual intentions from contractual undertakings which could be enforced in court. Western businessmen should therefore take care in concluding contracts. You might have the impression of making an agreement, but in reality the seller may not feel the obligation to supply the agreed goods in the agreed quality within the agreed time. And that is what matters in purchasing.

The most important legal systems of this category are Chinese law, Muslim law, Hindu law and Jewish law. Furthermore, there are some customary laws in different countries in Africa. All systems have to some degree been influenced by one or more of the systems described above. The roots of Chinese law, for instance, date from about 23 decades before Christ. Communist ideas were introduced with the Great Revolution and the 'civil code book' (1929–30) was inspired by a mixture of German, Japanese and Swiss law.[13]

Difficulties arising from different legal concepts

In this diversity of legal concepts there are some daunting conclusions to be drawn. Even within the same legal system there are differences in national rules of which no purchasing manager could reasonably be expected to have knowledge. It is absolutely impossible to be aware of all legal differences which could jeopardize the purchasing activities of purchasers operating on a worldwide basis. With constantly growing internationalism and the growing demand for flexible purchasing techniques, this is even impossible for experienced legal counsellors and solicitors when operating in an international field.

Figure 17.1 provides an overview of the economic and trade blocs which are apparent nowadays in the world.

SOME EXAMPLES OF DIFFERENCES BETWEEN COMMON LAW AND ROMANO-GERMANIC LAW

The penalty

Under Romano-Germanic law it is not considered improper for defaulting parties to pay a penalty for failing in their contractual obligations. In common law a clause is penal if it provides for a payment of a sum of money stipulated in order to perform the contract. Such a clause is disregarded by the courts. The reason behind this is to protect a weak party against a powerful one. The plaintiff cannot recover more than his actual loss. In common law, however, it is possible to enforce a liquidated damages clause if it represents a genuine attempt by the parties to estimate in advance the loss which will result from the breach. Such a clause is effective. In practice, this means that a purchasing manager operating in Europe who writes a penalty clause into a contract with a seller under common law might feel frustrated when, later, the seller is not prepared to pay the penalty, even in the case of default.

The moment a contract comes into force

Under Romano-Germanic law a message from one party to another is effective when the message arrives at its destination. In common law an acceptance (which is also a 'message') takes effect when posted. As these 'general rules' differ, the various consequences which are deduced from these rules differ. In practical terms it means that:

1 in common law a posted acceptance prevails over a withdrawal of the offer which was posted before the acceptance, but which had not yet reached the offeree when the acceptance was posted whereas under Romano-Germanic law, because the acceptance has not reached the offeree, there is no contract and therefore the withdrawal would be valid;[14]

2 in common law a posted acceptance takes effect even though it never reaches the offerer on account of it being lost in the post, whereas in Romano-Germanic law there is no contract in this event;

3 in common law the contract is taken to have been made at the time of posting, so as to take priority over another contract affecting the subject-matter made after the original acceptance had been posted but before it has reached the offerer, whereas in Romano-Germanic law the contract is concluded at the time the acceptance arrives at the

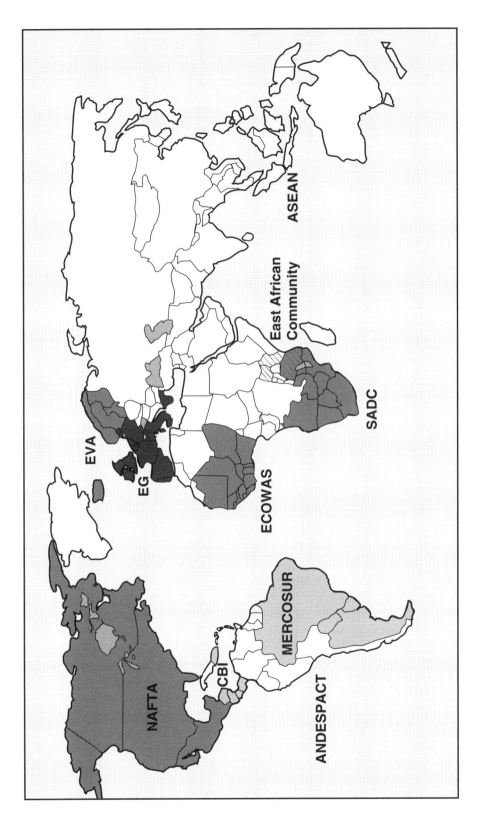

Figure 17.1   *World economic and trade blocs during the 1990s*

offeree.[15] A contract at an earlier date entered into with another buyer by a seller, affecting the subject-matter, takes priority over the contract which became effective by the receipt of the acceptance by the seller (see Figure 17.2).

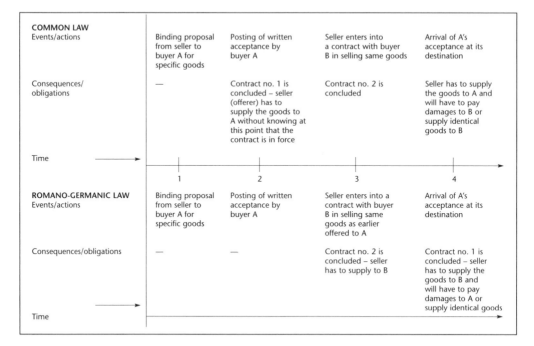

Figure 17.2   *The differences between Romano-Germanic law and common law in respect of the point at which contracts come into force*

Specific performance

Under Romano-Germanic law specific performance can be enforced. In common law damages are to be calculated and to be paid in cash to the plaintiff.

Good faith

Ideas about good faith differ as a function of time, place and legal system. Take, for instance, the clause agreed upon between a buyer and seller who, in some way – for instance by means of a co-makership relation – are rather dependent upon each other.

> The liabilities or obligations of each of us under this contract shall not be impaired or discharged by any provisions of this contract being or becoming void, unenforceable or otherwise invalid under any applicable law for any reason whatsoever as regards any of us or by the winding-up, amalgamation, reconstruction or re-organisation of any of us (or the commencement of any of the foregoing).

Such a clause is valid at common law. Parties declare to each other that, notwithstanding the ideas of lawyers in any applicable legal system ('under any applicable law') 'they shall keep their promises'. This is the way gentlemen agree.

At this point it is worth discussing the differences between the common law system and the Romano-Germanic system. The latter incorporates the rule that good faith has priority over agreed clauses. This could mean that, in the event that one of the clauses of the agreement happens to be in defiance of good faith, as interpreted by a court operating under one of the Romano-Germanic laws, that same clause could probably be declared 'void' and consequently 'unenforceable' and 'invalid'. Unfortunately this is exactly the kind of situation which the clause was drafted to prevent.

Difficulties within one and the same legal system

Even between two different states which operate within the same legal system, as described above, practical rules applied in purchasing practice may differ. Some of these are detailed below.

PRODUCT LIABILITY

Product liability in the USA requires much less proof in the courts than in England and the scale of damages which courts award on each side of the Atlantic also differ. Product liability in the USA has grown into a disproportionate burden of responsibility on manufacturers. In England the EC Directive 1985[16] which, by and large, is designed to protect consumers, is applicable.

PASSING OF TITLE

In French and Belgian law title passes at the conclusion of the purchasing contract. In the law of the Netherlands, title is passed at delivery of the goods. This consequently results in different regulations with regard to the risk to the goods to be delivered and different responsibilities for the seller and purchaser. For example, who is responsible for damages during transport – the buyer or the seller?

THE BATTLE OF FORMS

A classic problem in purchasing practice is the 'battle of forms'. The purchasing manager issues his order indicating that the purchasing conditions of his company are applicable. In his order confirmation, the supplier makes his sales conditions applicable to the same order. As this problem was not recognized in Napoleon's Civil Code, national courts within Europe have developed different solutions for this phenomenon.

In such circumstances the following possibilities exist for interpretation:

- The offerer's conditions apply.
- The conditions of the party that first mentions its conditions apply, unless the other party waives the first-mentioned conditions (law of the Netherlands, New Civil Code).
- The conditions of the accepting party apply.
- None of the conditions is effective; the judge takes as if only the law is in force (Belgian courts).
- As long as the parties exchange messages contradictory to each other's terms there is no agreement, because the parties' considerations are different on essential points until one of the parties (implicitly) accepts the 'last' message of the other party (common law courts).

- The party's conditions which are subject to the judge's opinion are valid in so far as they do not contradict the other party's conditions.
- General sales conditions and general purchasing conditions have to be accepted explicitly by the other party.[17]

When coming before court it is important to know beforehand which 'solution' has been adhered to in earlier cases. This depends upon the country where the case is brought before court.

Does the perfect contract exist?

As will be seen from the foregoing, doing business abroad involves risks with regard to:

- the process of negotiation
- closing the contract
- the seller and buyer satisfying the terms of the contract.

Earlier in this chapter examples of situations which may occur within an international buying context were discussed. As will have been seen, these situations will result in different interpretations depending on the kind of legal system that prevails.

However, not only the contract between parties itself has to be considered. The communication process may be influenced, among other factors, by the preliminary negotiations, by any practice which the parties have established between themselves during the foregoing years, and by the usages of the industrial or commercial sector in which they operate.

Given such complications, the reader might wonder whether it would be feasible to execute all buying–selling agreements in a 'perfect' manner. In order to be able to do this, a purchasing manager would need to have a perfect understanding of the specifics of business law of all his international suppliers. However, is it really necessary to close an agreement with a Chinese person according to Chinese law, just to be able to subpoena him in case of non-compliance with the contract? Just think of all the expensive and time-consuming work and effort which would be required in that case! Fortunately, in practice, many business contracts do not need to be that perfect, partly because they do not represent sufficient value to the company to warrant such a thorough treatment. In recognition of this fact, the purchasing manager will consequently tailor the right contracting strategy to fit the purchasing strategy which he is adopting. The instruments which are used in this respect need to be selected after a careful analysis of cost, benefits and effectiveness. Table 17.1 provides a minimum checklist for international contracts.

For example, where a number of suppliers are available in a market, the necessity to spell out every detail of the purchasing contract is less important than in a situation in which you have to deal with just one supplier who is crucial to your business. Where that is the case, it may help if, in case of potential delivery problems, you are able to point out clearly the eventual legal consequences for the supplier, which, in most cases, are not very attractive from his point of view. However, even in such a situation, alternative measures may be taken. The most effective policy is to let the supplier know that in the future you will also consider doing business with some of his competitors. Obviously perfect contracts are very effective in supporting the buyer in doing his job. However, they are not the only instrument! Good con-

Table 17.1 *Minimum checklist for international contracts*

- Contract parties
- Representatives
- Description of quality and quantity of goods
- Contract date
- Price
- Currency
- Payment conditions
- Invoicing
- Delivery terms (preferably INCOTERMS 1990)
- Delivery date
- Bank guarantee
- Transport
- Documents
- Taxes
- Customs regulations
- Insurance
- Packaging
- Inspection before shipment
- Inspection at delivery
- Re-inspection
- Industrial and intellectual property
- Warranties
- Passing and risk of property
- Indemnity
- Indemnity third parties
- Contract fulfilment
- Adjournment
- *Force majeure*
- Disbandment
- Damage
- Litigation
- Settlement of damage
- Interest
- Non-disclosure
- Applicable law
- Selling and buying terms
- Specific arrangements (safety/environmental/health)

---

tracts should never become an aim in themselves. An example (see Box 17.2) will illustrate this situation.

E-procurement law

Boxes 17.3 and 17.4 set out some case studies relating to e-procurement law.

Argos's argument that the website was not an offer, but an invitation to treat is correct under English contract law. However, under UK consumer protection laws, criminal prosecutions could have been brought under the Trade Descriptions and Consumer

---

Box 17.2   MoD case study

Recently a manufacturer of military trucks negotiated a contract with the Ministry of Defence of a foreign nation for the delivery of 300 heavy vehicles. At that time, as far as the buying country was concerned, it was only permitted to close the contract with the truck manufacturer according to its own national law. In the event of a conflict it was stipulated by law that, when a court's decision came to an appeal by one of the parties, the vice president of the government would come to an independent and final decision. Coincidentally, at the time the contract was made the vice president and the Minister of Defence of the country were the same man! Thus from the manufacturer's point of view this would imply that in case of difficulty the client would at the same time represent the ultimate judge! Clearly, this was not a very attractive clause in the contract as far as the manufacturer was concerned. Nevertheless, the truck manufacturer accepted and signed the contract. Later the trucks were delivered to the great satisfaction of the client. When accepting the contract the truck manufacturer had informed its ambassador in the country concerned about its weak contractual position. The ambassador was prepared, in case of difficulties, to support the truck manufacturer by exerting political pressure on the foreign government. Within NATO this case could have been made known, with all the likely negative consequences for the country. The risk that the MoD would stick to its legal position, while not giving the truck manufacturer a fair trial, was estimated by the supplier to be fairly low. Consequently, it accepted the legal position described above.

Protection Acts and if this had happened in a shop in the UK the retailer would have had to sell at the marked price. Complaints were settled out of court.

Online procurement exchanges and competition law

In 2000, investigations were continuing in the USA and starting in the European Union (EU) into online B2B ('business-to-business') exchanges – where companies can buy and sell goods and services in an Internet marketplace.

American antitrust officials argue there should be no difference between the competitive

---

Box 17.3   E-procurement law case study

(This case study is a summary of a real UK disputed.)

In 1999, the UK retail chain Argos appeared to be offering for sale on its website 21-inch Sony Nicam TV sets at the bargain price of 3 UK pounds (£). *The Times* newspaper reported that 'thousands of orders – reported to be worth at least 1 million UK pounds – had been placed', before Argos had discovered the mistake.

Argos refused to accept the orders on the basis that there was a clear mistake and they were not under a legal obligation to sell the TVs at 3 UK pounds (£). Argos argued that they did not accept the customers' orders and therefore they were under no legal obligation to supply.

Box 17.4   E-tendering: a public sector case study

The Electronic Tendering System (ETS) of the Hong Kong Government Supplies Department (GSD) was launched on 7 April and provides a secured electronic means for handling GSD's tenders and related matters with the use of Internet technologies.

The new system issues notification of GSD's tenders, specifications and documents to potential suppliers; receives submission of tender offers; and displays contract award notices.

Great importance is attached to security considerations of the ETS. To protect against unauthorized access, the most advanced encryption technology is used. Once a tender offer is submitted via the ETS, it cannot be accessed by any party – not even the GSD staff nor the tenderer himself – until the tender opening time.

In 2000, representatives from about 1,700 companies had shown an interest in the system by taking part in ETS seminars to familiarize themselves with the technical and subscription issues.

The service will not only bring in new tender bidders, but also achieve savings in time and expenses for the government as well as tender bidders.

The ETS site allows open access to government procurement opportunities to all small-, medium- and large-sized enterprises from anywhere in the world.

Interested suppliers should find the ETS cost-effective and user-friendly. As the system will operate 24 hours a day and seven days a week, subscribers can obtain tender information or submit their bids anytime of the day.

Instead of obtaining the information via mail, which used to take hours or days, they gain real-time access to tender specifications and can download tender documents with the click of a mouse button directly from the website in seconds. Submission of tender offers is also instantaneous. All these help save time and costs for printing, courier and mailing.

With the shortening of time for receiving and submitting tender documents, the new service allows suppliers more time to prepare their bids.

As for the government, the announcement of tender opportunities and results electronically will also reduce paperwork and costs related to distributing the information.

For a charge, subscribers can enter the ETS and enjoy a full year's benefits. Infrequent users who do not subscribe to the system can make use of the service too at a charge each time. The ETS has been contracted out.

Source: The Hong Kong GSD: sosr@gsd.gcn.gov.hk.

rules of the old economy and those of the new. They claim that there are only half a dozen forms of illegal conduct, and these apply to all businesses, electronic included.

In the digital age, wise procurement exchanges ensure that a visitor from the industrial age, a competition lawyer, supervises the discussions as a constant reminder that, even in cyberspace, the same old sheriff patrols the frontiers. For example, if suppliers to a steel B2B exchange meet for informal conversations about rising steel prices, this could possibly count in the USA as collusion. Caution must extend beyond the boardroom. Employees can also be accused of anti-competitive behaviour if they handle data about sensitive customer and supplier transactions. So, exchanges are recommended to restrict employees' access to data or outsource data-handling.

Legal action list for e-procurement

As demonstrated in the case study set out in Box 17.4, basic principles of contract law will apply to contracts made online ('e-contracts'). Therefore, buyers should consider legal contractual issues in relation to e-procurement, just as they do in relation to other methods of procurement to protect their rights and limit or avoid liability, but must consider the new electronic environment. Buyers must:

1   draft new terms and conditions for e-procurement, for example, define how they communicate electronically and when acceptance takes place in the e-contract
2   define how their terms and conditions are incorporated into the e-contract, for example, via their website
3   consider what other new terms and conditions need to be included and what existing ones need to be amended within their e-contract for e-procurement, for example, jurisdiction/governing law clause
4   review their terms and conditions more regularly
5   keep up-to-date with e-procurement legal developments, e.g. by subscribing to electronic legal update newsletters.

E-commerce is nothing new; EDI (electrical data interchange) has existed for many years. It is not the first or the last time that new technology will change procurement. It is not clear what new legal problems will arise from the rush towards e-procurement and e-tendering; B2B online procurement exchanges are already being investigated for anti-competitive practices. But what is clear is that buyers must learn and grasp the legal frameworks of the new millennium now!

Conclusions

The discussion in this chapter emphasizes that, when doing business in an international context, in order to be effective as a buyer, perfect contracts are not always necessary.

Of course, the fundamental question is what business arrangements do require a thorough legal approach? The answer to this depends on the importance of the contract to the company. Therefore, the contracting strategy which should be followed should be closely related to the overall purchasing strategy of the company and its approach towards its foreign suppliers.

Notes

1.   As John van der Puil was not available to rewrite the revised chapter, this chapter has been edited by Paul Abbiati, based on Taylor, M. (1985), 'Legal Aspects of Purchasing', in D. Farmer, *Purchasing Management Handbook*, London: Gower, pp. 367–81; second edition Aldershot: Gower, pp. 210–25.
2.   See also Zweig, S. *Die Welt von Gestern*, Chapter 1.

3. Here some limitations exist. In most countries the transfer of ownership of specific goods needs to be registered and witnessed by a public notary or a solicitor. Knowledge about ownership of buildings, ships, aircraft, shares, etc. needs to be publicly available.

    For example: when a ship at sea causes damage to your ship, you may note its name and its country, the latest made known by its flag. Now what to do? Just consult the register of ships in the referred country and you will learn the owner and his address; which enables you to claim damages.

    Consequently, transfers of ownership of ships have to be registered, the reason why many countries have arrangements to have 'sale/purchase' contracts registered and witnessed by a public servant (in some countries such a servant is a 'public notary', in some others a 'solicitor').

    Only some rules apply for ships, shares and aircraft. The rule has been created to maintain public order.

4. This is not entirely true. The government imposes regulations in terms of public order, quality, safety and public health. These regulations may relate to specific goods and services. The trend towards internationalization due to the opening up of the EU leads to an increasing number of regulations. As a result the margins within which to operate are becoming smaller for companies and institutions. The intensifying international competition forces companies to improve on product and service quality. This last-mentioned aspect is primarily a non-legal matter. The law does not force companies to sell and buy better-quality products than required by the law. As a matter of fact this aspect is some form of voluntary self-regulation by the international business community.

5. However, transactions which may negatively affect safety, hygiene, public health or the environment are subjected to government regulation. In these cases the government may take possession of goods or take ownership, for example where weapons or fireworks are involved.

6. Products without a CE-brand and for which this brandmark is required. Re: EC Directive 89/392/EC and 91/368/EC, Resolution of European Counsel, 21 December 1990, 90/C10/01. Proposal COM (91) 145 def -SYN 336, Eur. Publ. nr C160, 20 June 1991, pp. 14–17; products for which the European Union has prescribed uniform minimum technical requirements are: simple pressure vessels, toys, materials for construction of buildings, electromagnetic compatibility, machinery, means for personal protection, non-automatic weighing equipment, active electromedical apparatuses, gas equipment and consumer equipment for telecommunications. For all of these products EC Directives have been issued. For some 15 further products EC Directives are in preparation.

7. See for instance COM (90) 322 SYN 285, EC Publ. C 326/108, 16 December 1991 and COM (92) 66 def-SYN 285 (92/C 73/05) EC Publ. C 73/7, 24 March 1992. These EC publications strive to harmonize requirements aimed at protecting the consumers in the EU.

8. Taylor, 'Legal aspects of purchasing'.

9. Cohen Jehoram, H. (1968), *Over codificatie*, Deventer, the Netherlands: Kluwer.

10. Benger, A. (1978), *Rechtsgrundlagen für den Meister*, Berlin: Verlag Die Wirtschaft.

11. Keromow, D.A. (1977), *Philosophische probleme des Rechts, Staatsverlag der Deutschen Demokratischen Republik*, Berlin (German translation of original Russian text).

12. Enderlein, F. (1980), *Handbuch der Aussenhandelsverträge, Staatsverlag der DDR*, Berlin; see further Kemper, M. and Maskow, D. (1975), *Aussenwirtschaftsrecht der DDR, Staatsverlag der Deutschen Demokratischen Republik*, Berlin.

13. Tsien Tche-Hao (1982), *Le droit chinois*, Paris: Presses Universitaires de France.

14. In the International Conventions for harmonizing the law of contract this aspect has been considered. The Uniform Laws on the International Sales of Goods (1964) (ULIS), as well as the United Nations Convention on the International Sales of Goods (1980) (CISG), both give the same solution: a message has to arrive at its destination in order to have a legal impact.

15. Treitel, G. H. (1991), *The Law of Contract*, 8th edn, ed. London: Sweet & Maxwell, Stevens & Sons.

16. EC Council Directive concerning liability for defective products, no. 85/374/EG of 25 July 1985.

17. This is the position of both the ULIS as well as the CISG. Consideration was given to the fact that general conditions, which are drawn up in a legal system of a foreign party, are very difficult to understand in most cases

18 *Countertrade*

Simon Harris

There is no universally accepted definition of countertrade. All countertraders have their own ideas. What is clear is that countertrade is used as an inclusive term for all forms of trading mechanisms involving an element of reciprocity. The sale of goods (tangible or intangible) to an export market is made conditional upon the importing country receiving a reciprocal benefit through a link being made, directly or indirectly, with purchases of its own products and resources.

The element of reciprocity is designed around the importing country's desire to protect and stimulate its economy, primarily by balancing, at least partially, foreign exchange expenditures.

As an example, countertrade often occurs where a country lacks the convertible currency to pay for a priority import. Instead, export products are made available in settlement. These generate the necessary convertible currency to pay for the import.

Countertrade is therefore not necessarily trade without money, the exception being the few remaining cases of classic barter, involving the straight exchange of goods. All other forms of countertrade involve the use of money in some way.

The boundaries of what constitutes countertrade are forever widening as more and more complex and innovative transactions are contemplated. In particular, the ability to link countertrade with financial products and mechanisms enhances the ability to formulate non-conventional solutions to trade-related problems that would otherwise go unresolved.

Why countertrade?

Trade in its earliest form was based on countertrade. The exchange of goods for other goods under barter transactions formed the foundation of commerce as we know it and, arguably, the very survival of the human race.

Over many centuries barter was gradually overshadowed by the widespread use of money as the primary medium for exchange and valuation. Today, money continues to offer unequalled trading flexibility and liquidity, for those countries that can generate it in sufficient quantities.

The imperfections in the distribution of the world's resources and in its economic and monetary systems restrict and sometimes stifle the rate of growth and development of many less fortunate nations. In recent times many economies have been dominated by inflation, liquidity problems, local currency devaluations, huge balance-of-trade deficits, foreign exchange shortages, massive foreign indebtedness and, consequently, new financial regulations. As a result, a more subjective commercial environment has been created with many financial institutions around the world adopting a more conservative lending policy, both on an individual corporate and country risk basis.

Restrictions on the availability of traditional forms of trade financing, acute shortages of foreign exchange, wild fluctuations in commodity pricing and oversupply have caused some countries to turn to alternative methods of financing their trade, while at the same time attempting to achieve their economic objectives. Countertrade can obviate, ease or at least help contain such problems. The expertise of countertraders can be instrumental in the expansion of markets and enable importers and exporters alike to be brought together easily and with the minimum of risk.

ADVANTAGES TO A NATION OF A COUNTERTRADE POLICY

1 To implement a selective import programme in spite of foreign exchange shortages and credit restrictions.
2 To help balance overseas trade and achieve other economic objectives.
3 To clear surpluses of products at times of market oversupply.
4 To establish incremental sales of traditional products and/or to expand exports of non-traditional goods.
5 To exploit a buyer's market (in respect of the import) to negotiate the best terms and/or generate additional benefit for the economy.
6 To increase employment and generate prosperity.

Who countertrades and who doesn't?

LESS DEVELOPED COUNTRIES (LDCs)

Many countries turn to countertrade to help relieve economic pressures and most LDCs fall into this group. It largely comprises the LDCs in Africa, parts of the Middle East, Asia, Central and South America and some of the countries which were formerly part of the Soviet Union (see also Central and East European countries below).

These are the countries with limited resources, with infrastructure and industry in the early stages of development and, therefore, a restricted capacity to generate convertible currency to sustain ever-increasing import requirements and service possibly huge foreign indebtedness. They are the poorest and often the hardest hit when recession and unease shake the world markets and when demand and pricing fall in respect of their few staple products, which are their lifeline.

Countertrade is used to obtain priority imports, to clear surpluses of traditional products, create new export markets and balance foreign exchange expenditures. But the volume of business transacted in this way is often restricted by the limited availability of exportable products of an acceptable quality.

Some LDCs have specific countertrade policies, which should outline (i) the parameters within which countertrade is acceptable, and (ii) how a transaction should be progressed. For the countertrader, this should help lessen the often extensive organizational and bureaucratic delays experienced in obtaining the ministerial and central bank authorities which are usually required for countertrade transactions to proceed.

SEMI-INDUSTRIALIZED COUNTRIES (SICs)

SICs are vulnerable economies, mainly in the southern hemisphere, with a relatively young and growing industrial presence, probably dependent on substantial foreign debt and the import of large volumes of raw materials. They are hungry for new export markets, but their products face stiff competition from established foreign manufacturers.

Countertrade is used to develop new markets for industrial products (export-led countertrade) and/or for the procurement of raw materials (import-led countertrade) or to help balance foreign trade in an overall sense.

SICs engage in countertrade with Western industrialized countries in the northern hemisphere (North/South countertrade), but the development of business with LDCs is becoming increasingly important (South/South countertrade). The LDCs, with their limited industrial development, offer both new and less demanding markets for industrial products and ready sources of raw materials.

CENTRAL AND EAST EUROPEAN COUNTRIES

Countertrade has played an important role in the development of the countries of Central and Eastern Europe ever since the end of the Second World War and continues to do so.

Until recent years, countertrade with Western industrialized countries was based upon the concept of counterpurchase obligations: 'If we buy some of your goods, you must buy some of ours.' Often, an East European country's foreign trade, including countertrade, would be handled by a number of foreign trade organizations (FTOs) each of which had its own product sector to look after. Under a countertrade transaction a limiting factor was that the FTO handling the import of the Western products would usually also supply the counterpurchase goods for export (that is, within the same product sector). This meant a restriction in the products a country would supply to enable a foreign exporter to fulfil a counterpurchase obligation. Viennese banks and trading companies played an important role in such transactions, particularly by finding markets (often in LDCs) for East European manufactured goods and other products supplied by the FTOs.

A significant proportion of trade between East European countries and with some SICs (notably Brazil and India) and LDCs was often transacted by way of countertrade through bilateral trade agreements, using 'clearing currencies'.

Imbalances in trade under bilateral arrangements sometimes resulted from a deficiency in demand for East European products from the overseas trading partners. Such imbalances gave rise to a further specialized form of countertrade called 'switch trading', whereby a third-party Western nation could help reduce such an imbalance by shipping its preferred products to an overseas trading partner instead. Once again, the Viennese were often instrumental in this form of countertrade.

As a trading medium, these old bilateral trade arrangements were of fundamental importance to many East European economies. On the one hand, they provided a means of importing vital raw materials (notably oil and gas from the former Soviet Union) and, on the other, ready export markets for manufactured goods and products. In the early 1990s, however, the historic liberation of many of these nations and the dismantling of the Soviet Union was founded on a revolution of a different kind – the move away from communism and centrally planned economies towards democracy and market-based economies. But it also meant that the bilateral trading arrangements with their clearing currencies were suddenly gone and trade between East European nations and with all their overseas partners was wholly transferred over to hard currency.

Many countries, not surprisingly, had fairly modest hard currency resources, and the demise of the bilaterals made it difficult to pay for fundamental food and energy imports and, at the same time, stifled export markets. Political freedom and, in some cases, the strife that resulted, has also created new countries and states, particularly following the break-up of the former Soviet Union. The emergence of these new countries, major economic reforms and shortages of hard currency have meant a continuing role for countertrade in Central and Eastern Europe.

WESTERN INDUSTRIALIZED COUNTRIES

This group is based closely on the countries that belong to the Organization for Economic Co-operation and Development (OECD), notably the USA, Canada and European countries in the northern hemisphere and Japan, Australia and New Zealand in the southern hemisphere.

These are the more fortunate nations with the resources to generate sufficient convertible currency and the ready ability to raise and service credit to allow their foreign trade to proceed generally without a need to countertrade.

Countertrade is often not promoted and is sometimes actively discouraged because it is regarded as a threat to the multilateral trading system which is characterized by competition, free bargaining, openness and convertible currency.

The system is not perfect and some nations, including the USA and the UK, have adopted a middle-of-the-road attitude towards countertrade. This is generally for the following reasons.

1   They acknowledge that countertrade can play an important role in trade with LDCs, SICs and East European countries. They realize that in order to remain competitive, maintain and increase market share and create new markets, exporting companies must be prepared to be involved in countertrade and the more dynamic among them will even be adopting a proactive (as opposed to reactive) stance towards it. Some governments provide support and assistance on countertrade to exporters. In the UK the Department of Trade and Industry (DTI), through its Project and Export Policy Division, provides an advisory service in relation to countertrade matters.

2   Export credit agencies, such as the UK's Export Credits Guarantee Department (ECGD), have in general been opposed to countertrade. They would only consider a financing proposal incorporating an element of reciprocity, provided the credit risk could stand alone, independent of the countertrade even if in practice it would provide the primary source of repayment. Some export credit agencies are beginning to take a more pragmatic view of countertrade, both as a source of repayment for new credits and as a means of getting at least some of their money back under recovery situations. In August 1998, ECGD introduced its 'Good Projects' scheme under which they will consider the provision of support for viable new projects in markets generally off-cover for medium-term business. The key element of the scheme is that debt service must, from the outset, be secured by an existing, identifiable revenue stream flowing into an escrow account mechanism. Such revenue flows often come from the sale of goods and services.

3   Large, usually high-technology contracts between industrialized nations, particularly in

the defence and aerospace industries, often include an element of offset. (See 'Offset' later in this chapter.) This can offer the buying nation various reciprocal benefits including the generation of orders for its own products, increased employment, transfers of technology and the chance, at least partially, to balance foreign exchange expenditures.

4   Australia and New Zealand have both set in place specific countertrade policies, primarily based on offset. An element of reciprocity is called for in bids from overseas companies for public sector contracts. The policy is designed to promote technology and skills transfer to make the countries more self-sufficient and to increase export capacity.

5   Some countries, such as Greece, Portugal and Spain, recognize how countertrade can stimulate an economy, particularly through the preservation of foreign exchange resources, additionality and increased employment. Consequently, they open their doors to countertrade on a selective basis.

TYPES OF COUNTERTRADE

There are six widely discussed countertrade mechanisms:

1   barter and evidence account transactions
2   counterpurchase
3   compensation or 'buy-back'
4   offset
5   bilateral trade agreements
6   switch trading.

Although countertrade is a specialized, non-conventional trading medium, in practice it uses conventional banking services and trading tools, such as documentary letters of credit (L/Cs), bills for collection, international payment mechanisms and guarantees, to achieve its objectives and this should be borne in mind in considering the following detailed reviews.

BARTER AND EVIDENCE ACCOUNT TRANSACTIONS

It is a common misconception for the word 'barter' to be used as the generic term for all forms of reciprocal trade. This is incorrect. Barter is itself a form of countertrade.

It is the oldest, but now the least used countertrade mechanism – a simultaneous exchange of goods (tangible or intangible) for other goods without the involvement of money; often a once-only transaction bound by a single commercial contract.

In practice the supplier in country A (Figure 18.1) might delay shipment of its products until it is sure that country B's goods have been shipped first.

A more complex structure can be used to record the two-way flow of goods between commercial parties in countries A and B up to a specific total value (for example US$ 5 million each way) and over a fixed period of time (say 12 months). The two-way flow of trade would be recorded via notional *evidence accounts* maintained and mirrored by a bank in each country. It would be pre-agreed that imbalances in the value of goods shipped in either direction would be cleared periodically (each quarter perhaps) or within a stated period (90 days, for instance) following the end of the term of the arrangement, by settlement in convertible currency or by a balancing shipment of goods. This overall structure is similar in concept to government-to-government bilateral trade agreements.

Figure 18.1 *Barter*

COUNTERPURCHASE

Counterpurchase is the most extensively used form of countertrade. There are two distinct counterpurchase concepts:

- classic counterpurchase
- counterpurchase obligations.

Classic counterpurchase

Classic counterpurchase is often used in countertrade with LDCs and SICs.

An LDC lacks readily available convertible currency to pay for a priority import. Instead, the country makes available its own goods for export (the counterpurchase or offtake goods) the hard currency proceeds of which are specifically used to pay for the import (the principal products).

Normally two separate underlying commercial contracts are involved:

- one between the exporter of the LDC's counterpurchase goods and an overseas buyer; and
- one between the foreign supplier and the LDC importer in respect of the principal products.

Both contracts would probably be concluded between unrelated parties, that is, separate importers and exporters within the LDC and separate foreign buyers and suppliers.

The parties would be linked together by countertrade documentation, which would outline the purpose of the overall countertrade transaction, the responsibilities of the various parties involved and the banking structure for its implementation. The banking arrangements are often administered between a prime international bank (probably the principal banker to the transaction), in concert with the central bank in the LDC.

Settlement between importer and exporter within the LDC would be made in local currency via the central bank.

Counterpurchase goods can be overpriced or of an inferior quality by world market standards. In order to tempt a prospective buyer, an incentive must be given. The supplier of the principal products must subsidize the cost of the counterpurchase goods by paying a rebate or subsidy, sometimes known as a 'disagio', to the buyer.

In Figure 18.2 we see an example of a counterpurchase transaction. An LDC wishes to purchase buses from Germany. Coffee is made available in settlement. A buyer for the coffee is found in France.

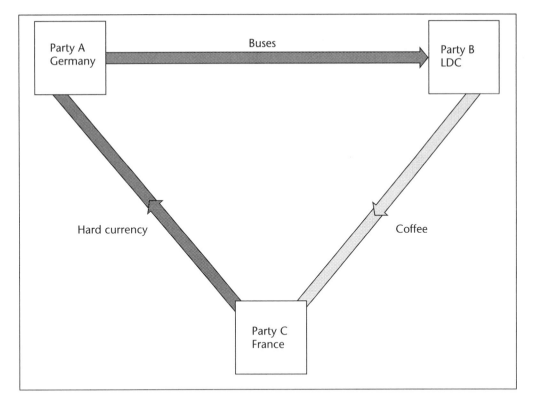

Figure 18.2   *A classic counterpurchase structure*

The coffee is shipped first, thus neutralizing the risk on the LDC. The buses are shipped, with settlement coming from the proceeds of the coffee sale.

Figure 18.3 relates to the same transaction with the banking structure superimposed. The overseas international bank would act as principal banker for the transaction. Let's look at the transaction again.

1   Once the coffee is shipped, the shipping documents are presented to the overseas bank under the coffee L/C. The documents are presented to the French coffee buyer against payment in convertible currency. Simultaneously, the bus manufacturer will pay the disagio to the coffee buyer.
2   The coffee proceeds are held by the overseas bank on an interest-bearing proceeds or 'escrow' account, until the buses are shipped in accordance with the terms of the bus L/C opened by the central bank in the LDC.
3   Upon presentation of (conforming) shipping documents for the buses, the German manufacturer is paid in convertible currency to the debit of the proceeds account. The shipping documents are passed to the central bank in the LDC.
4   Should the bus manufacturer fail to perform, the coffee proceeds would be held at the disposal of the LDC.

Counterpurchase obligations

'If we buy your goods you must buy some of ours' – counterpurchase obligations constitute simple reciprocity.

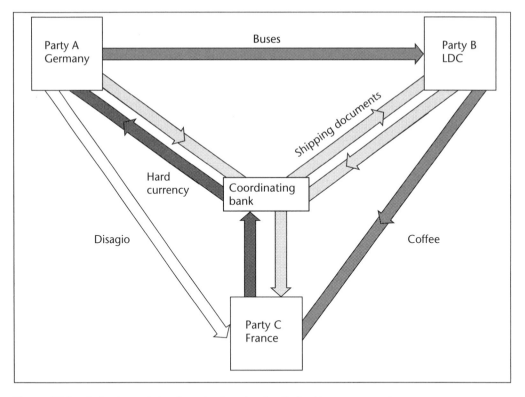

Figure 18.3   *A classic counterpurchase structure showing the banking arrangements*

In order to secure an overseas sales contract, a foreign exporter enters into an obligation to make reciprocal purchases of the importing country's own products and resources.

The counterpurchase obligation would be separate from, but run in parallel to, the supply contract for the principal products, which itself would either be concluded on a cash basis or have its own financing structure.

The value of an obligation is usually calculated as a percentage of the value of the supply contract for the principal products. It could be 25 per cent, 50 per cent, 100 per cent or more: the level is subject to negotiation. Much will depend on the eagerness of the foreign supplier to win the contract, the level of competition and the priority given to the purchase of the principal products by the importing country. The lower the value of the counterpurchase obligation, the lower the potential cost to the foreign supplier.

Counterpurchase obligations are often evidenced by a memorandum of understanding (MOU) outlining the terms of the arrangement. Fulfilment of the obligation would be through the purchase of probably part traditional and part non-traditional products, which would be listed in the MOU.

Whilst the MOU would be signed by the foreign suppliers, provision is usually made for the counterpurchase obligation to be fulfilled by a third-party trader on their behalf.

In its simplest and arguably cheapest form, an obligation might represent a simple statement of intent to purchase on a best endeavours basis. But it is more usual for a formal MOU to be involved which might call for a performance guarantee or at least a penalty clause to cover non-fulfilment. Non-fulfilment would probably harm the image of the foreign supplier at least in the eyes of the importing country.

Countries that have used countertrade policies based on counterpurchase obligations (for example, East European countries, India, Indonesia and Malaysia) can often raise credit in international financial markets. Their countertrade policy is used to increase exports, to find new markets for their products and help balance trade and therefore foreign exchange expenditures in an overall sense, rather than on a transaction by transaction basis (see also 'Offset' later in this chapter).

COMPENSATION OR BUY-BACK

Compensation, or buy-back, is an arrangement whereby the supplier of capital plant, manufacturing equipment or technology accepts payment, or part thereof, in goods subsequently manufactured by the equipment supplied.

This mechanism is often associated with large project-related and/or long-term contracts which can involve a lead-in time of several years before output begins. The sale of the relevant equipment would probably be the subject of a financing package in which case the proceeds of the plant output would be used in repayment.

The simple example in Figure 18.4 relates to the supply of a cement manufacturing plant by country A to country B. The suppliers accept payment in the form of 30 per cent convertible currency and 70 per cent in cement produced by the plant they supplied. They may find markets for the cement themselves or engage a trader to do so.

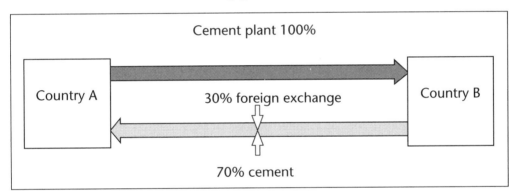

Figure 18.4   *Compensation or buy-back*

Through buy-back the purchasing nation can benefit from the development of its industrial base, technology transfer and assured export markets for the products subsequently manufactured.

OFFSET

Offset is a form of countertrade usually between industrialized nations and often associated with high-value contracts for the supply of civil or military aircraft, defence equipment and high-technology products.

The export contract, the subject of its own financing arrangements, is conditional upon the importing nation receiving a reciprocal benefit in return for making such a major purchase. The reciprocity could take the form of local investment, the transfer of technology or by orders being placed for the purchase of the importing nation's own products. The value of the offset would normally be calculated as a percentage of the value of the main supply contract.

Direct offset

Direct (related) offset is where the principal products being supplied and the reciprocal arrangements are related:

- where materials, components or systems used by the exporting company, possibly but not necessarily in the manufacture of the products to be supplied, are procured from within the importing country; and/or
- the supply contract incorporates an element of technology transfer; and/or
- the products to be supplied, or at least major sub-assemblies, will be manufactured under licence within the importing country.

An example some years ago was a much publicized £850 million contract for the purchase by the UK Ministry of Defence of American Boeing AWACS aircraft, which was conditional upon companies in the AWACS consortium placing orders in the UK for materials and products for a total value equivalent to 130 per cent of the value of the aircraft being supplied. The items procured in the UK did not have to be used in the manufacture of the aircraft, but had to be for use by AWACS consortium companies. Similar contracts for the purchase of Boeing AWACS aircraft by France and Saudi Arabia were also believed to have had offset arrangements attached.

Indirect offset

Indirect (unrelated) offset is where the exporting country agrees a programme of reciprocity, be it investment or the purchase of goods and services, which are unrelated to the principal supply contract.

For example, an exporter of high-technology communications equipment agrees to make purchases of unrelated industrial products from the importing country, which can either be sold on the home market or laid off elsewhere (perhaps by a trader).

Offset is becoming increasingly popular with certain importing countries seeking to accelerate industrial and technological development and increase export capacity. Australia, New Zealand and the Philippines set in place offset regulations several years ago. More recently, offset has become almost commonplace in the United Arab Emirates, Oman and (post-Gulf War) Kuwait, usually in relation to large public sector and often military contracts. The offset here often relates to indirect investment and can be based upon profit generation (rather than the investment value simply equating to a percentage of the value of the supply contract as is usual). Kuwait also has an interesting multiplier system, whereby the offset value is weighted depending upon the importance of the investment or purchase to the local economy.

Some potential advantages of offset to an importing country are:

- reduction in imported content of a contract
- elimination or at least reduction in the effect of a sizeable import on a country's balance of foreign trade and foreign currency reserves (a foreign exchange inflow could occur)
- transfer of technology and increased industrial development
- increase in exports and/or export capability

- creation of jobs
- stimulation of the economy.

BILATERAL TRADE AGREEMENTS

Although government-to-government trading mechanisms, bilaterals are still regarded as countertrade, the countries involved typically having centrally planned or controlled economies and foreign exchange shortages. Bilaterals offer them assured markets for exports, regular sources of raw materials for import and balance-of-payments benefits.

An arrangement can vary from a statement to develop mutual trade on a best endeavours basis to a formal agreement, often with the following features.

1   An agreed volume of goods would flow in each direction during a specified period of time (say 12 months).
2   The goods to flow in each direction would probably be specified.
3   Monetary settlement between the countries should normally not be involved. Instead the each-way flow of goods is monitored by the central bank in each country through notional 'clearing accounts' maintained in an independent 'clearing currency' (usually a convertible currency such as US dollars).
4   Any imbalances which occur, whereby one country ships more goods than the other, would be cleared periodically or at the end of the term of the agreement by a balancing shipment of goods (or by a payment in convertible currency).
5   Settlement between importers and exporters within each country would be made in local currency through the central or foreign trade bank.

Bilateral trade agreements have historically been an important feature of trade of East European countries between themselves and with LDCs and SICs. Notably, many East European countries had agreements with Brazil and India. With the moves away from centrally planned to market-based economies, the formal clearing-account-based bilaterals have largely fallen away. The technique could however become popular again in certain circumstances and Figure 18.5 shows an example of how a bilateral trade agreement worked

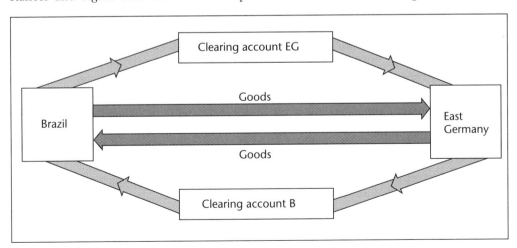

Figure 18.5   *Bilateral clearing accounts*

between the former East Germany and Brazil involving the use of clearing accounts, maintained by the central bank in each country, to record the two-way flow of goods.

When Brazil shipped goods to East Germany, instead of being paid in convertible currency it would be given a credit in the clearing account maintained by the East German central bank, equivalent to the value of the shipment. When Brazil received goods from East Germany the clearing account would be debited. The central bank in Brazil would do the reverse and therefore the two clearing accounts should mirror each other.

SWITCH TRADING

Despite this form of countertrade largely falling into disuse, it may still be helpful for the reader to gain an insight into how such transactions worked since such techniques might always arise again in response to any future regional economic crises. Switch trading was a specialized form of countertrade which related to the bilateral trade arrangements between East European countries and their trading partners and directly to the imbalances in trade that often occurred thereunder.

Using, once again, the example of Brazil and the former East Germany, Brazil might have shipped substantially more goods to East Germany than it had received in return, creating a large credit balance on the clearing account maintained in East Germany (mirrored by a similar debit balance on the account maintained in Brazil).

East Germany would be indebted to Brazil and should provide goods, or perhaps convertible currency, to settle the shortfall. In order to reduce this and bring the clearing accounts more into balance, it was sometimes possible for goods sourced from a third country to be shipped to Brazil instead.

An exporting company in a third country, say the UK, interested in using bilateral clearing mechanisms to penetrate overseas markets, in this case Brazil (with its stringent import regulations) would normally seek an introduction to a specialist 'switch trader'. These were banks and trading houses (many located in Vienna) experienced in handling trade with East European countries. They maintained close links with the FTOs and central banks and were able to monitor the surplus space on the large number of clearing accounts that existed. Once authorities had been obtained from the central banks in East Germany and Brazil, the switch trader was able to implement a switch operation to allow the UK goods to be shipped to Brazil.

Figure 18.6 shows an example. The switch trader stands in the middle. East German products (or possibly convertible currency) are made available to the switch trader who finds markets for them elsewhere. The proceeds are paid, less a disagio, to the UK exporter whose goods are shipped to Brazil. East Germany debits its clearing account with the appropriate value, Brazil passes a corresponding credit entry and the clearing accounts are brought more into balance. The whole operation is essentially a swap of East German goods for UK goods.

Some advantages of such switch trading were:

- The East European country benefited not only because its indebtedness to its foreign partner had been reduced, but also this had been achieved at an advantageous cost, since it probably provided goods to the switch trader for an equivalent value of less than 100 cents in the dollar.
- Whilst the third-party exporters received less than 100 per cent of the quoted price for their goods (reflecting the disagio costs of the operation), they were able to make an export that otherwise would not have been possible.

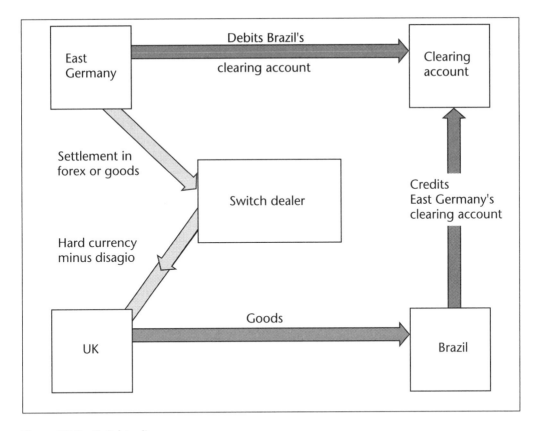

Figure 18.6 *Switch trading*

- The foreign partner (Brazil) received goods it had a preference for.
- The clearing accounts were brought more into balance.

Participants in countertrade: the 'countertraders'

The above review of the six basic countertrade mechanisms should only be regarded as a very general guide.

In reality, countertrade is very much an *ad hoc* activity. Every transaction is different and it is difficult strictly to categorize them. There are neither ground rules nor standard procedures and the mechanisms vary according to the needs of the individual transaction. It is the countertrader's job to engineer, or tailor, a countertrade solution to a particular set of trade-related circumstances. In doing so, the countertrader will consider such things as local regulations (including countertrade policy if there is one), the type of goods being traded and the requirements of the parties involved. The result could be a structure very similar to one of the six mechanisms reviewed; it might be a hybrid incorporating elements drawn from two or three of them or, perhaps, an innovative solution which breaks new ground.

It is often costly and difficult to put a transaction together and bring it to fruition and a successful conclusion. It is fraught with a seemingly endless catalogue of pitfalls, problems and delays. It is a minefield for the amateur.

An involvement in countertrade requires special skills and knowledge which should be introduced at the earliest opportunity. If introduced too late, much straightening out and undoing may be necessary to place the transaction on an acceptable footing and it could also mean that costs are higher than might otherwise have been the case. The introduction of a specialist countertrader early on could mean the difference between success and failure. Experience counts.

There are a few exporting companies, usually the major multinationals, which use their trading experience and worldwide network of resources and contacts to maintain an in-house capability to handle countertrade. They are seeking to maintain and expand export markets and therefore use it not only in response to requests from buyers, but also offer it as an extra incentive in order to win contracts. But, for the majority of those considering countertrade, it is usually essential to employ the services of a specialist. So who are the specialists, the 'countertraders'? Excluding the large corporates mentioned above, there are three principal types of player in the marketplace:

- large commodity traders
- banks
- independent consultants/agents.

These offer their expertise to exporters interested in countertrade.

LARGE COMMODITY TRADERS

Leading trading houses may specialize in trading a particular commodity or commodity group, be it metals, grains, fruit and vegetables, oil or whatever. Some have the capacity to handle a wide range of products and goods, including industrial products and consumer goods sourced from SICs.

Such traders can actively countertrade in the following ways:

1 They will use it selectively to maximize their trading returns.
2 Like other exporters they might be obliged to countertrade to penetrate a particular overseas market.
3 They use to advantage their worldwide trading ability to trade in those products offered under countertrade transactions. As buyers thereof they can reduce the costs and improve profit margins through the receipt of disagio payments.
4 They engineer countertrade transactions on their own behalf, using their in-house expertise to trade out the offtake products and look for suppliers of suitable return products who are willing to absorb the required disagio, in order to make an export which might otherwise not be possible.

Those most actively involved in countertrade can therefore provide a wide range of useful services and opportunities for the exporter.

1 They will help structure, negotiate and document the countertrade transaction and, most important, act as principals in contracting to purchase the offtake products. They are nevertheless reliant on their bankers to provide the necessary services which constitute the banking structure for the transaction.

2 They can simply act as buyers of and thus take title to, the offtake products. In so doing they are prepared to be a signatory to countertrade arrangements structured and administered by banks and large corporates.

3 For a market-related fee, they are willing to take over responsibility for the fulfilment of counterpurchase obligations.

4 The countertrade transactions engineered by the traders themselves can open up useful opportunities for exporters seeking to penetrate potential overseas markets which are short of foreign exchange and/or unable to raise credit and/or which have compulsory countertrade requirements.

BANKS

A common misconception is that banks are not countertraders at all, that their only use is as providers of traditional banking services and as administrators of proceeds accounts required under countertrade transactions arranged elsewhere. Let's look at the reality.

Banks have long-standing relationships with governments, central banks, companies and traders worldwide – in fact, all the parties likely to be involved in countertrade. However, although Viennese banks have been involved with East European countertrade for many years, it was only in the early 1980s, which saw a significant increase in the volume of countertrade, that some of the major international banks perceived the important role they could play in countertrade arrangements.

Today, some banks that have accumulated countertrade knowledge still take a relatively passive role. They will only go as far as assisting an exporter in an advisory capacity, preferring subsequently to make an introduction to a trading house which ultimately would be better placed to satisfy the exporter's requirements. However, whilst volumes of countertrade significantly reduced during the 1990s, there are a handful of very much more active banks that place themselves competitively in the forefront of the countertrade market. They have set up specialist units which can combine a comprehensive range of countertrade skills, traditional banking services and both conventional and non-conventional financing products to provide innovative solutions to trade-related problems.

Like everything else in countertrade, the role of such banks will vary from transaction to transaction, but the services they can provide include the following principal elements:

1 To review a company's export opportunities, identify potential for countertrade and implement a programme.

2 To introduce parties to a transaction, as appropriate, and bring them together in complete confidentiality.

3 To review the details of the underlying circumstances, propose how a countertrade solution should be pursued and suggest ways of overcoming operational difficulties and minimizing risks.

4 To structure the transaction and create the necessary countertrade documentation.

5 Those banks that have a trading capacity may act as principals in purchasing the offtake products.

6 To introduce, as appropriate, specialist suppliers and/or takers of specific products traded under countertrade transactions. (Through worldwide networks of clients and contacts, the banks have special relationships with product suppliers and end users as well as with the trading houses.)

7   To assist with the negotiation of the countertrade with the commercial parties involved and with the acquisition of the necessary government and central bank authorities and approvals that are usually necessary before a transaction can proceed.

8   To act as principal banker for the transaction, maintaining full control over its operation from start to finish and providing the required banking facilities to the parties concerned (subject to the bank's usual credit criteria). Such banking facilities could include the opening, advising and confirming of L/Cs, the operation of proceeds and/or evidence accounts and the issuing of bonds or guarantees, as appropriate.

9   To introduce finance into a transaction (see 'Financing', below).

10   To work closely with the private insurance market. It is possible to cover a number of non-bankable performance/political risks through specialized markets in London and New York. Policies can be tailored to a given set of circumstances.

11   To act as countertrade advisers to governments, central banks, development banks, companies and individuals worldwide.

One of a bank's primary strengths in countertrade is its ability to act as an impartial intermediary to both sides of the transaction. Although the bank will primarily be representing its client, whichever party that is, it can be viewed by all the parties to the transaction, be they importers, exporters, government ministries or central banks, as a major financial institution that will wish to ensure not only that the transaction proceeds satisfactorily, but that its own name and reputation remain unblemished. For this reason, a bank's involvement can often enhance the chances of a transaction being brought to fruition and successfully concluded.

Some banks have built up enviable reputations based on successfully concluded transactions and will handle all types of countertrade, from barter to switch. Their approach is often both reactive and proactive, with clients bringing deals to them and the banks engineering transactions to take to their clients.

INDEPENDENT CONSULTANTS/AGENTS

These are usually individuals or small companies. Some simply provide advice and assistance on countertrade matters, whilst others offer a more extensive range of services encompassing the structuring of transactions, the placing of countertrade products and the management of the arrangement. A few will consider taking title to countertraded products.

Most consultants may be dependent on the banks and trading houses to complement the services they can provide. At the same time they will also be competing with them for business.

For the exporter, consultants can provide valuable assistance, particularly those that specialize in particular types of countertrade (for example, product related buy-back or offset) or specific markets.

The costs (and the savings)

Each of the specialist countertraders will charge for their services. Their fees will vary according to the nature of the services provided and the size and complexity of the transaction, but they are competitively based and generally good value for the expertise and work involved. Out-of-pocket expenses, including any travel costs, may be extra. In addition, the exporter must also consider any banking cost of the operation which may fall outside the counter-trader's fees. The latter might include L/C fees, including any confirmation charges (which could be significant) and funds transmission costs. But the countertrader's fees can often be relatively insignificant when compared with the costs of selling the counterpurchase or offtake products into the world market. This is the real cost of countertrade.

LDCs and SICs will often not allow their staple, cash-earning products to be used for countertrade unless surpluses exist and/or new, additional markets are being created. It is more usual for second-string, non-traditional products to be offered, but these may be of an inferior or substandard quality in world market terms. In order to protect the existing export markets for their goods and ensure additionality, stringent destination restrictions may be imposed which make the placing of the goods even more difficult. To compound all of this, the supplying country will have its own idea of pricing for the goods, which is often in excess of the world market value.

So why should potential buyers change their normal purchasing pattern and consider countertraded goods? They must be given an incentive. In practice the supplier of the princi-pal products back into the country concerned will be responsible for paying a 'disagio' (that is, a subsidy) to the buyer of the offtake goods to bring their cost down to an acceptable level.

In Figure 18.3, for example, the French coffee buyer will have negotiated a price for the coffee with the supplier in the LDC. Based on this pricing, the French buyer must pay 100 per cent of the coffee proceeds into the proceeds account maintained by the coordinating bank (for the purpose of purchasing the buses). *Simultaneously* the German bus manufacturer will pay a disagio to the French coffee buyer to subsidize the cost of the coffee and reduce it to an acceptable level.

The cost of the disagio must be built into the costings of the suppliers of the principal products (the buses). They must consider how far they are prepared to reduce their profit margin to absorb the disagio cost and/or whether the price of the principal products to be supplied can be increased to compensate.

Unless an LDC can be persuaded to offer the counterpurchase goods at market price in the first place, it is generally unusual for the LDC to bear the cost of the disagio.

The size of the disagio would be negotiated between the buyer of the offtake goods and the supplier of the principal products. It will be calculated as a percentage of the LDC cost of the offtake goods and its size can vary considerably. The subsidy might be 3 per cent, 10 per cent, 30 per cent or even more. Much will depend on the original LDC cost of the goods, the quality and demand. It is when the disagio costs are realistically estimated and the full impact is known, that many potential countertrade transactions fall apart.

In theory, it follows that if good-quality, traditional products are offered for countertrade at a competitive price and at a time of buoyant demand, the subsidy required by the prospec-tive buyer should be a relatively small one. In practice it is rarely so simple.

Disagio costs might be reduced if the counterpurchase goods can be used in-house by the supplier of the principal products. Such opportunities are most likely to occur in relation to the offtake of goods under counterpurchase obligations or reciprocal orders for goods under offset requirements.

During the structuring and negotiation of a countertrade transaction a considerable amount of work is involved in identifying suitable counterpurchase products, finding a prospective buyer and estimating the likely level of disagio which must be absorbed. The definitive cost of the disagio will not be known until the final negotiations and contract signa-ture, although a reasonable estimate can usually be made early on in the negotiations.

However, counterpurchase obligations are different. Because of the nature of these obligations, it is not uncommon for them to be fulfilled by third-party traders who, given certain basic information, are often willing to quote what is tantamount to a market price for the business. An exporter negotiating for the supply of products to a particular country can therefore obtain an accurate estimate of the cost of the countertrade early on in the negotiations.

As regards 'the savings', it follows that, depending on how attractive the disagio is, it is possible for a manufacturing company to reduce costs by sourcing its raw materials through countertrade. The savings that can be made by buying offtake products and therefore taking advantage of disagio payments represent one of the main reasons why trading houses have developed their expertise in trading the types of goods offered by LDCs and SICs for counter-trade.

Some risks

DELIVERY/PERFORMANCE RISKS

Countertrade is a trading medium whereby a country's goods, rather than its precious foreign currency reserves, are being used to generate either settlement for specific imports or at least some form of reciprocal benefit. The risks therefore generally relate to non-delivery or non-performance in respect of the offtake goods, rather than directly to non-payment.

In the majority of cases such risks can be reduced, if not eliminated, by ensuring that the *counterpurchase goods are shipped first* and that the proceeds are held safely on the proceeds account with the coordinating bank, outside the country concerned, before the principal products are shipped. In the case of term transactions, involving a number of shipments of offtake goods, it would be a matter of ensuring that there are always sufficient funds on the proceeds account to cover work completed under the contract for the supply of the principal products. The coordinating bank might, however, be able to inject some flexibility into such a structure if it is prepared to add its confirmation to the LDC/SIC's letters of credit for the import of the principal products, thus allowing the suppliers to ship when they like, regardless of whether there are sufficient funds in the proceeds account to cover.

Risks that are more difficult to cover occur when it is agreed that the principal products should be shipped early on under a countertrade arrangement, with the counterpurchase goods, possibly perishable items, being supplied over a longer period of time, perhaps a number of years. It is possible to insure the associated delivery and political risks in the private insurance markets – such as Lloyd's of London and the American International Underwriters (AIU) – but the premium would be another significant cost which must usually be borne by the supplier of the principal products.

CONTRACT RISK

As a general rule it is not advisable for the supply of the principal products and the purchase of the offtake goods to be the subject of the same commercial contract. If, for example, a problem associated with the offtake goods occurred, then the whole contract could be endangered. Far better to have separate commercial contracts linked by the countertrade documentation. This way there would probably be a far better chance of solving the problem, perhaps finding a new buyer or substituting the offtake goods (which might even necessitate a completely new contract), without bringing down the whole structure.

THE OVER-ZEALOUS SALES EXECUTIVE!

There are many jokes about over-zealous sales executives who, in order to win supply contracts, readily sign on the dotted line to make reciprocal purchases of a country's own goods without in the slightest realizing the implications of what they are doing. It really does happen, even in the largest companies. Under normal circumstances, a contract for the offtake of goods should not be signed in isolation or without the countertrade being properly assessed and structured. The underlying commercial contracts and the countertrade documentation should preferably be signed simultaneously.

DISAGIO RISKS

There are two main areas of disagio risks.

1   Disagios are normally paid to the buyer of the offtake goods simultaneously with the remittance of the goods' proceeds to the coordinating bank for credit of the proceeds account.

   As mentioned above, to cover the delivery risk on the LDC, it is advisable to arrange for the offtake products to be shipped first. This means that the suppliers of the principal products would make the (first) disagio payment before their products have been shipped and therefore prior to their receiving any payment from the funds on the proceeds account. The disagio therefore represents a real up-front risk.

   In most cases the principal products would be shipped as soon as the funds are credited to the proceeds account, so that the disagio risk is short-lived. But this is not always the case. An advance payment under the supply contract, in convertible currency (possibly from the proceeds account), might be the best way of covering the disagio risk. An alternative could be penalty clausing in the supply contract providing for the payment of a penalty, equivalent to the disagio payment, from the funds on the proceeds account, in the event of default by the LDC.

2   Under countertrade transactions involving more than one shipment of offtake goods, it might not be in the buyer's interest to agree a fixed purchase price (and therefore disagio) at the outset of the contract covering all the shipments, which might be made over several months, if not years. A buyer will only be prepared to bear the pricing risk for a limited period of time, for example one, three or six months, depending upon the nature of the offtake goods and the relative market for them.

   This could mean periodic price negotiations and a fluctuating level of disagio, from shipment to shipment. It might also mean that shipment opportunities are missed because the disagio required is too great. The offtake of more goods must wait until the differential between the LDC pricing and the market value closes to an acceptable level. Hence the advisability of ensuring that there are always sufficient proceeds on the proceeds account to cover work completed under the contract for the supply of the principal products.

CURRENCY RISKS

An exporter should consider the risks in the usual way, but for the purposes of the smooth operation of the countertrade transaction, it is best for the whole structure (including both commercial contracts) to be denominated in a single convertible currency, for example US dollars. If, for example, a supply contract is denominated in the LDC's local currency, with the proceeds of the offtake products paid in convertible currency, a conversion formula for reference purposes can be built into the countertrade documentation, but it only leads to unnecessary complexities and potential problems. Far better to use a single convertible currency to avoid confusion.

Financing

Financing relates to the timing of payment, whereas countertrade involves the kind of payment.

A countertrade transaction often involves a country's products being used to generate payment in convertible currency, but finance can be introduced to add flexibility to the timing of the payment. Though financing is not strictly part of countertrade, the two can thus complement each other. Be it the simple provision of pre-shipment finance to an exporter, with repayment coming from the proceeds of the offtake products, or a large buy-back transaction involving an export credit, finance is an additional marketing tool which is playing an increasingly important role in countertrade transactions, particularly where banks are involved. However, the ability to introduce finance will depend very much on the bank's appetite for the credit and country risks involved.

EXAMPLE OF THE ROLE OF FINANCING

1   An LDC wishes to import chemicals, foodstuffs and spare parts (the principal products) for a total value of US$ 5 million, on 180-day credit terms.
2   The LDC offers settlement by way of shipments of sugar at the end of the 180-day period.
3   The exporter of the principal goods requires payment at sight, that is, upon presentation of the shipping documents.
4   A major international bank is introduced to structure a classic counterpurchase-type transaction.
5   The bank identifies a buyer for the sugar.
6   The bank agrees to advance funds to the supplier of the principal products, enabling him to extend 180 days' credit, against the following security:
    • an assignment of the sugar contract;
    • an assignment of the proceeds of the letter of credit covering the sale of the sugar; and
    • the guarantee of the central bank of the LDC covering the delivery of the sugar or, failing that, payment of the equivalent value in convertible currency.
    Repayment of the borrowing would come from the sugar proceeds.
7   The sugar buyer might arrange delivery risk insurance, in the private insurance market, covering non-delivery of the sugar. The bank would be named as the loss payee.
8   Recourse would be maintained to the supplier of the principal products for warranty and exclusions under the insurance policy.

A practical example of countertrade

Although a relatively simple transaction, based on the classic counterpurchase structure, the following example emphasizes what can be achieved through the clever use of countertrade. Figure 18.7 relates to a countertrade transaction for the redemption of overdue debt.

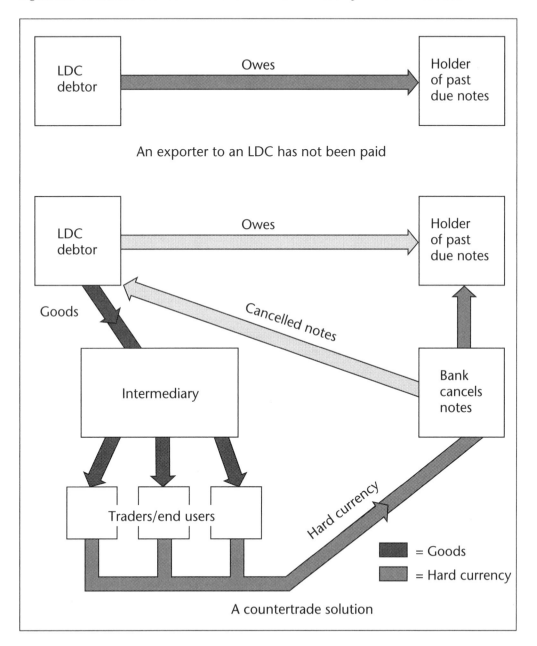

Figure 18.7 *Countertrade to redeem overdue debt*

An LDC owes money to a foreign supplier who is the holder of past due notes evidencing the debt. The foreign supplier has no idea when or if payment will be received.

An intermediary (probably a bank or trader) proposes a solution whereby:

1   the noteholder agrees to accept less than 100 cents in the dollar for cash now, or at least over an agreed period of time
2   the LDC debtor makes available non-traditional goods (or a mix of traditional and non-traditional goods) to the trader for export, the proceeds of which are used to:
    • pay off the notes and
    • pay the intermediaries' fees.

Figure 18.7 outlines the operation of the transaction. The importance of the banking structure is emphasized. The bank's role would be to:

• monitor the levels of LDC goods being traded
• handle the flow of shipping documents presented under the relative letters of credit
• receive the convertible currency proceeds and hold them in a proceeds account
• pay to the noteholder the agreed percentage of the notes (probably together with interest and overdue interest)
• cancel the overdue notes and pass them back to the central bank in the LDC.

The LDC benefits through a reduction in foreign debt, increased exports to new markets and the creation of new jobs.

Anatomy of countertrade

How is a transaction constructed? What are the stages which a countertrader must work through?

CONCEPTION OF THE PROPOSAL

An exporter might consider countertrade for any of the following reasons.

1   It might be required by the importing country which may have a well-established and controlled countertrade policy.
2   It might be the only way of selling to a nation short of foreign currency and unable to raise the necessary credit.
3   Reciprocity might be offered as an extreme incentive to win a contract.

Whatever the reason, a trading opportunity will present itself which is conditional upon settlement in goods, rather than money, and/or some other form of reciprocal benefit accruing to the country concerned.

Our example of classic counterpurchase (Figures 18.2 and 18.3) would probably fall under (2) above. The LDC has an urgent requirement for new buses, but does not have the necessary convertible currency available. Consideration is given to the provision of surplus staple products (coffee) in settlement.

RESEARCH AND ASSESSMENT

The following basic background information should be properly assessed in relation to the importing country:

- economic and political backdrop
- credit rating
- trading reputation
- performance record
- level of public sector involvement in foreign trade
- import and export regulations
- exchange controls
- export products, volumes, values and markets
- countertrade policy
- countertrade track record.

Through this exercise and previous knowledge and experience, the countertrader will be able to draw some initial conclusions as to whether a countertrade proposal is worth pursuing or not.

THE COUNTERTRADE PRODUCTS

In our counterpurchase example, the LDC has a priority import requirement for buses, but what goods can it offer in settlement? The following points should be considered.

1. Obtain a list of goods *available for countertrade.*
2. Who is responsible for the marketing of the goods *and* the allocation to a specific countertrade transaction?
3. Are the goods traditional or non-traditional? Traditionals should be the objective.
4. Consider the quality and grade of the product(s) by national and international standards.
5. Obtain specifications and, if possible, samples.
6. Ascertain quantity and availability for shipment.
7. Pricing – how does it compare with the world market value? What sort of disagio will be required?
8. Marketability – are there any destination restrictions?
9. Examine the LDC's infrastructure and its ability to perform.
10. Who might be prepared to buy these goods?
11. Do the goods really exist? Have they been sold several times over in the market? It does happen.

IDENTIFICATION OF THE PLAYERS

In our counterpurchase example, we have a manufacturer (exporter) and a buyer (LDC importer) of buses. It has been agreed that coffee will be made available in settlement and a coffee supplier (LDC exporter) has been identified. In this example, the coordinating bank, which is providing its specialist countertrade services to the bus manufacturer, has identified a prospective buyer in France for the coffee.

It is often at this point, when the counterpurchase products have been identified and are being assessed, a buyer for them is being sought and an estimation of the disagio is known, that many potential transactions fall by the wayside.

THE STRUCTURE

Once the parties have been identified, the countertrader can get down to formulating an operating structure for the proposed transaction. It should be kept as simple as possible. The countertrader will consider the following:

- the terms of the underlying commercial contracts
- the requirements of the parties to the countertrade
- local regulations (including any countertrade policy)
- timing
- how to minimize risks and overcome any operational difficulties
- any financing requirements
- how will the countertraders receive their fees?

The result will be a unique structure tailored to a unique set of circumstances.

THE COUNTERTRADE DOCUMENTATION

It has already been stated that there should be separate commercial contracts, one for the primary products (the buses), the other for the offtake goods (the coffee). The purpose of the countertrade documentation is to put a written legal framework around the countertrade structure. In so doing it will:

- link all the parties together
- state the purpose of the countertrade
- state the responsibilities of the parties
- outline how the transaction will operate
- seek to maximize the protection for the customer.

All countertraders will have their own method and style of documenting a transaction. The type and complexity of the transaction will dictate its format. There might be a single document or there could be several. Many countertraders have a preference for the existence of a separate document between the coordinating bank and the central bank of the LDC, outlining the *modus operandi* of the transaction (or what is often called 'the banking structure').

Some LDCs and SICs with an established countertrade policy provide their own countertrade documentation, which may or may not be negotiable.

NEGOTIATION AND THE AUTHORITY PROCESS

This is the most frustrating and troublesome stage, when another large proportion of proposed transactions fall apart. There are so many potential problems and pitfalls, that negotiations can take an inordinately long time and they can collapse at any moment. From inception of the proposal until signature and implementation of the transaction can take three months, six months, 18 months or even longer. Much will depend on the willingness of the parties to cooperate and compromise and on their appetite for success.

There are seemingly endless negotiations not only between the contractual parties, but also with government ministries and the central bank in the country concerned. A competent, well-connected local agent is a valuable asset and could represent the difference between success and failure.

Because of the nature of countertrade, its potential effects on a country's economy and its sensitivities, it is a government-led trading medium and various approvals and authorities may be necessary from within the LDC before a transaction is allowed to proceed. Commonly found requirements are as follows:

1 authorities from the ministry responsible for the import and the ministry responsible for the export
2 separate authorities from the ministry of foreign trade and/or the ministry of finance
3 final overall approval for a transaction to proceed, possibly from the prime minister or president himself
4 written evidence that the offtake products have been specifically allocated to this countertrade transaction
5 central bank approval for the non-repatriation of the foreign currency proceeds of the offtake goods where they are to be held on a proceeds account by a bank outside the country concerned.

OPERATION AND 'THE BANKING STRUCTURE'

Once all the authorities are in place and the commercial contracts and countertrade documentation have been *simultaneously* signed, operation of the transaction can begin. How trouble-free the transaction proves to be will not just depend on the integrity of the preparations, negotiations and agreements that have gone before.

A countertrade transaction can collapse at any time before or during implementation. It is never a success until the last nut and bolt has been shipped. The banking structure of the transaction and how professionally it is implemented are all-important.

This is where the countertrade units of the banks come into their own. They provide not only the specialist expertise to set up a transaction, but also:

- as a first-class financial institution they can stand in the middle as an independent intermediary giving integrity to the transaction and its operation
- they can provide, in-house, the necessary traditional banking services on which the transaction depends
- they may add flexibility to the transaction by the introduction of an element of finance
- above all else they are able to maintain close control over the operation of the transaction including the flows of shipping documents and payments.

Countertrade checklist

Even if specialist expertise is employed to handle a countertrade transaction, certain information will be required at the outset. Here is a list of points that the countertrader will need to know and which will help the exporters in their approach to a countertrade proposal.

1   Why countertrade and are there any alternatives?
2   What is the proposal and what are the benefits for the exporter?
3   Has the country any countertrade policy and/or a track record in countertrade?
4   What are the local import and export regulations?
5   What products are being offered for countertrade? In particular consider:
   • specifications and samples
   • quality (in world market terms)
   • volumes and availability
   • pricing (how does it compare with the world market value?)
   • infrastructure and ability to perform
   • marketability and destination restrictions
   • whether the goods really exist.
6   Who would buy such goods? Make sure the prospective buyer is willing to take all the risks involved in the purchase of the goods.
7   What disagio costs are likely to arise?
8   Have the offtake goods been specifically allocated, in writing, to this countertrade transaction?
9   Have the necessary government and central bank authorities been given for this business to be transacted on a countertrade basis? If not, what authorities will be required? Who has the last say as to whether a transaction will proceed or not?
10   Has the exporter's local agent the tenacity, motivation and connections to play a significant role in negotiations and in obtaining the necessary authorities?
11   What are the risks and how might they be covered?
12   What happens if the offtake goods are not forthcoming? If a proceeds account is used, make sure that there are always sufficient funds available to cover work completed under the supply contract should it be necessary to stop work at any time.
13   Consider advance payments or penalty clausing to cover up-front disagio costs.
14   Consider arbitration clausing in case things should go wrong.

Conclusion

So is countertrade just an unwelcome necessity when trade with certain developing countries is contemplated, or is it an innovative marketing tool?

Many companies shun countertrade, believing it to be more trouble than it is worth. They should not be deterred. In truth, it can be complex, expensive and fraught with setbacks and frustrations, but the rewards are there and a willingness and ability to countertrade can mean the difference between exporting, possibly even increasing market share, and not exporting at all. If a company cannot accept this point, it is likely that its competitors will.

But an increasing number of exporters acknowledge the rewards countertrade can bring and many adopt a proactive approach towards it. They know that the inclusion of an element of reciprocity in an offer can tip the balance. They realize that in order to penetrate some markets they must 'invest' in them rather than simply sell to them. They must give as well as take. This could mean two-way reciprocal trade, technology transfer or perhaps joint venture contracts with local entities, all of which are countertrade in their own way.

As a consequence of this positive approach to countertrade, its parameters are forever widening. The banks and traders respond to their customers' requirements with ever more innovative structures which combine reciprocity with both conventional and non-conventional financing techniques.

The tools are there. The choice is for the potential purchaser to make. Reactive or proactive?

Recommended reading

Francis, Dick (1987), *The Countertrade Handbook*. Cambridge: Woodhead-Faulkner. (Gives an overview of countertrade and offset techniques in general.)

Rowe, Michael (1997), *Countertrade*, 3rd edn. London: Euromoney Books, Euromoney Institutional Investor plc.

.

Evidence-based Practice in Purchasing Management

19 *Purchasing for SMEs*

Michael Quayle

Introduction

The assessment of facets of total quality leads to a focus on improvement behaviour (Saunders, 1994). The dynamic outcome of this can be the identification of action plans which are of mutual interest to both the supplier and purchaser. Developments in both product and process areas can enhance the value added by the supplier. Development opportunities can cover improvements in dimensions of performance other than just product quality, such as delivery and cost. The thrust of this kind of supplier development is for purchasing personnel to work with suppliers to improve all aspects of quality. The reinforcement of innovative behaviour to improve quality and to produce new products and services can be achieved through close cooperation and intensive interaction between supplier and customer. Incentives need to be given to suppliers to encourage their investment in improvement initiatives and to gain their support. Tangible rewards in the form of future business, but also more symbolic rewards, in the form of 'preferred supplier status' and 'awards of excellence', can play a part. Feedback of poor performance and the insistence that suppliers rigorously analyse causes of problems help to prevent complacency and a lax attitude. The development of potential suppliers cannot be excluded and can be undertaken in a similar manner to the benefit of purchasers and the local economy.

Local economies in Europe, however, are made up of a significant percentage of small and medium-sized enterprises (SMEs) – in many cases circa 80 to 90 per cent per country. Whilst these SMEs are looked upon with interest by purchasers who have coherent supplier development programmes, purchasing within the smaller firms receives little or no attention. There is a limited amount of in-depth analysis of purchasing in SMEs, but nevertheless anecdotal agreement on a number of points. In particular there appears to be scope for improving purchasing; there also appears to be a need to improve and develop credible methodologies for it.

Major purchasers appear to have improved their image, moving it along a continuum from a clerical function in the 1960s and 1970s, to a commercial activity of the 1980s and then to a strategic activity in the 1990s. Some purchasers have clearly made significant progress, and the impact on organizational competitive advantage has been positive. Some purchasers have wobbled a little, for example M & S, Sainsburys, ICI, Shell, Rover and BMW (Heller, 1999). Have small firms kept pace and/or been brought along by major purchasers in terms of purchasing expertise as the drive for competitive advantage continues? There are some fundamental issues associated with pursuit of competitive advantage. These include: instability through changes of ownership; changes in strategic direction and the speed of technological change; globalization of sources of supply for state-of-the-art products; the constant drive for product/service improvement, resulting in a tension between incremental approaches and radical innovation; the desire for cost reduction achievement to be now rather than later; risk exposure being pushed down the supply chain, resulting in an increase in constructual liabilities and, perhaps, frightening the small firm into paralysis about being a supplier to a major purchaser.

Critical factors emerge from the pursuit of competitive advantage. There is a need, for example, for board-level priority to be given to purchasing and, indeed, the whole supply chain. Effective purchasing needs resources and capital; capital availability, particularly for smaller firms, is a growing concern, leading perhaps to risk-averse behaviour. The emphasis placed on specification purchasing, particularly where it is over-precise, may stifle innovation where suppliers are not offered early participation in the design process. Smaller firms are often the minority partner within the supply chain; both purchasers and suppliers (some of these can be powerful) should focus on a fair and reasonable relationship – a non-'cheating' relationship. Linked to globalization and mobile markets is the logistics factor; the benefits of local sourcing need to be considered, and perhaps offset, by the risks of losing control of product knowledge and the creation of future sources of supply, which may turn into sources of competition. Another critical factor is the need for basic benchmarks for measuring purchasing (and supply chain) performance and avoid the 'it's too difficult/we cannot measure the un-measurable' syndrome/mind set. The final critical factor in the context of this research is training. Purchasing specialists are in short supply and perhaps there is a need for a cross-functional orientation to ease the shortage.

One of the outstanding characteristics of the small firm is the simplicity of its management structure. The typical small firm is directly managed by its owners, who themselves take nearly all important decisions and probably oversee their execution as well; only in the larger firms is there a subordinate managerial structure and even the delegation of specific functions such as marketing is comparatively rare. This direct dependence on the proprietor in every facet of the detailed running of the business is the source of most of the strengths, and many of the weaknesses, of small firms. The strengths stem largely from a rapid decision-making process and the weaknesses lie in the fact that the skills and experience of one person are necessarily limited. This weakness is not dangerous unless significant growth of the business is an objective and/or changes to the organization need to be made to ensure its survival.

Drawing evidence from 26 firms in five sectors, an ACOST (1990) report found that

> it is apparent that growth creates major management and organisational problems. The principal dimensions of this relate to the need to develop a balanced managerial team, which combines appropriate marketing, financial and technical skills; and the need to create and organisational structure, which supports an appropriate delegation of decision-making. Sometimes the inability of the founding entrepreneur to delegate becomes a major barrier to growth. A good organisational structure provides top management with some insulation from the day-to-day pressures, and the freedom to take a strategic view.

The importance of a relatively flat management structure is also stressed, as this will provide the short communication channels necessary to best support, and maintain the creativity and flexibility of the organization.

Strategic planning

Strategic planning typically refers to the process of producing written plans which describe the organization's chosen future direction, based on an assessment of the external environment, and specifies goals and objectives. Such plans can then be used to monitor the disparity, if any, between intended and realized strategy and assess the reasons for it.

There is much support for the claim that strategic thinking and planning supports growth in small businesses. This association of thinking and behaving strategically with the production of formal plans has not been proved and can be questioned. In smaller businesses especially, communication can be informal and personal, obviating the need for the development of formal plans and reports. Formal planning systems and documents are more commonly characteristic of large organizations. In the case of the small business, informality does not seem to equate with ineffectiveness. There is a need to relate the SME business strategy to its purchasing operation. This is encapsulated in Figure 19.1.

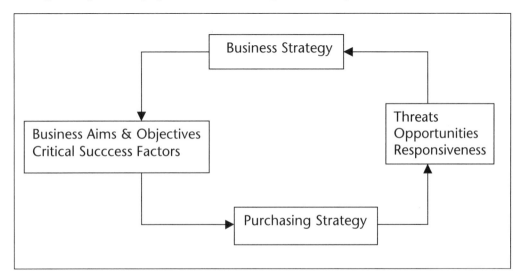

Figure 19.1   *Relating business and purchasing strategy*

This perhaps moves purchasing in SMEs from a passive to a forward-thinking function. Purchasing is the predominant outward-facing area of the enterprise and needs to gather market information and feed that information back into the overall business strategy. This will ensure that the strategy is refreshed and meaningful rather than the document used to negotiate the first bank overdraft ten years ago!

The potential problem for purchasing in SMEs is its relative importance within the organization and where it 'fits' with all other priorities and issues. This is illustrated in Figure 19.2.

The four issues (leadership, strategy, marketing, waste reduction) attracting the highest priorities in Figure 19.2 appear to be concerned with a relatively narrow vision of what is required for the business to survive. The issues which relate to innovation (R&D and EDI) are not considered as important. Issues of purchasing and purchasing-related activity (purchasing, subcontracting and supplier development) do not appear to be important; similarly, people issues, other than team working, such as staff development and Investors in People,

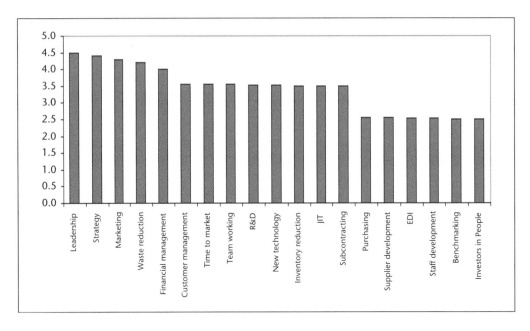

Figure 19.2   *Importance of issues at site*

appear to be recognized but given low priority. Why should this be? The answer lies in the SME's perception of what are real issues forced upon them by their customers. This in turn shapes the SME's attitude to its suppliers.These issues are reflected in Figures 19.3 and 19.4 respectively.

From Figures 19.3 and 19.4 it can be seen that companies perceive the priorities of customers and their suppliers to be very similar. The highest priorities are for quality, reliability and price. There is thus a contrast between the internal priorities of companies and the perceived demands of customers and suppliers. EDI, new technology and R&D, the innovative elements, again score low importance, along with purchasing expertise.

Purchasing activity in SMEs

Only 19 per cent of SMEs have a separate purchasing function. The function averages two buyers. However, 81 per cent have a designated employee (very often the owner-manager)

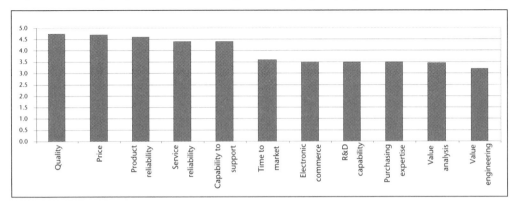

Figure 19.3   *Priorities of customers*

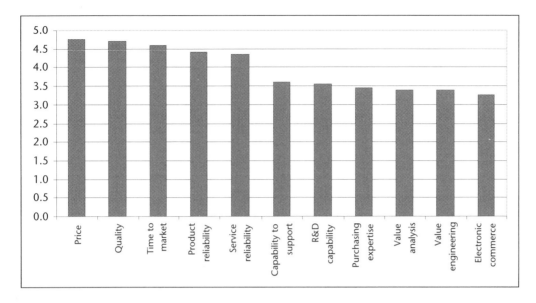

Figure 19.4 *Priorities for suppliers*

whose duties include purchasing. SMEs feel that purchasing is not a high priority; this in itself confirmed in Figures 19.3 and 19.4. There is a general view (65 per cent) that with little or no perceived purchasing power/leverage, there is little point in pursuing the activity through additional, already scarce, resource(s).

There is strong interest (74 per cent) in the use of a purchasing service. Some 36 per cent of SMEs considered they would use such a service for all purchases and 64 per cent considered they would use the service for part of their purchasing needs. Similarly there was strong interest in using the service as a consultancy (68 per cent) and for use in finding new or difficult-to-find products (78 per cent). Given the interest in the service it is perhaps inconsistent to note that only 32 per cent of SMEs would make available current purchasing costs to aid negotiation. There are consistencies in that price and quality are seen as the important issues.

It is clearly difficult for SMEs to organize themselves to cope with their purchasing activities. The effort has to be made. The need for a dedicated purchasing activity is axiomatic and a professional should be able to, at the very least, pay for themselves. By professional I mean an individual who has been educated and trained to do the job – not someone who is not very good at anything else, not someone who is given the job as an 'easy ride' before retirement. If the professional is recruited externally, sector experience would be helpful but is not essential. Purchasing is to a large extent generic. The products or services would need to be learned quickly to enable an early (not instant) impact on SME profitability.

To those already dedicated to purchasing in SMEs and who are not educated and trained, I say, go and get yourself educated and trained – and quickly. In the meantime, organize your purchasing activity. Identify where you (really) spend money, identify what are the (really) critical items or services in the success of your enterprise and devote some time to getting the supply arrangements right. Don't spend the same amount of time on everything – it will probably be 20 per cent of the items purchased that need 8 per cent of your time. You will not be able to organize your purchasing activity beyond that approach, but if you get it right, who knows, you might get some help! Oh yes, don't forget to tell your boss about the successes – he/she will already know about your failures from someone else.

Conclusions

The issues of highest importance at site for SMEs, as leadership, strategy, marketing, waste reduction and financial management, are perhaps enlightened. This finding may of course reflect the consultant's approach. The issues of lowest importance to the small firms are surprising. Purchasing (ranked 14 out of 19 where 1 is highest), supplier development, EDI, staff development, benchmarking and Investors in People are issues seen as ways to improve competitive advantage. Are these issues not being pursued by customers? Investors in People has recently been suggested as mandatory for suppliers used by the public sector. More significantly, the issues of lowest importance are those to do with innovation. Why should this be? The answer may lie in both the small firms' perception of their customers' requirements, and what small firms expect from their suppliers. The small firms' perception of their customers' requirements is interesting. The high priorities of quality, price, product reliability, service reliability and capability to support are the traditional buyer's results-oriented demands. The low priorities of time to market, EDI, R&D, purchasing expertise (ranked 9 out of 11 where 1 is the highest), value analysis and engineering should be of concern to customers, particularly those who have long-term relationships with smaller suppliers.

The small firms' priorities for their suppliers are not unexpected. High priorities of pricing, quality, time to market, product and service and reliability, and low priorities for capability to support, R&D, purchasing expertise (ranked 8 out of 11 where 1 is highest), value analysis, value engineering and EDI all suggest that the customer's message is not getting through or is not clear. In analysing small firms' purchasing activity and finding that 19 per cent have a purchasing function and 65 per cent view purchasing as not important, then arguably there is a lack of awareness that effective purchasing can affect profitability positively. A solution may be a small firms' purchasing service or consortium.

Overall, there are some enlightened approaches and awareness of what is critical to their success. This does, however, highlight the elements of innovation as having low priority in small firms; it also highlights that customers are not focusing on both results and capability development as part of their supplier development activity. Innovation is an overused term; the word means to introduce something new, to make changes. Innovation may therefore be used in the context of introducing purchasing professionalism, certainly in SMEs, probably in larger purchasers. Similarly, there may be an element of both SME and purchasers (customers) needing to manage themselves. The purchaser may need to consider whether they are simply managing suppliers and not really managing the interface.

The challenges ahead

E-commerce and indeed Internet purchasing represent a significant challenge. Food for thought here is that as the concept expands and more sources of supply become available, the desire to reduce the supplier base as part of strategic purchasing may not be as important as it is currently perceived to be; what this does not recognize, however, is the partnership/long-term business relationship, e.g. single sourcing and trust, which may have significantly more benefits to all concerned than maintaining a huge supplier base.

Given that 75 to 80 per cent of all organizations' purchases have a transaction value of £250 or less, there is a great deal to be said for e-commerce and the probability that transaction costs would be reduced. Perhaps the problem is that big purchasers have the power to 'persuade' small firms to comply with e-commerce. There are, however, very few real studies on the business case for e-commerce introduction in small firms. Small firms could benefit by using e-commerce, both as a strategic business tool and to facilitate small firms' purchasing consortia. It should be recognized that effective purchasing effects the all-important bottom line – both in the public and private sectors. Small firms do not appear to recognize this and hence do not see a problem with their own purchasing capability. Purchasing strategy is missing from many SME business plans. The need for a purchasing strategy is axiomatic but it needs to be linked to technology management, EDI and innovation. Purchasing consortia for small firms may be a solution to the lack of purchasing leverage.

Investors in people (IIP) represents not only a quality kitemark but also a process whereby SMEs can identify and satisfy true education and training needs, linked to their business objectives. IIP is about people, not paperwork systems. There is help available both in terms of money and free advice, particularly for SMEs. IIP is not easy, but it is useful and can only have a longer-term impact on profitability. It may also become mandatory for UK government contracts. SMEs contribute approximately 50 per cent to the UK gross domestic product and nearly 60 per cent to employment. They provide clear opportunities for economic development both locally and nationally. Developing SME purchasing expertise is essential to sustaining (and in some cases, achieving) competitive advantage.

The (often-repeated) fact that SMEs are not a homogeneous group is an important one. SMEs differ enormously not only in terms of size or what they do, the markets they serve and compete in, but also according to the aspirations and ambitions of their founders. The implications of this heterogeneity include the dangers inherent in offering generic support services. The high-tech firm is unlikely to be satisfied with the same package of support given to a wholesale greengrocer, or need the same resources as the owner of a group of residential care homes. This is not to say that firms are so different that there is nothing they cannot learn from each other – indeed there could very well be valuable lessons that readily apply across sectoral boundaries. For example, non-growth firms could imitate or adapt behaviours or activities more commonly associated with growth firms in order merely to maintain their market position or survival. Support or assistance packages must be grounded in the real needs and context of the individual, client enterprise (Gibb, 1996).

The second point to be made concerns the nature of the current state of research into SME growth. One weakness in the area is the marked inconsistency in the definition of key variables and criteria. For example, a number of different criteria are used to define growth: growth has been defined in terms such as: increase in employment; increase in sales; the rate at which growth occurred; or the increase in the owner's business earnings. This inconsistency serves to contaminate comparisons made across independent studies. Variables studied such as 'innovation', 'strategic planning' and 'business planning', for example, are defined in a number of ways or in the case of the last two the distinctions are perhaps blurred or ignored. This lack of consensus has introduced unhelpful confusion and inconsistency, and undermines the strength of the research. Studies also vary according to the time periods in which growth occurred and the size of samples from which findings are drawn, again reducing comparative power. Another important criticism is that many studies based on small samples offer sector-specific findings and are therefore not representative of the SME population. A major criticism that has been levelled at SME research is the reliance on quantitative (survey) data. This is problematic for a number of reasons: first, findings or conclusions tend to be drawn from aggregated results, which may bear no resemblance to any SME, or real facet of an SME (Gibb and Scott, 1985). The useful (or practical) application of such findings then becomes difficult or pointless. Second, quantitative data are useful in identifying which SMEs have grown and by how much, but produce data of insufficient depth to describe and understand the reasons for, or the processes involved, in achieving that growth.

With a few exceptions, the studies tend to use techniques which consider variables such as age of the SME, size or marketing strategy in isolation or independently, possibly promoting the misconception that such factors are functionally discrete. Research methodologies therefore preclude any real understanding of the relationship between variables and their relative impact. Critical success factors are just as likely to exist as, or within, the relationship between a number of variables or factors. For example an SME's success relies not only on the owner's ability to understand the market in which it operates but requires the production capability to deliver goods or services to satisfy the perceived need, in conjunction with the management talent to be opportunistic and make appropriate decisions at the right time. A number of essential areas for research have not been recognized or addressed fully, for example the role of chance in a firm's success. Is being there at the 'right time' completely lucky or is the successful entrepreneur somehow more able to spot opportunities? If so, how? To answer this a detailed understanding of how an entrepreneur makes sense of his/her environment is required. Linked to this is the need for a better understanding of how firms develop strategy. It would also be useful to understand the process by which an entrepreneur, and in turn the firm, learns and applies and modifies that learning over time. Finally, a further gap is the need for more research into the impact of network or supply chain relationships on the performance of SMEs. Overall the nature of SMEs is a major reason why defining a recipe for success is extremely difficult – perhaps impossible. One size does not fit all! Arguably, however, unless the SME gets its purchasing right it is unlikely to survive, let alone gain competitive advantage in its marketplace.

References

ACOST (Advisory Council on Science and Technology) (1990), *The Enterprise Challenge: Overcoming Barriers to Growth in Small Firms*, London: HMSO.

Gibb, A. (1996), 'Entrepreneurship and Small Business Management: Can We Afford to Neglect Them in Twenty-first Century Business School?' *British Journal of Management*, Vol. 7, No. 4, pp. 309–22.

Gibb, A. and Scott, M. (1985), 'Strategic Awareness, Personal Commitment and the Process of Planning in the Small Business', *Journal of Management Studies*, Vol. 22, No. 6, pp. 597–627.

Heller, R. (1999), 'Profit goes to the Swift and Lithe', *Management Today*, April, p. 32.

Saunders, M. (1994), *Strategic Purchasing and Supply Chain Management*, London: Pitman.

20 *Buying electricity and gas*

Ken Burnett

Introduction

As will be clear from reading the other chapters in this book, virtually all organizations need a purchasing function, whether this is a separate, stand-alone department or is subsumed within another department in the organization, such as finance. Whatever the status of purchasing within an organization, efficient purchasing procedures are paramount: professional buyers can achieve significant savings for their organization if they carry out the function in the correct manner.

Just as all organizations have a requirement for purchasing, so, obviously, do they all need energy, the costs of which may represent a considerable proportion of overall operational expenditure. Significantly, the opening up of the electricity and gas markets to competition in the 1990s has given buyers the opportunity to exercise their skills and produce significant savings for their organizations.

ENVIRONMENTAL FACTORS – THE CLIMATE CHANGE LEVY

We are all familiar with the problem of global warming, brought about by the emission of greenhouse gases, the most important of which is CO_2, much of which is energy-related.

The UK government, acknowledging this problem, agreed in the 1997 Kyoto Protocol to reduce emissions of the major pollutant gases to 12.5 per cent below 1990 levels over the period 2008–12. This figure is more stringent than the general EU target of 8 per cent. The USA agreed on a figure of 7 per cent.

The Kyoto summit also brought about a renewed focus on the desirability of introducing practical measures to tackle environmental problems; the Climate Change Levy is one of the outcomes. Unveiled at the March 2000 budget, it is based on the fundamental economic principle that increasing the cost of a product or service reduces the demand for it; it came into effect in April 2001. The rates are a flat-rate addition to the unit cost of fuel and have been set at 0.43p/kWh for electricity, and 0.15p/kWh for gas. However, it is not the government's intention that businesses should be penalized by the tax, the idea being that the money raised will enable cuts in National Insurance contributions to be made.

It is important to note that 'good-quality' CHP (combined heat and power plants) will be exempt from the new tax, although at the time of writing what constitutes 'good quality' has not been defined. Other exemptions to the levy include certain new forms of renewable energy, energy products that act as both a fuel and a feedstock within the same process, and electricity used in certain electrolytic processes – primary aluminium smelting, for example.

Predictably, companies are not best pleased at the prospect of this new financial burden. For instance, the UK arm of the Anglo-Dutch steel producer Corus has estimated that the levy will cost it £8m pa. There are, however, measures which can be taken to mitigate the effects of the CCL, for instance the government's IPPC (Integrated Pollution Prevention Control) scheme, particularly suited to companies with high levels of pollution that undertake to reduce energy consumption per tonne of whatever they produce by between 5 per cent and 20 per cent by 2010.

ELECTRICITY AND GAS IN CONTEXT

In recent years there has been a marked reduction in the use of oil and coal as generating fuels. In any event, neither of these fuels represents an area where the typical UK buyer is able to exercise his skills to any great effect, with coal being very much a minority fuel and a signifcant proportion of the cost of oil being tax and also subject to world price fluctuations and as such beyond his control.

REGULATION OF THE ENERGY MARKET

OFGEM (Office of Gas and Electricity Markets) is the regulatory body which replaced the former OFFER (Office of Electricity Regulation) and OFGAS (Office of Gas Regulation). For some time there had been a growing level of overlap between the two industries and it was therefore felt that they should be regulated by a single body.

Electricity

ELECTRICITY SUPPLY INDUSTRY – BACKGROUND

Privatization of the electricity industry took place in 1990, with competition being intro-duced into both generation and supply; generally speaking, buyers have been able to take advantage of this new competitive situation and the lower prices (in real terms) associated with it. Thus in 1996, for example, for medium-sized and large users of electricity, prices were less than 2 per cent up on the 1989 levels. To put this apparent increase in context, during this period inflation rose by more than 30 per cent.

This competition was promoted by the use of a pool system whereby companies wishing to generate electricity to send to the grid system were obliged to bid a price with only the lower bids being accepted . The Pool, established in April 1990, has been defined as 'the wholesale market through which all electricity from all but the smallest generators is bought and sold in England and Wales. Prices are volatile, changing every half hour subject to bid prices from the generators and the relationship between declared generating capacity avail-able and anticipated system peak demand' (Buckley, 1998.) The system was found to be par-ticularly beneficial to very large users with the ability to cut their consumption at times of high prices.

Key to the Pool was the SMP (System Marginal Price), paid to all generators under a pro-cedure monitored by the market operator. The two other components of the Pool selling price were capacity charges and uplift. The former, intended to promote investment in new plant, was added to the SMP and paid to all succesful generators; the combination was referred to as the Pool purchase price. Uplift prices were designed to introduce a 'real-world' element (in the form of extra costs in the system which were not taken into account in the theoretical mechanisms employed to establish the Pool purchase price).

NETA (NEW ELECTRICITY TRADING ARRANGEMENTS)

Shortly after coming to power in May 1997, the Labour government promised a major overhaul of the Pool mechanism. The outcome of their deliberations was NETA, whose reforms have been characterized by the DTI as 'allowing more opportunities for contracting, easier adjustment of contract positions, better risk management and the balancing and operation of the system'.

NETA, which is seen as being seen as broader in scope and of potentially greater significance than its gas industry counterpart (NGTA), is expected to lead to a higher level of competition between generators, and to reductions in wholesale prices.

NETA seeks to ensure that energy is traded on long-term bilateral contracts. Additionally, however, NETA has a short-term bilateral market operating from 24 to 3.5 hours ahead of delivery so that the parties can adjust their respective positions in the light of the latest information.

COMPONENTS OF THE ELECTRICITY PRICE

Buyers of electricity need to be familiar with the constituent elements of the price which they are paying and the electricity units used for calculating the basis of that price. The basic parameter is the kWh, which means quite simply the amount of power used in an hour. Larger units are the megawatt hour (MWh, equivalent to1000 kWh) and the gigawatt hour (GWh), equivalent to 1m kwh. The major element of the price is the energy charge, also known as the power station gate price. This price, together with the profit element, is negotiable. As will be seen elsewhere the other key variable is the time at which the electricity is consumed. The buyer will also need to be aware of the Climate Change Levy and the Fossil Fuel Levy (see below), although he will of course not be in a position to exercise any control over them.

Climate Change Levy

The origins and broad implications of the Climate Change Levy have been discussed above. As noted, the general effect, as with any levy, is to increase customers' bills in both the electricity and gas supply industries. Unlike the Fossil Fuel Levy, however, the CCL will be applied as a flat-rate surcharge on top of the unit rate. Initially the rate was set at 0.43p per kWh, offset by a reduction in employers' National Insurance contributions.

Fossil Fuel Levy

In addition, all electricity bills are subject to the Fossil Fuel Levy, first introduced in April 1990, since when, as Table 20.1 shows, it has been revised a number of times. The significant reduction in the rate since November 1996 is explained by the fact that with the privatization of some parts of the nuclear industry under British Energy it is no longer in need of a subsidy (originally, of the total revenue raised by the Fossil Fuel Levy, approximately 90 per cent was used to support the nuclear power sector).

As can be seen, the table applies to England and Wales. Scottish customers are also subject to the Fossil Fuel Levy; the rates, however, are different. In fact it reduced to zero from April 1999. However, it was decided in December of that year that the rate should be set at 0.8 per cent as from 1 April 2000, a decision which came as an unpleasant surprise to customers who had mistakenly construed the earlier zero date as representing the full abolition of the levy.

Table 20.1   *Fossil fuel rates in England and Wales since privatization*

Period	Rate of Fossil Fuel Levy (%)
1 April 1990–31 March 1991	10.6
1 April 1991–31 March 1993	11.0
1 April 1993–31 October 1996	10.0
1 November 1996–31 March 1997	3.7
1 April 1997–31 March 1998	2.2
1 April 1998–31 December 1998	0.9
1 January 1999–30 September 1999	0.7
1 October 1999–	0.3

Source: Energy Information Centre (2000), p. 29.

Metering and settlement

A compulsory half-hourly metering programme is now in operation for sites qualifying for the over 100 kWh market; for those below this figure half-hour metering remains optional.

Competition has been introduced to the metering supply sector, with customers being able to buy or rent their meters, but whatever their decision, they are responsible for the necessary maintenance and must ensure that such equipment is tested and registered with the settlements administrator no less than one month before supplies commence.

Another cost element is that of data collection and settlement (settlement is defined in the *Energy Purchasers' Yearbook* as 'the charge levied for collecting and handling a site's consumption data for billing purposes'. There are two site registration systems for data settlement – the Electronic Registration System (ERS) and the Public Electricity Supplier Registration System (PRS).

Procedures for ERS settlement charges for 2000–2001 show important differences from previously, with both ERS variable and fixed charges being set on a quarterly basis.

Transmission and distribution charges

Transmission charges are based on the concept of triads, that is to say the three highest periods of demand on the National Grid system over a 12-month period. The rules stipulate that these peaks must be at least ten days apart and would typically occur in late afternoon/ early evening on winter weekdays. Transmission costs are arrived at by multiplying the demand for these three half-hour periods by £1 per kilowatt charge. It will be obvious that buyers can achieve worthwhile reductions in transmission costs if they can persuade management to arrange to reduce demand at these peak times. Transmission charges which came into effect as from April 2000 represent on average a reduction of 2.5 per cent as compared to 1999–2000. However, wide regional variations exist; OFGEM is seeking to incorporate into NETA a system whereby regional differences are made less pronounced.

Distribution charges are payable to the RECs (regional electricity companies) for the use of their networks; these charges, which are reviewed annually, comprise a number of elements which may in some instances include a maximum demand charge, although these have now been dropped by many suppliers, who have moved towards a system of charging whereby the unit rate varies according to season and time of day.

Buyers should be aware that in the light of the RECs' monopoly status, distribution revenues are monitored and controlled by the regulator in accordance with the current Retail Price Index.

TENDERS AND CONTRACTS

The procedure is for a customer to give notice to his existing supplier. Such notice periods vary, but can be as much as three months. Ideally, 10–12 weeks should be set aside for obtaining the necessary information on new suppliers, and preparing the tender documentation; this will take into account the statutory 20 days (in effect four weeks) for the registration of a new supplier to take place.

Data required for tendering are as follows:

- name/address of company
- capacity and voltage
- details of REC
- details of the maximum demand reached during the previous 12 months – usually obtainable from invoices from the existing supplier, or from half-hour data
- return date for completed tenders
- type of offer required
- length of contract anticipated – normally a year, but can be longer (when considering the anticipated duration of the contract it is important for the buyer to bear in mind that a supplier who is competitive one year may not be so the next. In his own interests, therefore, the buyer should keep in touch with changes and developments in the market).

Potential suppliers need to be informed of the electricity consumption pattern. Normally the data which need to be supplied are the monthly usage for the preceding year, split into day and night-time slots. When half-hour meters are fitted, this can be a good source of data.

NEGOTIATION

Sound negotiating techniques are an essential part of the buyer's toolkit, whether he is purchasing energy or anything else. (It should be borne in mind that cosy partnership arrangements between trading partners, so familiar to many buyers in today's marketplace, are not a particularly prominent feature of the energy market.)

In negotiating with electricity suppliers, recommended strategies for buyers to get the best deal include:

- providing potential suppliers with as much consumption pattern information data as possible, including half-hour data when appropriate
- ensuring that all quotes are on a like-for-like basis
- ensuring that the organization has a reputation for prompt payment of bills
- giving plenty of time for the completion and return of tender documentation
- ensuring that approaches are made to a reasonable number of suppliers
- chasing potential suppliers when necessary, but the basic negotiating principle of not appearing over-interested should be borne in mind
- if the proposed contract start time is in the spring, considering arranging an 18-month deal to receive the benefit of two periods of low summer prices.

Unfortunately, even the most skilled buyer can sometimes come to grief at the contract preparation stage. Typical instances include:

- not leaving enough time for the project
- not checking half-hour data for any inconsistencies which may be present
- not adhering to basic negotiation principles
- not giving sufficient notice to terminate existing contracts
- failure of the new supplier to register sites in time to start supply on the agreed date.

Gas

GAS SUPPLY INDUSTRY – BACKGROUND

British Gas was privatized as long ago as 1984, but competition in the supply of gas did not really become significant until the early 1990s; the last 10–12 years have seen a dramatic increase in demand, largely at the expense of coal (see Table 20.2 for trends in consumption). However, at the end of 1997 the government took the steam out of the so-called 'dash for gas', putting a moratorium on the construction of any new gas-fired plant, the logic being that it was considered unwise to be overdependent on a single source of energy. However, in April 2000 the moratorium was lifted to take effect from October 2000.

Table 20.2   *Trends in gas consumption, 1994–98 (in million therms)*

	Industry	Commerce & public service	Domestic	Power stations	All users
1994	5,704	3,451	11,250	3,909	24,314
1995	5,993	3,750	11,123	4,974	25,782
1996	6,526	4,092	12,824	6,506	29,948
1997	6,370	3,991	11,790	8,304	30,455
1998	6,708	4,024	12,147	8,800	31,678
Five-year change (%)	17.6	16.6	8.0	125.1	30.3

Source: Energy Information Centre (2000), p. 40.

In 1997 shareholders gave approval to a plan to split the company into two – BG plc and Centrica, the former comprising Transco (defined in the *Energy Purchasers' Handbook* as 'the business unit responsible for operating the national pipeline network'). As a monopoly its charges and operations are overseen by OFGEM. Much of the company's assets are derived from exploration, whilst Centrica focuses on supply activities. Centrica reserves the right to use the names British Gas and BG plc. Nowadays, the supply arm of British Gas is just one of some 30 companies involved in selling gas in what is seen as a very competitive market-place.

Much of the gas consumed comes from the North and Irish seas via beach-head terminals, five on the east coast and one on the west. From there it is transported to the customer through Transco pipelines (see below for other key players in the supply chain); Transco sets out the terms for access to its pipelines for all those who ship gas. It is important to note that the end users and supplier deal with the shipper rather than with Transco, a procedure not without its inefficiencies and consequently under review. As for the future, reserves are limited – most are in the former USSR, the Middle East and Algeria, all areas, unfortunately, which are not noted for their political stability. This obviously has potential implications for the supply situation.

In October 1998 the Interconnector opened for business. This is a pipeline between Bacton (Norfolk) and Zeebrugge in Belgium. In the short term the pipeline was designed to export gas from the UK to the continent, with the direction of flow being reversed in the longer term. The pipeline is owned by a consortium, the principal member of which is British Gas.

NGTA (NEW GAS TRADING ARRANGEMENTS)

One of the principal reasons for the formation of NGTA was a growing awareness of the deficiencies of the Network Code, in particular the lack of an effective contractual relationship between end users and Transco, and exploitation by suppliers of the rules on capacity constraints.

NGTA has effected two key changes to the operation of the market: (a) introduction of an 'on-the-day' commodity market and (b) the use of capacity auctions as a way of allocating entry rights into the network.

CLIMATE CHANGE LEVY

The essential principles of this tax (for that is what it is) were outlined earlier in this chapter. As far as gas customers are concerned, it appears as a flat-rate addition to the fuel cost, scheduled at the 2001 budget to be 0.15p per kWh, or 4.4p per therm. Certain categories of user, notably good-quality CHP plants, will be able to claim exemption.

KEY PLAYERS

The principal players within the gas supply market are:

- producers
- transporters
- shippers
- traders
- suppliers.

Producers

Producers are the first link in the gas supply chain. They obtain their supplies mainly from the North Sea and Irish Sea; since as long ago as the late 1960s this natural gas, rather than coal gas, has been the principal heat source for home and industry.

Gas exploration and development activity is dominated by the major oil companies, notably Shell, Elf, BP and Mobil. Not surprisingly, as is the case with the oil market, the pattern of such activity is greatly influenced by the prices that can be achieved in the marketplace, with producers (a) selling on long-term wholesale contracts; (b) trading on spot/balancing markets; and (c) selling to final customers.

Transporters

To be accurate, one should not speak of transporters in the plural since the transport of gas is effectively a Transco monopoly; as such its activities are monitored by OFGEM. The precise breakdown of charges will vary according to circumstances, but typically transport costs amount to about one-third of the total. The delivery charges are levied by Transco on shippers, then passed on to suppliers, and ultimately on to the end user.

Transco runs six main input terminals with which serve as the key distribution points for individual consumers. The company has responsibility for ensuring that the system remains in balance, in other words always ensuring that sufficient gas remains in the system to ensure that supplies to customers are maintained. A buffer stock to assist in this process is achieved by some customers (those with a minimum usage of 200,000 therms pa) having so-called 'interruptible contracts', which means they are prepared to stop taking gas for a time; in practice those who have this arrangement rarely get interrupted for the full time specified in their contract.

Shippers

Defined as 'an operator licensed by OFGEM to move gas through the British Gas Transco's pipeline system in accordance with the Network Code, covering, for instance, daily balancing and procedures for changing customers. The principal responsibility is to secure space in the pipeline system to ensure that customers' needs are met.

Traders

Traders may be thought of as speculators in the gas market; they can also be suppliers. The principal methods of trading gas are as follows:

- traditional index life of field arrangements
- short-term spot markets
- futures contracts.

Marker prices for gas are produced by a number of bodies, one such being the *Petroleum Argus*. Variations in daily prices appear in the *Financial Times* alongside prices for both crude oil and refined products.

Suppliers

The traditional distinction between suppliers of gas on the one hand and electricity on the other is becoming increasingly blurred; as an illustration, according to a press report which appeared at the end of 2000, Centrica, trading under its former public sector name of British Gas, is expected to become the UK's biggest domestic electricity supplier. Following the same trend, suppliers of electricity such as TXU, owners of Eastern Electricity, are significant players in the domestic gas supply market.

Advice on dealing with suppliers, including supplier evaluation and procedures for changing suppliers, appears in later sections.

COMPONENTS OF COST

Traditionally, gas has always been priced in therms but is now invoiced, like electricity, in kWh. There are approximately 29.3 kWh in a therm.

The cost comprises two main elements – the beach-head cost, and a charge for delivering it through the Transco system. The wholesale cost can be identified by stripping out the transport costs so that the supplier charge can be accurately assessed. This element needs to be known with some accuracy when potential new suppliers are being considered. Transport costs will vary according to a number of factors, for example:

- annual volume used
- where gas is landed
- where customer is situated
- whether or not a supply is classified as 'interruptible'.

At the time of writing (February 2001) there have been considerable increases in gas whole-sale prices, reaching 26p per therm in October 2000 compared to only 11p just ten months previously (see Figure 20.1).

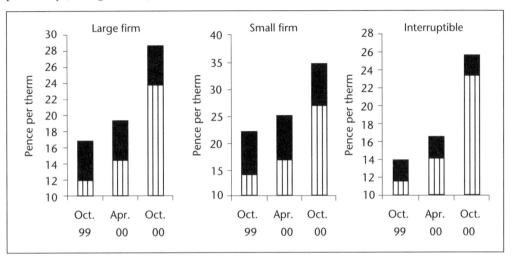

Source: EIC Seminar, October 2000.

Figure 20.1   *Autumn 2000 gas market – customer prices*

Various factors have been identified as being behind these hikes, not least the increase in the price of oil; possible price manipulation by suppliers is another factor.

APPROACHING AND EVALUATING SUPPLIERS

Price is obviously a key consideration when evaluating potential suppliers; in particular buyers should ensure that the supplier under consideration has based his quoted price on Transco data. However, other factors are also important; buyers need to be aware of:

- take or pay arrangements (i.e. paying for what you don't use)
- scheduling/balancing penalties
- cost issues: ensure that supplier has based his quoted price on Transco data
- short periods of validity (can be as little as half an hour!).

The recommendation is that buyers should maximize their range of options by getting a broad band of suppliers to quote; they should also be on the lookout for short offer periods.

Generally the recommendation is that, in general, energy buyers should go to the market in plenty of time when negotiating new contracts; a reasonable minimum is three months before the end of the existing contract. To streamline the process, measures should be taken to ensure that all site data are made readily available to the new supplier. It is also important to avoid confusion over the termination date of the existing contract.

Sites with over 200,000 therms' consumption pa can be supplied on an interruptible basis; suppliers can transfer their gas to the spot market at those times when gas is not required by customers under an interruptible supply arrangement.

Prices can vary with length of contract period; a contract spanning two summers and one winter should normally yield lower prices.

How can the buyer best deal with excessively high gas prices?

A general point is to shop around; even in a strong market of the type experienced in autumn 2000 prices will ultimately fall to more sustainable levels. Nevertheless, even in such a market situation some relatively good deals may well still be available. However, for those not wanting to be stuck with a contract at prices at unacceptably high rates, and who are able and willing to accept a somewhat higher level of risk, there are two alternatives: (a) to move to a short-term floating contract or (b) secure a temporary extension of the contract from the existing supplier. Under (a), buyers pay market rates plus a margin to begin with, and, at a later point in the contract, the option to transfer to a fixed price arrangement. Under (b) a customer will agree to remain with their existing supplier for a set period, say three months, after which they are free to go to the market again. Buyers should not, however, expect their extended contract period to be at the same rate as their old contract.

SUPPLIER SELECTION

Invitations to tender should be dispatched well before end of existing contract; a new supplier needs a month to organize the registration of the new site with Transco. Time is also needed to review the terms and conditions. Look particularly for clauses which cover:

- required maximum/minimum consumption levels per day/year, together with any penalties for breaching these
- in the case of interruptible suppliers, scale of penalty for non-compliance plus overall length of potential interruption specified
- consequential loss provisions arising from actions of either supplier or customer
- period of notice for contract termination
- payment terms (Buckley, 1998, p. 102).

Other issues to be considered, suggests Buckley, are whether or not extra sites can be added if necessary, the rate of interest levied on overdue accounts, and the speed with which the proposed supplier is able to address any problems which may arise within the term of the contract; for example, the proposed supplier may find difficulty in satisfying unexpectedly high consumption requirements. For this type of information, which the supplier himself is unlikely to volunteer, the recommendation is that buyers should approach existing customers of the supplier.

CHECKLIST FOR SEEKING GAS SUPPLY OFFERS

For all sites the full address and postcode must be given. A brief description of the type of business activity at the site is also required. For sites requiring a firm (i.e. non-interruptible) supply it is also necessary to give the following information:

- meter supply point 'M' number

- present supplier
- length of desired contract period
- history of gas consumption pattern
- site load factor.

In addition to the above data, buyers requiring an interruptible supply will also need to give an indication of the acceptable period of interruption which they envisage.

Before signing the contract, buyers should make sure the offer in question is still deliverable, and that the existing supplier has no reason for complaint as far as any overdue payments or notice period are concerned.

Glossary

(Definitions taken from *Energy Purchasers Handbook*, 2000.)

Arbitrage
A strategy used in both the gas and electricity markets – simply the well-established concept of buying cheap and selling in dear markets.

Capacity
Also known as the seasonal offtake quantity – in the gas supply industry a measure of maximum daily gas take for a site. It is used in the calculation of Transco delivery charges.

Competition clauses
Clauses which can appear in supply contracts which are of more than one year's duration, enabling customers to assess and evaluate prices in the market at each anniversary.

Energy Price Index (EPI)
In both the electricity and gas supply industries, a system developed by the EIC (Energy Information Centre) for the analysis of published tariffs.

Gas day
A 24-hour period commencing at 6 am and used as a basis for ensuring that shippers input sufficient gas to meet their customers' requirements. Fines are levied under the Network Code in the event of non-compliance.

Gas year
The gas year begins on 1 October, the start of the season of peak demand. Annual transportation charges normally change with effect from that date.

Load factor
In the gas industry, the relationship between daily average consumption and maximum consumption. The higher the ratio, the more predictable the consumption pattern and therefore more attractive to suppliers who are more easily able to plan and schedule their output levels.

In the electricity industry it is a measure of the relationship between consumption and maximum demand.

M number

In the gas industry, a unique identification number allocated by Transco to meters, enabling them to be easily identified and stored in its database.

Minimum consumption

A feature of many gas supply contracts, being defined as the least amount of gas a site would be likely to use in the contract year. Some suppliers stipulate that their customers must pay for this minimum level of consumption even if they do not use it.

Network code

The terms and conditions governing the use of Transco's pipeline system.

Nominated consumption

The total volume of gas which a site is expected to use in the course of a year.

Swing factor

The ratio between maximum daily flow of gas and average daily flow. The ratio serves to indicate the variability of the flow, which will in turn affect price.

Tariffs

In the gas industry, tariffs are price schedules, not subject to negotiation, available to SMEs and domestic users. In the electricity industry, these are price schedules available to users whose consumption does not exceed 10 MW.

Therms

A measurement of gas consumption. Multiplying kWh prices by the conversion factor (29.3071) gives the pence per therm equivalent.

Transportation

In the context of the gas industry, the movement of gas from the beach-head terminal through the gas supply system to the customer's meter.

References

Buckley, A. (2994), *Buying Electricity and Gas in the Competitive Marketplace*, Aldershot: Gower. CIPS (2001), *How to Buy Energy*, London: CIPS.

Compton, H. and Jessop, D. (2001), *The Official Dictionaryof Purchasing and Supply*, Liverpool: Liverpool Business Publishing .

Energy Information Centre (2000), *Energy Purchasers Handbook 2000*.

Energy Information Centre (2000), *How to Purchase Gas and Electricity - A Beginner's Guide*, EIC Seminar, Coventry, October.

21 *Buying IT*

Ken Burnett

One definition of IT is:

> the application of appropriate (enabling) technologies to information processing. Currently interest centres on computing, telecommunications and digital electronics. *(British Computer Society, 1995)*

Another definition, taken from *Purchasing* (Lysons, 1996), is:

> the acquisition, processing, storage and dissemination of vocal, pictorial, textual and numeric information by a microelectronics-based combination of computing and telecommunications.

IT in the purchasing department

It is widely accepted and recognized that the adoption of IT[1] in the purchasing department can bring about significant advantages. Among those identified by C.K. Lysons are:

- provision of accurate and up-to-date information necessary for routine purchasing activities such as expediting and order processing
- keeping staff levels and hence salary costs to a minimum
- ability to react rapidly to fluctuations in the workload
- cost savings resulting from high levels of efficiency in warehousing and inventory monitoring
- formalization and streamlining of standard procedures
- production of reports and analyses at appropriate intervals. These reports can cover a wide range of activities and parameters but typically may include:
  - overdue orders
  - vendor rating reports
  - stock movements
  - invoices received
  - stock values
  - capital project expenditure
  - list of suppliers in order of spend.

What is meant by buying IT

Buying IT systems and equipment, whether for the purchasing department or for the organization as a whole, is an area of fundamental importance to corporate well-being.

The *Buy IT Guidelines* suggest that the concept of IT procurement encompasses a number of key areas; in addition to the procurement of the IT system itself, consideration also needs to be given to installation, commissioning, testing and integration, as well as to ancillary support activities such as training, maintenance and support, and development of the system.

Typically, the IT system will include some or all of the following:

- databases
- transaction processing systems
- text processing and office systems
- communications and networks
- product design and product data systems
- data classification and storage systems
- software.

Before measures are put in hand to purchase any of the above, a statement of user requirements needs to be drawn up; this sets out the organization's IT requirements in non-technical terms. It is important to avoid any temptation to succumb to pressure from the supplier to buy the latest technology, only to find subsequently that it is too sophisticated for the application(s) that the buyer has in mind.

Requirements capture can be far from easy to achieve. In-depth consultations and discussions between all interested parties will need to take place, with the finalized Statement of Requirements being subject to approval by the manager of the department(s) intending to use the system. However, requirements and circumstances will inevitably change from time to time and it is essential therefore that the Statement contains provision for this.

In a perfect world there will be a good correlation between what is required and what is technically feasible. However life is rarely that simple and invariably there will be some degree of mismatch. Each situation will of course be unique as far as details are concerned, but in essence two scenarios may be identified:

- a match between some areas but not in others
- no match at all, in which case a radical review of the Statement of Requirements is indicated.

Once a Statement of Requirements has been drawn up, and a suitable supplier identified by means of an appropriate procurement process, attention should be given to drawing up the contract. This is, of course, primarily a legal document; however, in addition to legal aspects, it will also address all the relevant commercial and functional considerations. In short it will, if correctly drawn up, reflect the range of customer–supplier relationships from the one-off delivery of a single component through to a framework for a long-term partnering agreement.

The author of any dedicated software specified in the contract will seek to retain ownership of the software even though it may have been developed specifically in accordance with the buyer's instructions. Ideally, therefore, the contract should make it clear that ownership is transferred to the buyer, together with the source code. Where this is not possible, the supplier should be required to deposit the source code with a third party such as the NCC (National Computing Centre). For a further discussion of this arrangement (known as escrow), see below.

Contracts

Whilst model forms of contract for the purchase of IT systems are readily available, it is important to stress that these are inevitably somewhat general in nature, and it is therefore advisable, if the buyer is not an expert in IT procurement, to obtain legal advice when drawing up the precise terms of the contract for specific situations and circumstances. Having said that, there are certain features which are common to many contracts, as follows.

WARRANTIES

All reputable computer systems are sold with some form of warranty for a specified period. However, in the IT industry it is commonplace for a supplier to attempt to put right faults under the warranty but without feeling under any pressure or obligation as far as the time he takes to do this is concerned. Buyers should, therefore, seek to ensure that the contract incorporates a clause covering this eventuality.

LOSS

Clearly a buyer who is contemplating a claim under warranty is at risk from suffering loss – for instance, loss of profit from malfunctions in the computer system causing a bottleneck in the organization's operations.

Losses may be direct or indirect. In the case of direct loss many contracts seek to place a limit on liability; the limit often approximates to the value of the contract. In the case of legal disputes over the sum payable in the event of a claim, it is worth remembering that the insurance cover provides a good indication as to what the courts would consider to be a reasonable figure.

Indirect losses are more difficult to quantify and it is unlikely that in practice buyer and supplier will agree to a mutually acceptable figure in the event of a claim arising from loss of profit which is ultimately attributable to, say, a computer failure. For this reason computer contracts usually exclude liability for indirect loss.

PERSONAL INJURY

At first sight this may seem an improbable factor to include in a contract for the purchase of an IT system. However, IT has a vital role to play in today's cars and aircraft, for example and it is obvious that faulty or unreliable equipment in such environments can produce catastrophic consequences. Clearly claims under this contract term can be very high and this needs to be borne in mind by both parties at the time the contract is drawn up.

IMPLIED TERMS

In addition to the range of express terms outlined above, parties to the contract will be bound by the implied terms; that is, conditions which have to be satisfied under current statutory legislation.

Buyers of IT systems will need to be aware of statutory legislation such as the Sale of Goods Act 1979 and the Supply of Goods and Services Act 1982 which require the goods to be 'of satisfactory quality and fit for the purpose'. This underlines the importance of exercising care when drawing up the Statement of Requirements (see above). It is all too easy to purchase a piece of equipment which is perfectly acceptable in terms of quality, reliability and performance characteristics, but it will be a waste of money if it cannot perform the tasks for which it is purchased in the first place. It will not, in short, be fit for the purpose.

In the case of IT services (as distinct from goods), there is a requirement under the Supply of Goods and Services Act 1982 that these will be performed with due skill and care. This requirement is clearly applicable to IT consultants and providers of IT services under an outsourcing agreement.

One of the legal firms active in this field (Ormerod Wilkinson Marshall) has produced further practical advice on system procurement, as follows:

- If the system is large and expensive and its purchase is based on a written Statement of Requirements and Specification, ensure that the specification forms part of the contract itself. This will go a considerable way towards avoiding disputes and arguments at a later date.
- Even in the case of a smaller system, where a specification perhaps does not feature, try to ensure that a written record is made of any representations made verbally by the supplier.
- In cases where a system is purchased through a finance company, make sure that the latter is kept informed of any problems. All too often the buyer falls into the trap of thinking that it is only necessary to inform the supplier who in fact may not be liable for compensating the buyer.
- If the problems are sufficiently serious to justify the purchase of a replacement system, then this should be done as soon as possible. If the dissatisfied user delays replacing the faulty system, he may be held liable for not attempting to mitigate his losses at an earlier date.
- The contract should be checked carefully for any indication of an attempt to limit the supplier's liability for any consequential losses resulting from any defects in the system. Such clauses must stand the test of reasonableness in accordance with the Unfair Contract Terms Act 1977.

Supplier assessment

To minimize the risk of 'getting it wrong', whether it be for the purchase of hardware of software, or the recruitment of IT personnel, a rigorous supplier evaluation procedure is essential. A precondition is to appoint a project team responsible for implementing the supplier selection process. Typically, such a team should include:

- representatives from all the relevant departments within the organisation (finance and IT for example)
- representatives from senior management
- individuals representing the business users of the systems.

A typical supplier selection procedure begins with a long list of suppliers drawn up on the basis of such criteria as:

- financial viability
- implementation track record
- quality and relevance of reference sites
- project management capability
- ability to understand the business at the strategic and process level
- resource base of appropriate skills
- technical competence.

The process steps in a procurement decision need to be appropriate to the type of procurement being undertaken. Additionally, public sector purchasers need to proceed in accordance with the EC procurement rules.

Whether the procurement is taking place in the private or the public sector, a structured approach is essential. A checklist of key steps will typically include:

- identification of a 'long list' of potential suppliers who have the capability to meet the business requirements
- an initial approach to suppliers on the 'long list' to confirm their capability and interest in being involved
- issue of the statement of business requirements to the interested suppliers
- selection of 'short-listed' suppliers based on the assessment and ranking of supplier responses
- demonstrations of capability by the 'short-listed' suppliers
- selection of two or more preferred suppliers based on the assessment and ranking of their performances in the demonstrations (and any subsequent follow-up)
- specification of the functional and performance standards to be met, which more complex projects may be based on a pilot implementation of the preferred solution(s)
- issue of the ITT (Invitation to Tender) to those suppliers willing to comply with the contract terms
- final supplier selection, negotiation and award of contract.

Throughout each step of the process, the selection team should rank suppliers, eliminating those that do not meet the standard, as requirements are clarified and risks prioritized. This will result in a natural selection process leading to the appointment of the preferred, successful supplier. This will build consensus and commitment to the selected solution on the part of both the purchaser and the successful supplier.

Software – general considerations

Before proceeding with the purchase of software, the buyer will need to be aware of the software development cycle, not least because no matter how much care is taken in the purchase, the software will sooner or later need upgrading or replacing. At this time the buyer will once more need to exercise his purchasing skills. The main stages of the process are described in Table 21.1.

Table 21.1   *Stages in the purchase of software*

Stage	Description
System requirements	Identifying what the customer wants . . .
Software requirements	. . . and turning this into a software specification
Overall design	specifying the whole system
Detailed design	splitting it into containable modules
Module design	deciding what each part will do
Module production	. . . and turning this into a computer design
Module testing	making sure each module works alongside . . .
Integration and system testing	. . . and together with all the other modules
Acceptance testing	getting the customer to agree that it works
Release	the software is sold, or delivered to the customer
Implementation and operation	it works . . . or some parts do not have to be corrected
Maintenance	usually includes upgrading the software to meet new requirements

Source : Dictionary of Computer Terms (British Computer Society).

Software testing

In some cases, particularly where a critical application of the software is involved (the defence and aerospace industries are obvious examples) the buyer may, with permission of senior management, consider carrying out test routines. Management approval is necessary since testing can be an expensive process. In fact the cost of a single testing tool, or testing methodology, can run into several thousand pounds. When paying this kind of money the buyer will need to check carefully as to what he is getting in terms of testing tool performance.

A broad categorization of testing is as follows:

- *Integration testing*. This involves making sure that the various functional units work together satisfactorily.
- *Regression testing*. A test procedure which is applied after a fault has been identified and corrected; the purpose of regression testing is simply to ascertain whether or not the fault has been corrected.
- *Crash testing*. This is designed to detect any tendency for the system to crash if it is being used concurrently by more then a small number of people.
- *Acceptance testing*. As the name implies, this involves the final testing of the complete system.

- *Static testing*. This is a technique whereby the correctness (or otherwise) of the source code and other documentation is checked without actually running the program with automated tools; these can identify the presence of errors but cannot unfortunately establish whether faults are potentially serious or trivial.
- *Unit testing*. This involves testing the smallest component of a software program (a functional module to ensure that a given input produces the expected output), in other words that the program is doing what it is supposed to do.

Escrow

In the software procurement process, escrow is a useful device to bring into play in those cases where the supplier becomes, or in the view of the buyer is likely to become, insolvent. (Passing reference may be made at this point to the concept of key escrow, whereby, in e-commerce transactions, security keys are held by an independent third party as part of the contract between the trading parties.) In instances where the buyer has no reason to suppose that insolvency is in prospect, appropriate supplier appraisal procedures, which would normally include an assessment of the financial standing of the supplier, may often be sufficient, although as a back-up it may well be advisable before signing the contract to establish that a second source of maintenance is available if necessary. An effective insurance policy against software malfunction is also recommended.

Whilst astute buyers, as part of their supplier evaluation process, should be alive to the possibility of supplier insolvency, this is not always predictable. If the software purchased from a supplier who gets into difficulty is of the sort that does not require sophisticated maintenance, then the buyer should not experience any problems since the appropriate maintenance programme can be entrusted to another software house. On the other hand, it may be the case that the original supplier will be anxious to continue receiving the maintenance fees and will have incorporated a source code in the software to prevent unauthorized access. They will usually have spent a lot of time and money on software development and they will, understandably, wish to retain copyright. Retention of the source code is an effective way of ensuring this.

In such instances there is clearly a potential conflict of interest between the developer of the software (the licensor) and the user of it (the licensee). One solution to the problem is an escrow agreement whereby the source code is held by a neutral and disinterested third party. The best-known institution offering this service is the NCC (National Computing Centre), but some banks and other financial bodies now have also now entered the arena. Some legal firms also now offer such a service.

The escrow agreement may be between the licensor and the escrow agent (bipartite); the licensee may also be party to the agreement (tripartite). Whatever the format, it is vital for the licensee to make sure (if he has the technical expertise to do so) that he checks that the code which has been deposited is up to date. There have been many instances where the code which has been deposited is out of time and therefore completely useless for getting the software to perform as it should, particularly since, generally speaking, escrow agents will not assume responsibility for what has been deposited.

The interaction between the software supplier and the buyer is typically handled by an escrow agent who 'is responsible for the physical storage and/or timely distribution of the software code according to an escrow agreement'. The agreement can cover eventualities such as the software developer going out of business, legal disagreements during development, or unanticipated delay in the release of a software product.

The escrow principle brings into focus the key issue of who actually is the owner of the software and it is here that the question of intellectual property rights (IPR) arises. It is a widely held belief that once an individual or an organization has purchased software, then it is theirs to do with as they wish; this belief is particularly prevalent where a company has bought software specifically for its own use and may well have assisted in its development. In fact all that has been bought is the licence to use it; ownership of the copyright remains vested in the software house or the freelance programmer who was responsible for developing it (the word 'freelance' is significant – if a programmer is in paid employment, then it is his employer who owns the IPR). However now that IT systems, at varying levels of sophistication and complexity, are an essential feature of virtually all organizations, buyers and managers are now realizing that, at least as far as standard off-the-shelf shrink-wrapped software is concerned, the very act of removing the wrapping is construed as acknowledgement of the supplier's ownership of the IPR.

Intellectual property rights

The escrow principle throws into focus the important question as to who actually owns the software and it is here that the issue of IPR (intellectual property rights) raises its head.

Before becoming part of the OGC (Office of Government Commerce) the CSSA (Computing Services and Software Association) published guidelines for protecting the licensor's IPR. However, to an increasing extent these terms are being viewed as negotiable with, for example, buyers having the right to lay claim to a share of the revenue from the sale of the software that they have helped to develop. Furthermore, whilst the copyright Designs and Patents Act 1988 recognizes that the originator of the software enjoys full IPRs and the EU Software Directive provides among other things that the legitimate end user may take a share in any royalties, without needing the consent of the originator.

- make a back-up copy of the software where that is necessary
- examine the functioning of the software to determine its underlying principles
- decompile the software where that is 'indispensable' to achieve the interoperability of an independently created program with other programs.

SOFTWARE PATENTS

Companies devoting resources to developing software-related inventions will wish to gain some commercial benefit from their efforts. This is best achieved through the acquisition of patent rights, a process which offers far greater protection than copyright and which, unlike copyright, does not come into being automatically, but only after a rigorous application procedure.

To be eligible for patent status, an invention must be new (i.e. not readily available to the public) as well as being inventive – that is, it will not be obvious to qualified individuals in the relevant technical field. However, it must not fall within an excluded category – this is where the programs begin. Under existing UK and EU laws a patent cannot be granted for a computer program as such. In other words, a patent can only be granted in cases where the software has a specific practical application.

Those wishing to see software being given patent status take the view that copyright only provides protection for the code of software program and does not take account of the work and expertise which has gone into its development, not to mention the costs involved. A study undertaken in 1998 by IDC, the IT consultancy and research organization, estimated that even in 1996 the world software industry was worth about $95bn, and would increase at an annual rate of 13 per cent. It is not surprising that, at this level of expenditure, companies are anxious to protect their investment.

The IPR aspect of software is now (May 2001) under active review with increasing pressure being brought to bear to allow programs to be patented; the present somewhat anomalous situation is that whilst inventions which make use of software programs in their development can be patented, the software program itself is not eligible for patent status).

The situation is not helped by the lack of consistency with which existing patent legislation is applied within the countries of the EU; inevitably there are differences in the views which individual countries take as far as proposals to grant patent status to software programs are concerned, with Italy and Portugal for instance opposing patent status on the grounds that granting patent monopolies will have the effect of stifling competition. The contrary view, expressed by some Scandinavian countries, is that patent protection for programs will have the effect of stimulating competition.

Case studies – pitfalls in software procurement

A seminal case of which all buyers of software should be aware is that of *St Albans City Council* v. *ICL* (1996). The Council purchased software from ICL for the collection of the council tax. However, the software was defective and, as a result, the council tax figure was set too low, resulting in a considerable shortfall in Council revenue. The Council commenced proceedings against ICL, whereupon the defendants argued that it was not realistic to expect software always to be free of defects and that in any case any such defects could easily be rectified once the package became the property of the customer. However, statutory legislation requires that, unless there are express terms to the contrary, there is an implied contractual term that at the point of delivery the goods must be:

- of satisfactory quality and
- fit for their intended purpose.

Clearly, the software are supplied by ICL did not satisfy these criteria. The judge accordingly found in favour of the plaintiff and awarded substantial damages of over £1.3m.

Other instances involving ICL software have also been reported (*Computer Weekly*, 2 April 1998). One such case concerned Staffordshire Moorlands Council, which issued a High Court writ for over £500,000, claiming that the systems supplied by ICL for the collection of the council tax was 'a total failure'. In particular, the Council complained about the number of 'rollbacks' (i.e. instances where the data needs to be re-entered, and the need for manual intervention for supposedly automated software modules for the collection of council tax). The Council was reported as wanting reimbursement of its original costs, plus compensation.

WESSEX REGIONAL HEALTH AUTHORITY

In 1982 the decision was taken to develop an approach to an information system which would cover all information requirements within the Authority. This was known as the RISP (Regional Information Systems Plan), its precise object being 'to use modern technology in order to optimise the use of information in the continuing improvement of the effectiveness and efficiency of clinical and other health services'.

In September 1986 the contract for both the hardware and the software was awarded to an Andersen Consulting/IBM consortium, even though they had earlier been advised that their tender for the hardware alone had not been successful. Crucially, the contract did not contain any stipulations as to quality, nor did it specify a maximum price.

The principal problems with the project may be summarized as follows:

- poorly defined scope of the RISP
- poor general project management
- poor supervision of software consultants
- inadequate financial control.

The end result of the project was that the Authority still did not have the system that it considered essential for its long-term plans. It was estimated that about half of the £43m cost of the project was wasted.

LONDON AMBULANCE SERVICE

The computerized despatch system went live on 26 October 1992. However, within the first few hours it became apparent that the system could not handle the loads being placed on it. Among the specific problems arising were:

- failure of calls to reach ambulances
- incorrect vehicle locations
- failure to identify duplicate calls
- poor prioritization of error messages
- calls being lost in the system.

The system closed down the following day and, the day after, reverted to semi-manual operation. The chief executive resigned, and the Health Secretary ordered an internal inquiry. Whilst there were a number of factors leading to the disaster, poor procurement certainly played a part. In particular, although the software supplier (Systems Options) was a software house with a good reputation, it crucially did not have any significant experience in designing or developing packages for safety-critical command-and-control systems.

The inquiry team took the view that, given the very tight deadlines which were applied, not to mention the complexity of the system, the probability was that no software house, whatever its size, could have developed a suitable solution. However, it is reasonable to suppose that a larger, more experienced software house would have recognized the danger signals early enough to have taken some effective action.

This example has been taken from *Software Failure: Management Failure* by Stephen Flowers. Other cases discussed in the book are:

- PROMS (Performing Rights Society)
- the CONFOIRM Computerized Reservation System
- the VBA (Veterans Business Administration) – USA
- Socrates Reservation System (SNCF – French National Railways)

Outsourcing

It should be clear from what has been said above that purchasing, implementing and operating an IT system in-house is beset with potential problems. For those who would rather avoid such difficulties, outsourcing represents a possible answer (cynics would, however, suggest that deciding to outsource to an external provider is simply to exchange one set of problems for another – see below). That said, there are few who would dispute that outsourcing, particularly of IT, is now very much in fashion.

Contrary to the popular impression, IT outsourcing is far from a new idea. As long ago as the mid-1960s, for instance, computer services bureaux in the USA ran a range of programs for purchasing and finance departments. Customers of these services were mostly small and medium-sized firms.

Until the late 1980s one of the principal drivers for IT outsourcing was to facilitate cost-effective access to specialized or occasionally needed computer expertise or systems development activities. The first major step forward in the development of IT outsourcing was the decision by Kodak in the USA in 1989 to outsource its IT function. Subsequently, research has conclusively shown that IT outsourcing is not, as sometimes supposed, a 'flash in the pan' management fad, and that half of medium to large USA firms have outsourced or are considering outsourcing some of their IT activities.

ADVANTAGES OF OUTSOURCING IT

Different writers have different opinions as to what the key attractions of outsourcing the IT functions are. However, most reviews of the benefits of outsourcing include the following:

- *It enables a company to focus on its core competences.* It is generally accepted that a business should concentrate on its core function, as this is what it does best. Other activities such as IT, whilst vital to the day-to-day operation and long-term development of the organization, are peripheral to the central core and as such, it is argued, most efficiently operated by external experts in the field. To take a specific example, the UK Director of IT at Philips Electronics has been quoted as follows:

  Outsourcing something to a third party does not mean you lose control. There is a paradox in that you get more control because an external organisation that treats you as a customer can sometimes be more responsible than an internal organisation that does not have quite the same view of internal people as customers.

- *It gives access to new technology.* Developments in IT occur at a faster pace and on a broader scale than in most other areas of technology. Outsourcing IT to a specialist in the field means that a company is kept abreast of these developments, something that it might not have the time or resources to do if the IT operation were retained in-house.
- *It overcomes skills shortages.* Skills in the IT field are becoming increasingly specialized, and to keep up-to-date with the changing requirements would present the human resources

department with a difficult problem. A 1996 report by the IDPM (Institute of Data Processing Management) has noted that the UK is threatened with an IT skills crisis unless government, vendors, educational establishments and users can be forced to address the shrinking pool of experienced IT professionals. Against this background it makes good sense to employ an external organization which may be presumed to know what skills are in demand at that particular time and, just as important, what the going rate is.

- *It overcomes image problems.* In many organizations the IT department has suffered an image problem, with many MDs complaining that the department, with its esoteric jargon and technospeak, causes serious problems of communication. Outsourcing represents a convenient and cost-effective way of talking about the issue. In many cases it is found that the members of the erstwhile IT department are thereby freed to perform higher-value activities within the organization.
- *Fixed costs can become variable.* Under a typical outsourcing agreement, a company will sell its computer assets to the outsourcing company. The company then pays for IT services on a demand-led basis. This enables the IT budget to be reduced, thereby freeing up financial resources for other uses.
- *It gives greater flexibility.* No longer constrained by a fixed IT infrastructure, the company is able to respond more immediately to changes in the marketplace, whether positive or negative. If changes in IT requirements then follow, the IT service provider should have the resources and capability to respond accordingly.

DISADVANTAGES OF OUTSOURCING IT

Attractive option though it is in many situations, outsourcing the IT function also has its downside. The principal limitations include:

- *The use of inexperienced staff by the service provider* – particularly difficult to spot since the IT specialist companies are not going to advertise such deficiencies, if indeed they are even aware of them in the first place.
- *Outdated technology skills* on the part of the IT specialist.
- *Inflexibility on the part of the supplier* – in the IT industry in particular, organizations need to be able to react to and take advantage of new developments as and when they come about.
- *Hidden costs* – there have been numerous instances of companies being faced with the unexpected costs, not least the considerable management time, associated with setting up and running and outsourced IT operation.
- *Weak management* – poor management in the IT department can often be the real, if hidden, reason for MDs or CEOs to outsource the IT function. However, moving the problem is rarely an effective solution, since the inadequate managers will hardly be any better at managing an external provider.
- *Poor innovative capability* – using a supplier with this deficiency can easily cause an organization to lose both credibility and market share.

Clearly by no means all outsourcing situations will have all or indeed any of these deficiencies. However, it is important for executives considering outsourcing to be aware of their existence and if necessary undertake a cost–benefit analysis to establish whether or not the level or risk or expenditure is acceptable or indeed whether or not it makes better sense to retain the IT function in-house.

IF THE RELATIONSHIP BREAKS DOWN

As noted above, difficulties and misunderstandings can all too easily arise between buyer and supplier. The following observations by Bird and Bird, a large London law firm, may prove of interest, particularly to those involved in those cases where the supplier is at fault:

- *Misrepresentation.* A complaint often heard against suppliers is that of the customer stating that he bought a system on the advice of the supplier only to subsequently find it unsatisfactory. An obvious example is that of software bought on the understanding that it is Year 2000 compliant, only for it to later emerge that it is nothing of the sort.
- *Breach of contract.* In the case of a clear-cut, well-drawn-up contract, and when the deficiency is clearly identifiable (missing functionality, for example), the customer may well be able to demonstrate breach of contract and should therefore win his case relatively easily. However, if the complaint concerns something less easily quantifiable or identifiable, such as reliability or stability, he may have a much harder task.
- *Negligence.* This frequently applies to consultants but it can also apply to suppliers and providers of outsourcing services. The key question is: 'Did the consultant use reasonable care, skill and judgement in the advice and recommendations he gave to the buyer?' If the computer system that he recommended subsequently proved to be unsuitable for the specified application, he clearly is guilty of negligence. The difficulty may well lie in proving such negligence.

To conclude, if it becomes necessary to extricate oneself from an outsourcing contract and none of the above escape routes is applicable, legal advice needs to be sought.

Disposal of equipment and the EU Draft Directive on Waste Electrical and Electronic Equipment

Sooner or later even the best IT equipment comes to the end of its useful life, at which point the question of environmentally aware disposal arises. The size of the problem may be gauged from the fact that, according to ICL, a survey carried out in 1996 revealed that only 24 per cent of the 125,000 tonnes discarded each year is recycled. To help address the problem the company introduced a scheme – 'Recycle' – to assist any of its customers having any unwanted equipment that they wish to dispose of. The scheme provides a foretaste of future legislation which is expected to set recycling targets of between 80 and 90 per cent.

The legislation in question is the EU Draft Directive on Waste Electrical and Electronic Equipment (WEEE) recycling and is an important development of which buyers need to be aware. The proposed legislation also has significant implications for manufacturers who will have responsibility for taking back their products once they have reached the end of their useful life and arrange for recycling.

PRINCIPAL OBJECTIVES OF THE LEGISLATION

- To reduce the quantity and potential environmental impact of 'end-of-life' equipment.
- To aim for reuse or recycling wherever feasible.

On the basis that prevention is better than cure, the Directive proposes:

- reducing the usage of dangerous substances such as lead and cadmium
- reducing the range of plastics employed
- promoting design for recycling.

SCOPE OF THE DIRECTIVE

The Directive identifies 11 categories of equipment as follows:

1 Large household appliances
2 Small household appliances
3 IT equipment
4 Telecommunication equipment
5 Radio and television equipment; musical instruments
6 Lighting equipment
7 Medical equipment
8 Monitoring and control instruments
9 Toys
10 Electrical and electronic tools
11 Automatic dispensers

Category 3 – IT equipment – comprises the following:

(a) Centralized data processing
   - Mainframes
   - Minicomputers
   - Printer units

(b) Personal Computing
   - PCs
   - Laptops
   - Note-book computers
   - Note-pad computers
   - Printers
   - Copying equipment
   - Electrical and electronic typewriters
   - Pocket and desk calculators.

At the time of writing, the proposed Directive is still progressing through the various committees in Brussels, with debate being centred on whether or not it should be split in two, with the suggested introduction of a Directive on RoHS (Restrictions on the use of certain Hazardous Substances – lead, mercury, arsenic cadmium, etc.) in electronic equipment. The expectation is that the legislation will come into force in 2005.

References

British Computer Society (1995), *A Glossary of Computing Terms*.

Buy IT best Practice Group (1998), *The Buy IT Guidelines*, London: Buy IT.

Compton, H. and Jessop, D. (2001), *Official Dictionary of Purchasing and Supply*, Liverpool: Liverpool Business Press.

Flowers, S. (1998), *Software Failure, Management Failure*, Chichester: John Wiley.

Lysons, C.K. (1996), *Purchasing*, London: Pitman.

22 *Purchasing in the Higher Education sector*

Tom Chadwick

The higher education sector in the UK includes a very broad spectrum of institutions ranging from small specialist colleges of art, music or agriculture, through multidisciplinary metropolitan institutions, many with large medical schools and research activities, to the giant collegiate universities of Oxford and Cambridge.

The 160 or so institutions are autonomous and jealous of their independence. Many of the larger, older universities have highly devolved management structures that can make the aggregation of purchasing spend on common items difficult to achieve. Academic freedom is enshrined in law, and it can require particular skills from the head of purchasing to achieve the best overall value for money without compromising support for individual areas of specialization.

The resources available to universities and colleges remain under pressure, with expenditure constrained by the level of funds available. In the UK, over 60 per cent of the sector's income still comes from public funds so there is a need, not just to obtain value for money, but to be able to demonstrate that this is being achieved.

An important characteristic of purchasing in the higher education sector is the breadth of commodity and service requirements. A large research university teaching arts and social sciences, engineering and physical sciences, with a medical faculty and veterinary school, probably employing 5,000 staff and with an estate of teaching facilities, laboratories, libraries and residences to support 20,000 students, has a very significant demand for external resources.

History and context

The sector spends over £4bn annually, making it an important and attractive marketplace for suppliers.

The buying and selling interfaces between the HE community and the many thousands of suppliers are varied and complex. Just as there are many thousands of suppliers to the sector, so there are many thousands of buyers within the sector. Most institutions operate through systems of devolved financial management, and the authority to purchase goods and services frequently rests with colleges, schools or departments and, in many instances, with a number of staff and cost centres at a further level of devolution. This fragmented and uncoordinated buying dilutes institutional purchasing power and encourages sub-optimal decisions. There is considerable advantage to both buyer and seller if expenditure on supplies is professionally and efficiently managed. Progressive improvements in purchasing policies and practices have been made over the years and institutions have increasingly seen the benefits to be derived through collaborative arrangements.

In 1992 the Committee of Vice-Chancellors and Principals (CVCP – now Universities UK) sought to provide a focus for the development of best procurement practice in a structured and focused way. The establishment of the office of the Central Purchasing Coordinator was a significant step in the process of integration and aggregation of purchasing interests at institutional, regional and national levels.

During 1996 the CVCP, the Standing Conference of Principals (SCOP), the Committee of Scottish Higher Education Principals (COSHEP – now Universities Scotland), together with the three higher education funding councils, reviewed their respective activities in promoting good procurement practices in higher education institutions. They concluded that their activities in the field of purchasing should be brought together into one joint strategy under the control of a steering group – the Joint Procurement Policy and Strategy Group (JPPSG).

Public sector status and the National Audit Office reports

Although an increasing proportion of the income of institutions is from sources other than the government's higher education funding and research councils, they remain firmly within the public sector as far as accountability is concerned, and hence subject to the rules set out in the European Union Procurement Directives and the scrutiny of public audit.

The National Audit Office (NAO), the UK parliament's watchdog, published two reports in 1999. The first, *Procurement in the English Higher Education Sector* (NAO, 1999a), recorded substantial progress since the last audit in 1993, coming as a result of the existence now of a procurement strategy and the increasing employment of specialist heads of procurement in the sector. However, there were many areas where further improvement was considered necessary:

- Increase cooperation between institutions to make more use of the sector's purchasing power.
- Extend influence of procurement to all areas of non-pay expenditure.
- Extend training to all with procurement responsibilities.
- Increase adoption of procurement management systems.
- Develop performance indicators and benchmarks.
- Increase reporting on procurement performance.
- Increase use of approved suppliers.
- Increase aggregation of orders.

The second report, *Procurement of Equipment from Research Grants* (NAO, 1999b), presented five recommendations:

- Encourage universities to improve their estimating of equipment costs by requiring proposals for equipment funding to be fully evidenced, while recognizing, however, the effort required in preparing such proposals.
- Make applicants aware that, for research proposals of equivalent quality, those that have well-supported and realistic assessments of equipment costs are more likely to be fully funded.

- Encourage universities to follow best procurement practice, including that set out in the JPPSG 'Equipment Procurement' guidelines.
- Identify opportunities for coordinated purchasing between universities.
- Work with the other research councils and the higher education funding councils to continue to improve procurement and seek assurance that best procurement practice is being used and measures agreed to monitor progress in equipment procurement performance.

The Joint Procurement Policy and Strategy Group (JPPSG)

In September 1996 the JPPSG issued its *Procurement Strategy for Higher Education.* Over the years since then much progress has been made in improving procurement practices in higher education, but there is still a great deal to do.

To assist with this the JPPSG appointed a Director of Procurement Development in May 1998 to build on the work of the disbanded CVCP Central Purchasing Coordinators. The JPPSG recognizes that that the primary aims of institutions are to work towards providing excellence in teaching and research, and that effective procurement will support these aims by providing the best possible management of externally provided resources. The JPPSG strategy is to assist universities and colleges to secure effective procurement through the application of good management and practices, thereby achieving value for money from all non-pay expenditure, both capital and recurrent.

The elements of the strategy are:

- securing commitment to effective procurement from governing bodies, heads of institutions, and senior managers
- improving the training and skills development of all those involved in procurement
- improving the use of procurement management systems and information systems
- identifying and disseminating information and advice on good procurement practice
- promoting cooperative procurement arrangements within and between institutions
- promoting the development and use of performance measures
- promoting procurement practices which contribute to the sustainability of the environment.

The JPPSG Procurement Development Directorate produces, publishes and supports a wide range of guidance and model documents, and toolkits backed by training workshops and help-line support. The Directorate has been established as an accredited award centre for procurement and management courses at a range of levels under the National Vocational Qualification scheme. A deputy director of procurement development works with individual institutions and regional consortia to identify candidates for training within institutions.

Training can be provided directly to candidates, but the preferred option is to identify one of the institution's professional purchasing staff to learn the role first of a mentor and eventually a coach assessor, to cascade training throughout the college or university. This process has the significant benefit of building or reinforcing an effective network between the institution's purchasing office and the staff in external departments who actually carry out an important part of the purchasing function (McCulloch, 2000).

JPPSG also provides some project funding to stimulate or pilot procurement initiatives, including the establishment of affinity groups to look into collaborative opportunities related to expenditure on grants received from the research councils, and the pilot programme to test the national contracting protocol for greater cooperation among the regional purchasing consortia.

The Association of University Purchasing Officers (AUPO)

AUPO was formed around 1985 as an independent networking forum and has developed steadily into a well-regarded representative body for purchasing in the higher education sector.

Apart from a few exceptions, which are mainly in the largest institutions, the team dedicated to purchasing is small and the opportunities for sharing experience and finding moral support from immediate colleagues in the profession would be limited or absent without the Association of University Purchasing Officers. As well as the essential camaraderie, this very active network provides often ready access to a wealth of information and expertise.

A typical scenario would start with a telephone call or visit from a professor in the pathology department advising of their imminent, and usually apparently urgent, need to purchase a confocal laser scanning microscope or similar item of exotic equipment presumably fraught with specification and procurement risk. The well-meaning academic has at least contacted the purchasing office but may well be convinced that only one supplier can meet the requirements, and will almost certainly be anxious to complete the purchase virtually there and then. While it is unlikely that the purchasing office itself will have previous experience of a similar requirement, it is almost certain that colleagues in another institution will. An enquiry sent by e-mail around the AUPO circulation list will often produce a file of previous case histories, alternative suppliers and possibly a draft purchase specification within a small number of hours.

As well as this powerful if informal network, AUPO runs a website closely linked to, and complementary with, the main JPPSG site.

AUPO is run by a council of elected representatives from seven geographical regions covering Britain and Northern Ireland. There is an annual conference focused on aspects of current interest. Since 1999 AUPO has been formally affiliated with the Chartered Institute of Purchasing and Supply, removing the earlier anomaly of having two bodies trying to provide the same support activities for the same group of purchasing professionals. AUPO plays a full role in the various procurement advisory groups active in the sector, including areas like e-procurement, continuing professional development, and performance measurement and benchmarking.

The seven regional consortia

Most universities and colleges in the UK have organized themselves into regional purchasing consortia to share common interests and to aggregate expenditure on commonly purchased commodities where this can be seen to provide value for their members. There are seven consortia which are formally established covering the whole of Great Britain and Northern Ireland. There are variations in their size and in the management structure that they have set up to coordinate their activities. None of them is a buying agency as such, but work to facilitate the establishment of framework agreements normally via teams of commodity specialists drawn from member institutions. In addition to their role as facilitators of joint negotiations, the consortia offices provide a forum for the exchange of knowledge and experience. The heads of the regional consortia meet on a regular basis and have established a protocol and a national contracting strategy to examine the best approach to each major commodity and service area.

The seven consortia vary in their size and in the extent of the administrative support that they supply to their member institutions. In essence, however, they are similar in having a small administrative core consisting of one to seven full-time staff. Funding comes largely from subscriptions, which vary in their level and their relationship or not to the extent of the member's non-pay expenditure or size in terms of staffing. One consortium uses retrospective rebates from suppliers to substantially reduce membership costs. The concept of a low-cost permanent core facilitating and supporting collaborative working by specialists drawn from member institutions can be a very cost-effective way of resourcing cooperative procurement. Each regional consortia office is governed by a board of management drawn from member institutions, normally including a strong representation of directors of finance.

Each of the seven regional consortia provides a very valuable opportunity for both member institutions and suppliers to coordinate and optimize commodity supply chains to a high level of efficiency. However, as in all efforts to promote the benefits of collaboration among independent bodies, barriers can arise in the development of optimum effectiveness:

- the perception that in a grouping of unequals, which all the HE consortia are, large members benefit least of all
- the fact that HE institutions are themselves consortia with often highly devolved management structures – their powerful constituent parts may not be active willing participants
- actual or perceived loss of buyer–supplier relationships
- loss of status by insecure purchasing staff
- perceived threat to supplier base with unsuccessful tenderers tempted to try to divide and conquer.

The potentially negative effects of these perceptions is neatly illustrated in a series of sets of concentric circles which progressively built on each other. The inner core is red hot, representing the enthusiasm of a commodity team having just successfully awarded a contract to the best supplier after the usual tender and evaluation process. The next annulus is also red but not quite so hot, as the consortium office transmitted the information to the heads of purchasing in the institutions. The third ring is a bit more pinkish, as each institution's purchasing office passed the news and details of engagement on to the actual user. The outer circle is entirely blue, as the users who felt that they had not been considered, never mind consulted, received the news and possibly resolved to shelve the information and carry on with their locally chosen and friendly incumbent supplier. The situation is not as bad as described in *Reinventing Government* (Osborne and Gaebler, 1992, p. 318) where David Kearns, former CEO of Xerox and at that time an under-secretary of education, is quoted as saying that public education is 'the only industry we have where if you do a good job, nothing good happens to you, and if you do a bad job, nothing bad happens to you'. However, the higher education sector in the UK can have its moments of resistance to change.

Good communication, inclusive consultation, the highest standards of supplier selection and good marketing of ongoing supplier performance are essential to make cooperation work. The benefits in optimization of effort, selection of the very best suppliers and reduction in purchasing risk are not in doubt (Ritchie and Chadwick, 2000).

The national contracting protocol

The national contracting protocol is a mechanism that ensures that heads of regional consortia, or specialist national working groups making plans for a new contract, have a ready process to communicate their objectives and consult for possible collaboration with the sector as a whole. It does not mean, as some had first feared, that everything becomes a national contract controlled and dictated from some dreaded bureaucratic centre, but it does mean that the sector as a whole, by at least representative democracy, takes an overall view for each commodity group. A good example of this is the arrangement for library periodicals. The Southern Universities Purchasing Consortium took the lead in this because of all the regional consortia they had the most experience in this important commodity group.

Details of existing contract experience, though not price levels, and the regional split of probable contract value are ascertained from the heads of each regional consortium and any relevant national working group. For periodicals there were six major regional contracts in place with a range of expiry dates. The higher education sector is the largest customer in the UK in this field and hence must take account of the effect of its overall strategy on the market. The number of companies known to be able and interested in supplying the wide range of periodicals required is limited in number though the major players are international businesses with much of their turnover outside the UK. A risk analysis and an exploration of short- and long-term benefits are used to determine the best way forward for the higher education sector as a whole.

The use of the protocol enables clarification and much better understanding of important supply chain issues like review procedures, performance measurement and improvement targeting. Innovative ways of working can be explored and improvements in purchasing methodology and process sought to benefit the supply market as well as the higher education sector. As e-commerce continues to develop there are opportunities for change across all segments of commodity and service provision. However, the delivery of periodicals to libraries takes this to another dimension as the impact of fully electronic publications with or without accompanying hard copy challenges both the provision of the information and the working methods and the very *raison d'être* of academic libraries.

The national and interregional purchasing working groups

To supplement the work of the regional purchasing consortia and to bring specific focus to major areas of expenditure, a considerable number of national working groups meet regularly and formally to examine and discuss related procurement issues. Like the regional commodity groups, members are drawn from both procurement staff and academic or administrative staff. This cross-functional forum and the networking which develops provide more opportunities for procurement staff to show how their work can support and bring major benefits to even the most cloistered areas of academe.

Several specialist organizations also exist within the sector, like EduServ, providing a service to purchase software and datasets, and the Energy Consortium supporting collaborative purchasing of power fuels and water.

Purchasing in a typical institution

Figures 22.1. to 22.3. show expenditure levels and the range of commodities purchased in a typical institution.

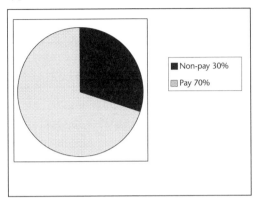

Figure 22.1   *Typical breakdown of expenditure in a small institution*

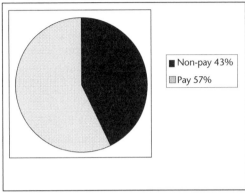

Figure 22.2   *Breakdown of expenditure in a large institution with a strong research commitment*

Opportunities for the purchasing office to play a strategic role

A few years ago the very mention of commercial planning or strategic objectives would have been met by no more than a cold stare of disdain in many academic circles. However, economic pressures and globalization penetrate even the hallowed walls of academe and nowadays a typical mission statement for an HE institution might include:

• to enhance its status as an internationally recognized research institution
• to provide excellence in teaching

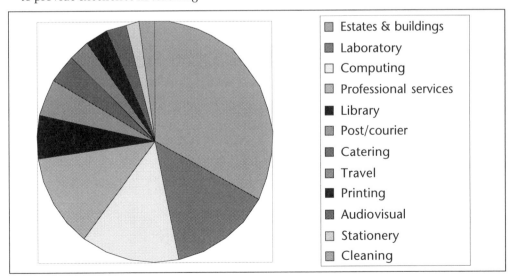

Figure 22.3   *Expenditure by commodity type in a typical medium-sized institution in a small institution*

- to recruit and retain excellent staff and improve their effectiveness through the provision of appropriate training and development
- to optimize the use of resources
- to achieve a level of income which will allow for balanced growth and future development.

A strategy for purchasing can make clear reference to the institution's overall strategic aims and objectives, with specific links to each of these where the impact of good management of external resources affects performance and fulfilment. The aim of the purchasing office will be to make a recognized and measurably cost-effective contribution to the success of the institution and the achievement of its strategic aims.

Purchasing is a key business skill (Kolchin, 1993) and purchasing staff should be able to bring knowledge and commercial input to help senior management plan for the success of the institution by:

- identifying and evaluating commercial issues affecting organizational planning (and organizational issues affecting commercial planning)
- evaluating supply market issues
- evaluating alternative commercial strategy options
- stepping back from the day-to-day operational concerns and thinking about the big picture.

The purchasing office should not necessarily do the purchasing. They should be involved in summarizing and sharing current and new knowledge, searching for improvements in the performance of suppliers (Womack and Jones, 1994). In this regard the devolved management structure of most institutions actually helps in removing much of the day-to-day order processing from the central purchasing office thus providing the opportunity to look across the needs of the institution as a whole.

A process benchmarking tool (e.g. Figure 22.4) provides an excellent mechanism to examine and develop current strategies (or devise them if none exists so far) by identifying the key stakeholders in the institution and bringing them together for a prepared and structured workshop on the role and way forward for purchasing.

Skills development and training

As well as having one of the largest procurement NVQ training schemes in the UK, with well in excess of 300 candidates progressing through units at levels 2, 3 and 4 of the nationally accredited programme, there is a strong and successful history of the use of sophisticated expenditure analysis, whole-life costing and procurement process benchmarking in many institutions around the sector. These toolkits have been developed either entirely within the sector, or by working groups supporting and directing external procurement consultants.

Expenditure analysis and benchmarking toolkits

The devolved management structure of many institutions and the very wide range of often non-recurring items purchased present a significant challenge to the effectiveness of

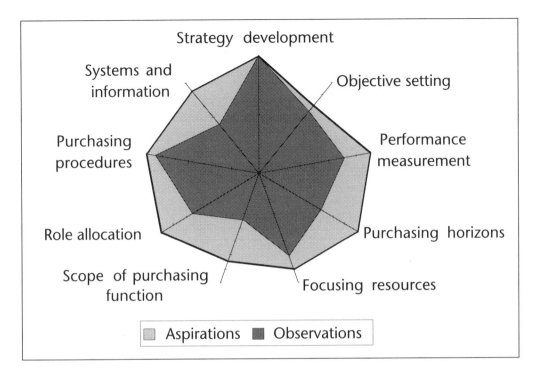

Figure 22.4   *The process benchmarking toolkit*

purchasing management systems. While the sector and its management information suppliers are progressing steadily in this regard, the expenditure analysis toolkits are based on the fail-safe principle that a start can be made with the simplest listing of supplier invoice payment totals. By sorting supplier expenditure in the last financial year into descending order and entering the names and amounts into the main analysis worksheet, opportunities are provided to assess the level of influence, or control, achieved by the institution's professional purchasing function on the business transacted with the selected supplier.

The supplier's expenditure is also analysed by the type of purchasing arrangement used to commit the funds: e.g. national; regional consortium; local agreement; tender/quotation; or other. This may be divided, in percentage terms, over as many of these headings as necessary.

The development of the 'Financials' toolkit from its origins in a small group of universities in Scotland and Northern Ireland is described by Florence Gregg (1999). The model emphasizes performance measurement rather than more popular 'traditional' benchmarking. Initially, the research involved a number of institutions prepared to share with each other the collected performance measurements, this approach being preferable to one where the project became a large-scale comparative exercise from which 'league'-type tables could be generated. The view was therefore focused, in the short term at least, on close collaboration between a small number of institutions.

Use of the 'Financials' toolkit at least ensures that the purchasing office begins to take an overview role in the total institution's dependence on external resources and can demonstrate awareness of where the money is being spent. The charts show clearly the extent of 'penetration' of the influence and control of the purchasing office in the activities of the devolved management structure that characterizes most institutions (see Figure 22.5).

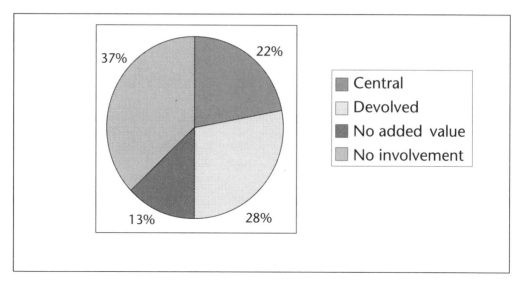

Figure 22.5   *Purchasing impact on analysed expenditure*

The tool provides the facility to use a set of basic coding letters to begin to sort suppliers by the type of commodity they supply. Supplier data can then be readily sorted to show how many are being used for each commodity range, providing a starting point for consideration of rationalization. Several institutions have now been using the 'Financials' toolkit over five or more years with a steady progression in effectiveness.

IBIS – Integrated Benchmarking Information System

In a further development of the work of the group in Scotland and Northern Ireland, funding was obtained to create a more complex toolkit which provides facilities to analyse additional factors to those covered by 'Financials'. These include:

- size, cost, staff qualifications and division of work in the central procurement office
- quality of service provided by the central procurement office as seen by users of the service
- quality of service provided by each supplier.

The increased sophistication of IBIS will help institutions further down the route to best practice, though its complexity and the new challenges it brings may take a little time to be universally accepted.

Process benchmarking

The process benchmarking toolkit used most in the sector is illustrated in Figure 22.4. It is a strategic-level tool which stimulates the need to identify the key stakeholders both for the purchasing process in the institution as a whole, and for any particular commodity or service range where a specific strategy is important.

The stakeholders are assembled to set aspiration levels for a whole panoply of purchasing criteria. The toolkit provides a series of descriptors from best practice in a scoring range from 1 'innocent' to 4 'world-class'. Realistic aspirations are discussed and agreed and become the first plot in a radial spider chart. The same stakeholders then work independently to record their observation mark for the current situation as they see it. Again a list of questions is used to produce the scoring. The average of these scores is used to produce the second plot in the radial chart. Conventional 'gap analysis' can then be used to target and address the largest differences between aspiration and observation.

As well as covering both institution and specific commodity-based strategies, the process toolkit has been developed to address sustainability in environmental, social and ethical purchasing performance.

The initial phase of identifying and assembling the key stakeholders immediately demands and delivers attention to purchasing from senior management in the institution. There is a challenge to the marketing skills and the professional knowledge of the purchasing officer involved, and as in all sectors there may be some who are nervous about raising their head above the safety of the parapet. Those that do and are able to engage effectively with key stakeholders have a real chance of achieving results and outcomes to affect the strategic objectives of their institution. This is the difference between just measuring process and measuring results. In *Reinventing Government* Osborne and Gaebler worry that when public organizations set out to measure performance, their managers usually draw up lists that measure how well they carry out some administrative process: how many people they serve; how fast they serve them; and what percentage of their requests are fulfilled within a set period of time (Osborne and Gaebler, 1992, p. 350).

Whole-life costing

This toolkit is also Excel-based and is designed to be as easy as possible to use and to fit into the normal provision process for significant purchases. There are six basic steps:

1 Enter background information and details of the options to be considered in the acquisition options worksheet.
2 Define the acquisition criteria and performance specification. A large number of suggestions are available from drop-down menus.
3 Select the criteria weighting for both user requirements and performance specification.

At this stage the normal tendering process is carried out.

4 Score the options.
5 Identify the cost profile over the item's lifecycle.
6 Select the preferred option based on scored qualitative criteria, user requirements and whole-life cost of the item or project.

This is a genuinely practicable toolkit and its benefits are readily demonstrable, even using fairly mundane but general-interest examples like car purchase. Good progress has been made in promoting its use for research grant applications and other projects. If purchasing officers can be encouraged to use it they also gain another valuable opportunity to break out of the confines of the purchasing office and engage with and share supporting skills with academics and researchers (Chadwick and Mee, 1998).

Value measurement and price tracking

The purchasing offices in many institutions use spreadsheets and tabular listings to record, track and report the contribution in 'added value' or 'savings' terms usually as an adjunct to management reports. As with other aspects of the HE sector, the highly devolved management structure makes this complex to keep track of outside the immediate areas of central responsibility, but improving management information systems are having a positive impact on this. Many purchases are non-recurring, so life is not as simple as monitoring repeated purchases of production materials against indices or targets for cost reduction.

A number of institutions and several consortia have worked with an external price-tracking agency to monitor shopping baskets of specific commodity ranges against prices paid by other users in the same sector and all other users subscribing to the database. This enables both good management of general purchasing results and provides the information to target areas that are not under control. Because it can be done at department level, it is an effective but non-interventionist means of keeping an eye on areas like general cleaning materials or food in the student halls of residence. However, price tracking can also be used to tackle high-level areas in both goods and services provision.

Procureweb, electronic purchasing and purchasing cards

The devolved nature of most higher education institutions lends itself quite neatly to the use of electronic procurement applications. The higher education sector has been using the Internet since its inception via the UK's Joint Academic Network (JANET). For many years there has been a website dedicated to purchasing information, guidance documents, downloadable toolkits and links to other major purchasing websites. This has steadily developed into a portal 'Procureweb' that will progressively allow universities and colleges to have direct access individually or collectively (as they see fit) to a wide range of selected suppliers. Electronic procurement is cutting transaction costs and shortening lead-times. The improved accuracy and currency of the management information provided gives a real chance to monitor supplier performance. Procureweb also provides access to an integrated supplier database 'Catalist'.

The concept behind 'Catalist' is to provide a readily accessible database of supplier information which can be maintained and kept up to date with minimal resource expenditure by the sector itself. If carried out effectively it obviates the need for individual institutions to replicate essentially the same information on many common suppliers many times over. It introduces a good standard by including all the criteria for supplier selection laid down in the European Union Procurement Directives. It benefits suppliers not just by putting their vital statistics directly in front of both existing and potential customers of their products or services, but also by eliminating the need for countless copies of current annual reports, quality assurance certificates etc. to be sent out every time any institution needs to go through a tendering process.

Recognizing the growing importance of e-commerce, JPPSG appointed an e-procurement adviser in 2001 to facilitate the development and adoption of e-procurement in the higher education sector, coordinate such developments within an overall strategy and act as a source of e-procurement expertise, advice and guidance on which institutions can draw. As well as a strong e-procurement best practice group, a number of initiatives are under way, including the use of both thick (managed catalogues) and thin (punch-out) marketplaces and sourcing tools (see Figure 22.6 for an overview of the e-procurement models used in the HE sector).

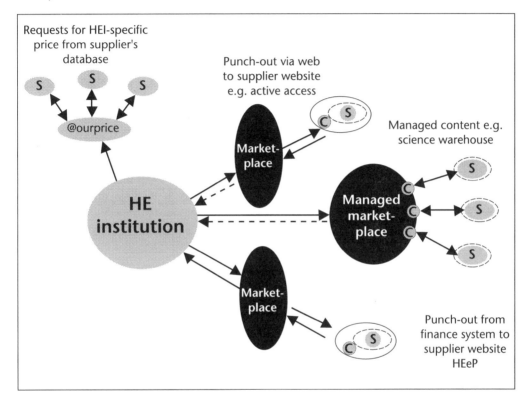

Figure 22.6   *E-procurement models*

Purchasing cards are used in a number of institutions both for low value orders with frequently used suppliers and single transactions with companies where no account has been established perhaps a stockist of a special book or very rarely asked for chemical.

The future of purchasing in the sector

Higher education in the UK will continue to anticipate reducing levels of income from public sources and an increasingly competitive environment in which to exist. There will be more and more scope for purchasing offices led by bold, capable and committed professionals to harness best practice and new techniques to make a real contribution to their institution's success and continuing existence. Proposed changes to the EC Procurement Directives will force increased transparency and challenge any shortfall in professional practice. Increasing adoption of e-procurement will help to reduce transaction costs and increase compliance with strategic contracts. Electronic auctions and increased use of dynamic pricing will provide a better environment for gaining best value.

References

Chadwick, T. and Mee, M. (1998), 'Whole Life Costing – Helping Buyers to Break the Confines of the Purchasing Office', *Proceedings of IPSERA Conference 1998*, pp. 112–19.

Gregg, F. (1999), 'Purchasing Performance in the UK's Higher Education Sector – Functional Measures to Aid in Strategic Development for the 21st Century', *Proceedings of IPSERA Conference 1999*, pp. 351–64.

Kolchin, G. (1993), 'Purchasing Education and Training: Requirements and Resources', CAPS, USA, Arizona State University, p. 47.

McCulloch, H. (2000), 'Getting to the Fundamentals in Procurement Training', in A. Erridge, R. Fee and J. McIlroy (eds), *Best Practice Procurement: Public and Private Sector Perspectives*, Aldershot, UK: Gower Publishing.

National Audit Office (1999a), *Procurement in the English Higher Education Sector HC 437*, 27 May, Norwich, UK: The Stationery Office.

National Audit Office (1999b), *Procurement of Equipment from Research Grants HC 494*, 23 June 1999 Norwich, UK: The Stationery Office.

Osborne, D. and Gaebler, T. (1992), *Reinventing Government*, Reading MA: Addison-Wesley.

Ritchie, J. and Chadwick, T. (2000), 'A Quart from a Pint Pot? Developing the Effective Use of Purchasing Consortia', in Erridge, A., Fee, R. and McIlroy, J. (eds), *Best Practice Procurement: Public and Private Sector Perspectives*, Aldershot, UK: Gower Publishing.

Womack, J.P. and Jones, D.T. (1994), 'From Lean Production to the Lean Enterprise,' *Harvard Business Review*, March–April, pp. 93–103.

23 *Purchasing transportation*

Kenneth Waters

Introduction

Transportation, in its many guises, has been an important element in the growth of civilization. It is necessary because even the simplest form of exchange will normally have an element of transportation within it to complete the transaction according to the needs and wants of the marketplace and to the satisfaction of the end user or customer. The formality of exchanges or trade has advanced the social and economic benefits to the inhabitants of the globe over many centuries. Even the earliest merchants realized the importance of adding value to their wares by making the products available at the point of consumption and thereby gain a competitive advantage over their rivals. The era of the great explorations of the thirteenth and fourteenth centuries were undertaken to discover not only new sources of supply, but also to find new and quicker routes for the conduct of trade. It should also be remembered that, over the centuries, transport was always the great instigator and innovator for the application of new technologies. As a result, merchant venturing and transport have always been associated with great entrepreneurial individuals such as Marco Polo, Columbus, Stephenson, Brunel, Cunard and organizations such as The East India Company, The Hudson Bay Company, the Liverpool to Manchester Railway, etc. Due to the importance of transport links to economic and social well-being, governments invested heavily in the protection of their interests through military means, which resulted directly and indirectly in the invention of quicker, safer and more economical transportation, e.g. the jet engine. Large organizations have and continue to use the functional area of transport within the vertical integration concept to maintain their strategic competitive advantage, e.g. oil companies, breweries etc.

As societies as a whole have become more sophisticated and demanding, the transport industry has had to adapt to their needs and wants. It has provided the means for freedom, whether individual personal mobility or the ability to engage in multifarious exchanges. It provides for the movement at an affordable cost of raw materials from supplier to producer over great distances and also for the supply of goods and services through a multiplicity of outlets. It provides a stimulus for the conduct of international trade with the potential for a more stable world economic order with its associated benefits for all. However, transportation does have negative effects on the environment, such as pollution, accidents, congestion, noise, land use etc. Only by balancing these conflicting issues will society benefit fully in the future. Therefore, the purchase of transportation in the future will become more onerous with the need to satisfy a variety of stakeholders.

The role of transportation within the organization

The costs associated with the transport of raw materials, semi-finished products within and between plants and finished products between the manufacturing facility and the customer can be very high and could therefore be a critical feature not only of the final price offered to the customer, but also the long-term profitability of the organization. The cost of transportation, in most cases, will partly be a reflection of the distances involved. For this reason, the location of sources of raw materials, manufacturing and market have become increasingly important in strategic thinking where there is an element of choice. However, many organizations do not have the opportunity or resources to indulge in this type of relocation to find cost savings. Consolidation/rationalization of depots etc. is an option but this will not achieve the fundamental change in substantially reducing the spatial gap which exists between the 'ideal' and the 'actual' situation. In these circumstances, the transportation purchaser has to maximize the efficiency of the system employed, which will inevitably involve trade-offs between the level of service and costs. Also, due to the growth of the 'globalization' of business, many more markets have to be serviced by the transportation function, and with growth in the complexity and sophistication of organizations, structures, products, services, legislation, codes, information systems and markets will bring additional problems for the decision maker. It is therefore vital that the strategic decision maker fully appreciates the relative importance of transport provision in policy making. Also, external forces such as the liberalization of international trade, trading blocs and governmental legislation will all have an impact on the strategic decision-making process and indirectly on the provision of transportation. The transport purchaser must also be aware of the interrelationships between transportation and the other elements in the business logistics chain. There is a direct link between the transit times and the cost of inventory carrying, for example. Lengthy transit times, although procured at a favourable rate, will lead to increased costs in the other elements of the supply chain.

To alleviate these problems, it is recommended that purchasers of transportation should think in terms of the 'total cost' concept where due consideration is given to the 'knock-on' effects of their purchasing decisions. This of course is not exclusive to logistics but will also affect other organizational functional areas, particularly production and marketing. For this reason, cooperation will be required between the various functional areas to achieve the level of service commensurate with the cost which the strategic plan encompasses. As a result, many organizations have been adopting the 'total cost' concept to provide a high customer service level at a competitive price, so gaining the necessary 'competitive edge' to compete successfully in the marketplace. The 'trade-offs' which this implies will mean that the transportation purchaser will have to develop strong negotiation skills both for internal constituents as well as for external transport providers. The setting of performance criteria, measurement, monitoring and control are also important issues.

When making decisions within the framework of logistical strategic planning, the transportation purchaser will have to be aware of the major issues involved. These are:

- modal choice
- carrier negotiations and selection
- rate determination
- required appropriate documentation
- insurance and claim procedures.

The modal split

The 'modal split' is the term given to the basic transport elements which make up the total transportation system. The main elements are, to a certain extent, dependent on their 'way' i.e. the medium through or over which they have to travel. The 'way' will, directly or indirectly, play an important role in the operational constraints of the transport system, whose major elements are:

1 road
2 rail
3 air
4 sea/inland waterway
5 pipeline.

The ownership of the transport infrastructure and the units employed may be either publicly or privately owned, or a combination of both. The global trend appears to be a transfer of publicly owned transport provision to the private sector, which may have implications for transport policy in many countries.

THE CHARACTERISTICS OF THE ELEMENTS OF THE MODAL SPLIT

Road

Road transport is flexible, relatively quick for localized transport needs and can provide a 'door-to-door' service without the need to use other transport modes. It can cope with a large variety of loads, from the smallest to the largest within the confines of the infrastructure and can transport unitized cargo easily. The units are highly manoeuvrable, giving access to confined places, which is very convenient to the customer. It is relatively cheap to operate in comparison with other modes and, due to the cost structures involved, has a relatively low barrier to entry. Specialist vehicles can be designed for operational effectiveness. The infrastructure, once established, is relatively easy to maintain. However, increasing congestion, competition for road space and access, and rising fuel and taxation costs will undoubtedly increase overall costs. There is also the political dimension with pressure to force loads on to more environmentally acceptable modes. The regulations which have to be complied with, such as plating, drivers' hours, weight/dimension restrictions, carriage of dangerous goods, etc. can be onerous. There is a relatively high risk of damage and pilferage.

Rail

Rail is capable of moving large volumes and is particularly cost-effective over longer distances. It has the potential of offering quick terminal-to-terminal transit times using exclusive, dedicated tracks, with a high degree of safety, little bad weather interruption and, with the right precautions, freedom from damage for the goods carried. Due to its inherent environmental credentials, it has become an important factor in transport policy, especially within Europe, with large capital investment programmes. However, it tends to be relatively expensive to maintain and operate, and the fixed costs are passed on to the user in the pricing structure, making it uncompetitive with road transport over short distances. The notion of 'wagon load' is obsolete in some national rail systems due to the concentration on freight movement by 'block trains', which is cited as evidence that rail management appears to be 'production/operational'-oriented rather than 'customer'-oriented. There is also the additional problem of the use of dedicated rail freight terminals and the subsequent movement to and from the rail head. Rail freight is also subjected to 'privatization, open competition and mergers' in many industrialized countries.

Air

Fast door-to-door services are possible with air, but at a price. However, in certain circumstances, e.g. urgent, high-value goods etc., the cost will be outweighed by the advantages of customer satisfaction, security, packaging cost reductions, lower insurance premiums and improved cash flow. Loads are consolidated to reduce costs. Some goods are prohibited due to their potential danger on an aircraft. The use of efficient dedicated cargo aircraft (e.g. MD-11, B-747 and the new A-3XX) by airlines which are separate from passenger operations (e.g. Lufthansa Cargo), centralization of stocks, customer need awareness, etc. have increased the relative importance of this mode of transport over the last ten years.

Sea/inland waterway

Cost is a major advantage by this mode compared with other forms of transport, although it is relatively slow. However, this is not such an important factor with bulk cargoes and international transport. Sea/inland waterway can accommodate all types of cargo, including containers. Goods are subject to a greater risk of damage and are therefore more expensive to insure. There is a wide provision of facilities in all coastal/river/canal physical environments to handle shipping and river/canal traffic. In many cases, it performs the role of a 'water bridge', using ferries, for example.

Pipeline

Pipelines are a very efficient method of moving liquids, and although they are initially expensive to construct, have relatively low operating and maintenance costs. Their use is very limited due to the physical properties of the product type required to be transported, i.e. liquid or gaseous.

The management of the transportation purchasing function

The fundamental concepts of purchasing management for transportation are the same as for any other service-related provision. However, it is not only the variety of providers but also the complexity of the transportation systems employed that makes the selection process a relatively complicated activity due to the high impact on an organization's performance and, ultimately, its profits. The costs of transportation are relatively easy to quantify but it is more difficult to judge whether the system/provider is the most effective in the prevailing circumstances. One reason is the relatively fragmented nature of the prime mover in the UK, the road haulage industry. Therefore, the transportation purchaser must be aware when formulating a decision that the choice or choices will have a fundamental impact on the organization's systems. One such reason for this is the growing awareness of the mutual benefits which accrue from a 'partnership' between organizations and their suppliers in general due to the introduction of modern production-efficient techniques.

Regulation of transportation

The movement of large, heavy and fast units of transportation is inherently dangerous and, for this and other reasons, it is heavily regulated. The major impetus for this attitude has been safety in transport and this has resulted in transport management and operations being innovative in operational practices and new technology. The regulatory framework for safety in transport targets specific areas of (a) the management of transport operations, (b) the personnel who are directly involved in the day-to-day operation of transport units, and (c) the design, construction and maintenance of the transport unit. There are various bodies set up by governments, intergovernmental as well as national, which control, monitor and investigate transport and other related activities.

Selecting the transportation mode

Before specifically investigating criteria in the selection process, it is an useful exercise to analyse the part and present use of the modal split in the UK (see Table 23.1).

Table 23.1   *Trends (tonne/km percentages) in movement of goods, 1980–98*

Year	Road	Rail	Water	Pipeline	Total (1980=100)
1980	51	11	32	6	100
1985	55	8	31	6	107
1990	62	7	26	5	125
1995	66	6	23	5	129
1998	65	7	23	5	140

Source: DETR Transport Statistics.

The table shows a steady growth in the UK's overall tonnage/distance ratio and an increase in road transport at the expense of both rail and water transport. The trends when considering the tonnage lifted (Table 23.2) are not so remarkable when compared with tonnage/distance, but roads take a greater proportion of the tonnage.

Table 23.2   *Trends (tonne/km percentages) in goods lifted, 1980–98*

Year	Road	Rail	Water	Pipeline	Total (1980=100)
1980	78	9	8	5	100
1985	80	7	8	5	102
1990	81	6	7	6	122
1995	81	5	7	8	120
1998	81	5	7	7	120

Source: DETR Transport Statistics.

Overall, the trends suggest that road transport is being used for longer trunk journeys, taking business away from rail. Also, changes in the generation of power from coal to gas have resulted in water transport losing some of its business. Consequently, the distance travelled has increased at a greater percentage than the goods lifted. Centralization of warehouses, depots and production plants, rationalization, etc. have also resulted in longer journeys.

The results from the interpretation above obviously have implications for transport policy in the UK. However, with a well-developed motorway and trunk road system, it would appear that at the present time road transportation will continue to be the prime mover of goods in the UK for the foreseeable future. However, it is increasingly likely that the EU will have a greater influence on pan-European transport policy in the future, with a tighter control on national policies. It is interesting to note that the modal split in other countries can by radically different to the modal split found in the UK, where greater transit distances, topography, natural waterways, climatic conditions, environmental pressures etc. assume a greater importance in formulating transport policies than in the UK. When purchasing transportation for overseas delivery, this factor must be recognized.

The criteria to be used in selecting the most efficient and effective transportation can be viewed as a two-stage decision process:

(a)   the mode (single or multi-)
(b)   the carrier.

The stages in the evaluation process should be:

1   Compare the available alternatives.
2   Repeat the comparison at predetermined intervals.
3   Use an in-depth comparative evaluation technique.
4   Use a rigorous and comprehensive selection process.

The choice of transport mode will depend on a multitude of parameters, both internally and externally generated. Some of the more important are listed below:

1   *The nature of the goods to be transported.* The physical state of the goods (i.e. solid, liquid, gaseous), volume, weight, shape, unit (i.e. bulk or packaged), type of packaging, value, hazardous/toxicity, perishability, fragility, number in consignment, suitability for unitization, subject to tainting (the property of some commodities such as tea to pick up odours which adversely affect their taste), special storage requirements, special handling requirements.
2   *Time factors.* Urgency (i.e. perishability), regularity, reliability, delivery schedules, seasonal factors (e.g. in winter the freezing over of waterways), cash flow, insurance premiums on high-value goods.
3   *Availability of transport.* Mode availability, suitability (e.g. for unitized cargoes, dangerous goods etc.), specialized vehicles, frequency, convenience of schedules, security, tracking in transit, geographic coverage, infrastructure (management expertise, investment, terminals, hinterland, communication systems, intermediaries).
4   *The cost.* The transportation cost as an integral part of the total cost equation, service/cost trade-offs.
5   *Contractual factors.* Sales contract, terms of delivery, Letters of Credit, Bills of Exchange, insurance provision, monitoring progress.

6   *Environmental factors.* Depot and customer locations, industrial relations, political, physical, economic, regulatory, technological (e.g. information technology).
7   *Market factors.* The customer, location, accessibility, relationship, power, importance, characteristics.

Once the modal choice is made, the purchaser has to consider two alternatives: either to purchase transport for the organizations own account or to use the services of a 'hire-and-reward' carrier. The criteria for making this decision (or to use a combination) depend not only on cost, but on the level of vertical and horizontal integration required by the corporate strategy. While the purchase of road vehicles is affordable by many organizations, the purchase of aircraft, ships, rail wagons or the construction of pipelines will be prohibitively expensive. It is only those organizations, where the core business will benefit from such investment in a vertical integrative structure, that will have the resources and commitment to such a strategy.

In the UK, therefore, it must be recognized that the purchase of transport for internal consumption will be restricted by the availability of a particular mode to undertake the required function. Apart from bulk loads, the decision would appear in most circumstances to favour road transport. The purchaser of road transportation does, however, have a choice between 'own account' and 'third-party' or a mixture of both. The general trend is towards outsourcing of transport to dedicated transport providers, often supplying a 'one-stop' logistics/supply chain solution.

If it is decided to purchase road transport vehicles for 'own account', the evaluation will have to include many of the criteria used for modal selection. The type and size of the vehicle, together with decisions concerning leasing, outright purchase, financing, vendor etc., will have to be carefully evaluated according to the needs of the organization.

Selecting third-party providers of transport can incorporate many of the concepts already used in the purchase of services. The more specific evaluation criteria which may be used for transport providers will include:

1   the transportation cost
2   transit time, including pick-ups and delivery
3   capability, e.g. the right vehicles, expertise, reliability, flexibility, guarantees, etc.
4   geographical limitations.

One other possibility is for the organization to employ a subcontractor to manage their own transport function.

The purchase of international transportation

The purchasing decisions concerning international transportation will, to a certain extent, be dependent on the organization's overall distribution strategy, e.g. centralized or de-centralized distribution systems to multi-country markets, use of intermediaries in the distribution chain etc. The options for the prospective purchaser are varied, so it is important that once again the decision process will have to meet the general objective of balancing the level of service and cost-effectiveness within the constraints of a general strategic distribution policy.

The modal choice is probably greater here than in the domestic market, although there are circumstances in which the choice will be severely restricted, e.g. lack of a well-implemented transport infrastructure in the export market. Purchasers of transport to Europe have a wide choice of third-party transport providers as well as the option of using own account, although this option may still be prone to difficulty in some countries. Options for pan-European transport from the UK will be further enhanced by the opening of the Channel Tunnel both for rail and accompanied/non-accompanied road haulage using 'Le Shuttle'. However, the purchaser should be aware of the imbalance in transport availability between the UK and the continent and vice versa, as there are more 'imports' than 'exports'. With keen competition between European transport providers, and the recognition of 'cabotage' in the EC, the purchaser has the option of buying a transport service from third parties which is both physically efficient and cost-effective. Note that duty is liable on the costs of freight.

For longer international transport services, some form of 'multi-modal' solution using unitized methods will probably be needed. In particular, all the major international transport systems of sea, road and rail use the ISO containers (20 foot or 40 foot) with 'around the world' scheduled (i.e. conference) liner container ships, coastal shipping 'feeder' services and 'landbridge' systems using rail or road for the land-based transport element, all of which can offer a 'door-to-door' service.

The use of intermediaries such as freight forwarders, parcel carriers, groupage services, dedicated transport providers, shipbrokers, export houses, etc. are options open to the purchaser. Rationalization within the industry has produced a concentration of large companies which now provide a 'door-to-door' integrated transport service by using strategies of forward and backward integration.

DOCUMENTATION WHICH ACCOMPANIES INTERNATIONAL TRANSPORTATION

Some transport-related documents are very important in the procedures which cover international transport operations, especially in view of the fundamental obligations which may be present in the definitive contract. Therefore the purchaser of international transport services must be fully aware of the significance of the various documents. The main documents which may accompany the international movement of goods are:

1   *Invoice.* This is evidence of the contract between the two parties. SITPRO produces a *pro forma* aligned document for this purpose. 'Legalized' or 'Consular' invoices are sometimes required by importing countries.
2   *Bill of Lading.* This can be a Marine/Ocean Bill of Lading issued by the shipping company or their agent or a House Bill of Lading issued by a freight forwarder, for example. The use of 'electronic Bills of Lading' is being considered. The Bill of Lading is important because it provides evidence of a contract for carriage, receipt for the goods, statement of the condition of the goods when accepted and can provide title to the goods. It can also play an important role in 'collections', as it is sometimes an integral part in procedures where Bills of Exchange and Letters of Credit are used in international payments.
3   *Sea Way Bill.* This is a document which gives details of the consignment and acts as a contract and a receipt, but is 'non-negotiable'. It can be used for shipments between a firm's subsidiary companies.

4   *Air Way Bill.* This is evidence of a contract and a receipt for goods. It is not a document of title.

5   *Road Consignment Note.* This is a receipt given by a road haulier which also serves as a delivery note. A CMR consignment note is internationally recognized for movement in European countries.

6   *Insurance Policy and/or Insurance Certificate.* These are evidence that insurance has been effected covering the goods during the transportation phase.

7   *Bill of Exchange.* This is issued by the seller's bank and 'accepted' by the buyer when it is signed. The Bill of Exchange can secure payment as the transport documents are not released to the buyer until payment is made, so the title to the goods remains the seller's.

8   *Miscellaneous documents.* Those that may accompany the transport process are Certificates of Origin, Health, Quality, Inspection, European Community documents, TIR documents, Standard Shipping Notes and other commercial documents.

INCOTERMS 2000

The transport purchaser who is involved with the overseas import or export of goods must be aware of their organization's obligations concerning the 'terms of delivery', i.e. when the seller is released from certain obligations concerning the transport phase in accordance with the contract of sale. The carriage of goods by international transport systems can be subject to misunderstandings and risks. For example, if goods are damaged or lost during the process of international transportation, who will be responsible for the claim? To facilitate thorough understanding of the commitments entered into by both major parties, some device must be incorporated into the contract between seller and buyer to allow for the responsibilities and obligations of each to be clearly and unambiguously stated.

In an attempt to standardize the procedures and practice involved in the terms of delivery in the 1920s, the International Chamber of Commerce (ICC) began an investigation into the possibility of using a common interpretation of shipping terms, which at the time were subject to individual national custom and practice. The first set of INCOTERMS (INternational COmmercial TERMS) was published in 1936 and has been subsequently revised on six occasions since, mainly to accommodate changes in transport systems, documentation and the introduction of information technology. The latest edition of INCOTERMS came into force on 1 January 2000. It replaced the previous edition, INCOTERMS 1990, which was a major revision to facilitate the incorporation of modern electronic methods of communication used in international trade, e.g. Electronic Data Interchange (EDI) and Electronic Data Interchange for Administration, Commerce and Transport (EDIFACT). One of the major objectives of the 1990 revision was to indicate clearly the obligations of the two major parties to the contract, namely the seller and the buyer. This is continued and refined in the 2000 edition. It has 'tidied up' some of the ambiguities in the responsibilities between seller and buyer by introducing consistency of language. Although generally the changes are minor, the most important changes refer to the terms FAS and DEQ (see the following subsection for an explanation of these). In the case of FAS, the seller rather than the buyer is obligated to arrange outward customs clearance and similarly, in DEQ, it is the buyer rather than the seller who is responsible for inward clearance.

INCOTERMS 2000 is broadly structured into two major groups of (a) carriage by sea (FAS, FOB, CFR, CIF, DES and DEQ) and (b) all forms of transport, including multi-modal (EXW,

FCA, CPT, CIP, DAF, DDU and DDP). These two basic groupings are incorporated into four major categories which are chosen to indicate (i) departure (ii) main carriage unpaid by the seller, (iii) main carriage paid by the seller, and (iv) arrival. In total, there are 13 specific terms.

To aid recognition, each specific term within each category uses the same letter at the start of the abbreviation as follows:

Group	Category	Term abbreviations
E	Departure	EXW
F	Main carriage unpaid	FCA, FAS, FOB
C	Main carriage paid	CFR, CIF, CPT, CIP
D	Arrival	DAF, DES, DEQ, DDU, DDP

The purchaser of transport has an interest in the terms of delivery incorporated in the contract of sale, as this will affect the purchasing decision on the choice of carrier and mode most appropriate to the circumstances. Therefore, it is important that the purchaser fully understands the obligations inherent in the specific INCOTERMS used in the contract.

SUMMARY OF INCOTERMS

Category E: Departure; contains only one term – ex works (EXW) (Figure 23.1)

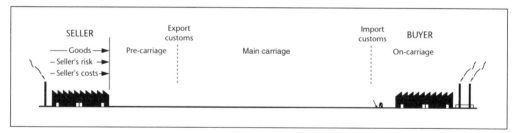

Figure 23.1   *EXW – Ex Works*

- *Seller's obligations*: to package, mark and make the goods available for collection by the buyer's carrier/agent at the seller's premises or other location at or on an agreed date/time.
- *Buyer's obligations*: to take delivery, arrange loading, provide and pay for the carriage to destination, insure the risk to destination, arrange customs clearances (export and import).

Category F: Main carriage unpaid; contains three terms – FCA (all modes), FAS and FOB (carriage by sea) (Figures 23.2–23.4)

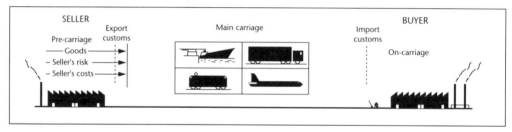

Figure 23.2   *FCA – free carrier*

- *Seller's obligations*: to deliver the goods to the carrier at the place nominated by the buyer, arrange export clearance, pay for pre-carriage.
- *Buyer's obligations*: to contract and pay for the carriage to destination from the agreed collection place, arrange to insure the risk from point of delivery, arrange import customs clearance.

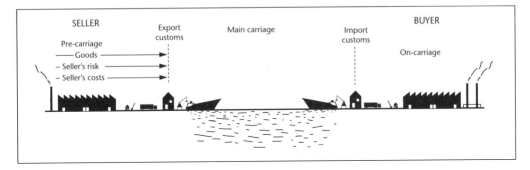

Figure 23.3   *FAS – free alongside*

- *Seller's obligations*: to deliver the goods alongside the ship at the named port, arrange, pay and insure for pre-carriage, arrange export clearance.
- *Buyer's obligations*: to nominate a carrier to the seller, arrange the loading of the goods on board the ship, contract for the carriage to port of destination, pay the freight, arrange and pay the insurance, arrange import clearance, provide onward carriage from the named port to the place of destination.

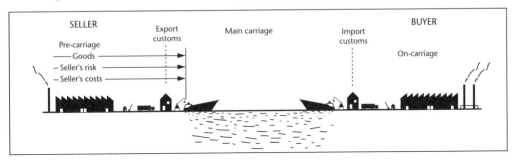

Figure 23.4   *FOB – free on board*

- *Seller's obligations*: to arrange pre-carriage to the named port of loading, deliver the goods on-board (when the goods pass the ship's rail), arrange and pay pre-carriage and insurance, arrange export clearance, provide a 'clean' on board receipt (e.g. an 'Ocean' or 'Marine' Bill of Lading), pay the loading charges not included in the freight.
- *Buyer's obligations*: to nominate a carrier and loading port to the seller, contract and pay the freight, arrange and pay insurance, pay discharging costs, arrange import clearance.

Category C: Main carriage paid; contains four terms – CFR, CIF (carriage by sea), CPT and CIP (all modes) (Figures 23.5–23.8)

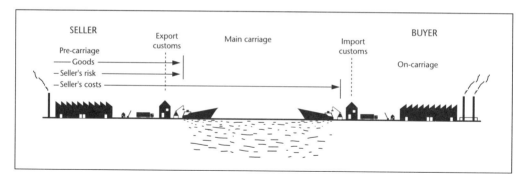

Figure 23.5   *CFR – cost and freight*

- *Seller's obligations*: to arrange pre-carriage to loading port, deliver the goods on board, contract and pay the freight to the named port of destination, obtain export clearance, pay the discharging costs at the port of destination.
- *Buyer's obligations*: to accept delivery of the goods on shipment, receive the goods from the carrier at the port of destination, arrange and pay for insurance for main and onward carriage, obtain import clearance.

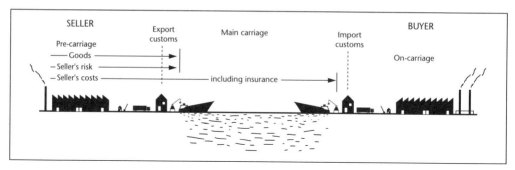

Figure 23.6   *CIF – cost, insurance and freight*

- *Seller's obligations*: to arrange pre-carriage to loading port, deliver the goods on board, contract and pay the freight to the named port of destination, obtain export clearance, arrange and pay pre-carriage and main carriage insurance premiums, pay the discharging costs at the port of destination.
- *Buyer's obligations*: to accept delivery of the goods on shipment, receive the goods from the carrier at the port of destination, obtain import clearance, arrange onward carriage.

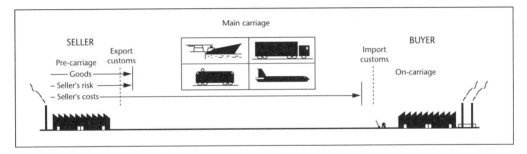

Figure 23.7   *CPT – carriage paid to*

- *Seller's obligations*: to contract for the carriage, cover the insured risk to delivery to first carrier, pay the freight to the buyer's named place of destination, deliver the goods into the care of the first carrier, arrange export clearance, pay loading and, subject to contract, discharge costs.
- *Buyer's obligations*: to accept delivery to the first carrier, arrange import clearance, insure the risk from delivery, receive goods from carrier at named place of destination.

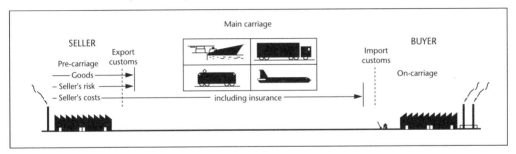

Figure 23.8   *CIP – carriage and insurance paid to*

- *Seller's obligations*: to contract for the carriage to the named place of destination, pay the freight to the named place of destination, deliver the goods into the care of the first carrier, provide export clearance, insure the risk for the main carriage and pay the premium, pay loading and, subject to contract, discharge costs.
- *Buyer's obligations*: to accept delivery of the goods when delivered to the first carrier, receive the goods from the carrier at the named place of destination, arrange import clearance.

Category D: Arrival; contains five terms – DAF (all modes), DES, DEQ (carriage by sea), DDU, DDP (all modes) (Figures 23.9–23.13)

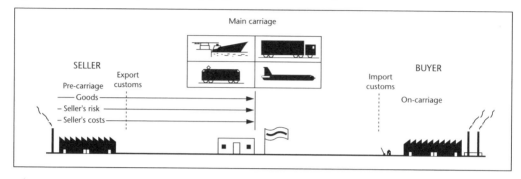

Figure 23.9   *DAF – delivered at frontier*

- *Seller's obligations*: to deliver the goods to the named frontier, obtain export clearance, insure the risk to the named frontier, arrange and pay for carriage to named frontier, assist the buyer in obtaining a through transport document.
- *Buyer's obligations*: to take delivery of goods at named frontier, arrange and pay for onward carriage, insure the risk from frontier to destination, arrange import clearance.

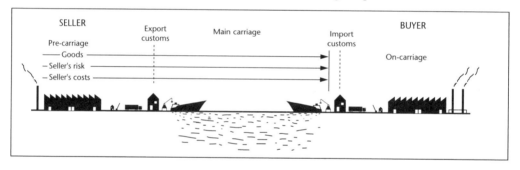

Figure 23.10   *DES – delivered ex ship*

- *Seller's obligations*: to deliver the goods on board the ship to the buyer at the named port of destination, arrange pre-carriage to loading port, arrange for the loading of the goods, contract and pay the freight to the named port of destination, obtain export clearance, arrange and pay insurance premiums, provide the necessary transport documentation.
- *Buyer's obligations*: to receive the goods from the carrier at the port of destination, arrange import clearance, arrange onward carriage, pay discharging cost.

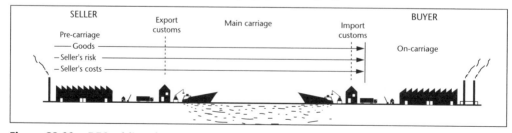

Figure 23.11   *DEQ – delivered ex quay*

- *Seller's obligations*: to deliver the goods on board the ship to the buyer at the named port of destination, arrange pre-carriage to loading port, arrange for the loading of the goods, contract and pay the freight to the named port of destination, obtain export clearance, arrange insurance premiums, pay the discharging costs at the port of destination.
- *Buyer's obligations*: to receive the goods from the seller 'ex quay', arrange import clearance, arrange onward carriage.

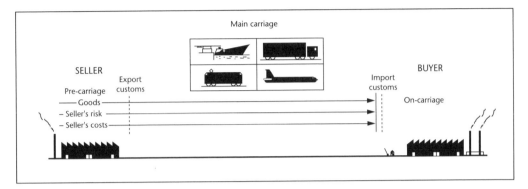

Figure 23.12   *DDU – delivered duty unpaid*

- *Seller's obligations*: to deliver the goods to the named place of destination, arrange export clearance, arrange for the carriage and pay the freight to the named place of destination, arrange and pay for insurance to the named place of destination, provide the buyer with the necessary transport documentation to take delivery.
- *Buyer's obligations*: to take delivery of the goods at the named place of destination, provide onward carriage, arrange inward clearance.

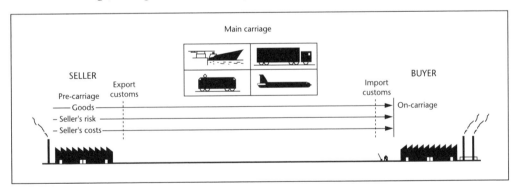

Figure 23.13   *DDP – delivered duty paid*

- *Seller's obligations*: to deliver the goods to the named place of destination, arrange for the carriage and pay the freight to the named place of destination, arrange and pay for insurance to the named place of destination, arrange both export and import clearance, provide the buyer with the necessary transport documentation to take delivery.
- *Buyer's obligations*: to accept the goods at the named place of destination.

24 Purchasing in the construction sector

Mark Smalley and Neil Jarret

Introduction

Sir John Egan's *Rethinking Construction* report (1998) to the deputy prime minister states that the UK construction industry is wasteful and inefficient. Egan argued that the underlying reasons for the waste and inefficiency and also the very low profit levels of the industry stem from the clients' procurement process. Clients traditionally hire designers to undertake design work in isolation from the construction team. Using price competition as the main criterion for selection, clients force contractors to submit very low tenders to win the contract. Once a contractor has secured the contract they strive to increase profitability by applying pressure on their subcontractors and suppliers to further reduce prices and searching for claims due to inevitable client changes and design errors. Egan (1998) argued that this inefficient system was not sustainable in the long term and had to change.

The many fragmented layers in the supply chain, with main contractors working with different suppliers selected on price for each project, gives rise to a lack of customer focus. Many organizations have little or no understanding of the end user clients' needs or aspirations. It is this lack of focus on the principal client that gives rise to problems of poor-quality products, late delivery and defects.

This process inevitably leads to acrimony and adversarial attitudes, with each party within the industry seeking to minimize the risk of losses. The result is an industry that has in the order of 126,000 contractors, subcontractors and suppliers; it suffers from a high number of liquidations, a high number of new entrants competing on price with very low profit levels and underinvestment in training and research and development.

Private sector clients such as BAA, Asda, Tesco and BP have demonstrated that increases in efficiency of at least 30 per cent can be achieved when clients make changes in the manner that they purchase from the industry. Better purchasing practice based on lessons from these clients has recently been supplemented by the experience gained from the MoD's Building Down Barriers pilot projects at Wattisham and Aldershot (Holti et al., 2000). Construction contractors were required to manage their supply chain in the way that is common in manufacturing. The Treasury now promotes the adoption of procurement processes by public sector clients which demands that their suppliers practise the following supply chain management principles:

1   long-term commitment to purchasing from suppliers
2   purchasing using collaborative contracts (including protected margins, open book, risk sharing and shared incentives)

3   supply chain involvement in design, planning and costing of new products and services
4   continuous improvement from project to project
5   development of skills for collaborative working.

All this is intended to lead to a collaborative approach to project delivery in which the clients are active members of the team seeking the delivery of the solution that is best value for money while helping to ensure that the industry participants receive a fair reward.

The purpose of collaborative purchasing is to increase customer satisfaction by fully utilizing the skills of the key supply chain members to optimize functionality and minimize cost by eliminating material wastage and labour and process inefficiency. In return they will win work not by submitting lowest bids but through the award of contracts based on commercial criteria as well as soft skills, including a sound understanding of supply chain management (SCM) principles and ability to work with key strategic suppliers.

Currently, however, few construction organizations have a strong vision for the way forward or the potential benefits of SCM in improving productivity and as a consequence reducing costs to their clients, while simultaneously increasing their own profitability to sensible commercial levels.

The immediate obstacle to the introduction of SCM is the relationship between the main contractor and key suppliers. Many contractors, while happy to negotiate contracts with leading clients (such as the MoD, BAA, and some retailers and local authorities), still need persuading of the advantages of abandoning the traditional approach of competitive tendering which views lowest cost as the only selection mechanism for suppliers. Worse, they have little idea of how to properly involve the supply chain in optimizing design to achieve optimal functionality and lowest cost. What is required is a commercial relationship that encourages the team of main contractor and key suppliers to work together.

The new public sector purchasing focus on SCM will enable the main contractors to shift their emphasis to management of the whole process in order to optimize cost reduction and waste elimination. Main contractors must therefore demonstrate their ability to manage an integrated design and construction service, involving supplier partners in design, scheduling and costing. The commitment to retain teams from project to project will offer clients benefits from the team's cumulative experience and the transfer of lessons between projects. The contractors will seek strategic relationships with first-tier suppliers in order to gain continued reduction in design and construction costs.

Purchasing from long-term suppliers

Main contractors have typically never had long-term suppliers. They may have used firms regularly but without any clear idea or drive to remove waste and inefficiency through continuous improvement. Now leading clients are expecting them to have or be in the process of forming long-term relationships with key suppliers who can play a critical role in delivering better projects at lower cost. Underpinning this requirement is the belief that long-term relationships can drive down costs through:

- the gradual establishment of better and more collaborative ways of working together
- early – and constant – involvement of supply chain partners in the planning and design of the project

- optimal selection and specification of equipment and materials and
- ensuring that the supply chain is fully involved in the development of cost calculations and the associated management of risk.

Supplier sourcing includes:

- limiting the number of suppliers
- taking care to select the best (only working with suppliers with the skills and attitude for collaboration) and
- developing and managing relationships with the key ones.

The products and services provided by the companies in the supply chain typically account for up to 80 per cent of the total cost of a construction project. The way in which those products and services are procured – and the way in which their delivery is managed – has a profound effect on the outcome of the project not only in terms of contract profitability for all parties but also in the extent to which the completed building meets the client's justifiable expectations of cost, quality and functionality.

One of the fundamental requirements of the public sector's new approach to the procurement of buildings is that appointed contractors must demonstrate their determination and commitment to forming long-term relationships with those companies which will be the major suppliers of products and services to a project. Underpinning this requirement is the belief that such long-term relationships can drive down both capital and through-life costs while also driving up quality through:

- the gradual establishment of better and more collaborative ways of working together so that the skills within the supply chain can be utilized more effectively and the building process optimized to eliminate waste of labour and materials, thus minimizing the cost of construction
- the contractor working with preferred suppliers to exploit the latest innovations in equipment, materials and building processes in order to develop collective expertise in particular building systems or approaches.

At the project level this means:

- ensuring that the supply chain is fully involved in the development of through-life cost calculations and the associated management of risk
- improving the quality and functionality of the final building through early – and constant – involvement of the supply chain partners in the planning and design of the project.

Such an approach to the mobilization of key members of the supply chain by the contractor has to recognize that there must be mutual benefit in the arrangement for all parties. This may take the form of working together to secure a greater market share as a result of being able to offer lower prices or better solutions to meet the client's needs, but it should also mean the routine achievement of better and more predictable profit margins while still delivering higher quality and lower cost to the client.

The nature of the construction industry, with projects geographically distant and unique in their detailed design, has led to the creation of a fragmented supply chain that responds only to local needs and lacks the financial strengths to invest in new product development or in new ways of working. As a result, and despite the fact that in some areas of the supply chain, such as roofing and cladding materials, manufacturers are generally large companies supplying the whole of the country, there has been little development of long-term relationships between contractors and what might be termed 'preferred suppliers'.

Instead, as we know, the relationships between contractors and suppliers are typically adversarial. The benefits which a carefully nurtured, financially secure and efficient supply chain could bring to improving the overall competitiveness and technological development of the construction sector have therefore been lost, not to mention the disadvantages that accrue to the customer in terms of high prices and poor quality.

Long-term supply chain relationships will only come about and deliver real benefit if contractors develop a sound process for the development of strategic relationships with the major organizations in the supply chain which deliver that 80 per cent of the value of any project.

DEFINING A STRATEGIC SUPPLY CHAIN PARTNER

Quite clearly, long-term relationships cannot be established with all the members of the supply chain who may be required on any large project. What is important is that long-term relationships, and the close working arrangements that will result, are formed by the contractor with those suppliers and subcontractors who play a critical role in working to deliver better projects at lower cost and with higher quality to the market. These we call strategic supply chain partners or 'first-tier suppliers'.

This inevitably means that the first step in developing long-term supply relationships is to define those aspects of a project in which suppliers or subcontractors will have a major impact on the outcome of a project. These might be, for example, members of the supply chain who would:

- account for the greatest elements of cost
- give a competitive advantage through the incorporation of their unique technical or process skills
- have the greatest potential impact on quality.

Having produced this list of initial criteria by which to make a selection of critical long-term strategic supply chain partners, companies which fulfil these roles (or have the capability to do so) can be identified. It is obvious that professionals – and in particular, architects – also make a major contribution to these factors and should therefore be considered as members of the supply chain.

SELECTING STRATEGIC SUPPLY CHAIN PARTNERS

The first step in selection is to establish the criteria which the supply chain members will have to satisfy if they are to become long-term, strategic supply partners. This is very different from suppliers selected in the traditional way because they have quoted the lowest price on the current project and where they are used again, only if they put in the lowest bid at the next time of asking.

Potential suppliers' strengths and capabilities should be evaluated and compared before selection for a strategic long-term relationship. Partners must be capable of supplying the products and services that they claim – and do so at competitive prices. But they must meet many other criteria if they are to be suitable long-term partners in a relationship which will deliver mutual commercial benefit through greater success in the market based on ever-more satisfied clients. These criteria include previous experience of supply chain collaboration, evidence of product and process innovation, ability to contribute to project design and planning, and people skills for collaborative working. The skills required for selection are discussed in detail below. Once supplies are selected, contracts should be established that promote the collaborative working through a 'win–win' arrangement.

Purchasing using collaborative contracts

Critical to the success of collaborative relationships is the approach to cost management and contracts which ensures that all parties are incentivized to deliver best value. Modern contract forms such as the Engineering and Construction Contract (ECC) enable the collaborative development of target costs and inclusion of gain/pain share arrangements to incentivize continual improvement. The main contractor, client and client's advisers should work together to develop a target cost (which will be developed from, but should be lower than, previously achieved costs) and then the target can be incentivized to keep on driving down costs.

The approach shown in Figure 24.1 has been adopted by many leading clients. An initial budget price is developed by the client, based on historical data of final project costs. Main contractors agree with their key supplier partners expected profits and overheads that are comparable to market rates, and these gross margins are then protected through the design and planning phase. Once all parties have agreed the gross margin, they are free to discuss openly the true costs of the project and commit to reducing as much cost as possible through value planning (which includes value management and value engineering) exercises.

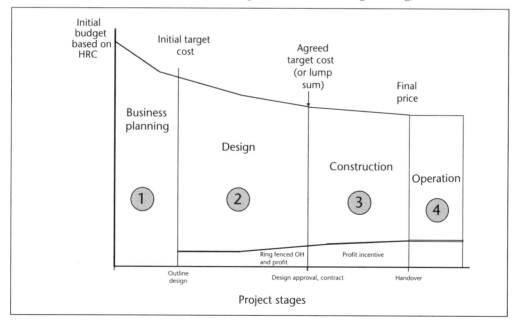

Figure 24.1   *The target cost approach*

Open-book accounting should be used to audit suppliers' costs. The open book must contain facts of costs broken down into material and labour, profit and risk as shown in Figure 24.2. Once margins are agreed and protected there is no reason for the open book to contain anything other than the facts since it merely lists auditable costs of labour and materials. Once auditable costs are exposed, they can be interrogated by the whole design team, so that waste and inefficiency can be reduced and costs minimized. Open book therefore establishes a collaborative approach to reducing costs.

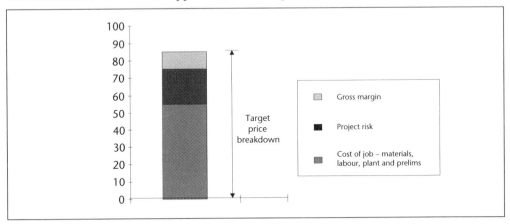

Figure 24.2   *Transparency in the build-up of costs helps everyone identify opportunities for cost reduction*

The principles for sharing risk and reward underpin the whole process of collaboration for mutual benefit and will be defined with each supplier. Leading clients are now starting to recognize that passing all risk to contractors does not lead to the lowest cost for the project. When it is beneficial to do so, contractors and suppliers should share financial benefits and risks with clients in proportions agreed at the outset of a contract.

INCENTIVIZATION

Effective incentive schemes need to be based on a mix of positive direct and positive indirect motivators. Ideally, there should be three strands to project incentivization: direct financial incentivization/disincentivization through the application of a gain/pain sharing where appropriate and indirect incentivization through the opportunity for long-term work. Disincentives are usually in the form of liquidated damages for non-completion of the construction works to agreed timescales.

Gain/pain sharing incentive schemes are intended to ensure the continuing delivery of optimum value for money to the client.

Incentives can be given to main contractors to reduce costs during design and construction. A major concern with the introduction of incentives at the design stage is that ideas will be 'held back' at the bidding stage and retained for design when the benefits can be shared with the contractor's team. Here clients expect that the incentive of maintaining the long-term relationship and the initial budget based on historic final project cost data will ensure that main contractors act in the client's best interest at all times.

Table 24.1 shows an example of the application of a gain and pain share scheme at the various stages of the project as developed by Portsmouth City Council.

Table 24.1   *Example of a gain and pain share scheme*

Stages	Tasks	Outputs	Gain share/pain share
Concept design	Undertake feasibility and concept design Obtain scheme funding	Brief, concept design Finance confirmed Budget set	Main contractor not appointed at this stage
Design	Detail design Value engineering Risk analysis	Design Risk matrix Final target cost	No gain share or pain at this stage
Construction	Construction Commissioning	Construction works Completed project	50/50 gain share and pain share Capped at 0% above and below target price

Managing the design and planning of schemes

Costs of construction cannot be adequately controlled without exploiting the expertise of the specialists in the supply chain, whose involvement will make up some 80 per cent of the final cost. That expertise has to be mobilized as soon as possible in the life of a project – and that obviously means during the design stage. And it must be used as thoroughly as possible – which means that sufficient time must be allowed for design to be done properly by fully utilizing the knowledge and practical experience of the experts from the various parts of the industry who will carry out the construction to complement the work of the consultant designers. And, similarly, the client and his user community also need to be involved in the design process if functionality is to be optimized and if the client is to make informed inputs to the choices and compromises that must inevitably be made during the design process.

Advanced construction purchasing ensures that the design process includes key suppliers' involvement in a fully integrated design team. Instead of imposing an input specification for a project, clients will produce output or performance specifications and will work with teams of suppliers to develop the best-value solution. Tools such as value management will be adopted to ensure that, at all times, the design team keeps a focus on the client's needs in coming to the final building solution. Client involvement will continue throughout the process, to ensure that client value and functionality are the basis of all design decisions.

As the design develops, the main contractors' entire design team (including suppliers) will agree all design outputs and the development of prices. The designers must share responsibility for every aspect of the product or service delivery (design, costing, planning, functionality etc.) with those who will deliver it. This entails the main contractor's strategic suppliers agreeing prices in a structured and methodical way so that all are committed to driving out all unnecessary cost, ensuring that quality is never jeopardized and that all parties make a fair and predictable profit.

All parties are members of the supply chain, which can be thought of as a continuum that encompasses the client, the users, the design consultants, the main contractor and all the specialist trade contractors and material and component suppliers who will jointly put the building together. They must form an integrated team, working within the disciplines of clear business processes to ensure the successful outcome of the project.

So suppliers and client must be involved if the design process is to deliver a project that:

- has optimum functionality
- will give the owner the lowest cost of ownership as a result of value for money being based on lowest through-life cost rather than just capital cost and
- can be constructed with the least amount of labour.

This combination of qualities can only be achieved if the design process is undertaken with rigour and sufficient time.

Management of construction to ensure Continuous Improvement

One of the key features of collaborative purchasing is that suppliers retain their preferred supplier status on the basis that they continually deliver cost savings through Continuous Improvement. This is the continual seeking of better ways of doing things, the objective of which is continuously to drive down costs while also driving up quality, safety and environmental performance. Effective purchasing must ensure that main contractors and their key suppliers have the capability to develop mechanisms for Continuous Improvement.

Continuous Improvement cannot be achieved over the life of one project – it has to be achieved over a period of time, and for that to happen it will be necessary for the client, main contractors and suppliers to capitalize on the long-term relationships. The use of Continuous Improvement as an intrinsic element of effective purchasing differentiates it from partnering (which can lack any drivers for consistent and determined action continually to drive down costs and drive up quality) and from design and build, where the long-term relationships which have to sustain Continuous Improvement may be lacking altogether.

Continuous Improvement application is twofold. It aims to driving out waste and inefficiency from the construction process. All the companies working on projects should contribute to identifying which activities can be improved and then to applying well-established problem-solving tools to find better ways of doing them. All organizations in the supply chain work with one another doing this, so that all the necessary talents and experience can be brought to bear in the analysis of each activity or process. The people from each company that make up the problem-solving teams are those who really understand where improvements can be made and what can be done to achieve it. They will include site foremen and site operatives from the various specialist construction trades.

That is Continuous Improvement at the individual project level. The same approach can be applied within each company so that internal processes can be improved. So Continuous Improvement operates not just within the project but is also an activity that goes on all the time in each company in the supply chain, with some or all of the savings it generates passed on in lower prices to the client.

Before selection, partner suppliers should have experience in the use of formal tools to deliver Continuous Improvement. These tools include process charts, brainstorming, Pareto analysis and Ishikawa diagrams. However, the tools on their own are not enough. Suppliers should be selected because they have a culture that:

- recognizes from the top that Continuous Improvement is fundamental to the future success of the company

- accepts that every employee can contribute to making things work better and will respond positively to being consulted in improvement activities
- recognizes that people can contribute effectively only if they are trained in problem solving
- ensures that good ideas are implemented
- acts on facts when taking decisions to reduce costs and when establishing the strengths and weaknesses of the company
- focuses all improvement activities on clear, consistent, measurable and time-related objectives aimed at giving customers a better deal and cutting operating costs.

Finally, Continuous Improvement cannot be done until present levels of performance have been established – or measured by some means.

People skills for collaborative working

A final key aspect of supplier selection is the emphasis that potential suppliers place on training to develop team facilitation behaviours and skills necessary to ensure that both design and construction teams operate in the most effective manner. Following supplier selection, all client and main contractor staff will need to undergo induction training to provide a common background to the working arrangements and a clear understanding of the role of both the individual and the integrated teams in carrying out the planned programmes of work. Organizations should operate a performance review discipline that allows staff to discuss with their managers their personal performance and agree development needs. This review procedure will allow career development and training to be tracked and measured.

Skills should be developed within main contractors' and key suppliers' staff to enable collaborative working. Training will be required, both to ensure that employees understand the new procedures demanded by collaborative working, but also to prepare them for a new work environment, which will include facilitation and teamwork. Some staff may find the new behaviours difficult to adopt and if, after suitable training and support, they are unable to perform satisfactorily, they may have to be reassigned from the project team.

The individual clients will hold teambuilding sessions to ensure that all participants in their schemes have an opportunity to meet and develop relationships with other team members. Key objectives of teambuilding events include the development of clear understanding of the key stakeholder's needs from schemes, the promotion of good communications and the development of best practice.

Concluding remarks on current construction industry purchasing

This chapter has set out at length the rationale for collaborative purchasing through the construction supply chain. It has been informed by the experience of leading clients such BAA, retailers and primarily the MoD's Building Down Barriers pilot projects at Aldershot and Wattersham. These almost certainly represent the best practice within the construction industry of complete practical implementation of supply chain management principles (albeit they posed some challenges to both pilot contractors and their suppliers that were too difficult to overcome on the first occasion).

Progress so far in the wider construction industry has been limited. We have found the following:

- While many people in construction are familiar with the term 'supply chain management', few understand its commercial objectives and its impact on every business process in both contractor and supplier companies.
- At present, lead contractors believe it is only possible to develop the strategic supply partnerships which are essential to deliver the benefits of supply chain management on negotiated contracts. This is because lead contractors believe that traditionally tendered contracts are invariably let to the lowest bidder and that they must therefore, in turn, award subcontracts to whichever supplier puts in the lowest price on that occasion. Worse, the traditionally tendered job is priced too quickly on the basis of an incomplete design in which the lead supplier (let alone his supply chain, which will do most of the building) has had little, if any, involvement. In such cases it is not possible for the lead contractor to work with his key suppliers in the structured way that supply chain management demands if the industry is to be able to mobilize all its expertise to satisfy the client.
- Suppliers, when approached to work collaboratively in a long-term relationship, are initially suspicious and cynical – but keen to try, since they see it as a far better way to do business in the future.

Many main contractors currently have a justifiable concern in their belief that sensible relationships with key suppliers are possible only when there is a negotiated contract with the client. This is one of the reasons that so many are now beginning to seek relationships with clients who understand the benefits that can accrue from a new approach to procurement. Fortunately, there is an increasing number of client organizations wanting to develop alliances with construction companies selected for capability rather than project tender prices.

Nevertheless, once relationships are established with key suppliers and once experience has been gained of working together, it is likely that the lead contractor will find that he can compete successfully for competitively tendered contracts without having to reduce his margins to win, as others without an established supply chain might well do.

Leading clients have demonstrated that supply chain management is a logical way in which to operate for the benefit of all. Major problems confront its implementation, ranging all the way from the suspicion of each other's motives for seeking change to downright hostility to a process that will require people to behave towards each other in ways that are very different from the ways that they have behaved hitherto – ways which have been seen as essential for promotion for many years.

References

Egan, Sir John (1998), *Rethinking Construction: The Report of the Construction Task Force on the Scope for Improving the Quality and Efficiency of UK Construction*, Department of the Environment, Transport and the Regions, Norwich: HMSO.

Holt, R. Nicolini, D. and Smalley, M. (2000), *The Handbook of Supply Chain Management*, London: Construction Industry Research and Inormation Association.

Further reading

Bachmann, R. and Lane, C. (eds) (2000), *Trust Within and Between Organizations*, Oxford: University Press.

Burgoyne, J. and Reynolds, M. (1997), *Management Learning*, London: Sage Publications.

Child, J. and Faulkner, D. (1998), *Strategies of Co-operation*, Oxford: Oxford University Press.

Clark, G. and Johnson, R. (2001), *Service Operations Management*, London: Prentice Hall.

Collins, D. (1998), *Organizational Change*, London: Routledge.

Colombo, M, (1998), *The Changing Boundaries of the Firm*, London: Routledge.

Cox, A. (1997), *Business Success*, Boston, UK: Earlsgate Press.

Cox, A., Sanderson, J. and Watson, G. (2000), *Power Regimes: Mapping the DNA of Business and Supply Chain Relationships*, Boston, UK: Earlsgate Press.

Croghlan, D. and Brannick, T. (2001), *Doing Action Research in your Own Organization*, London: Sage Publications.

Cummingham, I., Bennet, B. and Dawes, G. (eds) (2000), *Self-Managed Learning in Action*, Aldershot, UK: Gower Publications.

Curran, J. and Blackburn, R.A. (2001), *Researching the Small Enterprise*, London: Sage Publications.

Dawson, P. (1994), *Organizational Change*, London: Paul Chapman.

Eastham, J.F., Sharples, L. and Ball, S.D. (2001), *Food Supply Chain Management*, London: Butterworth Heinemann.

Ford, D., Gadde, L.E., Håkansson, H., Lundgren, A., Snehota, I., Turnbull, P. and Wilson, D. (1998), *Managing Business Relationships*, Chichester, UK: John Wiley.

Gadde, L.-E., and Håkansson, H. (2001), *Supply Network Strategies*, Chichester, UK: John Wiley.

Gattorna, J. (ed.) (1998), *Strategic Supply Chain Alignment*, Aldershot, UK: Gower Publications.

Gill, J. and Johnson, P. (1997), *Research Methods for Managers*, London: Paul Chapman.

Harvard Business School (2000), *Managing the Value Chain*, Boston, MA: Harvard Business School Press.

Hill, T. (2000), *Operations Management*, London: Macmillan Business.

Hines, P., Lamming, R., Jones, D., Cousins, P. and Rich, N. (2000), *Value Stream Management*, London: Prentice Hall.

Hughes, J., Ralf, M. and Michaels, B. (1998), *Transform your Supply Chain*, London: International Thomson Business Press.

Jessop, D. and Morrison, A. (1994), *Storage and Supply of Materials*, London: Financial Times/Pitman Publishing.

Johnson, P. and Duberley, J. (2000), *Understanding Management Research*, London: Sage Publications.

Kaplan, R. and Norton, D. (2001), *The Strategy Focused Organization*, Boston, MA: Harvard Business School Press.

Lamming, R. (1993), *Beyond Partnership*, Englewood Cliffs, NJ: Prentice Hall.

Lonsdale, C. and Cox, A. (1998), *Outsourcing*, Boston, UK: Earlsgate Press.

Morgan, G. (1997), *Images of Organization*, London: Sage Publications.

Noteboom, B. (1999), *Inter-Firm Alliances*, London: Routledge.

Osborne, S.P. (ed), (2000), *Public–Private Partnerships*, London: Routledge.

Remenyi, D., Williams, B., Money, A. and Swartz, E. (1998), *Doing Research in Business and Management*, London: Sage Publications.

Saunders, M. (1997), *Strategic Purchasing and Supply Chain Management*, London: Pitman Publishing.

Slack, N., Chambers, S., Harland, C., Harrison, A. and Johnson, R. (1998), *Operations Management*, London: Prentice Hall.

Taylor, D. (1997), *Global Cases in Logistics and Supply Chain Management*, London: International Thomson Business Press.

Van Weele, A.J. (2000), *Purchasing and Supply Chain Management*, London: Thomson Learning Business Press.

Appendix *Regional purchasing institutes**

Africa region

Morocco

Association des Professionnels des Achats et des Approvisionnements du Maroc – APAM

Mr Abdessamad Saddouq
c/o Secretariat
APAM
c/o Office National de l'Electricité
65, Rue Othmane Ben Affane
20 001 Casablanca
Tel: +212 2 66 80 66
Fax: +212 2 66 80 11
E-mail: Saddouq@one.org.ma

Tunisia

Assocation Tunisienne de Gestion des Approvisionnements et des Achats – ATUGA

Mr Taoufik Ben Salah
c/o Secretariat
ATUGA
78 Rue de Syrie
1002 Tunis
Tunisia
Tel: +216 1 788 113
Fax: +216 1 788 113
E-mail: badis@planet.tn
Website: www.stachanov.com/badis

Republic of South Africa

The Institute of Purchasing and Supply South Africa – IPSA

Mr Tony Mahood
Chief Executive Officer
PO Box 521
River Club 2149
Republic of South Africa
Tel: +27 11 706 3108
Fax: + 27 11 463 8132
Tel: +27 11 833 6221
Fax: +27 11 833 6224
E-mail: ipsa@mweb.co.za
Website: www.ipsa.co.za

Asia Pacific region

Australia

Australian Institute of Purchasing and Materials Management Ltd – AIPMM

AIPMM
Mr Les West
21 Ringwood Street, Suite 3
Ringwood, Victoria 3134
Tel: + 61 3 9876 9713
Fax: +61 3 9876 9714
E-mail:
leswest.aipmmwa@mail2.highway1.com.au
or   info@aipmm.com.au
Website: www.aipmm.com.au

*This list has been drawn from the IFPMM membership list.

Hong Kong

Institute of Purchasing and Supply HKG –
IPS HKG

IPS HKG
Mr Hoi-ming Cheng
Honorary Secretary
PO Box 72241
Hong Kong
Tel: +852 2231 5106
Fax: +852 2762 7297

India

Indian Institute of Materials Management –
IIMM

IIMM
Mr K.R. Rama Ayyar
Executive Secretary
Century Bazar Lane
405, Kaliandas Udyog Bhavan
Prabhadevi
Mumbai 400 025
Tel: +91 22 437 2820
Fax: +91 22 430 9564
e-mail: iimm@bom2.vsnl.net.in
Website: www.iimm.org

Japan

Japan Materials Management Association –
JMMA

JMMA
Mr Takashi Miyazawa
Chairman & Secretary General
Iwamotocho-Kita Bld 6F
1-8-15 Iwamoto-Cho
Chiyoda-Ku
Tokyo 101-0032
Tel: +81 3 5687 3477
Fax: +81 3 5687 3660
Website: www.jmma.gr.jp

Korea

Korea Purchasing & Materials Association –
KPMA

KPMA
Mr Jai Seog, Choi
Chairman
4th floor, Samwon Building
Chung-Ku Pil-Dong 1-ga 1 24-11
100271 Seoul
Tel: +82 2 2271 3691
Fax: +82 2 2277 2784
E-mail: kpma@kpma.or.kr

Malaysia

Malaysian Institute of Purchasing and
Materials Management – MIPMM

MIPMM
Mr Ang Hock Heng
Honorary National Secretary
Room 2.23, YMCA Building
211, Jalan Macalister
10450 Penang
Tel: +60 4 227 2188/3188
Fax: +60 4 227 0188
E-mail: mipmm@tm.net.my
Website: www.mipmm.org.my

New Zealand

New Zealand Institute of Purchasing and
Materials Management – NZ IPMM

IPMM
Mr Shaun McCarthy
PO Box 38 850
Wellington Mail Centre
Wellington
Tel: +64 028 224 9764
Fax: +64 4234 7770
E-mail: shaunmccarthy@xtra.co.nz

Philippines

Purchasing and Materials Management
Association of the Philippines, Inc. – PMMAP

PMMAP
Ms Miraluz Tan
Corporate Secretary
1706-A East Tower
Phil Stock Exchange Centre
Exchange Road
Pasig City
Philippines 1605
Tel: +63 2 634 5942
Fax: +63 2 634 6348
E-mail: pmmap@info.com.ph
Website: www.pmmap.org

Singapore

Singapore Institute of Materials
Management – SIMM

SIMM
Mr Raymond Choy
Honorary Secretary
Level 3, Pico Creative Centre
20 Kallang Avenue
Singapore 339411
Tel: +65 295 4427
Fax: +65 298 4012
E-mail: simmsg@singnet.com.sg

Singapore

Singapore Institute of Purchasing and
Materials Management – SIPMM

SIPMM
Ms Janice Ong
Registrar
165, Bukit Merah Central
#03-3685
Singapore 150165
Tel: +65 273 4172

Fax: +65 274 1132
E-mail: janice@sipmm.org.sg
or   info@sipmm.org.sg
Website: www.sipmm.org.sg

Prof. Philip Poh
School of Commerce and Management
Southern Cross University
c/o 30 Lilac Drive
Singapore 808220
Tel: +65 275 0686
Fax: +65 481 9135
E-mail: ppoh@scu.edu.au

Sri Lanka

Institute of Supply and Materials
Management Sri Lanka – ISMM

ISMM
Mr J. S. Anil Ponweera
Secretary
Professional Centre
275/75, Bauddhaloka Mawatha
Colombo 7
Tel: +94 1 584 302
or: +94 075 335 928
Fax: +94 1 584 302
E-mail: ismm@sltnet.lk

Thailand

Purchasing and Supply Chain Management
Association of Thailand – PSCMT

PSCMT
Ms Sirimetanon
54 Asoke Road
15th Floor, Room 1509
BB Building
Bangkok 10110
Tel: +66 2 260 7326
Fax: +66 2 260 7328
E-mail: pmat@thai.org
Website: www.thai.org/pmat

European region

Austria

Austrian Federation of Purchasing, Materials
Management & Logistics within ÖPWZ –
AFPMML

AFPMML
Ms Bibiane Sibera
Secretary General
Postfach 131
Rockhgasse 6
A-1010 Vienna
Tel: +43 1 533 86 36 56
Fax: +43 1 533 86 36 72
E-mail: bibiane.sibera@opwz.com
Website: www.opwz.com/Einkauf

Belgium

Association Belge des Cadres d'Achat et de
Logistique – ABCAL

ABCAL
Attn: Mr Marc Fourny
c/o Union Wallonne des Enterprises
Chemin du Stockoy, 1-3
B-1300 Wavre
Tel: +32 10 47 53 59
Fax: +32 10 47 51 80
E-mail: abca@acclivity-int.com
or   marc.fourny@acclivity-int.com
Website: www.truck-business.com/abca

Belgium

Vereniging voor Inkoop en Bedrijfslogistiek
– VIB

VIB
Mr Roger Gnat
Langemarkstraat 42
B-2600 Antwerp
Tel: +32 3 286 80 90
Fax: +32 3 286 80 98
E-mail: vib@bevib.be
Website: www.bevib.be/VIB

Denmark

Dansk Indkøbs- og Logistikforum – DILF

DILF
Mr Soren Vammen
Director
Dannebrogsgade 1
DK-1660 Koebenhavn v
Tel: +45 33 21 16 66
Fax: +45 33 21 15 66
E-mail: sv@dilf.dk
or   mail@dilf.dk
Website: www.dilf.dk

Finland

Suomen Logistiikkayhdistys – LOGY

LOGY
Mr Kari Litja
Managing Director
Katajanokankatu 5 D 14
FIN-00160 Helsinki
Tel: +358 9 179 546
Fax: +358 9 177 675
E-mail: logy@logy.fi
Website: www.logy.fi

France

Compagnie des Dirigeants d'Approvision-
nement et Acheteurs de France – CDAF

CDAF
Ms Cécile Masseron, Mr Michel Raffet
2, Rue Paul Cézanne
F-93364 Neuilly Plaisance Cedex
Tel: +33 1 43 08 20 20
Fax: +33 1 43 08 53 89
E-mail: cdaf@cdaf.asso.fr
Website: www.cdaf.asso.fr

Germany

Bundesverband Materialwirtschaft, Einkauf
und Logistik e.V. – BME

BME
Dr Holger Hildebrandt

Hauptgeschäftsführer
Bolongarostraße 82
D-65929 Frankfurt/Main
Tel: +49 69 30838 100
Fax: +49 69 30838 199
E-mail: holger.hildebrandt@bme.de
or   info@bme.de
Website: www.bme.de

Greece

Hellenic Purchasing Insitute – HPI

HPI
c/o HUMANTEC
Ms Anna Banaka
18 Iron Polytecniou Sq.
GR-145 64 Nea Kifisia
Tel: +30 1 62 09 726
Fax: +30 1 62 09 776
E-mail: humantec@compulink.gr
or   hpi@hol.gr

Hungary

Hungarian Association of Logistics,
Purchasing and Inventory Management –
HALPIM

HALPIM
Ms Anita Köhegyi
Director General
Veres Pálné u. 36
H-1053 Budapest
Tel: +36 1 317 2959
Fax: +36 1 317 2959
E-mail: akohegyi@matavnet.hu

Ireland

Irish Institute of Purchasing and Materials
Mangement – IIPMM

IIPMM
Mr Gerry Davis
Chief Executive Officer
5 Belvedere Place

IRL-Dublin 1
Tel: +353 1 855 9257
Fax: +353 1 855 9259
E-mail: iipmm@iol.ie
Website: www.iipmm.ie

Israel

Israeli Purchasing and Logistics Managers'
Association – IPLMA

IPLMA
Ms Bilha Karmon
12 Kaplan Street
PO Box 7128
61071 Tel Aviv
Tel: +972 3 696 6944
Fax: +972 3 691 9047
E-mail: iplma@doryanet.co.il
Website: www.doryanet.co.il/iplma

Italy

Associazione Italiana di Management degli
Approvvigionamenti – ADACI

ADACI
Mr Michele Anzivino
Secretary
Viale Ranzoni 17
I-20149 Milano
Tel: +39 02 400 724 74
Fax: +39 02 400 902 46
E-mail: segreteriasede@adaci.it
Website: www.adaci.it

Netherlands

Nederlandse Vereniging voor Inkoop
Management – NEVI

NEVI
Mr J.W. van der Meer
Director
PO Box 198
NL-2700 Ad Zoetermeer
Tel: +31 79 330 07 66

Fax: +31 79 330 07 60
E-mail: ver@nevi.nl
Website: www.nevi.nl

Norway

Norsk Forbund for Innkjop og Logistikk –
NIMA

NIMA
Mr Arne Hauge
Director General
PO Box 2602
St Hanshaugen
N-0131 Oslo
Tel: +47 22 20 14 00
Fax: +47 22 20 06 50
E-mail: Arne.Hauge@nima.no
Website: www.nima.no

Poland

Polskie Stowarzyszenie Logistyki
i Zaopatrzenia – PSLZ

PSLZ
Mr Artur Wozniak
Gen. J. Zajaczka 15-22
PL-01-510 Warszawa
Tel: +48 22 839 14 00
Fax: +48 22 639 86 27

Portugal

Associacao Portuguesa de Compras e
Aprovisionamento – APCADEC

APCADEC
Mr Joaquim F. Bapt. da Silva
Secretary General
Alameda das Linhas de Torres, 201-3° Dto.
P-1750 Lisboa
Tel: +351 21 758 5348
Fax: +351 21 758 5348

Spain

Asociación Española de Responsables de
Compras y de Existencias – AERCE

AERCE
Mr J. M. Fernàndez Fàbrega
C/: Rosselión 184 7° 4a
E-08008 Barcelona
Tel and Fax: +34 93 453 45 67 (Office site)
or   +34 93 322 69 84 (Secretary
General)
E-mail: secretaria@aerce.org
or   info@aerce.org
Website: www.aerce.org

Sweden

Swedish National Association of Purchasing
and Logistics – SILF

SILF
Ms Olwyn Ottenbring
Secretary General
Box 1278
SE-164 29 Kista
Tel: +46 8 752 16 90
Fax: +46 8 750 64 10
E-mail: il@silf.se
Website: www.iolservice.se

Switzerland

Schweizerischer Verband für
Materialwirtschaft und Einkauf – SVME

SVME
Mr Arnold Bachofner
Secretary General
Laurenzenvorstadt 90
CH-5001 Aarau
Tel.: +41 62 837 57 00
Fax: +41 62 824 60 45
E-mail: svme@svme.ch
Website: www.svme.ch

Mr Albert J. Gasser
PO Box
CH-4001 Basel
Tel: +41 61 262 02 77
Fax: +41 61 262 02 77
E-mail: ajg@bluewin.ch

United Kingdom

The Chartered Institute of Purchasing &
Supply – CIPS

CIPS
Mr Ken James
Chief Executive Officer
Easton House
Easton on the Hill
Stamford
Lincs PE9 3NZ
Tel: +44 1 780 756 777
Fax: +44 1 780 751 610
E-mail: info@cips.org
Website: www.cips.org

Latin American region

Argentina

Asociación Argentina de Compras y
Administración de Materiales – AACAM

AACAM
Mr Manuel Feito
Secretary
Tucuman 141-6 Piso
1049 Buenos Aires
Tel: +54 11 4 311 8421
Fax: +54 11 4 312 2178
E-mail: aacam@arnet.com.ar

Chile

Corporación Nacional de Ejecutivos de
Abastecimiento y Contratos – CORPAC

CORPAC
Mr Amador Auad Herezi
Santa Rosa 9412
Comuna de La Granja
Santiago
Tel: +56 2 541 9995
or: +56 2 546 6756
Fax: +56 2 541 9913
E-mail: c.butka@ctcreuna.cl

North American region

Canada

Purchasing Management Assocation of
Canada – PMAC

PMAC
Ms Jeanette Rennie, CPP
Executive Vice President
2 Carlton Street Suite 1414
Toronto
Ontario M5B 1J3
Tel: +1 416 977 7111
Fax: +1 416 977 8886
E-mail: info@pmac.ca
Website: www.pmac.ca

USA

National Association of Purchasing
Management – NAPM

NAPM
Mr Paul Novak, C.P.M.
Executive Vice President
2055 E Centennial Circle
P.O. Box 22160
Tempe
AZ 85285-2160
Tel: +1 480 752 6276
Fax: +1 480 752 7890
E-mail: pnovak@napm.org
Website: www.napm.org

USA

National Contract Management Association
– NCMA

NCMA
Mr James W. Goggins, CPCM, CAE
Executive Vice President
1912 Woodford Road, MS E-1
Vienna
VA 22182
Tel: +1 800 344 896
Fax: +1 703 448 0939
E-mail: goggins@ncmahq.org
Website: www.ncmahq.org

USA

National Institute of Governmental
Purchasing, Inc. – NIGP

Mr Rick Grimm
Executive Vice President
NIGP
151 Spring Street
Suite 300
Herndon
VA 20170
Tel: + 1 703 736 8900
Fax: + 1 703 736 9644
E-mail: rgrimm@nigp.org
Website: www.nigp.org

Index